THE COMPARATIVE HISTORIES OF SLAVERY IN BRAZIL, CUBA, AND THE UNITED STATES

This book is an introductory history of racial slavery in the Americas. Brazil and Cuba were among the first colonial societies to establish slavery in the early sixteenth century. Approximately a century later British colonial Virginia was founded, and slavery became an integral part of local culture and society. In all three nations, slavery spread to nearly every region, and in many areas it was the principal labor system utilized by rural and urban elites.

Yet long after it had been abolished elsewhere in the Americas, slavery stubbornly persisted in the three nations. It took a destructive Civil War in the United States to bring an end to racial slavery in the southern states in 1865. In 1886 slavery was officially ended in Cuba, and in 1888 Brazil finally abolished this dreadful institution, and legalized slavery in the Americas came to an end.

Laird W. Bergad was born and raised in Pittsburgh. He attended the University of Wisconsin, where he received his B.A. in history in 1970. He then lived and worked in various jobs in Puerto Rico before enrolling in graduate school at the University of Pittsburgh, where he received his Ph.D. degree in Latin American and Caribbean history in 1980. He has traveled widely through Latin America and has lived for extended periods in Puerto Rico, Cuba, and Brazil. He has written and published four previous books about rural slave-based societies during the eighteenth and nineteenth centuries in Puerto Rico, Cuba, and Brazil: *Coffee and the Growth of Agrarian Capitalism in Puerto Rico* (1983); *Cuban Rural Society in the 19th Century* (1990); *The Cuban Slave Market, 1790–1880* (coauthored, Cambridge 1995); and *Slavery and the Demographic and Economic History of Minas Gerais, Brazil, 1720–1888* (Cambridge 1999). Bergad has been the recipient of a Guggenheim Fellowship, two Fulbright Fellowships, and an NEH Fellowship, among other grants and honors. He is the founding director of the City University of New York's Center for Latin American, Caribbean, and Latino Studies.

New Approaches to the Americas

Edited by Stuart Schwartz, *Yale University*

Also published in the series:

Arnold J. Bauer, *Goods, Power, History: Latin America's Material Culture*
Noble David Cook, *Born to Die: Disease and New World Conquest,
1492–1650*
Herbert S. Klein, *The Atlantic Slave Trade*
Robert M. Levine, *Father of the Poor? Vargas and His Era*
Susan Socolow, *The Women of Colonial Latin America*
Sandra Lauderdale Graham, *Caetana Says No: Women's Stories from a
Brazilian Slave Society*

Forthcoming in the series:

John McNeill, *Epidemics and Geopolitics in the American Tropics*
Alberto Flores Galindo (translated by Carlos Aguirre and Charles
Walker), *In Search for an Inca*
Gilbert Joseph and Patricia Pessar, *Rethinking Rural Protest in Latin
America*
Eric Van Young, *Popular Rebellion in Mexico 1810–1821*

THE COMPARATIVE HISTORIES OF SLAVERY IN BRAZIL, CUBA, AND THE UNITED STATES

LAIRD W. BERGAD

Lehman College and
The Graduate Center
City University of New York

CAMBRIDGE
UNIVERSITY PRESS

CAMBRIDGE UNIVERSITY PRESS

Cambridge, New York, Melbourne, Madrid, Cape Town, Singapore, São Paulo

Cambridge University Press
32 Avenue of the Americas, New York, NY 10013–2473, USA

www.cambridge.org
Information on this title: www.cambridge.org/9780521872355

First published 2007

Printed in the United States of America

A catalog record for this publication is available from the British Library.

Library of Congress Cataloging in Publication Data

Bergad, Laird W., 1948–
The comparative histories of slavery in Brazil, Cuba, and the United States/Laird W. Bergad.
p. cm. – (New approaches to the Americas)
Includes bibliographical references and index.
ISBN 978-0-521-87235-5 (hardback)
ISBN 978-0-521-69410-0 (pbk.)
1. Slavery – Brazil – History. 2. Slavery – Cuba – History. 3. Slavery – United States –
History. I. Title. II. Series.
HT 1126 B 472007
306.3'62097 – dc22
2006101940

ISBN 978-0-521-87235-5 hardback
ISBN 978-0-521-69410-0 paperback

This book is dedicated to the memory of my mother, Ruth Bergad. Her life centered on her family, for whom she was a model of dedication, kindness, warmth, selflessness, dignity, humility, pride, toughness, and love. She embodied these basic human values, and they have inspired me throughout my life. Mom, I can see you putting this one on the shelf with the others, and I know you would have qvelled, as usual.

Contents

List of Maps and Figures   *page*   x

Introduction   xi

1   From Colonization to Abolition: Patterns of
     Historical Development in Brazil, Cuba,
     and the United States   1

2   The Diversity of Slavery in the Americas to 1790   33

3   Slaves in Their Own Words   64

4   Slave Populations   96

5   Economic Aspects   132

6   Making Space   165

7   Resistance and Rebellions   202

8   Abolition   251

Bibliography   291

Index   303

Maps and Figures

Maps

4.1	U.S. Old South and New South states	page 115
4.2	North, center, and south states in Brazil	122
4.3	West, center, and east in Cuba	130

Figures

5.1	Indexed slave price movements in New Orleans, Cuba, and Minas Gerais, Brazil, 1850–1860	158
5.2	Trend lines for indexed slave price movements in New Orleans, Cuba, and Minas Gerais, Brazil, 1850–1860	159
5.3	U.S. cotton production, Cuban sugar production, and Brazilian coffee exports by volume, 1821–1860	160
5.4	Indexed sugar, cotton, and coffee prices in the United States, 1850–1860, in real prices using U.S. "deflators"	161

INTRODUCTION

The African slave trade and slavery were among the great human tragedies in the development of the Americas. There were few colonies or nations founded by European powers where slaves of African descent were not found in significant numbers at some point in their histories. The institution of slavery and forced labor in one form or another was a part of all cultures – African, Asian, European, and in the indigenous societies of the Americas prior to European colonization. But it was only in the Americas that slavery developed as an institution based upon race. Although indigenous peoples were first enslaved by Spanish and Portuguese conquerors during the prolonged processes of discovery, conquest, and colonization initiated by the Columbus voyages of the late fifteenth century, by the 1550s only those of African descent could be enslaved according to legal codes. Scholars have debated why race-based slavery developed in the Americas on such a pervasive scale after 1500. They have arrived at the generalized conclusion that the European colonial powers became reluctant to enslave peoples who were racially similar to themselves, even though this had been the case for centuries within nearly all European cultures. Africans were so unlike Europeans from racial, religious, and cultural perspectives that it became morally and politically acceptable to enslave them. All kinds of philosophical and religious reasons were constructed by Europeans to justify the exclusive enslavement of peoples of African descent. These ranged from extraordinarily racist frameworks that depicted Africans as genetically inferior peoples who were fundamentally different from Europeans, to self-serving paternalistic concepts in which Europeans portrayed enslavement as a strategy for bringing culture, civilization, and religion to Africans. By the late eighteenth century, however, these justifications had come under scrutiny by religious figures, philosophers, humanists, and eventually politicians. Gradually it became morally and politically unacceptable to maintain African-descended peoples in slavery, and this dreadful system of human exploitation was slowly dismantled.

Brazil and Cuba were among the first colonial societies to establish slavery in the early sixteenth century. Approximately a century later British colonial Virginia was founded, and slavery became an integral part of local culture and society. In all three nations slavery spread to nearly every region, and in many areas it was the principal labor system utilized by rural and urban elites. Slavery developed nearly everywhere in the Americas, but the revolutionary upheavals of the late eighteenth and early nineteenth centuries gradually led to emancipation throughout the hemisphere. In French Haiti, slaves themselves abolished slavery through violent revolution and the formation of an independent nation in a series of wars that began in 1791 and ended only in 1804. The gradual emancipation of slaves took place in the northern states of the United States after the triumph of the American Revolution in the 1780s. The independent nations of Latin America that emerged in the 1820s after a series of revolutionary wars against Spain put into place laws that would forever abolish slave labor by the 1850s. In the early 1830s the British abolished slavery in their Caribbean colonies, and the French followed in 1848.

Scholars have debated why exactly slavery persisted for so long in the Americas. Explanations have varied considerably. Many have tied the end of slavery to the rationalism of the eighteenth-century French Enlightenment, the advent of democratic political forms in the North Atlantic world, and the development of capitalism as an economic system reflecting rational thinking and political democracy. In this view, slavery became obsolete as a labor system and ultimately was unproductive because of advancing industrialization and the widespread development of wage labor as a more economically rational way of organizing the labor force. Others have interpreted the demise of slavery in the context of the spreading humanitarian ideas that swept through Western Europe and the United States toward the end of the eighteenth and through the nineteenth century, as well as the religious revivalism that influenced broad population sectors during the same period.

Yet long after it had been abolished elsewhere in the Americas slavery stubbornly persisted in Brazil, Cuba, and the southern United States, and there was little inclination on the part of slaveholders or political elites to end this barbaric system of human exploitation. It took a destructive Civil War in the United States to bring an end to racial slavery in the southern states in 1865. Even in the aftermath of emancipation in the American South, slavery remained central to Cuba and Brazil until the 1880s, when a series of internal and external factors forced political elites to end the institution. In 1886 slavery was officially ended in Cuba, and in 1888 Brazil finally abolished this dreadful institution. After nearly five centuries, with its horrific toll in human lives destroyed or severely damaged, racial slavery was finally over in the Americas, although racism and systematic discrimination against those of African descent have remained to the present.

This book has been written as a general introductory history designed for those who are not familiar, or who are only vaguely familiar, with the theme of slavery in the Americas. It focuses upon the nations in which slavery lasted the longest and relies on the pioneering works of other scholars, which have been synthesized to consider some of the many general topics found in the historical literature of all three countries. Specialists will not find every aspect of the slave experience included here. General readers, information seekers, and undergraduate and beginning graduate students will encounter a broad array of themes that may whet intellectual appetites for more specialized readings.

The idea for this book was first put forth by Stan Engerman and Frank Smith, who had a somewhat different initial vision. At a conference organized in Rochester, New York, to honor Stan's pioneering and monumental body of work, I presented a paper on comparative slave markets in the three countries during the 1850s.[1] When my panel was over I walked to the back of the room, where Stan and Frank were sitting, and they called me over to suggest that I embellish my presentation into a short book. Herb Klein supported the idea, and without much hesitation I accepted. As I started thinking through how I would approach the topic, it quickly occurred to me that there was no general comparative history of slavery that focused upon the three nations. Accordingly, the chronological parameter of the book was

---

[1] The proceedings have been published in David Eltis, Frank Lewis, and Kenneth Sokoloff, editors, *Slavery in the Development of the Americas* (New York and London: Cambridge University Press, 2004).

broadened, and after work that proceeded in fits and starts over a four-year period in various locales, the book was completed. I want to thank Stan, Frank, and Herb for the original idea and for their encouragement. I also want to thank Jim Oakes for his careful reading of the chapter on abolition and his many invaluable suggestions that have been incorporated into the text in the sections on the United States.

Trancoso, Bahia, Brazil
August 2006

CHAPTER ONE

FROM COLONIZATION TO ABOLITION

PATTERNS OF HISTORICAL DEVELOPMENT IN BRAZIL, CUBA, AND THE UNITED STATES

BRAZIL[1]

Portuguese colonization of Brazil in the early sixteenth century was part of a long history of overseas expansion initiated in the early fifteenth century along the western coast of Africa. Portuguese merchants, often with ties to the crown, had established extensive seagoing commercial connections with the Islamic cultures of the North African Mediterranean dating from the thirteenth century. The Portuguese were skilled shipbuilders and ocean navigators, and through international trade they were well acquainted with a vast array of products from Asian spices such as cloves, peppers, and sugar to sub-Saharan gold and ivory. The techniques of sailing and navigating the comparatively difficult waters of the Atlantic were very different from those required to sail the Mediterranean. But during the fifteenth century, Portuguese sailors gradually became acquainted with the wind patterns and nuances of sailing into the Atlantic world.

In 1415, the Portuguese conquest of Ceuta, an Islamic commercial center on the Mediterranean coast of North Africa, opened sailing routes southward along the West African coast. Exploration was gradual, and it was not until 1487 that the Portuguese reached the Cape of Good Hope and opened routes to Asia through the Indian Ocean. Although they had little success, or even interest, in penetrating the African interior, the Portuguese established a series of trading depots (*feitorias* or factories) on key points along the coast. The purpose was to

---

[1] The major issues concerning slavery in each country are not considered at length in this chapter because they are the focal points of the rest of the book.

engage in trade for gold, ivory, slaves, and other products. They also began sailing farther into the Atlantic as wind patterns and ocean currents continually took them further westward before turning toward the south. These westward journeys led to the discovery, conquest, and settlement of various island groups that became the first European Atlantic colonies: Madeira, the Azores, Cape Verde, and São Tomé. It was on these islands, especially Madeira and São Tomé, that the first experiments with African slave–based sugar plantations were carried out.

In 1500, a large fleet heading for Asia left Lisbon following previously charted routes, sailing first toward the west before heading south. Commanded by Pedro Alvares Cabral, the fleet sailed further west than any previous trading mission and made unexpected landfall in north-eastern Brazil near the contemporary city of Porto Seguro. These new lands were claimed by Portugal, although little effort was made at set-tlement as the Portuguese were much too preoccupied with their extensive African and Asian commercial interests. Nevertheless, Brazil attracted some attention largely because of dyewoods, which could furnish a very marketable and lucrative red/purple dye ultimately des-tined for European textile centers such as Amsterdam.

The indigenous population was culturally and linguistically diverse, as was to be expected in such an extraordinarily large geographical area. There were no great imperial centers or overarching political entities such as Aztec Mexico or Inca Peru, which fell to Spanish conquerors in the 1520s and 1530s. Although Spanish explorers penetrated the Amazonian lowlands to the east of their Andean settlements, and explored the Río de la Plata region, they encountered little in the way of mineral resources or preexisting civilizations that could be system-atically looted, and thus had little interest in what would become Portuguese Brazil. Other European powers, however, did manifest interest, particularly the French, whose overseas expansion had been marginalized because of Spanish domination over the West Indies and access routes to mainland Central and South America, and Portuguese control of the African and Asian seagoing routes. French merchants entered the dyewood trade and on occasion established small settle-ments such as that in Guanabara Bay, contemporary Rio de Janeiro.

The Portuguese crown did not have the resources to directly control Brazil. The Brazilian littoral was explored, and on occasion missions penetrated the interior. But these found no gold of any significance and no great civilization that could attract them. There was concern about countering the French, and finally in 1532 the first official Portuguese settlement was established at São Vicente, the future São Paulo. But rather than taking direct control on the Spanish colonial model, the Portuguese decided to award fifteen huge swaths of land paralleling the equator and running from the north to the south of the colony, called captaincies (*capitanias*). These were bestowed upon private individuals in the hope that these grantees (*donatários*) would devote the resources necessary to maintain Portuguese sovereignty. Few were ever settled or successful, and only two, São Vicente in the south and Pernambuco in the north, maintained some permanence, largely because of the gradual development of an economic base, the cultivation of sugar cane and sugar export to Europe.

The Portuguese had extensive experience with sugar cane cultivation and sugar manufacture in Madeira and São Tomé, and their technologies, organizational methods, credit, and marketing infrastructures were transferred to these Brazilian settlements. African slaves were at first quite marginal, and indigenous slavery was the initial labor foundation upon which the sugar economies developed. But high death rates and the frequent large-scale abandonment of plantations made indigenous labor untenable, and the Portuguese turned to Africans.

By the middle of the sixteenth century, the Portuguese crown had made a decision to devote energies and resources toward the establishment of direct control over the fledgling colony. The *donatário/* captaincy system had been a failure, and in 1549 the first colonial governor was named to attempt to administer Brazil. Tomé de Souza was charged with building a colonial administrative capital at the mouth of the Bay of All Saints, which became the city of Salvador, Bahia. Ecclesiastical authorities, mainly the Jesuit order, established a presence in various regions throughout the colony, and this aided in the construction of some degree of nominal Portuguese control on various parts of the long Brazilian coast. The conflict with the French was ongoing, and they even established a major settlement in Rio de Janeiro in 1555. But by the mid-1560s they were expelled after a long Portuguese military campaign, and a second royal captaincy was officially established at Rio. The French, nevertheless, maintained a presence in Maranhão in the north of the country until the early seventeenth century, and founded the city of São Luis.

Thus, Portuguese colonial Brazil gradually emerged in fits and starts. There were no great wars of conquest as was the case with the Spanish, and this was largely because of the absence of any great imperial civilizations or large deposits of mineral wealth. In some ways the gradual occupation of various coastal regions of Brazil was similar to the process of British colonization of North America. Colonial Brazil by the early seventeenth century was more an archipelago of coastal settlements than any unified geographical entity. Centers of Portuguese control revolved around areas where economic activity and pre-occupation with taxation by the crown were strongest. In Bahia and Pernambuco, slave-based sugar export economies and colonial institutions developed. Sugar was also produced in the two other significant population centers, Rio de Janeiro in the center and São Vicente in the south. But most people were engaged in subsistence activities geared toward survival or small-scale local trade rather in the production of commodities for European markets. Cattle and other animals were raised, manioc root was cultivated, and a variety of foodstuffs were produced on small farms rather than the large *fazendas* or plantations that have become the paradigm of Brazilian history. The population of Brazil in 1600 is difficult to determine, but it has been estimated that there were around 100,000 people in this vast territory, of whom 30,000 were of European descent and the rest of African, indigenous, or mixed origin.[2]

During the first half of the seventeenth century political conflict defined the development of northeastern Brazil, although its impact was not as significant for the scattered settlements in the center and southern coastal regions of the country. The Portuguese and Spanish crowns were united from 1580 until 1640, and this facilitated Brazilian access to Spain's markets. But the union created enmity with the Dutch, who emerged during the sixteenth century as a naval power that rivaled and challenged the virtual Portuguese monopoly on African and Asian commerce. Raids on Portuguese settlements along the African coast began in the 1590s, and in 1604 Salvador was attacked. In 1624 the Brazilian capital was successfully seized by the Dutch, although the occupation was ended in the following year. However, in 1630 Pernambuco was conquered, and a huge swath of northeastern Brazil, from Ceará in the north to the São Francisco River in northern Bahia, was brought under Dutch control. This included the richest areas of the Brazilian sugar economy, which was modernized under Dutch tutelage.

2   Roberto C. Simonsen, *História Econômica do Brasil (1500–1820)*, 6th ed. (São Paulo: Editora Nacional, 1969) (Coleção Brasiliana, Série Grande Formato, v. 10), pp. 88, 271.

To guarantee slave supplies to the Brazilian northeast, the Dutch also successfully occupied the key Portuguese slave trading ports of Luanda and Benguela in Angola during the early 1640s.

The struggle to oust the Dutch in the northeast was the principal focus of the Portuguese colonial government in Brazil until their successful expulsion in 1654. But the center and south of the colony were only marginally affected by the war in the north. Isolated by the great distance from the colonial capital in Salvador and the Dutch-occupied regions of the northeast, the small population nuclei along the littoral developed separately, and in many ways independently. The relatively large indigenous populations of southern Brazil attracted missionary activity, mainly the Jesuits, and this was especially the case in the São Paulo region. The town itself was established in the mid-1550s and served as a base not only for missionary work but also for exploration of the vast Brazilian interior. A very different culture developed from that of northern or even central Brazil, and there was a great deal of cultural mixture, to the point that often Europeans or their mixed-race descendents adopted Tupi-Guarani (the dominant indigenous regional language) rather than Portuguese as the vernacular.

Slave-raiding missions and the constant search for rumored mineral wealth gave rise to bandeiras, or expeditions to the uncharted interior, which could last for years. The Spanish discovery of silver at Potosí in Bolivia (then known as Alto Peru) in the 1540s was well known, and there was the hope that Brazil possessed similar mineral deposits. In the second half of the seventeenth century, placer gold deposits were discovered in the distant and mountainous interior region that would become Minas Gerais. By the 1690s, long after the Dutch had been expelled, word spread that gold had indeed been discovered in significant quantities, and this news sparked a gold rush to the interior that transformed nearly every aspect of colonial society.

People poured into the mining regions in the early eighteenth century from all of the coastal population centers in the north, center, and south of the country. The fundamental institutions of colonial Brazil – slavery, export-oriented economic structures, political/administrative controls – were transferred to the interior of the colony for the first time. Infrastructural linkages emerged from coastal regions to move people, cattle, and consumer goods into the mining zones and to transport gold dust and bullion to the coast and export to Europe. From the north, these routes led from Bahia and Pernambuco along the São Francisco River. From the south, there was a long and tortuous network of trails that snaked up and over the Serra de Mantiqueira, the steep and difficult-to-penetrate mountain range that parallels the Brazilian coast from São Paulo to Rio de Janeiro, and then into the central mountain range, the Serra do Espinhaço, of Minas Gerais where the gold fields were located. The discovery of gold in faraway Goiás and Mato Grosso, and of diamonds to the north in the Diamantina district, intensified these processes.

The spread of cattle ranching, mule rearing, and foodstuff production to provision the mines and provide transportation affected areas as far north as Maranhão and as far south as Rio Grande do Sul on the border of what is today Uruguay. But perhaps most dramatic was the growth of the port city of Rio de Janiero and towns nearby such as Cabo Frio, Angra, and Paratí, which served as centers of an active contraband trade. These areas supplanted Salvador and Recife as Brazil's major import/export centers as the economic importance of the center and south of the country surpassed that of the northeastern sugar districts. Because of the gold cycle, Brazil was transformed from an archipelago of settlements into a colony in which diverse and vast regions were connected to one another for the first time.

There are no reliable statistical data that may be used to calculate the population of Portuguese Brazil at the onset of the mining boom in roughly 1700. It is likely that there were some 200,000 to 300,000 people, probably about a third of them of European descent, a third slaves, and another third of mixed race or indigenous origins. Over the course of the eighteenth century, the Brazilian population exploded because of immigration, a dramatic escalation of the African slave trade, and natural reproduction. There are no reliable immigration figures, or estimates of rates of population increase among the different Brazilian racial groups. But it is known that some 1.7 million slaves were imported to Brazil between 1700 and 1800. The overall population at the turn of the nineteenth century has been calculated at between two and three million people, an obviously imprecise estimate. But what ought to be emphasized is that the mining boom, the expansion into the interior and south of the country, and the end of the northeast's dominance in Brazilian history was accompanied by huge demographic changes. The eighteenth century was indeed one of radical transformation in the colony from every point of view.

The mining boom waned by the middle of the eighteenth century as gold reserves were gradually exhausted in region after region. The northeastern sugar economy suffered as well, principally because of competition from British and French Caribbean sugar producers – Jamaica, Barbados, and Haiti – which supplanted Bahia and Pernambuco as the largest sugar-producing economies in the world. But the shift in the economic and political matrix of colonial Brazil toward the center and south was highlighted by the transfer of the capital from Salvador to Rio de Janeiro in 1763.

The second half of the eighteenth century was a period of great transformation in Brazil. With the decline, not disappearance, of export products such as sugar and minerals, new economic activities emerged. Widespread food production and cattle ranching grew to provision the urban nuclei in the center-south of the colony that had developed during the mining boom. There was also the beginning of small-scale manufacturing such as textile and iron production and the emergence of new crops like cotton, coffee, and rice. Additionally, the formation of joint state/private capital enterprises charged with developing particular economic activities, such as cotton production, was a characteristic of this period; this were related to the reforms initiated by the Marquis of Pombal, who virtually ran the Portuguese government from 1750 until 1777 as secretary of state for overseas affairs. Pombal sought not only to revitalize the Brazilian colonial economy, but also to reassert Portuguese control, which had diminished during the mining boom because of a high degree of local autonomy. His efforts at directing the Brazilian economy, raising taxes, and controlling trade – much like the Bourbon reforms in Spanish America – provoked a nationalist reaction and the first stirrings of Brazilian national identity and sentiments for independence. An anti-colonial conspiracy seeking independence for Brazil known as the *Inconfidência Mineira* was discovered in Minas Gerais in the late 1780s, involving some of the most notable families of the region. It was brutally repressed.

The European crisis that followed the French Revolution of 1789 and the rise to power of Napoleon Bonaparte had profound consequences for Portugal and Brazil. The Napoleonic Wars, purportedly to spread democracy and freedom throughout Europe on the French model, spilled into Portugal in 1807 with a full-scale French invasion launched across northern Spain. In part this was because of the strong English influence and presence in Lisbon, for the British-French conflict was at the center of the European wars. When a French seizure of Lisbon was deemed inevitable, a British fleet evacuated the Portuguese monarch Dom João and the royal family, along with some 15,000 members of the political and economic elite. The destination was Rio de Janeiro, and the arrival and tenure of the Portuguese king between 1808 and 1822 changed the fundamental dynamics of Portuguese colonialism and paved the way for eventual Brazilian independence.

Under British pressure Dom João dismantled colonial monopolies on trade, and Brazil's economic system was opened to unrestricted commerce with friendly countries, which meant Great Britain. British merchants established a critical presence in Brazil's major commercial centers and came to play an important role as creditors and marketers to Brazil's import and export trade throughout the nineteenth century. The lifting of trade restrictions and of prohibitions on manufacturing led to an upsurge in exports of sugar and cotton as well as the expansion of coffee production in the valleys to the north and west of Rio de Janeiro. There was also a substantial increase in the importation of British manufactures, as well as increased indebtedness to banking and other commercial lenders.

The end of the European wars in 1814 created the possibility of Dom João's return to Lisbon, but he decided to remain in Rio and in 1815 elevated Brazil to the political status of a kingdom united with Portugal. This was not accomplished without conflict between Portuguese and Brazilian interests, and a separatist rebellion broke out in northeastern Pernambuco in 1817. Although it spread to neighboring provinces, it was successfully repressed by Portuguese troops. Yet Dom João was soon forced to turn his attention to Europe because of a wave of liberal political revolt that swept Spain and Portugal. In 1820, a liberal revolution triumphed in Portugal and established a government nominally representing the absent king. Dom João was forced to return to Lisbon or risk losing his position and reluctantly left Brazil in 1821. On his departure he designated his son, Dom Pedro, to act as prince regent in Brazil.

The Portuguese government attempted to reestablish direct control over Brazil by abolishing the kingdom status that had been declared in 1815, and indeed Portuguese troops were sent to Rio de Janeiro to enforce the return to colonial status. There was great resistance among local elites throughout the country, and Dom Pedro, responding to Brazilian pressures, made the decision to move toward independence, which was declared in 1822. Although there was armed conflict with Portuguese troops, formal recognition of Brazilian independence by Portugal occurred in 1825. Dom Pedro I became the emperor of a constitutional monarchy. Then, in 1831, he was forced from his throne and departed for Portugal, leaving behind his five-year-old son,

Dom Pedro II, as heir to the Brazilian empire. The period between 1831 and 1840 is known as the Regency, as Brazil was governed by three regents who ruled in the name of the young emperor, who assumed the throne as emperor of Brazil in 1840.

In 1819, when a census was conducted on the eve of independence, Brazil had a population of about 3.6 million people, of whom about one-third were slaves of African descent. The population was distributed fairly evenly throughout the coastal regions and Minas Gerais in the interior. About 38 percent of the total population lived in Minas Gerais, Rio de Janeiro, and São Paulo provinces in the south and center of the country. Nearly 30 percent resided in Bahia, Pernambuco, and Maranhão in the northeast. The slave population was also fairly evenly distributed, with 35 percent of all slaves residing in Minas, Rio, and São Paulo. Bahia, Pernambuco, and Maranhão together had about 34 percent of all slaves in Brazil. The geographical distribution of the population would move toward the south and center provinces by the time of the next Brazilian census in 1872.

Although the age of coffee had begun during the late eighteenth century, and production grew markedly after the 1808 free trade edicts, sugar remained Brazil's principal export until the 1830s. The older regions of the northeast, Pernambuco and Bahia, continued as major producers along with Rio de Janeiro and São Paulo. Gold and diamond exports continued at reduced levels, while cotton, tobacco, cattle by-products, and rubber found their way to European markets after 1850. A significant, if unknown, share of the national economy was oriented toward domestic markets. Food and small-scale textile production led the way. Cattle ranching, with its low demand for labor, and dairy-food production were widespread in nearly every region of the nation where there were natural pastures. But after 1840, coffee exports destined for U.S. and European markets dominated Brazil's export economy. Production spread from the Paraíba valley districts to the north and northwest of Rio de Janeiro into the state of São Paulo in regions contiguous to Rio, and then west to the frontier areas of São Paulo, which became the center of the nation's coffee production in the second half of the nineteenth century. Significant production also took hold in the southeastern regions of Minas Gerais known as the Zona da Mata.

As in the case of all of Brazil's previous export cycles, slaves provided the labor foundation upon which the coffee economy was constructed. The demand for labor increased markedly with the penetration of coffee into the Paulista frontier regions, and this resulted in an escalation of the transatlantic slave trade to Brazil, especially in the 1830s and 1840s. This was also a period during which the British pressured Brazil to end slaving and even forced several bilateral treaties that theoretically banned the African trade. Frustrated with Brazil's unwillingness to enforce these laws, British warships began their own systematic enforcement, and by the early 1850s the Brazilian slave trade was forcibly halted. With labor demands continuing upward, two solutions emerged for the coffee planters of southern Brazil. The first was the development of an internal slave trade from the northeastern and northern states to São Paulo. The second was the gradual turn to foreign immigrant workers from southern Europe, mainly Spain and Italy, although immigration escalated significantly only after the final abolition of slavery in 1888.

After 1850, there was a great deal of technological and infrastructural modernization in southern Brazil. New machinery for processing coffee was imported or manufactured locally. Port facilities in Santos, which served São Paulo, Rio de Janeiro, Salvador, and Recife, were improved to handle the increase in trade. Infrastructural links were forged to interior producing zones and market areas for imported goods. An all-weather road was built from northern Rio de Janeiro state to southern Minas Gerais. Railroad construction began in the 1850s, financed by British capital and utilizing British technology. Rubber and cotton production played a critical role in Brazil's export economy and was concentrated in the northern states of Maranhão and Amazonas. These activities also spurred the modernization of port facilities and internal infrastructure to facilitate exports.

Imperial Brazil under the tutelage of Dom Pedro II functioned as an oligarchic state in which the national government brokered conflicts between regional elites but geared its policies to favor the elites of the powerful southern states of Minas Gerais, Rio de Janeiro, and São Paulo. Elections were held for positions in state and local government, but the electorate was miniscule, limited by property qualifications and literacy requirements. More important to the structures of power were kinship networks, personal connections among the economic and political elites, and old-fashioned political patronage. The Catholic Church did not play the same kind of pivotal role in politics or society as was the case in Spanish America, and the military was under the tight control of the monarchy until the Paraguayan War, or the War of the Triple Alliance, which raged between 1864 and 1870. In this dreadful war, in which Brazil, Argentina, and Uruguay were aligned against Paraguay, Paraguay was devastated, and in its victorious aftermath the political position of the armed forces in Brazil was enhanced.

The end of the war in 1870 was followed by the rise of republicanism as an important political force in Brazil, especially in urban areas. The gradual modernization of the economy, the growth of cities in the south of the country, and the emergence of an urban middle class that was by and large frozen out of power by the oligarchic constitutional monarchy, led to pressures for reform and an opening of the political system to create space for these new social sectors. A shift in the composition of the officer corps of the armed forces, from landed elites to middle-class professional soldiers, also resulted in pressures for political change. Additionally, there was the growth of abolitionist sentiment among progressive Brazilians, and this led to the first efforts to dismantle slavery. In 1871, the Rio Branco Law declared that all children born to slave mothers would henceforth be free people, although they would remain under the control of their masters.

In 1872, a very detailed national census was published, revealing that the nation had a population of almost 10 million people, of whom about 15 percent were enslaved. The regional distribution of the overall population had moved slightly toward the south, although it is conspicuous that Minas Gerais, Rio de Janeiro, and São Paulo had about the same percentage of the total population (37 percent) in 1872 as in 1819. The same may be observed about the total population of Bahia, Pernambuco, and Maranhão provinces, which had 29 percent of the total in 1819 and 26 percent in 1872, a slight decline. However, the matrix of slavery shifted substantially toward the southern states, which were the centers of coffee production and export. Minas, Rio, and São Paulo accounted for 35 percent of all slaves in 1819 and 57 percent in 1872, while Bahia, Pernambuco, and Maranhão's share declined from 34 percent to 26 percent.

Brazil was a nation in transition during the 1870s and 1880s. New social classes had emerged with economic expansion, urbanization, and the beginning of large-scale immigration, especially in the south of the country. An educated urban middle class had evolved, and the officer corps of the armed forces had been professionalized. Political movements representing these new social forces emerged and demanded space and representation within an increasingly antiquated monarchical political system. Accordingly, republicanism became an important force, and by the 1880s there was also the dramatic growth of an abolitionist movement advocating the complete end of slavery. The emperor Dom Pedro, in fact, nurtured antislavery sentiment. In 1888, Brazil abolished slavery, the last nation in the Western Hemisphere to do so. The following year the monarchy was replaced by a republican government that was federalist in nature. The centralized empire gave way to a governmental structure in which states in the new republic acquired an enormous amount of discretionary power. This system lasted until 1930, and the period between 1889 and 1930 is known as the First Republic.

CUBA

Several weeks after making landfall in the Bahamas in early October 1492, Columbus sailed along the northeastern coast of Cuba and claimed the island for the Spanish crown. Columbus had sailed repeatedly down the African coast and was familiar with the ocean currents and wind patterns that carried ships south from Europe and then toward the west and the various island groups: the Cape Verdes, the Canaries, and Madeira, where he owned a sugar plantation. In many ways his voyage of discovery, as it has been labeled, simply extended well-known navigation routes further westward to the future Americas. He was convinced that the lands discovered in 1492, and on three subsequent voyages, were part of Asia and thus the name Las Indias, or the Indies, which the new Spanish possessions were called.

Cuba had little importance in the slowly emerging Spanish Caribbean colonies of the late fifteenth and early sixteenth centuries. The center of Spanish settlement, administration, and economic activity was Española, the contemporary nations of Haiti and the Dominican Republic. Significant placer gold deposits in the interior Cibão region drew colonists and authorities intent on tax collection, and Spain established its first new American port city and colonial administrative structures at contemporary Santo Domingo, which was built in the late 1490s. A substantial indigenous population, the Arawaks, living in sedentary villages with clearly defined political and social structures, was forced to labor in the mining districts and on farms that produced foodstuffs or sugar cane.

Toward the end of the first decade of the sixteenth century, the gold deposits of Española began to wane; the indigenous population had been reduced by disease and overwork; and the growing number of colonists arriving from Spain found themselves competing for shrinking resources. Accordingly, preparations were undertaken to occupy the two islands to the east and west, Puerto Rico and Cuba, in search of new sources of wealth. The conquest of Cuba began in 1511. By 1515 the entire island was under Spanish control, and settlers had established population nuclei in various regions, including the sites of the future cities of Havana, Santiago, and Trinidad, among others. Santiago in eastern Cuba, a day's sailing distance from Santo Domingo, became the capital city of the new colony.

As in Española, placer gold deposits were discovered in various regions, and indigenous labor was exploited by colonial authorities and miners. By 1520 the gold had all but given out, and the indigenous population had begun its catastrophic decline. But by then Cuba had begun to assume an important role in the ongoing Spanish explorations of the South and Meso-American mainland, and this activity was expanded after the conquest of Mexico in 1521 and of Peru in the early 1530s. Cuba became a critical supply area for seagoing exploratory missions and wars of conquest. Cattle ranching thrived, with its low labor demands, and the need for food production to provision the small ports and the voyages launched to the west stimulated significant agricultural development near coastal towns. Small-scale artisan-based industries also emerged to service the ships that docked in various harbors on the north and south coasts of the island.

But in the aftermath of the conquest of the Aztec and Inca empires of Mexico and Peru, and the discovery of enormous wealth that dwarfed the relatively meager gold deposits of the Caribbean islands, Cuba and the other islands were converted from major centers of settlement to way stations for travelers crossing the Atlantic destined for the mainland. Additionally, extant populations systematically abandoned Cuba for the more lucrative Mexican and Peruvian colonies. By the middle of the sixteenth century, Cuba had been depopulated and reduced to an insignificant role in the emerging Spanish colonial system.

This changed dramatically in the 1570s with the inauguration of the Spanish fleet system, armed convoys that sailed twice yearly from Panama and Vera Cruz to transport Mexican and Peruvian gold, silver, and other products back to Spain. With the dispersal of the news that wealthy empires had been conquered by Spain in the New World, English, French, and Dutch privateers began plying the waters of the Caribbean intent on attacking Spanish settlements and seizing Spanish ships laden with American wealth. Defensive measures to protect port cities and ships became a major undertaking of the Spanish crown.

Fortifications were built in key ports cities such as Cartagena, Colombia; Vera Cruz, Mexico; Santo Domingo, and Havana, which had replaced Santiago as the colonial capital in the 1550s. More importantly, Havana, with its fortifications and well-protected natural harbor, became the official rendezvous point for the fleets from South America and Mexico. Twice yearly for over two centuries the fleets were garrisoned in Havana bay before setting sail for Spain. This meant the influx of thousands of people into the city each year, all of whom had to be lodged, fed, and entertained while awaiting embarkation. The ships of the fleet were repaired in newly constructed shipyards, and they had to be supplied with food, water, and other provisions before departing for Europe.

Havana was gradually transformed during the seventeenth and eighteenth centuries from a small port of limited significance into a central cog within the Spanish colonial system and one of the great cities of the Spanish empire, superseded in population only by Mexico City and Lima, Peru. The demands of the fleet shaped the activities of the city itself and the surrounding countryside, and even extended into the plains of central Cuba far from the capital, where cattle were raised to provision the city and the fleet itself. Agricultural development was extensive and fairly diversified.

Cuba is usually associated with slave-based sugar production, but sugar did not become the central focus of the Cuban economy until the early nineteenth century. During the seventeenth and through most of the eighteenth century, Cuba's economy was extraordinarily diversified for a predominantly agricultural society. Food crops were cultivated in all regions contiguous to the great port city to provision its population and the fleet. Commercial crops, such as tobacco and sugar cane, were grown and marketed by merchants for export to Spain on the fleet's many ships. Salted meat was produced for local consumption and export. Hides and tallow for making candles and other products were sent back to Spain. Small-scale manufacture emerged to provide basic consumer goods and to service the needs of the shipping industry. In all of these occupations slaves and free laborers worked side by side, and slave labor was not concentrated in any one sector of the Cuban economy.

The development of the Havana region and its environs because of the economic activity revolving around servicing the city and the fleet led to geographically skewed patterns of development that had a lasting impact on Cuban history. Western Cuba became the colony's center of economic dynamism, while the eastern half of the island lagged behind. Although the production of export crops, such as small-scale sugar production and tobacco cultivation, took hold in the seventeenth and eighteenth centuries, the eastern regions of Cuba were zones where cattle ranching and subsistence agriculture predominated. There was also widespread trade with the English and French, although according to Spanish colonial law this was illegal and labeled as smuggling. Nevertheless, the contraband trade was fundamental to eastern Cuba.

It is difficult to determine the exact size of the Cuban population until the late eighteenth century, when systematic population censuses were undertaken. In 1650, the island may have had somewhere around 30,000 inhabitants, of whom around 5,000 were slaves. The population may be estimated at near 50,000 in 1700, but thereafter there was steady population expansion, and in 1774, when the first reliable population data are available, there were over 170,000 people living in Cuba, 26 percent of them (44,000) enslaved.

By the middle of the eighteenth century, Cuba's colonial economy and society had begun moving in new directions. The British West Indian colonies occupied from the 1620s, such as Barbados, and then Jamaica in 1655, had become the world's great centers of slave-based sugar production, along with the French colony of St. Domingue (Haiti) on the western half of the island of Española. For the Cuban-born elite that had grown prosperous because of commercial opportunities connected to Havana's broader role as a key port within the Spanish colonial system, the British and French islands became models to emulate. Sugar had been produced from the sixteenth century in Cuba, but most production was for local consumption rather than for export. Slave labor was essential to the colonial system, but it was highly diversified, and slaves were found in every economic activity, urban and rural. Attempts at stimulating large-scale sugar production had not been successful for varied reasons. *Ingenios*, or sugar mills, were founded continuously, but most were short-lived enterprises, and the sugar economy had difficulty sustaining any long-term growth prior to the middle of the eighteenth century. During the 1740s this began to change, however, and the mills established to produce sugar for export did not close or disappear so quickly. The sugar industry became a permanent fixture in the economic and ecological landscape of western Cuba, especially in zones close to the port of Havana.

Yet sugar did not dominate the Cuban economy and society until the 1820s. In the eighteenth century tobacco cultivation and export were critical to Cuba's rural society, and coffee cultivation took hold late in the century as well. Much of Cuba's eighteenth-century agricultural development was linked to efforts by the crown to stimulate economic growth. In 1700 the Hapsburg dynasty, which had ruled Spain from the sixteenth century, ended and the French-origin Bourbon family assumed the Spanish throne. Gradually over the course of the eighteenth century, the Bourbon monarchs attempted to establish more effective controls over all of the Spanish colonies and to enact policies designed to produce economic expansion and increased revenues for the crown. In Cuba this took the form of establishing government-sponsored mixed private/state enterprises. In 1717, the Royal Tobacco Factory was established and granted a monopoly over production and commercialization of tobacco, although there was much resistance on the part of small-scale producers, who succeeded in maintaining control over the many tobacco farms throughout the colony. In 1740, an effort to curb the contraband trade with English, French, and Dutch merchants, the crown created a monopoly company with exclusive rights to control the import and export trade of the island – the Royal Commercial Company of Havana. These restrictive policies were successful from the Spanish point of view, but engendered much resentment and animosity among Cuban-born elites and popular sectors.

The virtual end of state-sponsored monopoly companies began in 1762 with the successful British attack and occupation of Havana. This was provoked by Spain's entry on the French side against Great Britain in the Seven Years' War (1756–1763) – known as the French and Indian War in the United States. Although the British occupied Havana for only ten months, the long-term economic and political impact of the occupation was monumental. For the first time in its history, Cuba was opened to unrestricted free trade with foreign markets, principally British. This meant the flooding of Cuba with a wide array of consumer goods; the large-scale purchase of Cuban products such as sugar, tobacco, hides, and coffee by British merchants; and a significant escalation of the Cuban slave trade because of the freedom given to British slave traders to enter Havana slave markets. Although local elites made repeated patriotic declarations in favor of Spain, they were delighted at the economic opportunities bestowed upon them by English free-trade policies. When the British finally withdrew, Spain had little choice but to begin dismantling the government monopolies and restrictive trading policies that had prevailed prior to the British occupation.

The dramatic influx of slaves and new access to European markets stimulated the expansion of the sugar economy and heralded Cuba's economic future. Between 1762 and 1792, land planted in sugar cane soared from about 10,000 acres to over 150,000 acres. Most of the expansion was around Havana and in fertile lands to the south and east of the Cuban colonial capital. The slave population increased from around 44,000 or 26 percent of the total population of 172,000 in 1774, to 85,000 or 31 percent of the total population of 270,000 in 1792. Cuba had begun the march toward becoming the slave-based sugar-producing society that characterized the nineteenth century.

In some ways Cuba's economic history was similar to the histories of the eighteenth-century British and French West Indian colonies. Sugar plantations dominated physical and economic landscapes, although there were fundamental differences in colonial political and social structures. The most important was that a Cuban-born elite social class with extraordinary entrepreneurial skills dominated the insular sugar economy, although they were very dependent upon Spanish, British, and to some extent U.S. creditors and markets. They also relied on foreign technological innovations in cane processing and transportation, especially when a sophisticated railway system was constructed during the 1840s. In British Barbados, Jamaica, and the Leeward Islands, as well as in French St. Domingue, sugar production was controlled by European-based absentee producers. Accordingly, the Cuban elite played a relatively important role in colonial political structures and decision making.

Cuba was poised to become the Caribbean's premier sugar colony when the Haitian slave revolt exploded in 1791. The French colony was the world's leading exporter of sugar and coffee, and the rebellion – the only successful slave revolt in the Western Hemisphere, which led to Haitian independence in 1804 – was accompanied by the destruction of the sugar and coffee-producing infrastructure. As Haitian production collapsed during the early 1790s, prices for sugar and coffee on world markets soared, stimulating the expansion of Cuban output. Sugar colonized land that had been formerly dedicated to tobacco and marched methodically toward virgin frontier soils to the east and southeast. Coffee planting expanded as well, and in fact until the 1830s the value of coffee production rivaled that of sugar. There was also the migration of French-origin planters who fled the Haitian slave revolt, bringing with them the techniques utilized by coffee and sugar planters on St. Domingue as well as large numbers of slaves. They had a very important impact on the economy and society around the Santiago region of eastern Cuba, just across the fairly narrow strait separating Haiti from Cuba.

The successful American Revolution and the disruption of international commerce caused by Europe's Napoleonic Wars, which ended only in 1815, also favored Cuban expansion as the island's entrepreneurs successfully sought markets for their products. This meant British and North American markets above all and the continued growth of sugar and slavery. In some ways the relative prosperity experienced by Cuba's elite helps explain why Cubans did not rebel early in the nineteenth century when the rest of Latin America was struggling for its autonomy. The Latin American independence wars broke out in 1810 and lasted until 1825. At the end of the fighting, only Cuba and Puerto Rico remained Spanish colonies. One more factor that led to Cuba's becoming the leading world's sugar exporter in the nineteenth century ought to be noted. In the 1830s the British ended slavery in their West Indian colonies, and this resulted in the decline of sugar economies in the British possessions, especially Jamaica.

The overall population, and particularly the slave population, expanded dynamically. There were over 700,000 people in 1827, and nearly 41 percent (287,000) were slaves. By 1846 there were 324,000 slaves, 36 percent of the general population of 899,000. The free population – white, mulatto, and black – had begun to increase faster than the slave population, and this trend continued until the next population census of 1862, when the entire population was nearly 1,400,000, with 370,000 slaves, or 27 percent of the total. Thus, while the number of slaves increased in absolute terms, they declined as a percentage of Cuba's overall population.

Cuba's history in the early and mid nineteenth century was defined by sugar and slavery. The island developed into the world's premier sugar export economy, and constant technological innovation made it the most productive and profitable as well. In 1838 Cuba inaugurated its first railroad line, and during the 1840s and after, the most sophisticated railway network in all of Latin America was constructed almost exclusively to serve the sugar economy. Lines were built linking fields to mills, and more importantly, mills to port cities. Steam engines were imported to run the great cane-grinding machines, and vacuum evaporators were installed to convert the cane juice to crystallized sugar ready for export to U.S. and European markets. Cane planting spread to the great plains in western Cuba east of Havana and toward the south coast in the center of the island as well. Cane farming even became important in eastern Cuba. Yet it was western Cuba that was the center of the island's wealth. In 1862, nearly 80 percent of all the sugar mills on the island were concentrated in the western districts of the island. All of this led to a skewed pattern of wealth distribution, with eastern Cuba remaining relatively impoverished while western Cuba prospered.

Through the course of the sugar revolution that began during the eighteenth century, a separate Cuban national identity emerged among elite groups in much the same way that national identities developed in all of the Western Hemispheric colonies that became independent in the late eighteenth and early nineteenth centuries. Although the Spanish colonial system was absolutist, Cuban-born elites had a significant degree of both economic and political power on the island. They were among the most important sugar planters, held appointed political positions at the municipal council level of local government, were regularly awarded noble titles by generations of Spanish monarchs, and created social, political, and economic institutions that represented them on the island. In the 1790s two key organizations of the Cuban elite were founded: the Sociedad Económica de Amigos del País and the Real Consulado de Agricultura y Comercio de la Habana.[3] However, a sense of Cuban identity was one thing, political separatism was something else. Cuban elites were closely tied to Spanish extended families on the peninsula and to Iberian political and economic elites as well.

There was another factor that precluded any real aspirations for independence in the early nineteenth century. Cuba had a large and growing slave population, and the African slave trade was fundamental to the sugar economy. The fear of slave revolt on the Haitian model was an effective brake on the development of any real separatist movement, at least until the 1860s. If the kind of armed rebellion that was sweeping through the other Spanish colonies during the 1810s and 1820s broke out, there was the danger that more could be swept away than Spanish colonialism. The fear of what was called over and again *"otro Santo Domingo"* (another Haiti) kept any separatist inclinations of Cuba's powerful elite effectively in check, at least during the first half of the nineteenth century.

Yet Cuban society and the Cuban economy changed radically precisely because of sugar prosperity. Spanish officials poured into the

[3]   The "Economic Society of Friends of the Nation" and the "Royal Council of Agriculture and Commerce of Havana."

island charged with enforcing efficient tax collection policies. More important was the arrival of a powerful Spanish merchant class that eventually dominated the import/export trade of the island and, more ominously, the credit system that sugar planters relied upon to finance their operations. There was no effective banking system in nineteenth-century Cuba, and although some wealthy Cuban planters had lines of credit that extended to London or New York, most depended upon Spanish merchants with operations in Havana and the other major port cities such as Matanzas, Cárdenas, Cienfuegos, and Santiago. Many of these Spanish-born merchants also founded sugar estates, or took possession of them because of unpaid debts.

The powerful and controlling role that Spanish-born officials, merchants, and planters came to play in Cuba by the 1840s and 1850s gave rise to the resentment that led to separatism and eventually to the rebellion for independence that exploded in 1868. Another critical factor was related to the sharp geographical division with respect to wealth distribution that had been part of Cuban economic history from the founding of the fleet system in the sixteenth century. Eastern Cuban–born elite groups, away from the centers of power and wealth of western Cuba, were marginalized and did not derive the kinds of benefits from sugar prosperity experienced in the west. Resentment toward the Spanish element on the island and a greater sense of a separate Cuban identity characterized the attitudes of elite groups in eastern Cuba, who would become the leaders of the revolution.

There was not, however, a linear march toward rebellion. The fear of slave revolt continued as an inhibiting factor. There were also attempts at reforming the colonial system so that a more representative role could be played by powerful Cuban families in shaping Spanish policies. During the 1840s, there was even the short-lived rise of a political movement that favored annexation to the United States as a strategy for breaking the Spanish colonial system, bringing representative government to Cuba on the U.S. model, and guaranteeing the stability of the Cuban slave system, on the model of the southern states. The Reformist Party was founded in 1865 by progressive Cuban elites who sought formal representation in the Spanish parliament as well as less onerous tax burdens. But in the end their grievances against the colonial system were not effectively addressed by Spain, which in fact raised tax obligations and ignored pleas for reform. In eastern Cuba, elite groups turned away from reform and toward revolution. In October 1868 they rose in arms declaring Cuban independence and beginning what few had anticipated: a ten-year struggle for independence that changed the history of Cuba despite its eventual suppression in 1878.

The Ten Years' War (1868–78) was the great watershed in nineteenth-century Cuban political history. It marks the birth of the intellectual concept of Cuban nationhood in a very graphic way and the beginning of militant Cuban nationalism as a powerful political ideology. This first war for independence also heralded the end of Cuban slavery, for the republic in arms, or Cuba Libre, declared the abolition of the slave system in zones under their control by the early 1870s and offered slaves freedom if they reached rebel lines. This forced Spain's hand. To avoid mass desertions, Spain began dismantling slavery by enacting a law in 1871 that freed children born to slave mothers. Since the Cuban slave trade had been ended in 1867, this meant the eventual end of slavery on the island. But the war was ultimately a failure. The rebellion had solid support among elites and masses in eastern Cuba, but it was never able to enlist support in the rich sugar districts of the western half of the island. The powerful Cuban-born elites who had great economic investments in sugar and slavery sided with colonialism and did not support the revolution.

The death toll was horrendous. The overall population of Cuba declined from about 1.4 million people in 1862 to 1.2 million in 1877. But the sugar economy emerged from the Ten Years' War intact. The institution of slavery, however, did not. Under abolitionist pressure from the outside after the end of the U.S. Civil War in 1865 and emancipation, and continued pressure from British abolitionists, it was impossible to continue slavery in Cuba. Puerto Rican slavery had been abolished in 1873, and a powerful abolitionist movement emerged in Spain itself. In 1880, an emancipation law was passed freeing all Cuban slaves but requiring them to work for eight more years as contract laborers. There was great resistance among Cuban slaves, and in 1886 final abolition was proclaimed.

United States

Although Viking settlements are known to have been established in Newfoundland around 1000 A.D., the territory that would become the United States was first explored by Spanish conquerors with bases in the Caribbean and Mexico during the early sixteenth century. In 1513, the first permanent settlement of Europeans on the North American mainland was established in St. Augustine, Florida. Various Spanish exploratory missions sailed north along the Pacific coast of Baja California and the western United States during the 1530s and 1540s. Other expeditions moved through the U.S. Southwest from Mexico or set out from Florida exploring the southern tier of the future nation. No significant sources of wealth were discovered to attract settlement on any major scale, although the Spaniards established a series of mission towns such as Santa Fe in the southwest. Fortified military outposts were built along the Florida coast during the late sixteenth century with the objective of protecting the fleet, which sailed north from Havana before turning east to cross the Atlantic destined for Spain.

British claims to North America date from 1497 and the voyage of Giovanni Caboto, a Venetian sailor better known as John Cabot, who was commissioned by the British crown to discover, explore, and establish British sovereignty over any new lands found. He made landfall in contemporary Newfoundland, although no permanent settlement was established. Other explorers made landfall on the eastern coast, most notably the French-commissioned Giovanni da Verrazano, who landed on the Carolina littoral in the mid 1520s and sailed north toward New York. In the 1530s, the Frenchman Jacques Cartier penetrated the St. Lawrence River in search of a water link to the Pacific, the legendary Northwest Passage. He established the basis for French claims in North America, and indeed a French colony was established at Quebec.

The first attempt at English settlement was made in the early 1580s, when Sir Walter Raleigh led a small group of colonists to Roanoke Island near the North Carolina coast. It was abandoned as unviable after several years. In 1607, however, a permanent colony was established in the Chesapeake Bay region at Jamestown. It was an endeavor of the Virginia Company, a mixed state/private capital enterprise, and despite great turmoil and hardship the colony survived. A second settlement was founded in what is now Richmond, Virginia, several years later. Although they had dreams of encountering mineral wealth, colonists turned quickly to agriculture for survival, and more importantly to the cultivation of tobacco as a commercial crop for export back to England. Commercial tobacco production meant the need for labor, and in 1619 the first African slaves were imported to the Chesapeake from British Caribbean colonies, primarily to labor on tobacco farms.

Exploration of the mainland continued with Henry Hudson's voyage into New York harbor and the river named after him in 1609. Hudson was in the service of the Dutch East India Company, and the Dutch followed by establishing a colony at New Amsterdam (contemporary New York) in the 1620s. Further north, a group of settlers led by Puritans who had been persecuted in England for their religious beliefs established a colony in Massachusetts in 1620. They had set out for Virginia from England, but were blown off course by a storm and landed on Cape Cod. Immigration and settlement continued, and in the early 1630s Maryland was established on the east side of Chesapeake Bay.

In some ways the settlement of coastal North America was similar to Brazilian colonization. Private companies and individuals were granted charters endowing them with various rights and privileges, in contrast to the Spanish system of direct crown control. Settlements were isolated from one another in various areas along the littoral, as was the case on the Brazilian coast. There were no great indigenous civilizations on the order of the Aztec or Inca empires with extant wealth that could immediately be exploited. This forced settlers to become self-sufficient and to create new sources of wealth. Tobacco cultivation and export took hold in the Chesapeake in the same way that a sugar-export economy developed in the Brazilian northeastern settlements.

However, the economic, social, and cultural structures of the British North American colonies were altogether different. Above all, the land rights conferred to most free settlers distinguished colonial North America from Brazil and Cuba, where land was monopolized by a small elite beholden to the Spanish and Portuguese monarchies. Extensive plantations developed in Brazil and Cuba, and although these also developed in the southern British colonies, the percentage of the population that owned land was much greater in the future United States. Family farms dominated the rural landscape in most regions and coexisted with plantations in areas where extensive agriculture developed. The emergence of political institutions that gave extraordinary decision-making powers to local populations through town councils and representative assemblies, chosen through elections in which only males were permitted to vote, was another contrasting feature of British colonial America.

Racial structures and labor systems were extraordinarily different as well. Although the Portuguese in Brazil utilized free labor to some extent, slavery became the dominant labor system in nearly all regions. In Barbados and other smaller Caribbean islands, the British experimented with indentured labor, in which free people signed labor contracts for extended time periods. But the sugar export economies that took hold in Barbados and Jamaica in the seventeenth century became almost exclusively slave-based. This was in contrast with the major areas of settlement in British North America, which were destinations of large numbers of free migrants from Europe during the seventeenth century. Perhaps half of these were indentured servants, and although their conditions of life could be harsh, they were nominally free and could have access to land if they survived their contracted servitude. Although slaves were imported to the tobacco-growing regions of the Chesapeake, they were dwarfed in number by free peoples from Europe. By 1700, only about 10 percent of Virginia's population was of African descent. This meant a racial structure that was overwhelmingly dominated by whites, although this would change in the Chesapeake due to the escalating slave trade during the eighteenth century. Because of comparatively greater slave imports in Brazil and Cuba, peoples of color – slave and free blacks and mulattos – almost always outnumbered whites in nearly all regions.

The population of the British colonies on the eastern seaboard of North America is estimated to have been around 250,000 in 1700, and about 90 percent of the free population was from England. Slaves made up less than 10 percent of all inhabitants. During the eighteenth century new European migrant groups arrived, changing the religious and ethnic character of some regions. The Irish and Scotch-Irish were the most numerous migrants, most settling in the mid-Atlantic colonies of Pennsylvania, New Jersey, and New York. German migrants were numerous as well in southeastern Pennsylvania. But above all the slave trade to the Chesapeake region, and to colonies farther south, changed the racial/ethnic make-up of the southern colonies. It has been estimated that around 150,000 free people migrated to British America between 1700 and 1775. During the same period, over 275,000 Africans were imported via the transatlantic slave trade. Only about 20,000 slaves had arrived prior to 1700. On the eve of the American Revolution in the early 1770s, about half of the population of the Chesapeake region was made up of enslaved Africans, a drastic change from the seventeenth-century demographic structure of the area. Africans were imported in such large numbers because of the demand for labor by tobacco plantations of the Chesapeake. In Georgia and South Carolina rice cultivation took hold, and this also meant slave imports on a significant scale. Even in the northern colonies, especially New York, slave labor was important. In 1750, about 20 percent of New York City's population was enslaved, although in New England and Pennsylvania the percentage was much smaller.

The eighteenth century was one of demographic transformation, and it was also a period of rapid economic growth and political change. Great Britain surpassed the Netherlands during the eighteenth century as Europe's most dynamic economy and international commercial power. British North American agriculture and industry were integrated into the British international commercial system. Tobacco from the Chesapeake was a source of great wealth to the planter class and to English merchants who imported the crop and reexported it to European markets. The accompanying demand for labor fueled the African slave trade and brought riches to British slave-trading merchants. A shipbuilding industry of significant scale developed in New England to meet the demand for ships by British merchants involved in international trade. Cities such as New York, Boston, Philadelphia, and Charleston grew and prospered and constituted great markets for food products and a diverse array of consumer goods produced in the colonies or imported.

The political system that developed in the British North American colonies during the eighteenth century conferred extraordinary rights, privileges, and participation compared to colonial Cuba and Brazil. Although these should not be exaggerated, as propertied white males were the major beneficiaries of these freedoms, in comparative perspective they were truly remarkable. Representative assemblies chosen through male suffrage had a great deal of local power and control. Freedom of expression and religious tolerance were extraordinary compared to the Spanish and Portuguese colonial systems.

British sovereignty, however, was increasingly challenged by French control over a huge, if sparsely populated, swath of North America. All of Canada was in French hands, as well as the areas west of the Appalachian Mountains all the way to the south into contemporary Louisiana. Conflicts between the French and English in border regions such as western Pennsylvania were rife during the early 1750s and exploded into full-blown war in 1756. In that conflict, known as the Seven Years' War in Europe and the French and Indian War in the British North American colonies, the British decisively defeated the French and their indigenous allies by 1763. This meant that the size of the British-dominated regions more than doubled as the defeated French were forced to cede a huge amount of territory to the British, from Canada south to all of the areas east of the Mississippi River. Irrespective of the fact that these regions were inhabited by indigenous peoples, British sovereignty was established, and this marked the beginning of significant westward expansion of European-origin peoples into the North American continent.

Changes in the colonies in the aftermath of the victory over the French in 1763 led directly to the American Revolution of the 1770s and early 1780s. Great Britain had emerged as an imperial power and was faced with a wide array of administrative tasks, ranging from defense issues to raising revenues for the support of colonial government. Fundamental to British designs was the goal of imposing tighter controls over the colonies and reigning in the semiautonomy that had been forged by the colonists. The same kinds of challenges faced the Portuguese in Brazil and the Spanish in Cuba. The general response of all three European powers was to enact reforms designed to assert imperial control and to raise revenues by enacting colonial taxes. These efforts proved fatal to imperial designs in the long run and sparked revolutionary responses throughout the hemisphere. In British North America new taxes, especially the Stamp Act of 1765, which required taxes to be paid on all legal documents and publications, produced extraordinary resentment toward the British and widespread public outcry.

The issues of taxation without representation and basic human liberties led to organized resistance against British colonial abuses, and after a new round of taxes in 1767 confrontations were exacerbated. These exploded in Boston in 1770, when British troops opened fire on a demonstration protesting the seizure of an American-owned ship. Five people were killed. Known as the Boston Massacre, this event heightened anti-British sentiments throughout New England. This was followed by an onerous tax levied upon tea imports in 1773, again provoking the colonists' ire. The Boston Tea Party was the American response, a revolutionary act in which some three hundred colonists boarded ships in Boston harbor, dumping overboard some three hundred crates of tea. The British Parliament responded by passing the so-called Coercive Acts, a series of repressive measures including the closure of the port of Boston until the tea was paid for. Confrontation continued, and in September 1774 a meeting of representatives from the various colonies known as the Continental Congress convened in Philadelphia. During the spring of 1775 armed revolt broke out in New England, and the American Revolution had begun. In July 1776, the Declaration of Independence was proclaimed by the Second Continental Congress. A year later, in 1777, the Articles of Confederation, which governed the states during the revolutionary war, were drafted by the Congress. This document granted few powers to a national government and bestowed sovereignty upon each of the thirteen states. War raged until 1783, when the British surrendered and the United States emerged as an independent nation. New York City became the nation's first capital in 1789.

The population of the new United States had increased dramatically in all regions from its size at the turn of the eighteenth century, when it had stood at about 250,000. On the eve of the revolutionary war there were nearly 2.2 million inhabitants, and when the first census was taken in 1790 the new nation's 13 states and western territories were home to 3.8 million people, of whom approximately 700,000, or 18 percent, were enslaved. About half of the population lived in the southern states, and about 25 percent each in the mid-Atlantic and New England states. Over 90 percent of the total slave population of the new republic was concentrated in the southern states.

The Constitution adopted in 1787 to replace the Articles of Confederation was paradoxical in many ways. Although a national government was created with real powers to tax and to regulate commerce, and with other prerogatives, each state was endowed with extraordinary rights, such as the ability to legalize or outlaw slavery. Human liberty was proclaimed, and although the word "slavery" is not found in the Constitution, it was implicitly recognized and legally sanctioned. The rights of indigenous peoples, slaves, and women were not recognized, and indeed they could not vote for elected representatives. The Bill of Rights was added to the Constitution in 1791 at the behest of state governments concerned that the national government could possibly infringe upon the sovereignty of states and the freedom of individuals.

From its inception the United States began expanding toward the west despite the fact that indigenous peoples had considered these regions their ancestral homelands. Huge swaths of land to the east of the Mississippi River and west of the Appalachian Mountains had been acquired by the British after the French and Indian War in 1763 and were claimed at independence by the thirteen states. These were frontier regions inhabited largely by indigenous peoples, and after peace had been established in the early 1780s they became objectives of colonization by land-hungry farming families. A major issue confronting the national government was how to organize and control these distant regions. One strategy was the successful establishment of public domain lands in the largely unsettled western territories that had been ceded to the national government by each state. The U.S. government then established a series of policies concerning settlement, sale of land at affordable prices, and procedures for eventually admitting these territories into the union as states through a 1787 law, the Northwest Ordinance.

Expansion toward the west continued to be a fundamental dynamic of the new nation. In 1803, through the Louisiana Purchase from France, the United States doubled its geographical size by purchasing all of the land west of the Mississippi River to the Rocky Mountains in the north and center of the continent and to the Texas border in the south. Lands further west and in the contemporary Southwest of the United States were Spanish territory and had become part of Mexico when that nation won its independence in the 1821.

The settlement of Texas in the 1820s and 1830s created the conditions for conflict between the two nations, which exploded when settlers from the United States declared independence from Mexico in 1836. After trying unsuccessfully to become part of the United States, they established Texas, or the Lone Star State, as an independent nation. This lasted until 1845, when Texas was admitted into the United States The final expansion into Spanish territory and the extension of U.S. boundaries to the Pacific Ocean occurred in the late 1840s with the U.S. victory in the Mexican War. Settlers from the United States had steadily migrated to California and by 1846 wanted to emulate the Texas experience through incorporation into the United States. This precipitated war with Mexico, which raged from 1846 to 1848 and ended with a U.S. military invasion of Mexico, occupation of the Mexican capital, and the Treaty of Guadalupe Hidalgo. This treaty forced Mexico to cede the entire Southwest and West of the contemporary United States By 1848, when gold was discovered in California, the region comprising the continental forty eight states had come under the jurisdiction of the U.S. government in Washington.[4]

The territorial expansion of the United States was paralleled by impressive population growth, due principally to natural reproduction and the immigration of some four million people between 1840 and 1860. By 1860, on the eve of the U.S. Civil War, the total population

[4]   The issue of extending slavery into these new territories was part of an ongoing debate and political struggle that led to the Civil War. This will be addressed in Chapter 8.

was just over 31 million people, of whom 3.9 million (13 percent) were enslaved. New York, Pennsylvania, and Ohio were the largest states, with 3.8 million, 2.9 million, and 2.3 million people respectively. The southern slave states accounted for about one-third of all inhabitants, and New England and the mid-Atlantic states had about the same portion of the population. About a quarter of all inhabitants lived in the Midwest states, and the remainder were scattered about the sparsely populated western and southwestern states and territories.

Through the course of the nineteenth century the U.S. economy was one of the fastest growing in the world. Prior to the Civil War its basic structures became highly diversified, extraordinarily productive, and self-sufficient in agricultural and industrial production. The United States also became a leading force in the international economy because of an extraordinary growth of exports fueled by the European industrial revolution's demand for raw materials such as cotton. Many factors accounted for the economic transformation. Among them, the impressive growth of infrastructural linkages was primary. Rivers, roads, canals, and railroads connected the interior agricultural-producing regions of the nation with eastern cities and export centers such as New York, Philadelphia, Boston, and Baltimore. Road and canal building were widespread in the early nineteenth century, and the flagship project was the construction of the Erie Canal, completed in 1825, which connected the Hudson River and the great port of New York with the Great Lakes region. This meant lower transportation costs and the possibility of moving bulky agricultural products such as wheat and other grains from the interior of the United States on ships rather than overland.

There was also technological innovation in transportation, especially the steamboat and the railroad. Steamboats proliferated: on the Hudson River from New York to Albany after Robert Fulton's pioneering trip on the *Clermont* in 1807, on the Mississippi River, and on the sea between port cities on the East Coast. Railroad construction began in 1828, and by 1850 there were about 7,500 miles of railroad track constructed in the United States. During the 1850s, railroad building to the interior of the country mushroomed, and by 1860 there were approximately 30,000 miles of railway lines running mostly east/ west in both the North and the South of the nation. These infrastructural linkages facilitated the spread of market mechanisms and commercial life to all regions of country. With European population growth, industrial expansion, and urbanization, internal markets grew and export markets for U.S. products expanded.

Manufacturing increased after independence in the northeastern states. After the War of 1812 – an unsuccessful attempt by Great Britain to reassert control over its former colonies – cotton textile mills were founded in Massachusetts, and these began the development of a modern factory system utilizing mostly female labor. Shoe and clothing factories were established as well, and these catered to the growing domestic market for basic consumer staples. Food processing industries developed in New England and in neighboring New York and Pennsylvania, and the presence of coal and iron ore spurred the development of tool making and capital goods production. Lumber and wood processing were other important industries.

The agricultural economy of the United States became one of the most highly productive in the world during the nineteenth century in both the North and the South of the country. In the North, the highly fertile soils found in the western regions beyond the Appalachian Mountains sustained the large-scale migration of land-seeking farming families, who were aided by the federal government's policy of making affordable land available for ownership. Infrastructural linkages to eastern markets fueled commercialization and market mechanisms and led to rising incomes. In the South, westward movement was linked to the continually rising demand for short-staple cotton by textile factories in the northeastern United States and Great Britain. Land on the western frontier of the southern United States was also extraordinarily fertile and drew settlers continually throughout the pre–Civil War, or antebellum, period. The South's agricultural economy was slave-based, in contrast to the North's, and while cotton was the principal resource, tobacco, rice, and sugar were other important products.

The slave trade to the United States was ended in 1808, but the slave population continued to grow dynamically because of impressive rates of natural reproduction. Although the northern states had gradually abolished slavery in the aftermath of the revolutionary victory of the 1780s, slave labor was the mainstay of the southern rural economy. The issue of extending slavery into the frontier regions of the nation was contentious and divisive from the onset of westward expansion. Antislavery sentiments in the North spawned an important abolitionist movement seeking to end slavery completely. However, the major political issue that led to the Civil War was not slavery itself, but whether new states to be incorporated into the United States would be slave or free. To political elites, the importance of this issue was not moral or humanistic. The principal question was whether the national government in Washington would be controlled by southern Democrats from slaveholding states or by northern politicians from free-labor states. This issue became a center of political conflict pitting North against South during the 1840s and after.[5] To southern slaveholding elites, slaves were a form of property; they interpreted slave ownership as a right guaranteed by the constitution. The southern economy had prospered based upon slave labor and continual westward movement into frontier regions. To forbid slavery in western territories threatened the economic future of the south. If the western territories were admitted to the union as free states, the regional balance of power in the republic would shift and deprive the southern slaveholders of their historic power and influence at the national level.

The Republican Party, which would see its candidate, Abraham Lincoln, elected president in 1860, emerged only in 1854, and one of its main political issues was that slavery should not be extended into western territories or future states. Neither Lincoln nor the Republicans were against slavery and by no means stood for its abolition prior to the Civil War. Nevertheless, the slaveholding elites of the southern states interpreted Lincoln's election as a threat to their economic and political future and came to the conclusion that the only way to ensure their survival was the creation of a free and independent nation. Secessionist sentiment spread quickly through the South among whites of all social classes, and before Lincoln assumed the presidency in March 1861 the Confederate States of America was formed as an independent nation by seven southern states. In April 1861, the Civil War began in Charleston harbor in South Carolina when the federal Fort Sumter was attacked by the Confederacy.

Although the war was initially not about slavery, but rather about its extension into new territories, the Union's leaders quickly realized that slavery would have to be permanently destroyed if the Confederacy was to be subjugated. The slave population of the South also worked to sabotage slavery when Union forces approached, principally through mass desertions. In January 1863, Lincoln signed the Emancipation Proclamation freeing slaves within the Confederacy. This was a limited law, because slaves in areas under Union control or in loyal slave states such as Delaware were not freed. Yet it heralded the future, and slavery

---

[5]   These questions will be addressed in detail in Chapter 8.

became impossible to sustain as the war progressed. The Civil War was transformed from a war to save the integrity of the United States into a war that envisioned making a fundamental change in human relations by ending slavery once and for all. In December 1865 the Thirteenth Amendment to the Constitution was passed by Congress forever ending legal slavery in the United States.

CHAPTER TWO

THE DIVERSITY OF SLAVERY IN THE AMERICAS TO 1790

The word "slavery" inevitably conjures up a series of images: the cotton-picking slave of the U.S. South; the sugar cane–cutting slave gangs of the Caribbean and Brazil; and perhaps the domestic servants or house slaves present in all slave societies. These may be accurate for particular places during specific periods, but they are only partially indicative of the slave experience in the Americas. This is because of the extraordinary diversity of what it meant to be a slave in different epochs and regions. The patterns of daily life for a slave laboring on the Texas cotton frontier in the 1840s were dramatically different from those of a slave working in the eighteenth-century Chesapeake region, or a slave living in urban Richmond, Virginia. Aside from the horrifying and degrading reality of being treated and regarded as property – a powerful communality, no doubt – it is important to recognize that slavery was a complex institution with enormous variations as it developed and evolved regionally in the Americas from the early sixteenth century until slavery was finally abolished in Brazil in 1888. Despite popular perceptions and imagery, there are few generalizations about the slave experience that may be universally applied. Before turning to the comparative histories of slavery in the United States, Brazil, and Cuba, a summary of slavery's development in the Americas is needed so that slavery in these nations may be understood in its proper historical context.

The rhythms of European exploration, conquest, colonization, and economic development determined where and when Africans would be forced into the transatlantic slave trade and, if they survived the rigors of the middle passage, enslaved in the Americas. The first slaves to cross the Atlantic were the indigenous peoples of the Caribbean, sent to

Seville by Columbus during the 1490s to be sold on Iberian slave markets. Gold discoveries on Hispaniola during the 1490s, and shortly thereafter in Puerto Rico and Cuba, meant substantial labor requirements if the gold fields were to be profitably developed. Indigenous forced labor was initially utilized, but high death rates due to ruthless exploitation and the ravaging impact of European diseases resulted in the importation of African slaves in increasing numbers by the first years of the sixteenth century.[1]

African slavery developed on a small scale in early Spanish settlements on these islands even after gold resources had been virtually exhausted during the 1520s and 1530s. Sugar cane was planted by settlers, and African slaves were utilized in sugar production. However, this sixteenth-century Caribbean sugar economy should not be confused with the large-scale plantation environments that would emerge in the seventeenth and eighteenth centuries. Cane farms and sugar production were on a modest scale; labor demands were not extensive; and production for export was minimal after 1550. African slaves were present on all three Spanish-controlled islands, but slavery was not a labor institution of great significance because of the rudimentary level of economic development. One exception to this was Havana, Cuba, which after 1570 gradually grew into an important urban center after it became the rendezvous point for the fleet system that monopolized trade to and from the Spanish Americas. Because of this economic function within the broader colonial system and the resulting demand for labor in a diversified array of occupations, skilled and unskilled, slavery developed on a significant scale in Havana and its environs.

The importation of Africans to the Caribbean continued the well-established practice dating from the 1440s of Portuguese explorers and merchants who had gradually made their way southward along Africa's west coast. Slaves were readily available in most of the sophisticated

[1]   On death rates among indigenous peoples in the Americas after conquest, see Alfred W. Crosby, Jr., *The Columbian Exchange: Biological and Cultural Consequences of 1492* (Westport, CT: Greenwood Press, 1972), and his *Ecological Imperialism: The Biological Expansion of Europe, 900–1900* (New York: Cambridge University Press, 1986). Also see Noble David Cook, *Born to Die: Disease and New World Conquest, 1492–1650* (New York: Cambridge University Press, 1998), and Noble David Cook and W. George Lovell, editors, *"Secret Judgments of God": Old World Disease in Colonial Spanish America* (Norman: University of Oklahoma Press, 1991).

African coastal societies encountered by the Portuguese, and they were procured and purchased from powerful African brokers with the objective of exporting them to regions with labor demands and profit opportunities.[2] Lisbon and southern Portugal were important slave markets for Africans during the second half of the fifteenth century, and as the various island groups in the Atlantic were occupied and colonized – Madeira, the Azores, the Cape Verdes, the Canaries, and São Tomé – African slaves from the mainland were purchased and exported to meet labor needs in a wide variety of occupations, rural and urban.[3] The Caribbean discoveries and conquests meant that this process was shifted far westward. Additionally, the occupation of enclaves in northeastern Brazil – contemporary Bahia and Pernambuco – after the Portuguese made landfall there in 1500 led to the first small-scale presence of African slaves on the eastern coast of mainland South America during the early sixteenth century.

The continued push westward from the Caribbean islands across the Gulf of Mexico and then south through Mesoamerica and South America was accompanied by the spread of African slavery in each area of Spanish discovery, conquest, and colonization. The defeat of the Aztec empire in 1521 led to an early large-scale presence of Africans on the newly discovered continent, and it ought to be noted that several hundred slaves accompanied Hernán Cortes in his final attack on Tenochtitlán, the Aztec capital that today is Mexico City. This established a pattern of African slave participation in

[2]   For one of many considerations of the critical role of African merchants in the slave trade, see John Thornton, *Africa and Africans in the Making of the Atlantic World, 1400–1680* (Cambridge: Cambridge University Press, 1992). On the extent of slavery in Africa prior to the arrival of Europeans in the fifteenth century, see Paul Lovejoy, *Transformations in Slavery: A History of Slavery in Africa* (Cambridge: Cambridge University Press, 1983), and Patrick Manning, *Slavery and African Life: Occidental, Oriental, and African Slave Trades* (New York: Cambridge University Press, 1990). For an important recent survey of the slave trade, see Herbert S. Klein, *The Atlantic Slave Trade* (New York: Cambridge University Press, 1999). Also see his *African Slavery in Latin America and the Caribbean* (New York: Oxford University Press, 1986).

[3]   It ought to be noted that between the beginning of African slaving by Europeans in 1444 until 1600, more Africans were exported to Old World destinations, principally to the islands noted here and to Iberia, than were sent to the Americas. For the classic statistical consideration of slave destinations, see Phillip Curtin, *The Atlantic Slave Trade: A Census* (Madison: University of Wisconsin Press, 1969).

subsequent conquests, the most important being that of the Inca empire of contemporary Ecuador, Peru, and Bolivia in the 1530s and 1540s. On all of the Spanish- and Portuguese-led missions of exploration, war, and conquest during the sixteenth century, African slaves were present as soldiers, craftsman, baggage carriers, cooks, personal servants – in nearly every occupation in which free men labored as well.

With the establishment of relatively stable colonial systems in most areas of Latin America and the Caribbean over the course of the sixteenth century, the evolution of slavery came to be conditioned by economic cycles and labor demands. Three major focal points of African slavery developed: Mexico, Peru, and northeastern Brazil. The former two were centers of densely populated hierarchical imperial societies, the Aztec and Inca empires, with sophisticated mechanisms of labor mobilization that the Spaniards recognized and quickly took advantage of. Even after the great demographic collapse of indigenous peoples in the sixteenth century, they remained the most abundant source of labor exploitation. The situation was quite different in the Brazilian northeast, where the Portuguese encountered indigenous civilizations on a smaller scale that had never developed broad over-arching political structures or social systems designed to mobilize large labor reserves.

The number of African slaves imported to Mexico and Peru was initially quite small. The Spaniards first enslaved or found other coercive means to force indigenous laborers to serve the European-conceived urban centers they set about developing in the former Aztec capital, in the newly developed port town of Lima, Peru, and elsewhere. However, three interrelated factors resulted in increased labor demands, and these led to a significant rise in African slave imports by the mid sixteenth century. The first was the discovery of extraordinary silver reserves in northern Mexico and highland Bolivia during the 1540s.[4] The second was the dramatic demographic collapse of indigenous populations, primarily because of epidemics and pandemics. The third

---

[4]   See Peter J. Bakewell, *Silver Mining and Society in Colonial Mexico: Zacatecas 1546–1700* (New York: Cambridge University Press, 1971), and his *Miners of the Red Mountain: Indian Labor in Potosi, 1545–1650* (Albuquerque: University of New Mexico Press, 1984). For the broader impact of these silver discoveries, see Artur Attman, *American Bullion in the European World Trade, 1600–1800* (Gotenberg: Kungl. Vetenskaps- och Vitterhets Samhället, 1986).

was the spread by Europeans of new crops such as sugar cane, grapes, and a variety of grains, often grown in ecological zones in which indigenous laborers were scarce or suffered high mortality rates. This was especially the case in tropical lowland areas. Additionally, the introduction of cattle, pigs, horses, goats, and other European animals and crops led to a demand for labor skills that were lacking among the indigenous populations.

The onset and development of silver production in Mexico and the Andes created complex colonial economic systems stretching far beyond the mining regions. Transportation routes were forged through major urban colonial cities and towns; along Pacific and Gulf coast shipping routes to Havana, Cuba, which became the rendezvous point for a convoy system of transatlantic transportation; and finally to Spain, where silver entered Europe and led to transformations in economy and society.[5] An extraordinary array of ancillary industries, from food production to the small-scale manufacture of a wide variety of tools and consumer goods, developed to serve the mining economies. There were few regions of settled Spanish America that were not affected by the mining-based colonial economic systems. Economic expansion led to extraordinary labor demands, and these simply could not be met by indigenous communities suffering from the catastrophe of death and destruction wrought by European diseases to which they had no immunological response. It was within this social and economic context that Africans were imported to sixteenth-century Mexico and Peru, the first colonial societies with significant numbers of African slaves in the Americas.[6]

After indigenous peoples, African slaves were the second most numerous population sector in the colonial capitals of Mexico City and

[5]   For an important consideration of the impact of the discovery and export of American silver on European economies, see Earl J. Hamilton, *American Treasure and the Price Revolution in Spain, 1501–1650* (Cambridge, MA: Harvard University Press, 1934).

[6]   For considerations of slavery in colonial Mexico and Peru, see Gonzalo Aguirre Beltrán, *La Población Negra de México, 1519–1810: Etudio Etnohistórico* (México, D.F.: Ediciones Fuente Cultural, 1946); Colin A. Palmer, *Slaves of the White God: Blacks in Mexico, 1570–1650* (Cambridge, MA: Harvard University Press, 1976); Ben Vinson III, *Bearing Arms for His Majesty: The Free Colored Militia in Colonial Mexico* (Stanford, CA: Stanford University Press, 2001); and Frederick P. Bowser, *The African Slave in Colonial Peru, 1524–1650* (Stanford, CA: Stanford University Press, 1974).

Lima, Peru, for most of the sixteenth century. And their presence extended to every region of colonial Spanish America, rural and urban, from Buenos Aires to the northern Mexican frontier.[7] Enslaved African men and women worked in every occupation. They were employed in the mines; raised cattle, sheep, pigs, and goats; were muleteers moving merchandise to and from markets; grew wheat and corn; served as sailors; loaded and unloaded ships in port cities; labored in highly skilled trades as jewelers, goldsmiths, iron workers, and carpenters; and worked as house servants, cooks, laundresses, and drivers. They worked extensively in tropical lowland areas where sugar cane cultivation was introduced, and where indigenous peoples could not survive because of the disease environment. Without their labor, early Spanish colonial societies could not have functioned.

This was especially true as the demographic disaster among indigenous communities deepened over the course of the sixteenth century, when nearly 90 percent of pre-conquest populations in most areas died because of viral and bacterial infections introduced by Europeans. The importance of indigenous labor during the sixteenth century should not be minimized, for there were still many communities whose labor was requisitioned in a variety of ways after Indian slavery was abolished.[8] Yet African slaves were critical in providing labor for the colonial system during the sixteenth century. Population recovery among indigenous peoples would begin in the seventeenth century owing to the dramatic growth of a mixed-race, or mestizo and mulatto, population. This led to improved labor availability throughout Spanish America, and slavery gradually declined in importance in the principal Andean and Mesoamerican colonial regions, although in cities and in certain economic sectors slavery persisted through the colonial period.

Northeastern Brazil was to become the principal destination of the transatlantic slave trade later in the seventeenth century, and this

---

[7]   For slavery in Chile, see Rolando Mellafe R., *La Introducción de la Esclavitud Negra en Chile: Tráfico y Rutas* (Santiago: Universidad de Chile, 1959). For Argentina, see George Reid Andrews, *The Afro-Argentines of Buenos Aires, 1800–1900* (Madison: University of Wisconsin Press, 1980).

[8]   The Spanish crown, in a series of early sixteenth-century laws, forbade the enslavement of indigenous peoples, although royal officials often turned their backs on labor practices that resembled slavery. This all meant that race-based slavery emerged in the Americas. Only Africans or those of African descent born into slavery could be legally enslaved.

was largely because of the extensive development of slave-based sugar cane cultivation and sugar manufacture for European markets. Through most of the sixteenth century, however, Africans, although present in small numbers, were of marginal importance to the development of the Brazilian northeast. Portuguese settlers experimented with various possibilities for generating wealth, first exporting the by-products of a wood used as a source for textile dye – Brazil wood, which gave the future nation its name. Sugar cane was also planted, for the Portuguese had extensive experience with its cultivation in Madeira and elsewhere. Although slaves were utilized on cane farms of all sizes, they were for the most part indigenous peoples rather than Africans.

However, indigenous slavery could not support a large-scale sugar industry for a variety of reasons. First and foremost, as in Spanish colonial America, European diseases resulted in catastrophic death rates among indigenous slave laborers. Second, those who survived abuse, horrific exploitation, and disease often fled to the vast internal frontier that was unknown and impenetrable to the Portuguese. Finally, these factors, as well as the unwillingness of native slave laborers to submit to the seasonal discipline and regimentation that was necessary in order for sugar cane cultivation to be a profitable venture, led to the abandonment of indigenous slavery in favor of African slaves after the 1570s.[9]

The Portuguese, because of extensive experience and commercial linkages along the African coast dating from the mid fifteenth century; their profitable utilization of African slave labor on Madeira and São Tomé sugar estates; and their long-standing access to European markets, where sugar could be sold for extraordinary profits, made the decision to develop a large-scale sugar industry in northeastern Brazil supported by the importation of African slaves. By the 1580s the colony was rapidly developing the prototypical American model of the slave-based sugar plantation, and Brazil became the principal supplier of sugar to European markets, a position it would maintain until the middle of the seventeenth century. Although there were still more slaves in Mexico, Peru, and throughout the rest of Spanish America at the end of the sixteenth century, thereafter Brazil would

[9]   See the classic study by Stuart B. Schwartz, *Sugar Plantations in the Formation of Brazilian Society: Bahia, 1550–1835* (New York: Cambridge University Press, 1985).

become the leading African slave importer in the New World, a position it would maintain for some 250 years until the Brazilian slave trade was ended in the early 1850s. The colony also became the first true slave society in the Americas.[10]

Thus, by 1600, over a century after the fateful voyages led by Columbus, African slavery was well established in the three major colonial regions of the Americas controlled by Spain and Portugal – Mexico, Peru, and Brazil. It has been estimated that approximately 150,000 Africans had been imported to the Spanish colonies, and although slaves were found everywhere in peripheral areas, most were concentrated in Mexico and Peru. Some 50,000 slaves had also been imported to northeastern Brazil, with very few disembarking south of Bahia prior to the seventeenth century.[11] Slavery was a labor institution of enormous diversity, even in the Brazilian northeast, the one area where a specialized economic system revolving around sugar production was developing. African slaves labored in every economic sector – urban and rural, skilled and unskilled – and their occupational structures in each region paralleled those of free workers. Yet their legal status as property with few rights and privileges, and the often harsh and arbitrary treatment meted out by abusive owners, clearly distinguished them, along with their race, from the rest of the

---

[10] In his *Ancient Slavery and Modern Ideology* (London: Chatto & Windus, 1980), Moses I. Finley made a distinction between societies with slaves and slave societies, the latter defined in general terms as societies that depended upon slave labor for basic production and the generation of profits for elite groups, who were almost always slave owners. Additionally, slavery was a defining factor in nearly all social relationships because of the sharp legal distinctions between slaves and free; slaves were regarded and treated as property in addition to serving as laborers. Societies with slaves have been found in nearly every culture and region at some time through history. However, according to Finley, in these cases slave labor was not predominant but supplemented other types of free or coerced labor. Finley regarded the Caribbean, Brazil, and the U.S. South as slave societies. He identified ancient Greece and Rome as the two others. Finley's ideas have been challenged by some scholars who have observed that the experiences of slaves as human beings may have been very similar in both dichotomous conceptualizations.

[11] Curtin's statistical estimates of slave imports presented in 1969 in *The African Slave Trade: A Census* have been revised by David Eltis, "The Volume and Structure of the Transatlantic Slave Trade: A Reassessment," *William & Mary Quarterly*, 3rd series, vol. 63, No. 1 (January 2001), p. 46, Table 3. Eltis drew upon the work of many other scholars.

population. The Portuguese and Spanish monarchies had ruled that indigenous peoples could not be enslaved. But material conditions in their communities throughout the sixteenth century, when disease, suffering, and death were so pervasive, were probably much worse for commoners than conditions experienced by surviving Africans, despite their slave status.

Slavery in the Americas experienced major transformations during the seventeenth century, and these will be considered later in this chapter. During the eighteenth century the changes became quite dramatic as new critical matrices of the slave trade emerged in the British Caribbean and North America, in the French colonies, and later in Spanish Cuba. But before proceeding to consider the spread of slavery in these new areas, we should pause to consider some of the dynamics of African slave life and their multiple impacts on the first slave-importing colonies.

Too often contemporary observers tend to examine African slavery in the Americas from U.S., British, or French Caribbean perspectives, ignoring the fact that there were no slaves in any of these regions prior to 1600. This was more than a century after some 200,000 slaves had arrived in the Americas and had formed slave communities and cultures with particular dynamics and characteristics. These early colonial Mexican, Peruvian, and Brazilian slave societies established cultural parameters, legal and customary traditions, and patterns of slave life that would later be found in a variety of forms in the slave cultures that would eclipse them in size and importance during the eighteenth century. But from the vantage point of the early seventeenth century, slavery in the Americas had a particular set of meanings and dynamics that set the stage for the institution's later development in the Western Hemisphere. That Africans in the New World were heavily concentrated in the mainland Spanish colonies has not been emphasized in scholarly studies of slavery. The Caribbean was unimportant as a center of slavery, and Europeans had not yet established settlements in the future United States and Canada.

African slaves played critical social and cultural roles in the development of these Spanish colonial societies and northeast Brazil. In major urban areas of Mexico and the Andes they usually outnumbered Spaniards, and while they were nominally Catholic, owing to legal and social pressures or mandates, African religious beliefs and cultural practices were maintained even if hidden from local secular and religious officials.[12] Slaves were extraordinarily resourceful in carving out as many prerogatives as possible within the confines of a repressive system and subordinate legal status. They struggled to assert their humanity at every turn in a variety of ways, both visible and hidden from view.

Although approximately 60 percent of imported slaves were males, there were enough slave women that legal marriage or consensual cohabitation was found in all of these early colonial slave societies. In most regions this was encouraged and recognized by authorities and masters as a means to create stability and maintain control, a pervasive preoccupation for elites always fearful of resistance and rebellion. One theory was that if slaves were bound by wives, husbands, and children they would be less likely to run away or be disruptive to masters in different ways. However, slave owners could be wary of marriages or informal relations, especially between slaves living at some distance from one another, which they feared would encourage too much physical mobility, authorized or not. Nevertheless, the formation and maintenance of slave families, regardless of the attitudes of slave owners, was of extraordinary importance to slave populations them-selves in their never-ending quest to affirm individual and collective identities, optimism and spirit, and to establish links to the future through their children, whom they surely hoped would lead better lives and perhaps become free. The possibilities of forming family structures, nuclear and extended, should not be romanticized or misinterpreted as an attempt to portray slavery as humane in any way. Rather, they are testimony to the intelligence and resilience of Africans in the New World in creating their own lives, institutions, traditions, communities, and subcultures within the framework of the most degrading and brutal of all human conditions.

Possibilities for the creation of slave families and kinship networks were much more pronounced in urban centers because of a fairly even distribution of men and women. In the Mexican and Peruvian cases there were large concentrations of urban slaves, especially in colonial and provincial capitals. In rural areas, slave family possibilities were determined by a variety of factors. The ratio between men and women

[12]   See Roger Bastide, *The African Religions of Brazil: Toward a Sociology of the Interpenetration of Civilizations* (Baltimore: Johns Hopkins University Press, 1978) (originally published in French in 1960), and Fernando Ortíz, *Hampa Afrocubana: Los Negros Brujos* (Madrid: Librería de F. Fé, 1906).

was critical, and this was often determined by the type of rural economic activity in which slaves labored. It must be kept in mind that slaves lived and worked on small-scale food producing farms, in livestock enterprises, raising pigs and goats, growing export crops such as tobacco, in mines, as muleteers, and in nearly every other rural activity. During the sixteenth and early seventeenth centuries, with the exception of the Brazilian northeast, it was rare to find most slaves working in male-dominated plantation environments with large concentrations of slaves, despite the stereotypical image of the slave-based plantation that has been fairly pervasive.

The great majority of these rural slaves were owned in small lots of fewer than five slaves during the first century of African slavery in Latin America, and this was the case in both rural and urban environments. Near equal numbers of men and women were common, obviously a critical factor in family formation. However, a different set of demographic, social, and cultural dynamics governed the sugar plantation zones developing in northeastern Brazil in its formative phase during the late sixteenth century. As owners exhibited an overwhelming preference for males, sex imbalances reduced the possibilities for marriage, cohabitation, and families. But even more critical were the higher death rates for slaves found in tropical plantation regions, especially in the areas of Brazilian sugar production during the late sixteenth and early seventeenth centuries and after. Demographic studies have not been precise for the sixteenth century in any region, but in the Brazilian case we do know that there was an imbalance in the sex ratio heavily in favor of males, and thus that there were relatively small numbers of slave children, a certain indicator of poorly developed family structures.[13]

It must also be kept in mind that even when slave families and extended kinship networks emerged, slaves had no ultimate power over the lives of their children, spouses, and other relatives. The slave-owning class exerted complete legal control over every aspect of slave existence, and this could be brought into sharp and painful focus by the arbitrary and cruel decision to sell off spouses, parents, children, or other members of family units with utter disregard for human values or emotions of any sort. These powers were backed by colonial judicial systems and the state, which enforced laws that assumed property rights

[13] See Schwartz, *Sugar Plantations in the Formation of Brazilian Society*, Chapter 14, "The Slave Family and the Limitations of Slavery," pp. 379–412.

to be sacrosanct. It was without question psychologically wrenching for slaves to marry or cohabit, to have children, and to always know that upon the master's whim their families could be destroyed. Yet we don't know how pervasive the practice of separating families was in Latin American slave societies during any time period, or whether there were any social or cultural taboos on such inhumane behavior that may have restrained masters from this dreadful practice.

In addition to forming families and communities, slaves asserted their humanity in other very graphic ways. While many slaves were treated decently by masters everywhere, systematic patterns of physical degradation and humiliation were also found in all early Latin American colonial slave societies. Yet it is difficult to generalize on the pervasiveness of good or poor treatment, or on the degree of paternalism, humanism, or sadism prevailing in any locale or region, since slavery was so diverse and conditions varied according to place, gender, occupation, and time period. It is certain that there were great variations in the treatment of slaves, ranging from the worst possible forms of abuse to respect for the basic dignity of human existence. It is likely, of course, that most slaves were neither treated benignly nor abused systematically, and that both situations could be found existing side by side in the same places and time periods.

Yet slaves who were abused in a variety of ways, and even those who simply could not tolerate the indignity of being regarded and treated as property in addition to the ruthless exploitation of forced labor, practiced various forms of graphic or subtle resistance. The most common form was simply running away in search of freedom. In every colony, in both urban and rural zones, slaves fled bondage so frequently that the profession of slave bounty hunter emerged as a full-time occupation. Where daily or weekly newspapers were published, as was the case in most large cities, advertisements for runaway slaves were usually found on the first or second page, and in nearly every issue. Sometimes slaves ran away in groups after elaborate planning, while in other instances individuals fed up with various forms of systematic abuse, or no longer able to tolerate the humiliation of perpetual enslavement, spontaneously made their way to areas of perceived refuge. Slave flight was common in both rural and urban zones, and while there is no statistical record that suggests how many slaves, or what portion of the slave population, fled, it was clearly a widespread phenomenon.

Urban slaves often made their way to city or town enclaves in which sympathetic free black and mulatto communities had emerged, and where they could not so easily be identified as slaves simply because of their race. Rural slaves as well sometimes fled to cities and towns seeking these communities where they hoped to blend in and perhaps avoid recapture. The other possibility was fleeing in groups or as individuals, to remote and inaccessible areas where other slaves had established communities of runaways. These maroon communities (*palenques* in Spanish and *mocambos* or *quilombos* in Portuguese) could be quite large, although most were established on a modest scale.[14] Their long-term survival, with some exceptions, was quite precarious, since they had to create an infrastructure that assured sources of food and shelter as well as security. This often mandated contact with colonial population nuclei in search of basic supplies – tools, seed, animals, clothing, and sometimes weaponry. Raids on established farms or population centers was one form of such contact, a risky and often desperate enterprise because local militias or slave bounty hunters would thereby be alerted to a nearby presence. Or there could be attempts to purchase supplies from local populations, although this required some form of specie or goods to barter and was fraught with the danger of exposure. Isolation and self-sufficiency were difficult to maintain over an extended period of time, although it was not unheard of.[15]

These maroon communities were almost always discovered and eventually attacked by authorities in organized raids, or individuals or groups were captured by the ubiquitous bounty hunters. Upon return to masters, punishment could be extraordinarily harsh. Debilitating and horrendously painful whippings, often done in public; confinement in wooden or iron stocks for extended periods of time; deprivation of food and water; subjection to extreme heat or cold; and even amputation of limbs as a deterring lesson to fellow slaves were some of the punishments meted out by enraged or calculating slave owners.

[14] See the essays in Richard Price, editor, *Maroon Societies: Rebel Slave Communities in the Americas* (Baltimore: Johns Hopkins University Press, 1979).

[15] The most famous example of a large-scale *quilombo* that survived for much of the seventeenth century was that of Palmares in the Pernambuco region of Brazil. It had a sophisticated state structure, a taxation system, and even a standing army for defense. Repeated Portuguese military campaigns finally destroyed it in the 1690s. There are many accounts of Palmares, and a good survey is Edison Carneiro, *O Quilombo do Palmares, 1630–1695* (São Paulo: Editora Brasiliense, 1947).

But again, information is fragmentary as to the number of runaways, *palenques* or *quilombos*, or about the frequency or duration of the kinds of punishments just noted.

Resistance, individual or collective, against abusive masters or in some case against slaveholding elites as a group, could take violent forms. It was not uncommon for abused slaves or those against whom some injustice had been perpetrated, such as unwarranted punishment or the selling off of a family member, to attack overseers or their masters in acts of calculated or spontaneous violence. Individual murders committed by slaves were noted periodically, and slave rebellions date from a 1522 uprising in Santo Domingo.[16] During the sixteenth century, notices of slave uprisings in the Spanish colonies were pervasive in central and peripheral areas of settlement where slaves were found. Additionally, bands of *cimarrones*, or runaway slaves, were found in all of the major Spanish-controlled Caribbean islands in the sixteenth century.

Despite their legal and social status slaves never abandoned the hope of securing freedom for themselves and their family members, whether through flight or by utilizing other strategies. During the exploration and conquest phase of Spanish incursions into New World societies, warfare was constantly being waged as bands of soldiers moved into new regions confronting indigenous peoples. As indicated previously, slaves were nearly always present on these missions, often serving as able soldiers who distinguished themselves by their bravery, and were not simply utilized as menial laborers. Europeans brought to the Americas an entire range of customs and traditions, some legal and others rooted in long-standing practices, on the manner in which elite groups behaved toward slaves and other subalterns. In many medieval European societies, Iberian included, it had been customary to free slaves for acts of valor, bravery in battle, or extraordinary service in war, and this was long before slavery had become racially based in the Americas. In this way, during the conquest phase of Iberian expansion, many slaves secured their freedom, although there is no way to know the quantitative dimensions of this during each time period of the ongoing conquest. What is important to emphasize is that from the very beginning of conquest, colonization, and the development of slavery in the Americas, there were freed Africans present in every region.

---

[16]   See José Luciano Franco, *Afroamérica* (Havana: Publicaciones de la Junta Nacional de Arqueología y Etnología, 1961).

Thus, in all American slave societies, communities of free blacks and mulattos gradually emerged from the very beginning of colonization, and this would change the way in which the complex question and conceptualization of race evolved. In the region that would later become known as Latin America, to be black was not necessarily to be a slave. Additionally, unlike racial concepts that would develop much later in the United States after settlement during the seventeenth century, there was never a black/white dichotomy, precisely because of the process of race mixture that became so widespread throughout the region.

Spanish colonial officials initially attempted to keep the races separate, and in the aftermath of conquest they experimented with the creation of two legally distinct colonial worlds, one inhabited by Indians, the other by Spaniards.[17] Slaves and free people of color would, paradoxically, inhabit the Spanish "republic." This separation was, of course, impossible to maintain not only because of the widespread employment of indigenous peoples by Spanish conquerors and colonizers in Spanish cities and towns, and Spanish incursions into Indian villages, but also because of the almost immediate creation of new racial configurations resulting from unions, forced or voluntary, between Spanish men and indigenous women. The *mestizo*, or person of mixed Spanish/indigenous heritage, would eventually represent the great majority of populations in Mesoamerica and the Andean region.

The racial mosaic became more complex through the formative sixteenth century, for not only did a *mestizo* population grow in numbers, but a mulatto population of every possible skin tone, some free and others enslaved, evolved on a significant scale as well. Offspring of Spanish men and African slave women often resulted from rape, but there were consensual relationships as well. It should be kept in mind that a mixed-racial population emanating from European/African unions was not an innovation of sixteenth-century colonial Latin America. Similar populations had evolved from the mid fifteenth century all along the African coast in enclaves that the Portuguese had established to trade with African kingdoms, and on the islands conquered and occupied by Portugal and Spain such as the Azores,

[17] For a consideration of this and the general theme of race in Latin America, see Magnus Mörner, *Race Mixture in the History of Latin America* (Boston: Little, Brown, 1967).

Cape Verdes, Madeira, the Canaries, and São Tome. In many instances these mixed-race populations were Europeanized to varying degrees in that they spoke Portuguese in addition to African languages, sometimes dressed in European clothing, became Catholic, or in other ways adopted aspects of European culture. In Portugal itself, where some 10 percent of the population was of African heritage before Columbus set out on his fateful voyage in 1492, a more widespread phenomenon of race mixture had long been under way.[18] It is impossible to generalize about these populations of free or enslaved mulattos and blacks from cultural, religious, or any other perspectives because there was such diversity. The point to be kept in mind is that prior to the epoch of European conquest and colonization, whites had become accustomed to living with and interacting with free people of color, and with mixed-race slaves. Long before the beginnings of slavery in the future United States, multiracial societies had developed on a significant scale in Latin America and the Caribbean.

The importance of these communities of free people of color, some born in the Americas and others in Africa, to the slave population should be stressed. We don't know the degree of interaction between slaves and free blacks and mulattos, but in all likelihood there were extensive connections. This is suggested by the emergence of ethnic-based African social, cultural, and religious organizations, often legally recognized by colonial authorities.[19] What may have been most important to slave populations, however, was the example of ex-slaves and other blacks and mulattos living in freedom, even if there was segregation and discrimination. There is little question that for slaves the hope and aspiration of eventual freedom was an integral part of their lives, even if the probability was small in most cases. Flight and rebellion were options often exercised in this quest. But an inherited practice dating from Roman slave codes, filtered through Iberia to the African enclaves of the Portuguese in the fifteenth century, and later to Latin America, was of extraordinary importance to slaves as well. This was the legal or customary recognition that slaves had the right to own property and, perhaps surprisingly, to purchase their freedom through

[18]   A. C. de D. M. Saunders, *A Social History of Black Slaves and Freedmen in Portugal, 1441–1555* (New York: Cambridge University Press, 1982).

[19]   See Philip A. Howard, *Changing History: Afro-Cuban Cabildos and Societies of Color in the Nineteenth Century* (Baton Rouge: Louisiana State University Press, 1998).

an institution known as *coartación* – literally, "self-purchase". Slaves were not required to purchase themselves outright, but rather could pay for their freedom over time in small payments.

When a slave made a down payment on his or her freedom, or the freedom of children, that slave's legal classification was transformed from slave to *coartado*. This does not mean that the person ceased being enslaved and subject to forced labor, but it did entail a whole new series of rights that could be challenged through the judicial system if violated. First and foremost, the ultimate price of freedom was frozen, even if slave values were to rise or decline in future years. A master set the price of freedom, and this could not be altered. Second, at least theoretically, a *coartado* could not be sold without his or her permission, and a new master would have to accept the extant contractual arrangements for self-purchase, including the final cost of freedom. These contracts were almost always recorded by local notary publics present in every Spanish city and town, and thus there was a legal and public record that slaves could utilize if there were later disputes. Slaves themselves probably insisted on the recording of these documents, which were their only ultimate legal protection. Even if they were illiterate in Spanish, which was often the case because of the absence of education, they knew someone who could read. Historians have made extensive use of these records to reconstruct this aspect of slavery.

This institution was of extraordinary importance to the slave population. Quite clearly, access to cash or goods for barter was of critical importance, since it was the key to purchasing freedom. Slaves were often permitted to cultivate garden plots in rural areas, and they had the prerogative of selling merchandise, a practice that was widespread and legally condoned in the sixteenth and seventeenth centuries. In urban areas, slaves with highly sought skills were rented out by their masters and often, as an incentive for efficient labor, were permitted to keep a portion of the rent. The percentage of the overall slave population that was able to take advantage of such opportunities is unknown, nor do we know how many slaves who became *coartados* achieved ultimate freedom. Yet it is important to emphasize these dynamics of the slave experience in sixteenth-century Latin America, not as an attempt to portray human bondage as anything but ultimate brutality, but to understand the diversity and complexity of slavery during its formative period in the region. What is especially critical to comprehend is that slaves were people, not a mass of faceless humanity, and that within this horrendous institution they had normal everyday human strivings and inclinations that they struggled to realize, utilizing whatever physical, legal, or psychological space was available, however small. To be free was without question the most important objective.

Slaves were sometimes freed by their masters for a variety of other reasons. It was not uncommon for dying slave owners, perhaps wracked with guilt and having to face ultimate divine judgment, to free certain slaves in last wills and testaments. These slaves may have been mistresses or concubines, or even their children, who were sometimes legally recognized. We know by surviving census reports that within communities of free people of color, women made up about 60 percent of the overall population.

Care must be exercised when considering the possibilities of freedom during this formative phase of slavery in Latin America. The tradition and practice of some access to freedom continued until ultimate abolition in the various regions, the last occurring in Brazil in 1888, but we cannot generalize about the pervasiveness of self-purchase or the forms of voluntary manumission by masters in every locale and every time period. There were enormous variations throughout Latin America and the Caribbean, and when slavery developed on a massive scale in the British and French colonies during the seventeenth and eighteenth centuries, opportunities for freedom were almost nonexistent, sometimes even foreclosed by legal codes outlawing the granting of freedom or self-purchase.

During the seventeenth century New World slavery was transformed, and by the eighteenth century the massive slave trades to the British and French Caribbean colonies had changed the meaning of being a slave in the Americas, decisively altering the Spanish and Portuguese sixteenth-century colonial institutions just described. Slavery evolved intensively in Brazil as well after 1600 with the growth of a full-blown slave/sugar plantation complex in the northeast and its spread to other regions of the colony. But slavery gradually waned as a labor system of critical importance to the Spanish mainland after 1600 with the beginning of indigenous population recovery along with the rapid growth of a *mestizo* population whose labor could be harnessed by the colonial regimes in each region. Some 340,000 Africans had been imported to the Spanish colonies by 1650, nearly as many as would be imported over the entire history of the slave traffic to the future United States, but this trade plummeted thereafter.

Another 225,000 slaves had been imported to Brazil, largely to the northeast regions.[20] But the future destinations of transatlantic slaving followed transformations in the political and economic history of Africa, Brazil, and the Caribbean.

After 1600 slavery spread to new areas, and this was above all tied to the successful challenges to Spanish and Portuguese exclusivism in the Americas by the Dutch, British, and French. The Dutch led the way from the early seventeenth century, first contesting the Portuguese-controlled African and Far Eastern trades, and then in the early 1620s focusing on the Caribbean and Brazil, where a Dutch commercial presence dated from the 1590s.[21] The formation of the Dutch West India Company for the specific purpose of promoting and consolidating commerce with the Americas was a defining feature of this period.[22]

Amsterdam had long been a major center of sugar refining and marketing, but the Portuguese had established a near-monopoly over the production of raw sugar in the Brazilian regions of Pernambuco and Bahia. It is thus not surprising that the Dutch launched a series of attacks beginning in 1624 and by 1630 had occupied the major sugar-producing zones of the Brazilian northeast in the regions around Pernambuco, which they controlled until the early 1650s. This was complemented by African ventures that lead to successful domination of Gold Coast and Angolan slave-trading enclaves during the 1630s and 1640s, thus ending both Portuguese control over both raw sugar production and slaving.

The Dutch enterprise in Brazil was marked by technological advances in sugar refining and the creation of a transatlantic slave trading infrastructure. However, Portuguese settlers or their offspring controlled the planting and supply of cane in the Brazilian northeast. When it was expedient from an economic point of view, they cooperated with the occupiers. But when the Portuguese mounted serious efforts to end Dutch control, local residents supported the

---

[20] Eltis, "The Volume and Structure of the Transatlantic Slave Trade: A Reassessment," p. 46, Table 3.

[21] Charles R. Boxer, *The Dutch Seaborne Empire, 1600–1800* (New York: Knopf, 1965).

[22] The Dutch first began trading in the Caribbean during the 1590s. For the most complete histories, see Cornelis Ch. Goslinga, *The Dutch in the Caribbean and on the Wild Coast, 1580–1680* (Assen, The Netherlands: Van Gorcum, 1971), and Johannes Menne Postma, *The Dutch in the Atlantic Slave Trade, 1600–1815* (New York: Cambridge University Press, 1990).

reestablishment of Portuguese rule, and the Dutch were finally expelled in the 1650s.

Dutch colonizers dispersed to various regions after the Portuguese reconquest. Some came as far north as the future New York, establishing the New Netherlands in 1624. The colony of Surinam (Dutch Guiana), to the north of Brazil, was intensely developed as a slave-based sugar economy much like the Brazilian northeast. More importantly for the future of slavery in the Americas, Dutch settlers moved to the small, recently occupied British colonies of Barbados and St. Kitts, bringing with them slaves, equipment, and a sophisticated technological knowledge of the methods of sugar production. The French and the British, along with the Dutch, had been making tentative forays into the eastern Caribbean from the early seventeenth century, but it was only during the 1620s that permanent settlements were established. Often various islands were occupied briefly by some combination of these European powers, but eventually each established control over specific islands.

Neither sugar nor slave labor was initially important in these early island colonies. In Barbados and St. Kitts, tobacco was grown as the principal export crop during the 1620s and 1630s, and white settlers, many of them indentured servants, predominated, although small numbers of African slaves were also present. But by the 1650s Barbados was gradually being converted into a slave/sugar colony, in part because of Dutch influence, settlement, and the model of the African slave-based sugar plantation complex that had developed in Brazil. This model would gradually spread to the rest of the Caribbean in different waves of expansion, the last of which occurred in Cuba during the late eighteenth and nineteenth centuries. In this manner the slave trade and slavery shifted from its almost 150-year concentration in the Spanish mainland colonies and Brazil to the British and French Caribbean. The late seventeenth century marked the onset of most active period in the history of the transatlantic slave trade, due in large part to British and French colonial imports, as well as to the upsurge in the volume of slaves imported to Brazil.

The institution of slavery, from the Caribbean perspective, was closely bound up with sugar from these seventeenth century beginnings through the nineteenth-century Cuban sugar cycle. Without question, the association between sugar and slavery is an accurate portrayal from the British, French, Dutch, and nineteenth-century Cuban perspectives. But the slave/sugar complex has erroneously been seen in the popular imagination as a paradigm for understanding Latin American and Caribbean slavery in general. African slavery was well developed a century and a half prior to the onset of the Caribbean sugar cycle, and it was a very different institution, especially in the Spanish colonies. Two distinguishing features, of many, may be highlighted.

First, there was no occupational concentration of slaves, although in Brazil during the early seventeenth century quite clearly the sugar/slave plantation model was developing. However, the majority of all African-origin slaves were found in the Spanish mainland colonies prior to 1650, and they labored in every conceivable occupation, skilled and unskilled, in both rural and urban areas. This was even the case in sugar-producing Brazil. There were few large-sized concentrations of slaves, as would be the case in the developing Caribbean plantation model of the seventeenth and eighteenth centuries, and most slaves lived and labored alongside a relatively small number of fellow slaves, often in concert with free laborers of all racial categories.

Second, slavery developed in the Spanish colonies, and even in Brazil during the sixteenth and seventeenth centuries, within societies in which they were not the majority of all inhabitants and where they were often a small minority. These demographic environments were extraordinarily diverse racially and ethnically, with large numbers of indigenous peoples, mestizos, free blacks and mulattos, and even growing numbers of slaves who had been born in the colonies to African women. By the early seventeenth century there were large numbers of these American-born slaves, although no studies to date have determined their precise statistical profile in any region.

It ought to be noted that sharp distinctions were drawn between African-born and American-born slaves by the slaves themselves as well as by owners and free people in general. Slaves born in the New World had no experience or direct knowledge of what is was like to live as free people. They were born and raised within the confines of European-dominated structures of power and cultural systems, including languages, religions, ways of dress, customs, rituals, and traditions, even if these were imposed by masters and colonial states. Often they were of mixed racial backgrounds, and this could have resulted from forced sexual relations, consensual unions, concubinage, or even (in exceptionally rare cases) marriage. American-born slaves were most commonly found working in urban environs, skilled trades, or as house servants, and this was equally true of men and women.

The British and French Caribbean variants of slavery were so different that some historians have indicated that they were in reality part of a second American slave system, quite distinct from the first.[23] Not only did the trade in slaves during the eighteenth century dwarf the previous levels, but in the British and French Caribbean colonies slaves were the vast majority of all inhabitants. There were relatively few free laborers; communities of free blacks and mulattos were tiny; there were no indigenous peoples; mechanisms for acquiring freedom were nearly nonexistent; occupational diversity was minimal in comparative perspective; there were high death rates, especially among young children; and slave populations were constantly "Africanized" because of continuous large-scale importation. The Caribbean islands developed as black/white societies in which to be black was almost always to be a slave, and to be a slave was to be part of the great majority of the population.[24]

From St. Kitts and Barbados the British and French gradually moved to dominate nearly all of the Leeward Islands of the eastern Caribbean during the seventeenth century. The French established control over Martinique and Guadeloupe. The British dominated Nevis, Antigua, and Montserrat, which along with St. Kitts collectively replaced Barbados during the first half of the eighteenth century as the most important sugar-exporting colonies. But it was English-dominated Jamaica, occupied in 1655, and French-controlled St. Domingue, established after 1697 with the seizure of the western half of Hispaniola from Spain, that would become the epicenters of Caribbean slavery and sugar production by the mid eighteenth century. In large part these colonies created the lasting association of slavery with sugar, despite Spanish colonial antecedents that were so very different.

---

[23]   See the essay by P. C. Emmer, "The Dutch and the Making of the Second Atlantic System," in Barbara L. Solow, editor, *Slavery and the Rise of the Atlantic System* (New York: Cambridge University Press, 1991), pp. 75–96.

[24]   For example, in Barbados in 1773 some 78 percent of the total population of nearly 88,000 inhabitants was enslaved. In Antigua, St. Kitts, Nevis, and Montserrat in 1775, 92 percent of nearly 89,000 residents were black. See Jerome S. Handler, *The Unappropriated People: Freedmen in the Slave Society of Barbados* (Baltimore: Johns Hopkins University Press, 1974), p. 18; Richard B. Sheridan, *Sugar and Slavery: An Economic History of the British West Indies, 1623–1775* (Baltimore: Johns Hopkins University Press, 1973), p. 150; and Hilary McD. Beckles, *White Servitude and Black Slavery in Barbados, 1727–1715* (Knoxville: University of Tennessee Press, 1989).

By the 1750s Jamaican slave imports, which had begun on a significant scale during the 1670s, surpassed those of the all the other British Caribbean island colonies combined; and, not surprisingly, so did sugar exports. A similar trajectory was followed by French St. Domingue. On the eve of the great slave revolt of 1791 it was the world's greatest exporter of both sugar and coffee and a Caribbean center of slavery rivaling Jamaica. The two colonies alone imported nearly 1.6 million slaves between 1701 and 1800. During that same period the other French and British Caribbean colonies imported another 1.1 million slaves. These numbers are extraordinary when compared to sixteenth- and seventeenth-century Spanish and Portuguese colonial slave imports. It is because of this massive volume of Africans unwillingly brought to the New World by the British and French during the eighteenth century that the earlier history of slavery in the Americas has been relegated to the background of historical perception.

The settlement of the Caribbean by the British during the 1620s was paralleled by the establishment of the first population centers on the North American mainland. The Chesapeake region was one focal point of settlement, and slaves were among the first residents of a slowly emerging colonial society. Most slaves, however, were initially imported from the Caribbean, not directly from Africa, and a great majority of them were born in the New World. Until the last two decades of the seventeenth century, slavery was of marginal importance to settlements in Virginia and Maryland as most labor was performed by a diverse combination of indentured servants, family labor, and salaried employees in addition to slaves, who rarely surpassed 5 percent to 10 percent of the total population. These slaves lived in very small concentrations, most on family-run farms.

In some respects slavery in the formative phase of the Chesapeake area in the mid seventeenth century resembled the Spanish colonial experience in that slaves were only a small part of a varied labor force and populace. Slavery could be as brutal and dehumanizing as it was anywhere else. But there was also a series of prerogatives available to slaves similar to those found in the Spanish colonies, such as access to provision grounds or garden plots, an ability to market products and accumulate small amounts of cash, the accompanying possibility of acquiring freedom through self-purchase, the establishment of recognized families, and the development of communities of free people of color, which were acknowledged, if often resented, by political and social elites.[25] There was also a varied occupational structure among slaves within this emerging rural society.

Slaves were also found in early seventeenth-century northern colonial settlements of the future United States, but again slavery was not a labor system of widespread importance, nor were slaves demographically more than a small sector of the local populations of New England, New York, New Jersey, and Pennsylvania. New Amsterdam, controlled by the Dutch until 1664, was the largest center of northern slavery during the seventeenth century, but it was a diverse institution there as well, with slaves laboring in nearly every occupation alongside free laborers and with the same kind of relative social and economic fluidity that existed in the rural Chesapeake. Most slaves in the Dutch-controlled future New York were also born in the New World rather than having been imported directly from Africa.

If slavery was a comparatively unimportant institution in the history of British North America during the first half-century of settlement, this began to change decisively during the late seventeenth century. The spread of tobacco cultivation in the Chesapeake region, particularly in Virginia, increased labor demands and led to the first direct large-scale slave imports from Africa. The specialized slave-based plantation slowly took form, although it was initially on a fairly small scale. Planters gradually abandoned using European indentured servants, and they turned to the transatlantic slave trade from Africa rather than to the Caribbean for their labor needs. The transformations in economy, society, and culture were extensive by the early eighteenth century. The slave population was slowly "Africanized." Slaves had been almost insignificant in demographic terms through most of the seventeenth century, but by the 1740s they comprised over 40 percent of the overall population in tobacco-growing zones. Their numbers would grow dramatically over the eighteenth century through imports and an

---

[25]   An important general survey of these processes is found in Ira Berlin, *Many Thousands Gone: The First Two Centuries of Slavery in North America* (Cambridge, MA: The Belknap Press of Harvard University Press, 1998), pp. 29–46. Also see three other important works: Edmund S. Morgan, *American Slavery, American Freedom: The Ordeal of Colonial Virginia* (New York: Norton, 1975); Phillip D. Morgan, *Slave Counterpoint: Black Culture in the Eighteenth-Century Chesapeake & Low Country* (Chapel Hill: University of North Carolina Press, 1998); and Allan Kulikoff, *Tobacco and Slaves: The Development of Southern Cultures in the Chesapeake, 1680–1800* (Chapel Hill: University of North Carolina Press, 1986).

extraordinarily impressive process of natural reproduction that would be a defining demographic feature of the North American slave system. By the 1750s, remarkably, some 80 percent of all slaves in the Chesapeake had been born there, fairly large-scale imports of Africans notwithstanding.

There was also a curbing of most, if not all, of the prerogatives slaves had previously enjoyed when they made up a small portion of the total population. The growing number of Africans in the overall slave population in the late seventeenth and early eighteenth centuries induced fear and concern for security among planters, as well as within the broader white society. Absolute control became a major priority, and slaves were subjected to severe discipline. Limitations were imposed over their mobility, and a harsh regime of exploitation ensued. It became more difficult to form stable families, and to maintain extended kinship networks and communities, and the avenues to acquiring freedom were blocked by newly created legal codes. Free communities of blacks and mulattos were reduced vis-à-vis the ever-growing slave populations, especially in districts where tobacco was cultivated. The early dynamics of North American slavery in the Chesapeake were a distant memory by the mid eighteenth century. Slaves struggled continuously under this harsh regime to assert their humanity, and this led to increased incidents of resistance and running away, a concerted struggle to keep families together, and always the difficult quest to be treated as people rather than the faceless chattel that they were regarded as by the master class.

Further to the south, in coastal South Carolina, Georgia, and in the very southern littoral of North Carolina, another zone of slavery developed in British North America, although the timing, the driving economic forces, and significant other aspects of its development were very different from those found in the Chesapeake. These regions were settled more than a half-century after Virginia and Maryland, and during the 1660s and 1670s they were still sparsely populated. The process of colonization may also be contrasted with that of the Chesapeake in that early settlers brought with them fairly large numbers of slaves. Most were of Caribbean origin, rather than African, but rather than making up a marginal portion of overall inhabitants, slaves were well over 25 percent of colonial populations from the onset of settlement.

The "Lowcountry," the name applied to this region, was transformed by export-oriented rice cultivation, which told hold during the 1690s and spread continuously through the eighteenth century to the eve of the American Revolution. Rice needed to be grown on fairly extensive farms in order to be economically viable. This meant larger labor requirements on each farm compared to tobacco, which could be grown profitably on farms of all sizes, from small parcels to large plantations. The labor demands of rice production lead to the large-scale importation of slaves directly from Africa, but this occurred on a significant scale only after 1700, later than in the earlier-settled Chesapeake. The development of indigo production in interior areas also fueled slave demand. Accordingly, one of the great differences found in the Lowcountry was that the African slave trade was larger in volume and sustained for a longer period, with significant imports through the 1770s, after these had waned in the Chesapeake.

Although the slave populations of South Carolina and Georgia would also experience the pattern of natural increase found in the Chesapeake, this would occur mainly in the second half of the eighteenth century. Because of the sustained African slave trade to the Lowcountry that continued through the 1770s and 1780s, when the trade to the Chesapeake had diminished considerably, African-born slaves were a larger part of the region's slave population than in Virginia or Maryland. This meant that African cultural practices and customs remained an important part of slave life in the Lowcountry as the constant importation of slaves from Africa reinforced a wide variety of traditions even within the confines of human bondage.

Another important difference was the larger number of slaves found in the overall population, a pattern that was established from initial settlement. As the slave population increased through natural reproduction and the continuing slave trade, it was common to find Lowcountry regions in which slaves comprised well over 50 percent of all inhabitants. In intense rice-producing zones slaves could make up over 90 percent of the population from the 1760s through the 1790s, a proportion not found in Virginia, the largest slaveholding colony. This made South Carolina, and some regions of Georgia, the only British North American areas that emulated to some extent the population distribution patterns of the British and French Caribbean colonies, with their large percentages of slaves within the total population.

Finally, the rice-producing Lowcountry was distinguished from the Virginia and Maryland tobacco colonies by the development of a major city and the parallel growth in urban slavery, with its greater occupational diversity. Charleston, South Carolina, became one of the largest cities in the colonies by the second half of the eighteenth century; by 1770, with its population of over 12,000, it was surpassed in size only by New York, Boston, and Philadelphia. In part this was because of the desire of plantation owners to maintain residences for their families away from the intense disease environments prevalent in the tropical lowland regions where their plantations were located.[26]

There were two other areas on the North American mainland where slaves were found prior to the American Revolution, in Spanish Florida and French Louisiana. Neither of these areas was a major importer of Africans, nor was slavery important during the colonial period. This would change with the development of sugar production in Louisiana during the 1790s, and later with the growth of New Orleans as a center of slave trading during the nineteenth century.

The tobacco and rice economies of the British North American colonies were creating new markets for the African slave trade and new centers of slavery in the Americas by the late seventeenth century. The colonization and economic development of the British, French, and Dutch Caribbean set the stage for the great upsurge in the volume of the slave trade that occurred during the eighteenth century. Similar processes were occurring in Brazil, although they were driven by different economic forces.

As indicated previously, African slavery in Brazil prior to the late seventeenth century was concentrated in the sugar-producing zones of the northeast, although wherever settlements were established slaves were present on a small scale. Many of these slaves were not Africans but indigenous people, and this was especially the case in extreme southern Portuguese population enclaves such as São Paulo, still a small town during the seventeenth century. The geographical parameters of African slavery and the volume of the slave trade to the colony were decisively transformed by the discovery of gold and diamonds in the interior regions of Minas Gerais during the 1690s. When it became clear that the rugged mountainous regions some 300 kilometers north of Rio de Janeiro possessed the largest gold reserves ever discovered in the Americas during the colonial period, a veritable invasion of wealth-seeking adventurers ensued. Since the zone was populated only by a very small indigenous population, African slaves had to be brought in for the development of the mining economy. Accordingly, the "gold rush" to

[26] Peter Kolchin, *American Slavery, 1619–1877* (New York: Hill and Wang, 1993), p. 25.

Minas Gerais was paralleled by the importation of large numbers of Africans, and by the 1720s another major center of New World slavery had emerged in the Brazilian interior.[27] Gold and diamonds were also discovered in other areas further inland, such as Goiás and Mato Grosso, and slavery developed in these regions as well.

The mining zones were first supplied with slaves from the northeastern sugar-producing centers, principally Bahia, which is contiguous to Minas Gerais and linked to the gold region by the São Francisco River. But by the early eighteenth century a small port town on the Bay of Guanabara, Rio de Janeiro, had developed as a major commercial center for the importation of Africans and the export of precious minerals to Portugal. Winding overland transportation routes for mule trains were forged through the high Mantiqueira Mountains separating Rio from the gold- and diamond-producing zones, and a regularized commercial system gradually developed connecting the port to the interior.

The development of this eighteenth-century economic system in southeastern Brazil shifted the matrix of slavery in the colony toward these new regions of settlement and economic growth. Rio de Janeiro grew into a major port city and slave-trading center, and urban slavery there developed impressively. From the beginnings of the Brazilian slave trade until the 1720s, the northeastern centers of Bahia and Pernambuco had been the principal slave-importing regions for the colony. While slave imports to the northeast continued at fairly high levels, Rio de Janeiro became the single most important slave-trading Brazilian port by the second quarter of the eighteenth century.[28] The city's growing economic and political significance was underlined in 1763 when it replaced Salvador as the colony's capital.

As population increased in southern Brazil during the mining boom, regional social and economic systems emerged in which African slavery was central. Surrounding Rio de Janeiro, the development of agriculture and ranching to provision the growing city and to supply the mining zones with staple products fueled the demand for slaves. Sugar cane was grown as well, to provide the city's population with *cachaça*

---

[27]   For the history of this region, see Laird W. Bergad, *Slavery and the Demographic and Economic History of Minas Gerais, Brazil, 1720–1888* (New York: Cambridge University Press, 1999).

[28]   See the Eltis data in "The Volume and Structure of the Transatlantic Slave Trade: A Reassessment," p. 46.

(cane brandy) and raw sugar and for export to foreign markets. Mules, important to the expanding internal transportation system, were raised in the interior of São Paulo, which began to increase in population during the eighteenth century, providing surrounding farmers with markets requiring substantial labor inputs. Within Minas Gerais itself during the gold boom, which waned by the 1750s, a varied range of agricultural, pastoral, and manufactured goods was produced to supply the mining centers and the urban zones developing throughout the interior. This demand led to the expansion of all kinds of economic activities, and slaves were needed to labor in every one.

By the time the mining boom had run its course during the second half of the eighteenth century, Brazil had developed the largest and most diversified slave labor system in all of the Americas. Urban slavery, with its varied occupational structures, was well entrenched; slaves labored in mines and small-scale cottage industries; and a wide array of rural activities, from export-oriented sugar production to local food-crop cultivation, used slave labor extensively in nearly every region of the colony.

Additionally, Brazil developed the largest free black and mulatto populations in all of the Americas over the seventeenth and eighteenth centuries. From initial settlement these "free peoples of color," as they were labeled in both the Spanish colonies and Brazil, were integral to the emerging Portuguese colonial society. Many were ex-slaves who had acquired their freedom in a variety of ways, from self-purchase to grants of liberty by masters in last wills and testaments. These free blacks and mulattos were often more numerous than whites or slaves, and their communities were nurtured by impressive rates of natural reproduction in nearly all regions. This diversified racial structure, where to be black or mulatto was not necessarily to be a slave, was in sharp contrast with the British- and French-controlled Caribbean and North America, where free peoples of African descent were few and far between. This would be a defining feature distinguishing the British and French variants of slave societies in the Americas from the Spanish and Portuguese regions.

Table 2.1 provides some recent estimates of the volume of the slave trade to various American markets before 1800. Table 2.2 estimates the slave populations of the Americas toward the end of the eighteenth century.

The stage has now been set for understanding the contrasting patterns of slavery in the United States, Cuba, and Brazil, the last slave

Table 2.1. *Slave trade volume and destinations, 1519–1800*

	1519–1600	Percent	1601–1700	Percent	1701–1800	Percent	Totals	Percent
Spanish Colonies	151,600	75.2	194,700	19.9	131,500	2.5	477,800	7.3
Brazil	50,000	24.8	396,200	40.4	1,780,900	33.3	2,227,100	34.1
British North America	0		12,100	1.2	275,500	5.1	287,600	4.4
British Caribbean	0		236,900	24.2	1,807,900	33.8	2,044,800	31.3
French Caribbean	0		38,100	3.9	984,500	18.4	1,022,600	15.7
Guianas	0		91,000	9.3	291,100	5.4	382,100	5.8
Other Americas	0		11,600	1.2	80,400	1.5	92,000	1.4
TOTAL	201,600	100.0	980,600	100.0	5,351,800	100.0	6,534,000	100.0

Source: David Eltis, "The Volume and Structure of the Transatlantic Slave Trade: A Reassessment," *William & Mary Quarterly*, 3rd series, vol. 63, No. 1 (January 2001), p. 46, Table 3.

Table 2.2. *Estimates of slave populations in the Americas, c. 1790*

Brazil	1,500,000
United States	694,000
French Caribbean	675,000
British Caribbean	480,000
Peru	90,000
Venezuela	87,000
Cuba	64,000
Colombia	35,000
Argentina	15,000
Chile	12,000
Mexico	10,000
TOTAL	3,662,000

societies in the Americas, after 1790. But before turning to the various themes to be considered in the following chapters, it is important to understand one of the dilemmas faced by the social scientist or humanist considering slave history. The scholar must analyze slavery's sad and tragic past using objective analytical tools, and these are absolutely necessary if we are to understand how this dreadful institution emerged and developed in the Western Hemisphere, especially from comparative perspectives. But what is often lacking in these considerations is an appreciation for the individual life experiences of the millions of human beings who had the misfortune to be enslaved and to suffer through the pain and degradation of human bondage. Most slaves, tragically, died anonymously, leaving no written record or oral testimony. However, in each of the societies some slaves were somehow able to escape slavery, become literate, and leave a written record. In some instances governmental officials, scholars, or the descendants of slaves were able to gather testimonies and to preserve them in a variety of forms for contemplation by future generations. In the next chapter we will "listen" to slaves speak about different aspects of their lives.

CHAPTER THREE

SLAVES IN THEIR OWN WORDS

None but those who resided in the South during the time of slavery can realize the terrible punishments that were visited upon the slaves.[1]

New World slavery has been observed and analyzed from a variety of perspectives in thousands of published volumes in numerous languages. These date from Columbus's voyages of the 1490s, which opened the Americas to European colonization and initiated the transatlantic African slave trade. Yet, despite sympathy or disdain, intimate contact or distance in space and time, and regardless of academic discipline or methodological approach, few observers, present or past, have been able to answer the fundamental, and clearly horrific, question of what it was like to live one's life as a slave. This is a daunting task, and it would hardly be daring to suggest that no one except a slave, of any race or sex regardless of sensitivity or empathy, could possibly answer this query. Only slaves themselves had the ability to convey an accurate portrayal of their sufferings, pains, degradations, struggles, hopes, aspirations, joys, and sorrows. Through their written records, we now will "listen" to slaves speak about various aspects of their experience. These testimonies will provide the most valuable insights into their

---

[1] So begins the testimony of the slave Charlotte Brooks as transcribed by Octavia V. Rogers. Octavia V. Rogers Albert, *The House of Bondage or Charlotte Brooks and Other Slaves Original and Life-like, as they Appeared in their Old Plantation and City Slave Life; Together with Pen-Pictures of the Peculiar Institution, with Sights and Insights into their New Relations as Freedmen, Freemen, and Citizens* (New York: Hunt & Eaton, 1890), p. 1. This narrative may be found on the internet at <http://docsouth.unc.edu/neh/albert/albert.html>.

lives, for the following chapters of this book will use historical sources produced by others to map out various parameters governing slave life. Yet we must keep in mind the points made in the previous chapter. These poignant testimonies are set in particular places and times and must be located within the broad context of slavery's evolution in the Western Hemisphere. While they reflect particular slave experiences, they may not be used to represent the parameters of slavery for all slaves.

Surviving slave narratives and the other written records left by the enslaved are found principally in the United States.[2] These consist mainly of autobiographies of slaves who escaped bondage, became free, and were literate. Many of them were written and published as part of the antebellum abolitionist movement, and others were heavily influenced by organized religion as testimony to the virtues found by slaves or freed men and women who had converted to Catholicism or Protestantism. The U.S. written slave record was substantially enhanced during the 1930s by the collection of over 2,300 testimonies of ex-slaves by the Federal Writers' Project of the Works Progress Administration. A fascinating retrospective of imagery stored in the collective memory of those who lived and survived as slaves is found in these impressive volumes.[3] It is unfortunate that similar documents are not available for any other slaveholding society in the Americas, Brazil and Cuba included, although some insightful sources have been preserved.

Let us begin by listening to Octavia Victoria Rogers's account of the life of Charlotte Brooks, the daughter of slave parents who acquired an education after emancipation and attended Atlanta University. Ms. Rogers was a teacher and in 1879 befriended an illiterate ex-slave, Charlotte Brooks, who had been born in Virginia and sold as a child to a

---

[2]   For an analysis of U.S. slave narratives, see Marion Wilson Starling, *The Slave Narrative: Its Place in American History* (Boston: G. K. Hall, 1981). Also see the internet web site <http://docsouth.unc.edu/neh/neh.html>, which contains the electronic texts of a large number of slave narratives.

[3]   Seventeen volumes were compiled between 1936 and 1938. They were microfilmed in 1941 by the Library of Congress under the title *Slave Narratives: A Folk History of Slavery in the United States from Interviews with Former Slaves*. There are now available on the internet under the title *Born in Slavery: Slave Narratives from the Federal Writers' Project, 1936–1938*, at <http://memory.loc.gov/ammem/snhtml/snhome.html>. For an analysis of the reliability of these, see Paul D. Escott, *Slavery Remembered: The Twentieth-Century Slave Narratives* (Chapel Hill: University of North Carolina Press, 1979).

slave owner in Louisiana, where she lived her life on a sugar plantation. Rogers's book was based on transcriptions of lengthy conversations with Ms. Brooks, and it provides a series of remarkable insights into life as a slave woman within the context of the Louisiana plantation economy.[4] The following are direct quotes ascribed by the author to Ms. Brooks.

Why, old marster used to make me go out before day, in high grass and heavy dews, and I caught cold. I lost all of my health. I tell you, nobody knows the trouble I have seen. I have been sold three times. I had a little baby when my second marster sold me, and my last old marster would make me leave my child before day to go to the cane-field; and he would not allow me to come back till ten o'clock in the morning to nurse my child. When I did go I could hear my poor child crying long before I got to it. And la, me! my poor child would be so hungry when I'd get to it! Sometimes I would have to walk more than a mile to get to my child, and when I did get there I would be so tired I'd fall asleep while my baby was sucking. He did not allow me much time to stay with my baby when I did go to nurse it. Sometimes I would overstay my time with my baby; then I would have to run all the way back to the field. O, I tell you nobody knows the trouble we poor colored folks had to go through with here in Louisiana. I had heard people say Louisiana was a hard place for black people, and I didn't want to come; but old marster took me and sold me from my mother anyhow, and from my sisters and brothers in Virginia.

I have never seen or heard from them since I left old Virginia. That's been more than thirty-five years ago. When I left old Virginia my mother cried for me, and when I saw my poor mother with tears in her eyes I thought I would die. O, it was a sad day for me when I was to leave my mother in old Virginia. (pp. 3–4)

Later in the narrative we learn that the child referred to was fathered by her master's son. The poignancy of these passages reflects the tragic life experiences that were all too common because of the inter-regional slave trade from the Old South to the New South during the

[4]   Octavia V. Rogers Albert, *The House of Bondage or Charlotte Brooks and Other Slaves Original and Life-like, as they Appeared in their Old Plantation and City Slave Life; Together with Pen-Pictures of the Peculiar Institution, with Sights and Insights into their New Relations as Freedmen, Freemen, and Citizens* (New York: Hunt & Eaton, 1890).

nineteenth century as the cotton frontier pushed westward.[5] It was commonplace for children to be sold off with little respect for slave family integrity and complete disregard for any moral value system. Charlotte would never see her mother again, and this was a common fate among slaves sold to traders who marched them in coffles, often chained together, to be marketed in New Orleans or other slave-trading centers along the way. The basic structures of slave families were shattered, and slaves found themselves in complete isolation without immediate family, extended kinship, or even friendship ties in new environments that afforded few choices but to adjust in some way if they were to survive. Here Charlotte describes her hope, anxiety, and desperation for news of her family when she learns that a slave from Virginia has recently arrived at a nearby plantation:

Four years after I came to Louisiana the speculators brought another woman out here from my old State. She was sold to a man near my marster's plantation. I heard of it, and, thinks I, "That might be some of my kinsfolks, or somebody that knew my mother." So the first time I got a chance I went to see the woman. My white folks did not want the "niggers" to go off on Sundays; but anyhow my old marster let me go sometimes after dinner on Sunday evenings. So I went to see who the woman was, and I tell you, my child, when I got in the road going I could not go fast enough, for it just seemed to me that the woman was one of my folks. I walked a while and would run a while. By and by I got there. As I went in the gate I met a man, and I asked him what was the woman's name; he said her name was Jane Lee. I went around to the quarters where all the black people lived, and I found her. I went up to her and said, "Howdy do, Aunt Jane?" She said, "How do you know me, child?" I said, "I heard you just came from Virginia; I came from that State too. I just been out here four years. I am so glad to see you, Aunt Jane. Where did you come from in Virginia?" "I came from Richmond. I have left all of my people in Virginia."

Aunt Jane was no kin to me, but I felt that she was because she came from my old home. Me and Aunt Jane talked and cried that

---

[5]   This will be considered later in this book. For a provocative consideration, see Michael Tadman, *Speculators and Slaves: Masters, Traders, and Slaves in the Old South* (Madison: University of Wisconsin Press, 1989).

Sunday evening till nearly dark. Aunt Jane said she left her children, and it almost killed her to ever think of them. She said one was only five years old. Her old marster got in debt, and he sold her to pay his debts. I told her I had left all of my people too, and that I was a poor lone creature to myself when I first came out from Virginia. (pp. 7–8)

It is impossible to conceive of the enormous emotional pain and suffering experienced by "Aunt Jane," sold without her children, who she undoubtedly would never see again – a horrendously common fate among slaves forced into the interregional slave trade. She, Charlotte, and the tens of thousands of slaves in similar situations were then faced with the prospect of somehow coping with the work regime:

The white folks did not take the niggers for nothing more than brutes. They would take more time with fine horses, and put them up to rest. We poor darkies were never allowed to rest. I have split rails many and many a day, and sometimes my back would almost break when I'd have to roll logs, but I had to keep pulling along. When night came I could hardly drag one foot before the other. I'd go to my bed, and it would be wet where it leaked through the top of the house, and I'd just fall in it and would not know it was wet with water till next morning. I'd find leeches sticking to my legs, and blood would be all on my feet. I'd get them in the woods cutting wood. I tell you, if you get a leech on you it will draw like a blister. When I came to my house at night I was too tired to eat. I went to bed a many time hungry – was too broke down to cook my supper after working all the day hard. (pp. 43–4)

The conditions of slave life in the Louisiana sugar plantation districts where Charlotte Brooks lived and worked were among the harshest that slaves had to endure. However, the material parameters of slavery, as well as the attitudes of masters toward slave family life, varied enormously, and this is revealed by Tempe Herndon Durham's recollections of her life as a slave in and around Durham, North Carolina.[6]

---

[6]   This narrative is contained in George P. Rawick, editor, *The American Slave: A Composite Autobiography* (Westport, CT: Greenwood Publishing Company, 1972–79), vol. 14, pp. 284–90. It may be found on the internet at <http://xroads.virginia.edu/~hyper/wpa/durham1.html>.

Ms. Herndon Durham was interviewed in the late 1930s when she was 103 years old, and within her oral testimony the following passages are found.[7]

> My white fo'ks lived in Chatham County. Dey was Marse George an' Mis' Betsy Herndon. Mis Betsy was a Snipes befo' she married Marse George. Dey had a big plantation an' raised cawn, wheat, cotton an' 'bacca. I don't know how many field niggers Marse George had, but he had a mess of dem, an' he had hosses too, an' cows, hogs an' sheeps. He raised sheeps an' sold de wool, an' dey used de wool at de big house too. Dey was a big weavin' room whare de blankets was wove, an' dey wove de cloth for de winter clothes too. Linda Herndon an' Milla Edwards was de head weavers, dey looked after de weavin' of da fancy blankets. Mis' Betsy was a good weaver too. She weave de same as de niggers. She say she love de clackin' soun' of de loom an' de way de shuttles run in an' out carryin' a long tail of bright colored thread. Some days she set at de loom all de mawnin' peddlin' wid her feets an' her white han's flittin' over de bobbins.
>
> When I growed up I married Exter Durham. He belonged to Marse Snipes Durham who had de plantation 'cross de county line in Orange County. We had a big weddin'. We was married on de front po'ch of de big house. Marse George killed a shoat an' Mis' Betsy had Georgianna, de cook, to bake a big weddin' cake all iced up white as snow wid a bride an' groom standin' in de middle holdin' han's. De table was set out in de yard under de trees, an' you ain't never seed de like of eats. All de niggers come to de feas' an' Marse George had a for everybody. Dat was some weddin'. I had on a white dress, white shoes an' long while gloves dat come to my elbow, an' Mis' Betsy done made me a weddin' veil out of a white net window curtain. When she played de weddin' ma'ch on de piano, me an' Exter ma'ched down de walk an' up on de po'ch to de altar Mis' Betsy done fixed. Dat de pretties' altar I ever seed. Back 'gainst de rose vine dat was full or red roses, Mis' Betsy done put tables filled wid flowers an' white candles. She spread down a bed sheet, a sho nuff linen sheet, for us to stan' on, an' dey was a white pillow to kneel down on. Exter done made me a weddin'

---

[7] The interviewers transcribed many of these interviews phonetically, rather than in grammatically correct prose, and this has been preserved here.

ring. He made it out of a big red button wid his pocket knife. He done cut it so roun' an' polished it so smooth dat it looked like a red satin ribbon tide 'roun' my finger. Dat sho was a pretty ring. I wore it 'bout fifty years, den it got so thin dat I lost it one day in de wash tub when I was washin' clothes.

Uncle Edmond Kirby married us. He was de nigger preacher dat preached at de plantation church. After Uncle Edmond said de las' words over me an' Exter, Marse George got to have his little fun: He say, "Come on, Exter, you an' Tempie got to jump over de broom stick backwards; you got to do dat to see which one gwine be boss of your househol'." Everybody come stan' 'roun to watch. Marse George hold de broom 'bout a foot high off de floor. De one dat jump over it backwards an' never touch de handle, gwine boss de house, an' if bof of dem jump over widout touchin' it, dey won't gwine be no bossin', dey jus' gwine be 'genial. I jumped fus', an' you ought to seed me. I sailed right over dat broom stick same as a cricket, but when Exter jump he done had a big dram an' his feets was so big an' clumsy dat dey got all tangled up in dat broom an' he fell head long. Marse George he laugh an' laugh, an' tole Exter he gwine be bossed 'twell he skeered to speak less'n I tole him to speak. After de weddin' we went down to de cabin Mis' Betsy done all dressed up, but Exter couldn' stay no longer den dat night kaze he belonged to Marse Snipes Durham an' he had to go back home. He lef' de nex day for his plantation, but he come back every Saturday night an' stay 'twell Sunday night. We had eleven chillun. Nine was bawn befo' surrender an' two after we was set free. So I had two chillun dat wuzn' bawn in bondage. I was worth a heap to Marse George kaze I had so many chillun. De more chillun a slave had de more dey was worth. Lucy Carter was de only nigger on de plantation dat had more chillun den I had. She had twelve, but her chillun was sickly an' mine was muley strong an' healthy. Dey never was sick.

Ms. Herndon lived and labored on a fairly diversified farm that not only produced a wide variety of agricultural and pastoral products, but also manufactured cloth for textile production. This was an ecological and human environment altogether different from that of the tropical specialized sugar plantations of Louisiana, and master/slave relations were in sharp contrast with those recounted by Ms. Brooks. Herndon's vision of the past may have been somewhat distorted by time, but her testimony suggests some of the paradoxes and the enormous diversity of the slave experience in the United States. Clearly her master ran a well-organized and efficient plantation, and owned many slaves whose labor was exploited for profit. She emphatically notes her particular "value" to her owner because of the large number of children she bore. But her master and his wife also demonstrated the kind of paternalism that had long been trumpeted by southern slaveholders as a justification and apology for slavery. "Marse George" organized a big wedding for Ms. Herndon and actively participated in the ceremony and following celebration. Although her husband could spend only weekends with her, since he was owned by a master on a neighboring plantation, they had eleven children, and it may be assumed that the family remained together until slavery was abolished by the Civil War as there is no mention of children being sold off.

Brooks and Herndon were women who suffered through the unimaginable humiliations and indignities of being enslaved, but their lives were very different and perhaps represent the extremes of slave conditions. Brooks experienced the graphic destruction of her family in the interregional slave trade, and her narrative clearly indicates that this emotional trauma accompanied her throughout her life. Herndon seems to have led a more stable existence, maintained her family intact until emancipation, and does not use a bitter word to describe her master or mistress or the working conditions she was subjected to. It is likely that most slaves found themselves living somewhere between these two extremes: paternal treatment by masters, respect for slave family integrity, and tolerable working conditions, on the one hand; and utter disregard for the most fundamental aspects of human existence, ruthless exploitation, harsh labor conditions, and unmitigated suffering, on the other.

There are only two surviving published narratives by Cuban slaves, and these provide important insights into some of the dynamics of slave life in nineteenth-century Cuba. Let us begin by listening to one of the best-known testimonies by Esteban Montejo, who was interviewed in 1963 by a Cuban scholar when he was probably over 100 years of age. The passages quoted are Montejo's recollections of various aspects of his life as a slave in the last decades of slavery in Cuba, during the 1860s and 1870s.[8] He was born in Cuba, and thus

---

[8]   All of these selections are drawn from Esteban Montejo, *The Autobiography of a Runaway Slave* (New York: Pantheon Books, 1968).

his experiences were in all likelihood quite different from those of imported Africans. He was also a slave who worked on a sugar plantation, and thus his memoirs reflect a particular milieu in which about 60 percent of all Cuban slaves lived and worked by the 1860s. His observations reveal extraordinary aspects of the daily routines of slave life.

> Like all children born into slavery, *criollitos* as they called them, I was born in an infirmary where they took the pregnant Negresses to give birth.... Negroes were sold like pigs, and they sold me at once, which is why I remember nothing about the place. ... the picture of another plantation comes to mind: the Flor de Sagua. I don't know if that was the place where I worked for the first time, but I do remember running away from there once. ... But they caught me without a struggle, clapped a pair of shackles on me (I can still feel them when I think back), screwed them tight and sent me back to work wearing them. (p. 18)

> All the slaves lived in barracoons. ... The barracoons were large, though some plantations had smaller ones: it depended on the number of slaves in the settlement. Around two hundred slaves of all colours lived in the Flor de Sagua barracoon. ... There were barracoons of wood and barracoons of masonry with tiled roofs. Both types had mud floors and were as dirty as hell. And there was no modern ventilation there! Just a hole in the wall or a small barred window. The result was that the place swarmed with fleas and ticks, which made the inmates ill with infections and evil spells, for those ticks were witches. ... In the central patio the women washed their own, their husbands' and their children's clothes in tubs. ... There were no trees either outside or inside the barracoons, just empty solitary spaces. The Negroes could never get used to this. (p. 22)

> The bell was at the entrance to the mill.... At four-thirty in the morning they rang the Ave Maria ... and one had to get up immediately. At six they rang another bell ... and everyone had to form up in a place just outside the barracoon, men one side, women the other. Then off to the canefields till eleven, when we ate jerked beef, vegetables and bread ... Then at sunset came the prayer bell. (p. 23)

When time passed and ... the slaves' issue of clothing began to wear out, they would be given a new one. The men's clothes were made of Russian cloth, a coarse linen, sturdy and good for work in the fields – trousers which had large pockets and stood up stiff, a shirt, and a wool cap for the cold. The shoes were generally of rawhide, low-cut with little straps to keep them on. The old men wore sandals, flat-soled with a thong around the big toe. This has always been an African fashion. ... The women were given blouses, skirts and petticoats, and if they owned plots of land they bought their own petticoats, white ones, which were prettier and smarter. ... These plots of land were the salvation of many slaves, where they got their real nourishment from. ... Everything grew there: sweet potatoes, gourd, okra, kidney beans ... yucca and peanuts. They also raised pigs. And they sold all these products to the whites who came out from the villages. ... I learned to eat vegetables from the elders, because they said they were very healthy food, but during slavery pigs were the mainstay. (pp. 23–4)

Strange as it may seem, the Negroes were able to keep themselves amused in the barracoons. They had their games and pastimes. They played games in the taverns too, but these were different. (p. 25)

The taverns were near the plantations. There were more taverns than ticks in the forest. They were a sort of store where one could buy everything. The slaves themselves used to trade in the taverns, selling the jerked beef which they accumulated in the barracoons. They were usually allowed to visit the taverns during the daylight hours and sometimes even in the evenings. ... There was always some master who forbade the slaves to go. ... The taverns were made of wood and palm-bark. ... They sold rice, jerked beef, lard and every variety of bean. ... They noted down anything you bought in a book: when you spent half a peso they made one stroke in the book, and two for a peso. This was the system for buying everything else: round sweet biscuits, salt biscuits, sweets the size of a pea ... water-bread and lard. (p. 27)

Sunday was the liveliest day in the plantations. I don't know where the slaves found the energy for it. Their biggest fiestas were held on that day. On some plantations the drumming started at midday or one o'clock. ... The excitement, the games, and children rushing about started at sunrise. The barracoon came to life in a flash; it was like the end of the world. And in spite of work and everything the people woke up cheerful. (p. 29)

As soon as the drums started on Sunday the Negroes went down to the stream to bathe. ... It sometimes happened that a woman lingered behind and met a man just as he was about to go into the water. Then they would go off together and get down to business.

Shaving and cutting hair was done by the slaves themselves. ... The women arranged their hair with curls and little partings. ... They liked the excitement of fixing their hair one way one day and another way the next. One day it would have little partings, the next day ringlets, another day it would be combed flat. They cleaned their teeth with strips of soap-tree bark, and this made them very white. All this excitement was reserved for Sundays.

Everyone had a special outfit that day. The Negroes bought themselves rawhide boots ... from nearby shops where they went with the master's permission. ... (pp. 31–2)

These passages are quite astounding in many ways. Montejo's observations on the cold brutality of being born a slave and simply sold off by his master with few qualms or reservations are central, for they underline the ultimate barbarity of the slave system. After comments on the horrendous living conditions of the barracoons, the slave barracks that were typical on plantations with large numbers of slaves, there is an interesting shift in the prose to aspects of life that are not usually part of the imagery associated with slavery. These revolve around a series of daily routines – work rhythms, food consumption, clothing worn, the frequenting of taverns, and finally Sunday celebratory rituals. While Montejo recalled all of this from his selective memory long after these events or incidents had taken place, the fact that they stand out in his recollection is indicative of their importance to the slave population in their daily lives.

What is most striking is the "space" that slaves had been able to carve out for themselves to act as quasi-independent human beings by the 1860s, even within the framework of a fully developed slave-based plantation society. There is no way to know the historical antecedents, processes, and struggles leading to the prerogatives that the plantation slaves among whom Montejo lived insisted upon. Nor can we ascertain whether or not these were typical, although in all likelihood they were widespread. Yet it is clear that slaves moved fluidly to and from the many taverns surrounding the plantations and that they had at their disposal goods to barter, or cash to pay for the various kinds of merchandise described as available in general stores. There was a small-scale but apparently pervasive and regularized commercial life in which slaves actively participated, and this was central to such important matters as the acquisition of food, clothing, drink, and general entertainment. The descriptions of the Sunday fiestas are revealing as well. Slaves took pride in their appearance, cleanliness, and public presentation, and they refused to allow their subjugation and exploitation to dominate their lives, especially their ability to enjoy many aspects of life.

Care must be exercised in the interpretation of these passages. They are emphatically not testimonies to the humaneness of slavery, nor are they suggestive of a benevolent paternalism on the part of masters. The ultimate barbarity of the slave system was not mitigated by Sunday parties or the ability to steal off to taverns. Montejo's memoirs have a more important message, for they tell us that slaves insisted on acting and being treated as individuals with the same kinds of behavior patterns and material, emotional, and psychic needs as people everywhere, regardless of their legal and physical status and condition. Slaves asserted their ultimate and fundamental humanity and no doubt insisted that the prerogatives they had carved out be explicitly or implicitly acknowledged and respected by owners or overseers. The processes of negotiation carried out over time between the enslaved and those who ultimately controlled them – masters, overseers, the colonial state apparatus – are largely unknown. But it is clear that within this most horrifying of all human conditions, slaves struggled to be treated as human beings, not simply as objects to be bought and sold. Let us continue to listen to Montejo reminisce about other themes of importance to slave life.

> I knew of two African religions in the barracoons: the Lucumi and the Congolese. The Congolese was the most important. It was well known at the Flor de Sagua because their magic-men used to put spells on people and get possession of them. ... I got to know the elders of both religions after Abolition. (p. 33)

The Congolese were more involved with witchcraft than the Lucumi, who had more to do with the saints and with God. ... The difference between the Congolese and the Lucumi was that the former solved problems while the latter told the future. They did this with *dilogunes*, which are round, white shells from Africa with mystery inside. ... (pp. 34–5)

The other religion was the Catholic one. This was introduced by the priests, but nothing in the world would induce them to enter the slaves' quarters. ... Those Negroes who were household slaves came as messengers of the priests. ... The fact is I never learned that doctrine because I did not understand a thing about it. I don't think the household slaves did either, although, being so refined and well-treated, they all made out they were Christian. The household slaves were given rewards by the masters, and I never saw one of them badly punished.

The Lucumi and Congolese did not get on. ... it went back to the differences between saints and witchcraft. The only ones who had no problems were the old men born in Africa. They were special people and had to be treated differently because they knew all religious matters. (pp. 36–7)

In the plantations there were Negroes from different countries, all different physically. The Congolese were black-skinned, though there were many of mixed blood with yellowish skins and light hair. They were usually small. The Mandingas were reddish-skinned, tall and very strong. I swear by my mother they were a bunch of crooks too! They kept apart from the rest. The Gangas were nice people, rather short and freckled. Many of them became runaways. The Carabalís were like the Musungo Congolese, uncivilised brutes. (p. 38)

The Cuban slave trade continued through the 1850s and 1860s at fairly high levels, and the island was the last importer of slaves from Africa to the Americas. This meant that Africans from different ethnic groups continued to arrive, reinforcing African religions and cultures long after direct African imports had ceased to other regions.[9]

[9]   The U.S. and English slave trades had ended in 1808; the French large-scale West Indian trade was virtually halted by the 1791 slave revolt in Haiti but

Montejo's observations on religion underline several themes of importance for understanding nineteenth-century slave society in Cuba and probably elsewhere. The utilization of the term "African" to describe slaves from that continent was not a reference point used by slaves, who continued to conceive of their identities from the vantage points of highly differentiated ethnic, cultural, and religious groups. "African" in the broadest sense was a simplistic reference to skin color used by the colonial powers and elite groups, for whom it was usually synonymous with "black" and "slave."

To understand slavery it is important to comprehend the terminology of elites, but it is even more critical to understand how slaves identified themselves. Montejo refers to two general African religions – Lucumi and Congolese – and he indicates several other ethnicities, underscoring the physical and some times behavioral differences between them. These references suggest the way in which the slave population conceived of itself as consisting of varied groups who were very distinct from one another. Differentiation was made among slaves not only according to ethnic origins but also by slave occupation. Montejo suggests that Catholicism was an unimportant religion despite the presence of priests who dared not enter the slave quarters. Their emissaries were "household slaves. . . . so refined and well treated . . . and never punished badly" but whom Montejo believed merely pretended to be Catholic as a way to curry favor. An inevitable undercurrent of resentment toward these privileged slaves may be noted. But what is most important to observe is the great distinction drawn by slaves themselves between common laborers and the house slaves at the top of the slave hierarchy. In the barracoons, slaves clearly had a way of identifying themselves that was very different from the labels used in the great houses where the master class dwelled.

All the plantations had an infirmary near the barracoon, a big wooden hut where they took the pregnant women. You were born there and stayed there till you were six or seven, when you went to live in the barracoons and began work, like the rest. There were Negro wet nurses and cooks there to look after the *criollitos* and feed them. If anyone was injured in the fields or fell ill, these women would doctor him with herbs and brews. They could cure

continued on a smaller scale into the 1820s to other destinations; and the Brazilian slave trade ceased in 1851.

anything. Sometimes a *criollo* never saw his parents again because the boss moved them to another plantation, and so the wet-nurses would be in sole charge of the child. . . . A child of good stock cost five hundred pesos . . . that is the child of strong, tall parents. Tall Negroes were privileged. The masters picked them out to mate them with tall, healthy women – and shut them up together in the barracoon and forced them to sleep together. The women had to produce healthy babies every year. I tell you, it was like breeding animals. Well, if the Negress didn't produce as expected, the couple were separated and she was sent to work in the fields again. Women who were barren were unlucky because they had to go back to being beasts of burden again, but they were allowed to choose their own husbands. It often happened that a women would be chasing one man with twenty more after her. The magic-men would settle these problems with their potions. (pp. 38–9)

I saw many horrors in the way of punishment under slavery. That was why I didn't like the life. The stocks, which were in the boiler-house, were the cruellest. Some were for standing and others for lying down. They were made of thick planks with holes for the head, hands and feet. They would keep slaves fastened up like this for two or three months for some trivial offence. They whipped the pregnant women too, but lying face down with a hollow in the ground for their bellies. They whipped them hard, but they took good care not to damage the babies because they wanted as many of those as possible. The most common punishment was flogging; this was given by the overseer with a rawhide lash which made weals on the skin. They also had whips made of the fibres of some jungle plant which stung like the devil and flayed the skin off in strips. I saw many handsome big Negroes with raw backs. After-wards the cuts were covered with compresses of tobacco leaves, urine and salt. (p. 40)

Life was hard and bodies wore out. Anyone who did not take to the hills as a runaway when he was young had to become a slave. It was preferable to be on your own on the loose than locked up in all that dirt and rottenness. In any event, life tended to be solitary because there were none too many women around. To have one of your own you had either to be over twenty-five or catch yourself one in the fields. The old men did not want the youths to have women. They said a man should wait until he was twenty-five to have experiences. Some men did not suffer much, being used to this life. Others had sex between themselves and did not want to know anything of women. This was their life – sodomy. The effeminate men washed the clothes and did the cooking too, if they had a 'husband'. They were good workers and occupied themselves with their plots of land, giving the produce to their 'husbands' to sell to the white farmers. It was after Abolition that the term 'effeminate' came into use, for the practice persisted. I don't think it can have come from Africa, because the old men hated it. They would have nothing to do with queers. To tell the truth, it never bothered me. I am of the opinion that a man can stick his arse where he wants. (pp. 40–1)

You caught a lot of illnesses in the barracoons, in fact men got sicker there than anywhere else. It was not unusual to find a Negro with as many as three sicknesses at once. If it wasn't colic it was whooping cough. . . . But the worst sicknesses, which made a skeleton of everyone, were smallpox and the black sicknesss. Smallpox left men all swollen, and the black sickness took them by surprise: it struck suddenly and between one bout of vomiting and the next you ended up a corpse. (pp. 41–2)

In these quotations more of the harsh realities of slave life are revealed, and in many ways they provide a counterweight to the suggestive sections on taverns and Sunday celebrations. The taboo subject of "breeding" is broached, making it clear that masters were concerned with reproduction and the economic benefits to be derived from expanding their slave populations through natural increase. The dreadful punishments meted out to slaves accused of one infraction or another are underlined in horrific detail. Variations in attitudes and sexual practices among slaves are suggested, particularly the pervasiveness of male homosexuality. And finally, the dreadful chronic disease environment of the plantations, which often made them places of illness and death when struck by various epidemics, is revealed.

In these reminiscences Montejo has provided us with brief glimpses of the mundane aspects of daily life for Cuban slave populations laboring in plantation zones in the 1860s. Far from a faceless mass of chattel, slaves are revealed to have lived complex lives with greater variation than extant stereotypical images would suggest. Perhaps the

one simplistic conclusion that can be drawn from his testimony is that it
is impossible to generalize about common aspects of slavery owing to the
great diversity and many contradictions and paradoxes found in slave
life. The ultimate indignity, brutality, barbarity, and inhumanity of
slavery must be kept front and center. But the admirable ingeniousness
of slaves in asserting their humanity within these horrendous parameters must also be recognized and acknowledged.

The second Cuban slave narrative, written by Juan Francisco Manzano, reflects the experiences of an urban domestic slave who served one
of Cuba's wealthiest families.[10] Despite periods of enormous suffering
that in some ways paralleled those of Montejo, his perspectives on
slavery are extraordinarily different. Both expressed a driving quest for
freedom – Montejo by running away, and Manzano by finding a
mechanism to purchase his freedom and join the ranks of Cuba's urban
free population of color, which he eventually achieved because of a
wealthy benefactor. Yet the dynamics of daily life for these two people,
despite their being enslaved, could not have been more diametrically
opposed. Manzano enjoyed a relatively privileged position, and this is
reflected quite graphically in his recollections of his childhood.

> ... my mistress, the Marchioness de Justiz, by then an elderly lady,
> adopted me as a form of entertainment. They say she held me in
> her arms more than my mother, who, with all her titles from
> handmaid to half-time nurse, had married the head house servant
> and provided her mistress with a Creole. ... I grew up alongside
> my mistress without leaving her side except to sleep, for she never

[10]   For the most recent edition, see Juan Francisco Manzano, *The Autobiography
of a Slave | Autobiografía de un esclavo. A Bilingual Edition* (Detroit: Wayne
State University Press, 1996).The original edition was published in 1840 by
the English abolitionist Richard Robert Madden, who clearly was inspired by
Manzano's intellectual gifts and his story's usefulness in the abolitionist
campaign waged by the British. See R. R. Madden, *Poems by a Slave in the
Island of Cuba, recently liberated; translated from the Spanish by R. R. Madden,
M.D., with the History of the Early Life of the Negro Poet, written by Himself; to
which are prefixed two pieces descriptive of Cuban Slavery and the Slave Traffic*
(London: Thomas Ward and Co., 1840). The full text of the original edition
may be found on the internet at <http://docsouth.unc.edu/neh/manzano/
manzano.html>. Manzano was born in the house of Don Juan Manzano and
his wife, Doña Beatriz de Juztiz, a wealthy family from the province of
Matanzas.

even traveled to the countryside without taking me along in the coach. (p. 47, Shulman edition) ... When I was almost six, and more clever than the others, I was sent to school at the home of my baptismal godmother, Trinidad de Zayas. I was usually brought home at midday and in the evening so that the marchioness might see me, for she refrained from going out before I arrived. If she ever did leave, I raised such a fuss, crying and screaming, that I should have received a beating, but nobody dared do that. ... On one occasion my father shook me harshly for being quite unruly. My mistress found out, and that was enough for her to refuse to see my father for several days. (p. 49, Shulman edition)

Living within the protected environment of one of Cuba's colonial elite families; sent to be educated in a fine school; and having constant contact and interaction with his parents, who worked in the household, clearly meant that Manzano's childhood bore little resemblance to the lives of the great mass of slaves, urban or rural. His recollections also underline the clear hierarchy by occupation among Cuban slaves described by Montejo. They also serve as an interesting background for understanding the paternalistic justifications for slavery periodically offered by a master class whose perspectives were warped by their ongoing contacts and sometimes intimate connections with slaves who served them in the confines of their own homes. For the marchioness, the institution of slavery was personified by Juan Francisco, his parents, and the other domestic servants with whom she interacted on a daily basis in the same household. These slaves had a number of privileges and prerogatives unknown to rural slaves, especially those working within the plantation environments that dominated rural Cuba by the 1840s.

Juan Francisco himself would have contact with the masses of rural slaves, who lived, worked, and suffered in an ambience unknown to him, only after his mistress died and he entered adolescence. The Justiz/Manzano family owned one of Cuba's most productive sugar mills, El Molino in the province of Matanzas, where Manzano spent considerable time when he was still a boy. He apparently had a penchant for getting into mischievous trouble, and while this could be ignored when he was a young, by the time he was twelve or thirteen years old any violation of plantation discipline could not be tolerated by overseers and was followed by severe punishment irrespective of background, upbringing, or relative privilege. He describes in the following passages his conditions of punishment for repeated infractions of rules:

> For the least childish mischief, I was locked up for twenty-four hours in a coal cellar without floorboards and nothing to cover myself. . . . after suffering brutal lashes, I was locked up with orders that anyone who might give me even a drop of water was to be severely punished. Such an order was so feared in that house that no one, absolutely no one, dared give me as much as a crumb even if there were an opportunity to do so. What I suffered in that jail is unimaginable, afflicted as I was with hunger and thirst, and tormented by fear.
>
> It was a place as silent as it was removed from the house, in a backyard next to a stable and alongside a stinking, rotting garbage heap, which was near an outhouse, as infested as it was damp, and always foul, separated from me solely by a few hole ridden walls, which were the lair of deformed rats that incessantly ran over me. . . .
>
> I would scream so much, begging for mercy, that they would remove me, but only to punish me anew with as many lashes as their strength permitted, and than I was locked up again. (pp. 57–9, Shulman edition)

Yet despite these periodic punishments for various infractions, Manzano continued to live a life of relative comfort, illustrating quite graphically the vast gulf in all aspects of existence that separated domestic and field slaves. He never was away from his biological family for any extended period of time; he was instructed in all kinds of educational venues, from reading and writing to drawing and painting; and his work as a page within the household brought him into contact with some of Cuba's most powerful sugar-producing elite families at the ubiquitous dinners and social occasions he frequented as part of his domestic work obligations. From an early age his talent for writing and reciting poetry was recognized by many of these families. In this context he met Domingo del Monte, scion of one of the colony's wealthiest families, who had become a patron to literary figures as well as an ardent abolitionist. Del Monte eventually raised the funds to purchase Manzano's freedom.

Manzano and Montejo offer us suggestive fragments of the diversity of the slave experience in nineteenth-century Cuba. Neither of these narratives may be utilized to construct an overarching paradigm that will help us to understand Cuban slavery. However, both may be employed to underline the impossibility of conjuring up a single, universal, stereotypical image of what it meant to live one's life as a slave in the nineteenth-century Caribbean.

Let us now turn to the only known published memoir of an African slave imported to Brazil. Mahommah Gardo Baquaqua was a Muslim from an interior region of the Bight of Benin who arrived on a slave ship in Pernambuco in northeastern Brazil sometime in the 1840s. He was purchased by a baker and worked in various occupations, including an important stint as a sailor on a ship that regularly traded between Rio de Janeiro and the southernmost province of Rio Grande do Sul. He eventually traveled to New York on a vessel working as a slave and somehow made his way to freedom there. Later he settled in Haiti and eventually became a convert to Catholicism. Let us listen to Mahommah describe his arrival in Brazil.[11]

> The only food we had during the voyage was corn soaked and boiled. I cannot tell how long we were thus confined, but it seemed a very long while. We suffered very much for want of water, but was denied all we needed. A pint a day was all that was allowed, and no more; and a great many slaves died upon the

---

[11] Mahommah Gardo Baquaqua, *Biography Of Mahommah G. Baquaqua, A Native Of Zoogoo, In The Interior Of Africa. (A Convert To Christianity,) With A Description Of That Part Of The World; Including The Manners And Customs Of The Inhabitants, Their Religious Notions, Form Of Government, Laws, Appearance Of The Country, Buildings, Agriculture, Manufactures, Shepherds And Herdsmen, Domestic Animals, Marriage Ceremonials, Funeral Services, Styles Of Dress, Trade And Commerce, Modes Of Warfare, System Of Slavery, &C., &C. Mahommah's Early Life, His Education, His Capture And Slavery In Western Africa And Brazil, His Escape To The United States, From Thence To Hayti, (The City Of Port Au Prince,) His Reception By The Baptist Missionary There, The Rev. W. L. Judd; His Conversion To Christianity, Baptism, And Return To This Country, His Views, Objects And Aim. Written And Revised From His Own Words, By Samuel Moore, Esq.* (Detroit: Geo. E. Pomeroy & Co., Tribune Office, 1854). The original may be found on the internet at <http://docsouth.unc.edu/neh/baquaqua/baquaqua.html>.

Also see Robin Law and Paul E. Lovejoy, editors, *The Biography of Mahommah Gardo Baquaqua: His Passage from Slavery to Freedom in Africa and America* (Princeton, NJ: Markus Wiener Publishers, 2001).

passage. There was one poor fellow became so very desperate for want of water, that he attempted to snatch a knife from the white man who brought in the water, when he was taken up on deck and I never knew what became of him. I supposed he was thrown overboard.

When any one of us became refractory, his flesh was cut with a knife, and pepper or vinegar was rubbed in to make him peaceable (!) I suffered, and so did the rest of us, very much from sea sickness at first, but that did not cause our brutal owners any trouble. Our sufferings were our own, we had no one to share our troubles, none to care for us, or even to speak a word of comfort to us. Some were thrown overboard before breath was out of their bodies; when it was thought any would not live, they were got rid of in that way. Only twice during the voyage were we allowed to go on deck to wash ourselves – once whilst at sea, and again just before going into port.

We arrived at Pernambuco, South America, early in the morning. ... All that day we neither ate or drank anything, and we were given to understand that we were to remain perfectly silent, and not make any out-cry, otherwise our lives were in danger. But when ... the anchor dropped ... we were permitted to go on deck to be viewed and handled by our future masters, who had come aboard from the city. We landed a few miles from the city, at a farmer's house, which was used as a kind of slave market. The farmer had a great many slaves, and I had not been there very long before I saw him use the lash pretty freely on a boy, which made a deep impression on my mind, as of course I imagined that would be my fate ere long, and oh! too soon, alas! were my fears realized.

When I reached the shore, I felt thankful to Providence that I was once more permitted to breathe pure air, the thought of which almost absorbed every other. I cared but little then that I was a slave, having escaped the ship was all I thought about. Some of the slaves on board could talk Portuguese. They had been living on the coast with Portuguese families, and they used to interpret to us. They were not placed in the hold with the rest of us, but come down occasionally to tell us something or other.

These slaves never knew they were to be sent away, until they were placed on board the ship. I remained in this slave market but a day or two, before I was again sold to a slave dealer in the city, who again sold me to a man in the country, who was a baker, and resided not a great distance from Pernambuco.

When a slaver comes in, the news spreads like wild-fire, and down come all those that are interested in the arrival of the vessel with its cargo of living merchandize, who select from the stock those most suited to their different purposes, and purchase the slaves precisely in the same way that oxen or horses would be purchased in a market; but if there are not the kind of slaves in the one cargo, suited to the wants and wishes of the slave buyers, an order is given to the Captain for the particular sorts required, which are furnished to order the next time the ship comes into port. Great numbers make quite a business of this buying and selling human flesh, and do nothing else for a living, depending entirely upon this kind of traffic. (pp. 43–5)

In these passages the author reveals with clarity the sufferings and abuses of the "middle passage," a voyage that could be of four to eight weeks duration. Arrival in Brazil was greeted with relief, simply because of escape from the ship's hold and the ability to breathe freely. This was the likely reaction of captives surviving the horrors of the transatlantic crossing despite their enslavement. The mechanisms of buying and selling, multiple times, are described, and the disdain felt for the slave traders is quite graphic. The distinction made between acculturated slaves who could speak Portuguese and worked on the slave ships and Africans being transported to Brazil for sale should be underlined. Here Mahommah recounts his first experiences as an enslaved laborer:

I had contrived whilst on my passage in the slave ship, to gather up a little knowledge of the Portuguese language, from the men before spoken of, and as my master was a Portuguese I could comprehend what he wanted very well, and gave him to understand that I would do all he needed as well as I was able, upon which he appeared quite satisfied.

His family consisted of himself, wife, two children and a woman who was related to them. He had four other slaves as well as myself. He was a Roman Catholic, and had family worship regularly twice a day, which was something after the following: He had a large clock standing in the entry of the house in which were some images made of clay, which were used in worship. We all had to kneel before them; the family in front, and the slaves behind.

We were taught to chant some words which we did not know the meaning of. We also had to make the sign of the cross several times. Whilst worshiping, my master held a whip in his hand, and those who showed signs of inattention or drowsiness, were immediately brought to consciousness by a smart application of the whip. This mostly fell to the lot of the female slave, who would often fall asleep in spite of the images, crossings, and other like pieces of amusement.

I was soon placed at hard labor, such as none but slaves and horses are put to. At the time of this man's purchasing me, he was building a house, and had to fetch building stone from across the river, a considerable distance, and I was compelled to carry them that were so heavy it took three men to raise them upon my head, which burden I was obliged to bear for a quarter of a mile at least, down to where the boat lay. Sometimes the stone would press so hard upon my head that I was obliged to throw it down upon the ground, and then my master would be very angry indeed, and would say the cassoori (dog) had thrown down the stone, when I thought in my heart that he was the worst dog; but it was only a thought, as I dared not give utterance in words. (pp. 45–6)

These sections revolve around three themes. First, Mahommah was extraordinarily intelligent, quickly realizing the advantage of learning Portuguese and accomplishing this in short order. Second, he lived within the framework of a rather typical slaveholding family along with four other slaves. This was a milieu that bore little resemblance to the plantation environment of rural Cuba described by Montejo. In fact, despite the prevailing image of the plantation slave, most slaveholders owned fewer than five slaves, and this was the case in Brazil, the United States, and Cuba. His master insisted that symbolic deference by paid to Catholicism despite the fact that recently imported Africans had little knowledge of the rituals and symbols they were forced to pay homage to under the threat of the whip. Finally, the labor itself, hauling stones for the construction of a house, was little short of backbreaking. But Mahommah's condition would improve temporarily, in part because he had learned Portuguese.

I soon improved in my knowledge of the Portuguese language whilst here, and was able very shortly to count a hundred. I was then sent out to sell bread for my master, first going round through the town, and then out into the country, and in the evening, after coming home again, sold in the market till nine at night. Being pretty honest and persevering, I generally sold out, but sometimes was not quite so successful, and then the lash was my portion.

My companions in slavery were not quite so steady as I was, being much given to drink, so that they were not so profitable to my master. I took advantage of this, to raise myself in his opinion, by being very attentive and obedient; but it was all the same, do what I would, I found I had a tyrant to serve, nothing seemed to satisfy him, so I took to drinking likewise, then we were all of a sort, bad master, bad slaves.

Things went on worse and worse, and I was very anxious to change masters, so I tried running away, but was soon caught, tied and carried back. I next tried what it would do for me by being unfaithful and indolent; so one day when I was sent out to sell bread as usual, I only sold a small quantity, and the money I took and spent for whiskey, which I drank pretty freely, and went home well drunk, when my master went to count the days, taking in my basket and discovering the state of things, I was beaten very severely. I told him he must not whip me any more, and got quite angry, for the thought came into my head that I would kill him, and afterwards destroy myself. I at last made up my mind to drown myself; I would rather die than live to be a slave. I then ran down to the river and threw myself in, but being seen by some persons who were in a boat, I was rescued from drowning. . . .

After this attempt upon my life, I was taken to my master's house, who tied my hands behind me, and placed my feet together and whipped me most unmercifully, and beat me about the head and face with a heavy stick, then shook me by the neck, and struck my head against the door posts, which cut and bruised me about the temples, the scars from which savage treatment are visible at this time, and will remain so as long as I live.

After all this cruelty he took me to the city, and sold me to a dealer, where he had taken me once before, but his friends advised him then not to part with me, as they considered it more to his advantage to keep me as I was a profitable slave. I have not related a tithe of the cruel suffering which I endured whilst in the service of this wretch in human form. The limits of the present work will not allow more than a hasty glance at the different scenes which took place in my brief career. I could tell more than would be pleasant for "ears polite," and could not possibly do any good. I could relate occurrences which would "freeze thy young blood, harrow up thy soul, and make each particular hair to stand on end like quills upon the fretful porcupine;" and yet it would be but a repetition of the thousand and one oft told tales of the horrors of the cruel system of slavery. (pp. 46–7)

Because of his intelligence, clever obsequiousness, and ability to speak Portuguese, Mahoomah became what was known as an *escravo do ganho*, or itinerant peddler. Unlike the case in the U.S. South, or in rural Cuba, it was quite common to find slaves selling a wide variety of products for their masters in urban areas of Brazil. These slaves were on their own in daily routines and were not accompanied by masters or overseers. They would be provided with a quantity of merchandise to sell – in Mahoomah's case, bread – and were expected to deliver the cash proceeds to their masters at the end of the workday. This was a privileged position because it allowed wide-ranging flexibility in the rhythms of daily life as long as the stipulated amount of money was delivered at the end of the day. Slaves in similar positions could fraternize, socialize, and form liaisons of all types with each other and with the large free black and mulatto populations found in all Brazilian urban centers. Most importantly, they could accumulate small amounts of cash, using their ingenuity by charging a bit more to their customers than the amount ultimately due to their owners. This was extraordinarily important to these urban slaves because of the possibility of self-purchase described in the preceding chapter, and also because it allowed slaves to partici-pate in marketplace activities that could improve their lives, although this should not be exaggerated. Still, more food could be acquired, as well as better clothing and other consumer goods, because of this small-scale access to specie.

These activities and prerogatives must be kept in perspective. Most slaves, especially those in rural environments, had little hope of leading this kind of life. Although the *escravo do ganho* was clearly privileged, Mahoomah's narrative reminds us that life could become quite dreadful at the whim of his master. Any perceived shortcoming was met with brutality, arbitrary and ruthless corporal punishment, degradation, and ultimately being sold off to a new master. Mahoomah was driven to despair by this situation, and he started drinking heavily. After contemplating the murder of his owner he attempted unsuccessfully to run away, which was followed by more punishment and abuse of dreadful proportions. Thus, even a slave who lived a relatively privileged life could not sustain this existence without ultimately being subjected to "the horrors of the cruel system of slavery." Mahoomah was sold off to one master and then to another. He found himself working for a ship owner who transported merchandise back and forth from the south of Brazil to Rio de Janeiro. Here recalls this period in his life:

After a few weeks he shipped me off to Rio Janeiro, where I remained two weeks previous to being again sold. There was a colored man there who wanted to buy me, but for some reason or other he did not complete the purchase. I merely mention this fact to illustrate that slaveholding is generated in power, and any one having the means of buying his fellow creature with the paltry dross, can become a slave owner, no matter his color, his creed or country, and that the colored man would as soon enslave his fellow man as the white man, had he the power.

I was at length sold to a Captain of a vessel who was what may be termed "a hard case." He invited me to go and see his Senora, (wife.) I made my best bow to her, and was soon installed into my new office, that of scouring the brass work about the ship, cleaning the knives and forks, and doing other little matters necessary to be done about the cabin. I did not at first like my situation; but as I got acquainted with the crew and the rest of the slaves, I got along pretty well. In a short time I was promoted to the office of under-steward. The steward provided for the table, and I carried the provisions to the cook and waited at table; being pretty smart, they gave me plenty to do. A short time after, the captain and steward disagreed, and he gave up his stewardship, when the keys of his office were entrusted to me. I did all in my power to please my master, the captain, and he in return placed confidence in me. . . .

Our first voyage was to Rio Grande; the voyage itself was pleasant enough had I not suffered with sea sickness. The harbor at Rio Grande is rather shallow, and on entering we struck the ground, as it happened at low water, and we had great difficulty in getting her to float again. We finally succeeded, and exchanged our cargo for dried meat. We then went to Rio Janeiro and soon succeeded in disposing of the cargo. We then steered for St. Catharines to obtain Farina, a kind of breadstuff used mostly by the slaves. From thence, returned again in Rio Grande and exchanged our cargo for whale oil and put out again to sea, and stood for Rio Janeiro. The vessel being very heavily laden, we had a very bad time of it; we all expected that we should be lost, but by lightening the ship of part of her cargo, which we did by throwing overboard a quantity, the ship and all hands were once more saved from the devouring jaws of the destructive element. Head winds were prevalent, and although within sight of port for several days, we could not make the harbor, do all we could. (pp. 47–9)

After great labor and toil we were landed in perfect safety. During this voyage I endured more corporeal punishment than ever I did my life. The mate, a perfect brute of a fellow, ordered me one day to wash down the vessel, and after I had finished, he pointed to a place where he said was a spot, and with an oath ordered me to scrub it over again, and I did so, but not being in the best of humor he required it to be done a third time, and so on again.

When finding it was only out of caprice and there being no spot to clean. I in the end refused to scrub any more, when he took a broom stick to me, and having a scrubbing brush in my hand I lifted it to him. The master saw all that was going on, and was very angry at me for attempting to strike the mate – He ordered one of the hands to cut a piece of rope for him; he told me I was to be whipped, and I answered "very well," but kept on with my work with an eye continually turned towards him, watching his movements. When I had set the breakfast ready, he came behind me before I could get out of his way, and struck me with the rope over my shoulders, and being rather long, the end of it swung down and struck my stomach very violently, which caused me some pain and sickness; the force with which the blow was struck completely knocked me down and afterwards he beat me whilst on deck in a most brutal manner. . . .

When the cargo was landed, an English merchant having a quantity of coffee for shipment to New York, my master was engaged for the purpose, and it was arranged, after some time that I should accompany him, together with several others to serve on ship board.

We all had learned, that at New York there was no slavery; that it was a free country and that if we once got there we had nothing to dread from our cruel slave masters, and we were all most anxious to get there. (pp. 50–1)

Noting that he was sold multiple times and once had almost been sold to a free person of color, Mahoomah reveals that slaveholders were by no means exclusively white. In fact, ownership of slaves by free people of color was commonly found in all regions of Brazil, although the great majority of slaveholders were white. This was the case in Cuba as well, and to a lesser extent in the United States. The determining factor in slaveholding was not race but economic power, and this is made graphically clear in Mahoomah's narrative.

Once on board ship, and involved in the day-to-day routines of transporting jerked beef and manioc flour (*farinha*) from Rio Grande do Sul in southern Brazil to Rio de Janeiro, Mahoomah experienced the kinds of paradoxes and uncertainties that were in all likelihood common among slaves. His diligent work, responsibility, and intelligence earned him promotions from menial laborer, to understeward, and finally to head steward on his master's ship. Yet despite his position he was above all a slave, and this placed him at the beck and call of the ship's mate. After a physical confrontation in which Mahoomah defended himself from the mate's abuse, his master brutally beat him. The violence and arbitrary nature of the slave system, even for slaves who worked in skilled occupations, was part of the common everyday experiences for all slaves, regardless of their position in the slave hierarchy.

The final observations in these passages are extraordinarily revealing in that they demonstrate that the slave population had access to and disseminated among themselves information not simply of local news or events, but even of what was taking place internationally. Mahoomah and his fellow slaves knew very well that there was no slavery in faraway New York, and they were excited at the prospect of sailing to a place where perhaps there was the possibility of acquiring freedom, which indeed was what eventually would occur. Let us turn to his account of how freedom was secured once there.

The first words of English that my two companions and myself ever learned was F-r-e-e; we were taught it by an Englishman on board, and oh! how many times did I repeat it, over and over again. This same man told me a great deal about New York City, (he could speak Portuguese). He told me how the colored people in New York were all free, and it made me feel very happy, and I longed for the day to come when I should be there. ...

The pilot who came aboard of our vessel treated us very kindly, – he appeared different to any person I had ever seen before, and we took courage from that little circumstance. The next day a great many colored persons came aboard the vessel, who inquired whether we were free. The captain had previously told us not to say that we were slaves, but we heeded not his wish, and he, seeing so many persons coming aboard, began to entertain fears that his property would take in their heads to lift their heels and run away, so he very prudently informed us that New York was no place for us to go about in – that it was a very bad place, and as sure as the people caught us they would kill us. But when we were alone we concluded that we would take the first opportunity and the chance, how we would fare in a *free* country.

One day when I had helped myself rather freely to wine, I was imprudent enough to say I would not stay aboard any longer; that I would be free. The captain hearing it, called me down below, and he and three others endeavored to confine me, but could not do so; but they ultimately succeeded in confining me in a room in the bow of the vessel. I was there in confinement several days. The man who brought my food would knock at the door, and if I told him to come in he would do so, otherwise he would pass along, and I got no food. I told him on one occasion that I would not remain confined there another day with my life; that out I would get; and there being some pieces of iron in the room, towards night I took hold of one of them – it was a bar, about two feet long – with that I broke open the door, and walked out. The men were all busy at work, and the captain's wife was standing on the deck when I ascended from my prison. I heard them asking one another who had let me out; but no one could tell. I bowed to the captain's wife, and passed on to the side of the ship. There was a plank from the ship to the shore. I walked across it and ran as if for my life, of course not knowing whither I was going. I was observed during my flight by a watchman who was rather lame, and he undertook to stop me, but I shook him off, and passed on until I got to a store, at the door of which I halted a moment to take breath. They inquired of me what was the matter, but I could not tell them, as I knew nothing of English but the word F-r-e-e. Soon after, the lame watchman and another came up to me. One of them drew a bright star from his pocket and shewed it to me, but I could make nothing of it. I was then taken to the watch-house and locked up all night, when the captain called next morning, paid expenses, and took me back again to the ship along with him. The officers told me I should be a free man, if I chose, but I did not know how to act; so after a little persuasion, the captain induced me to go back with him, as I need not be afraid. This was on a Saturday, and on the following Monday afternoon three carriages drove up and stopped near the vessel. Some gentlemen came aboard from them, and walked about the deck, talking to the captain, telling him that all on board were free, and requesting him to hoist the flag. He blushed a good deal, and said he would not do so; he put himself in a great rage and stormed somewhat considerably. We were after-wards taken in their carriages, accompanied by the captain, to a very handsome building with a splendid portico in front, the entrance to which was ascended by a flight of marble steps, and was surrounded by a neat iron railing having gates at different points, the enclosure being ornamented with trees and shrubs of various kinds; it appeared to me a most beautiful place, as I had never seen anything like it before. I afterwards learned that this building was the City Hall of New York. When we arrived in the large room of the building it was crowded to excess by all kinds of people, and great numbers stood about the doors and steps, and all about the court-yard – some in conversation, others merely idling away the time walking to and fro. The Brazilian Consul was there, and when we were called upon I was asked if we wished to remain there or go back to Brazil. I answered for my companion and myself that we did not wish to return; but the female slave who was with us said she would return. I have no doubt she would have preferred staying behind, but seeing the captain there, she was intimidated and afraid to speak her mind, and so also, was the man, but I spoke boldly out that I would rather die than return into slavery!! After a great many questions had been asked us, and answered, we were taken to a prison, as I supposed it was, and there locked up. A few days afterwards we were taken again to the City Hall, and asked many more questions. We were then taken back to our old quarters the prison-house, I supposed preparatory to being shipped off again to Brazil, but of that I am not sure, as I could not understand all the ceremonies of locking us up and unlocking us, taking us to the court-house to ask questions and exhibit us before the audience there assembled – all this was new to me; I, therefore, could not fully understand the meaning of all this, but I feared greatly that we were about to be returned to slavery – I trembled at the thought! Whilst we were again locked up, some friends who had interested themselves very much in our behalf, contrived a means by which the prison-doors were opened whilst the keeper slept, and we found no difficulty in passing him, and gaining once more "the pure air of heaven," and by the assistance of those dear friends, whom I shall never forget, I was enabled to reach the city of Boston, in Massachusetts, and remained there under their protection about four weeks, when it was arranged that I should either be sent to England or Hayti, and I was consulted on the subject to know which I would prefer, and after considering for some time, I thought Hayti would be more like the climate of my own country and would agree better with my health and feelings. I did not know exactly what sort of a place England was or perhaps might have preferred to have gone there, more particularly as I have since learned that nearly all the English are friends to the colored man and his race, and that they have done so much for my people in the way of their welfare and advancement, and continue to this day to agitate anti-slavery and every other good cause. As it was, I determined to go to Hayti; accordingly, a free passage was procured for us, and considerable provisions were collected for my use during the voyage. (pp. 55–7)

Although Mahoomah's narrative is a matter-of-fact account of how he became a free man, it is remarkable that he was actually able to consummate his liberty in this way. This was not a common experience for any slave population, much less among Brazilian slaves. Yet it is instructive with respect to the dynamics of the northern abolitionist movement in the United States, which aided him; the perception of independent Haiti as a haven for freed men and women; and the newly discovered affection for the English because of their crusading antislavery activities. Mahoomah's good fortune was exceptional, and his life's story is fascinating. But we must keep in mind that by no means did this one surviving slave narrative reflect in any way upon the overall dynamics of the slave life or the possibilities of freedom in Brazil.

These narratives have provided insights into some aspects of slave life in the United States, Brazil, and Cuba during the nineteenth century. As solitary voices, they may or may not be more generally reflective of the experiences of the great masses of slaves who left no testimonies, written or verbal. Yet written records relating to slavery were produced in enormous quantities by the slaveholders themselves as well as by government bureaucrats. Slaves were extraordinarily valuable property worth millions of dollars, pesos, or *milreís*, and they had to be counted, accounted for, and kept track of on a continuous basis. When they were bought and sold, notary publics meticulously recorded details of their sales. When their owners died, they were carefully inventoried, as all property was, to be divided among heirs. If they ran away, announcements in local newspapers were published and detailed descriptions provided of each slave, who had suddenly become a specific individual rather than a member of a depersonalized mass of laborers. Government officials were concerned with monitoring how many slaves lived and worked in each district and region, and thus censuses were periodically undertaken and sometimes published. Marriages, if they took place, were often recorded by secular and religious authorities.

Elite-produced documentary collections preserved in archives and libraries in all three countries have been extensively examined by historians to reconstruct aspects of slave life and the multitude of social, political, economic, and cultural parameters governing the lives of slaves. Many of these themes will be explored throughout this book. In the next chapter we will begin by looking at how slave populations fared through time between 1790 and abolition in each of the three countries. Some slave communities or societies expanded through natural reproduction. Others suffered enormous death rates and had to be nourished by continuous imports from Africa or through interregional slave trades if slavery was to be maintained. Let us turn to the demographic aspects of these three slave societies.

CHAPTER FOUR

SLAVE POPULATIONS

Historians of slavery in the Western Hemisphere have long recognized the unique characteristics of slavery in the United States. Among the major American slave societies it was the only large-scale slave system in which the slave population grew in extraordinary numbers through natural reproduction. Every other slave society in the Western Hemisphere relied on the transatlantic slave trade to increase the availability of slave labor, since slave populations did not experience net reproduction on their own. General statistical data clearly illustrate this.

Before the slave trade to the United States was curtailed in 1808, it has been estimated that approximately 360,000 slaves were imported to the United States, a figure representing less than 4 percent of the total volume of the slave trade to the Americas.[1] Prior to the outbreak of the Civil War in the United States, the 1860 national census indicated that the slave population stood at nearly four million, more than ten times more slaves than had been imported from Africa.[2] By way of contrast, nearly four million African slaves were imported to Brazil before the slave trade there was halted in the early 1850s, which represents nearly 40 percent of all slaves forced to cross the Atlantic and more than ten times the number of slaves sent to the United States. Yet the 1872

[1] See Phillip D. Curtin, *The Atlantic Slave Trade: A Census* (Madison: University of Wisconsin Press, 1969), and revisions to Curtin's data in David Eltis, "The Volume and Structure of the Transatlantic Slave Trade: A Reassessment," *William & Mary Quarterly*, 3rd series, Vol. 58, No. 1 (January 2001), p. 46, Table 3.

[2] See the data in the 1860 census of the United States found on the internet on the United States Historical Census Data Browser at <http://fisher.lib.virginia.edu/census/>.

Brazilian national census enumerated approximately 1.5 million slaves, 38 percent of the imported total; and by the final abolition of slavery there in 1888, the slave population had fallen to about 720,000.[3] For Cuba, it has been calculated that about 780,000 slaves were imported before the Cuban slave trade was finally ended in 1867, more than twice as many as were brought to the United States and about 8 percent of all African slaves brought to the Americas. The Cuban census of 1862 indicated that there were nearly 370,000 slaves on the island, about half of the total number imported. By 1877, three years before the final emancipation law of 1880 was enacted, the slave population had fallen to nearly 200,000.[4] Although the timing of the final abolition of slavery was different in the three countries – 1865 in the U.S., 1886 in Cuba, and 1888 in Brazil – just prior to the end of slavery in each nation only the United States had more slaves than had been imported.

If there is no immigration or out-migration, populations increase only when birth rates exceed death rates. Since the forced importation of slaves to the United States ended in 1808 and there was no significant export of slaves from the United States thereafter, the slave population expanded precisely because more slaves were born than died. Two years after slaving had been halted, the United States census of 1810 revealed that the nation had a total of slightly more than 1,100,000 slaves. By the time of the 1860 census, this slave population had more than tripled to 3,950,000 slaves.[5] This meant that on the eve of the U.S. Civil War most slaves had been born domestically, and very few had been born in Africa.

---

[3] For Brazilian slave population data, see *Estatísticas Históricas do Brasil. Séries Estatísticas Retrospectivas. Volume 3: Séries Econômicas, Demográficas e Sociais, 1550 a 1985* (Rio de Janeiro: Instituto Brasileiro de Geografia e Estatística, 1987), p. 30. Also see Robert Wayne Slenes, "The Demography and Economics of Brazilian Slavery: 1850–1888" (Ph.D. dissertation, Stanford University, 1976), pp. 697–8 for 1887 data.

[4] Although the emancipation law was promulgated by Spain for its Cuban colony in 1880, slavery was not definitively abolished until 1886. For Cuban slave population data, see Laird W. Bergad, Fe Iglesias García, and María del Carmen Barcia, *The Cuban Slave Market, 1790–1880* (New York: Cambridge University Press, 1995), p. 39. For 1877, see Fe Iglesias García, "El Censo Cubano de 1877 y sus Diferentes Versiones," *Santiago*, Vol. 34 (June 1979), pp. 167–211.

[5] See the data for 1810 and 1860 found on the internet on the United States Historical Census Data Browser at <http://fisher.lib.virginia.edu/census/>.

This pattern of natural reproduction is so exceptional because of the stark contrasts with slave population dynamics found in the tropical British, Spanish, and French Caribbean colonies, and in Brazil. Scholars have generally agreed that there may have been fairly high birth rates among slaves in most of these colonies, and perhaps in some cases birth rates were even comparable to those found in the United States. However, death rates, especially among infants and young children, were greater than birth rates, and this precluded the possibility of net natural growth among slave populations.[6] Thus, in contrast to the situation in the United States, the only way to increase the number of slaves was through constant imports from Africa. Faced with these extraordinary demographic differences in American slave systems, one important focus of slavery studies has been to identify the various factors that would help to explain the ability of U.S. slaves to reproduce in such prodigious numbers. Another fundamental issue has been to determine what this pattern of natural increase indicates about the conditions of slave life in the United States compared to those prevailing elsewhere.

There are a multitude of complex natural and social factors that affect birth and death rates among all populations, enslaved or free. One critical variable is the general health of females of childbearing age, since this affects the ability to conceive and the frequency of conception, as well as the survival possibilities of newborns if pregnancies are carried to term. Health is affected by diet, disease environments, and in the case of slaves, the treatment afforded by owners, among other factors. Technical studies of slave diets in the United States have found, perhaps surprisingly, that in general slaves, especially those of working age, had access to adequate food supplies in comparative terms. In fact, there seems to have been a higher per capita consumption of meat, grains, and other sources of calories and protein among adult U.S. slaves when compared to most European free populations during the nineteenth century, although free people in the United States

---

[6] See the technically detailed studies of slave demography in the British West Indies by Barry W. Higman in *Slave Populations of the British Caribbean, 1807–1834* (Baltimore: Johns Hopkins University Press, 1984), and for Trinidad by A. Meredith John in *The Plantation Slaves of Trinidad, 1783–1816: A Mathematical and Demographic Inquiry* (New York: Cambridge University Press, 1988). For the French Caribbean, see Gabriel Debien, *Les Esclaves aux Antilles Françaises (XVIIe-XVIIIe Siècles)* (Basse-Terre: Société D'Histoire de la Guadeloupe and Fort-de-France: Société D'Histoire de la Martinique, 1974).

consumed more food per capita than slaves.[7] There also seems to have been a greater per capita level of food consumption among U.S. slaves than that found among slaves throughout Latin America and the Caribbean.

Greater food consumption not only would account for higher birth rates among U.S. female slaves, since they were generally healthier because of better diets, but also helps to explain comparatively lower infant and childhood mortality rates and longer life expectancies among U.S. slaves when compared to their enslaved brethren in Latin America and the Caribbean.[8] Adequately nourished mothers would mean higher birth-weight and healthier babies, increasing survival possibilities during the most vulnerable period of infancy, when death rates were often very high.

Further evidence of better diets among U.S. slaves has been generated by studies that have measured slave heights and compared them to those of free peoples and slaves from other regions. These have found that U.S. slaves were taller on average than slaves studied elsewhere in the Americas, and in many cases they were taller than free European populations, although free U.S.-born northern whites were found to be

---

[7] See Robert William Fogel and Stanley L. Engerman, *Time on the Cross: The Economics of American Negro Slavery* (Boston: Little, Brown, 1974), pp. 109–117, whch argued that U.S. slaves were well fed. There is by no means complete agreement among scholars on the quantitative or qualitative aspects of slave diets. For a view that contradicts that of Fogel and Engerman, see Richard Sutch, "The Care and Feeding of Slaves," in Paul A. David, et al., *Reckoning with Slavery: A Critical Study in the Quantitative History of American Negro Slavery* (New York: Oxford University Press, 1976), pp. 231–301. For diets of Caribbean slaves, see Kenneth F. Kiple, *The Caribbean Slave: A Biological History* (New York: Cambridge University Press, 1984), especially "Plantation Nutrition" and "Malnutrition: Morbidity and Mortality," pp. 76–103. Also see Kenneth F. Kiple, "The Nutritional Link with Slave Infant and Child Mortality in Brazil," *Hispanic American Historical Review*, Vol. 69, No. 4 (1989), pp. 677–90.

[8] As in all of these sweeping generalizations, caution is mandated. There may have been lower death rates among U.S. slave children compared to slave children elsewhere. However, death rates among U.S. slave children under five years old were much higher than those among white children during the nineteenth century, and it was only upon reaching adulthood that death rates among slaves seem to parallel death rates among the free population. See Sutch, "The Care and Feeding of Slaves."

on average taller than slaves.⁹ Since body size and nutrition are closely linked, the greater height of adults offers additional evidence of better diets among U.S. slaves during childhood and adolescence.¹⁰

Climate and the natural environment are other important factors that impact death rates. Although slavery in the United States was by and large confined to the southern states during the nineteenth century, slaves labored in diverse environments – temperate, tropical, and semi-tropical – as slavery spread to vast regions throughout the South and westward. This was not the case in the Caribbean islands or in the Brazilian littoral regions in which slavery originally took hold, and where environments are uniformly tropical. It has been generally recognized that a wide variety of diseases with high mortality rates proliferated more readily in tropical environments before the advent of modern medicine in the twentieth century, and that these resulted in higher death rates among all population sectors, irrespective of race or legal status.¹¹ Although West Africans were by and large immune to

9   See Richard H. Steckel, "Work, Disease, and Diet in the Health and Mortality of American Slaves," and Robert A. Margo and Richard H. Steckel, "The Nutrition and Health of Slaves and Antebellum Southern Whites," in Robert William Fogel and Stanley L. Engerman, editors, *Without Consent or Contract: Conditions of Slave Life and the Transition to Freedom, Technical Papers, (Volume 2)* (New York: Norton, 1992), pp. 489–507, 508–21. Also see the studies on slave heights found in *Social Science History*, Vol. 6, No. 4 (Fall 1982), especially Robert A. Margo and Richard H. Steckel "The Heights of American Slaves: New Evidence on Slave Nutrition and Health," pp. 516–38, and Gerald C. Friedman, "The Heights of Slaves in Trinidad," pp. 482–515.

10 As is the case for all general observations about slave populations, these sweeping conclusions may not be applied to all slaves at all times and in all places. Regional and temporal variations will be considered later in this chapter. It also should be stressed that while slaves in general seem to have had adequate diets that resulted in a health environment favoring natural reproduction, this factor cannot be utilized to justify slavery in any way, nor can it be viewed as mitigating that tragic and horrendous condition of being enslaved.

11 There is an extensive literature on disease in the Americas after European conquest and colonization, and among slave populations. Some important works are Kenneth F. Kiple and Virginia Himmelsteib King, *Another Dimension to the Black Diaspora: Diet, Disease, and Racism* (New York: Cambridge University Press, 1981); Kenneth F. Kiple, *The Caribbean Slave: A Biological History*; Philip D. Curtin, *Death by Migration: Europe's Encounter with the Tropical World in the Nineteenth Century* (New York: Cambridge University Press, 1985); Noble David Cook, *Born to Die: Disease and New*

two of the deadliest tropical diseases, malaria and yellow fever, slave populations were vulnerable to numerous chronic and infectious diseases that struck in periodic epidemics throughout these tropical regions.[12] Among the most devastating were cholera, tuberculosis (often referred to as consumption), typhoid, gastrointestinal illnesses (such as dysentery), tetanus, lockjaw, and leprosy, although there were many that which could be lethal or cause severe physical debilities.

U.S. slaves were susceptible to these same diseases, and indeed as slavery spread through southern tropical lowland regions death rates in these areas may have been comparable to those found among slaves in the Caribbean and Brazil. But with generally poorer diets and living almost exclusively in tropical regions where infectious diseases spread more readily, Caribbean and Brazilian slaves of all age categories experienced significantly higher death rates than U.S. slaves. This is the critical factor explaining the inability of these slave populations to increase naturally and the parallel need for the constant importation of Africans until the slave trade to the tropical Caribbean and Brazil was finally terminated.

This continued reliance on the slave trade from Africa is, perhaps ironically, another factor that explains the inability of slave populations in these tropical regions to increase through natural reproduction. Specialized studies have found relatively greater death rates and lower birth rates among African-born slaves compared to American-born slaves throughout the hemisphere. Immunities to recurring infectious and viral diseases were gradually developed by American-born slave populations, along with their inherited resistance to malaria and yellow fever, and these permitted a greater likelihood of survival through childhood as well as longer life expectancies. Children born to Africans generally did not have the same inherited immunological responses to American diseases, and thus death rates were in all likelihood significantly higher among slave children with two African-born parents. Since the U.S. slave population during the nineteenth century was increasingly, and eventually almost exclusively, U.S.-born, overall

World Conquest, 1492–1650 (New York: Cambridge University Press, 1998); and Noble David Cook and W. George Lovell, editors, "Secret Judgments of God": Old World Disease in Colonial Spanish America (Norman: University of Oklahoma Press, 1991).

[12] On West African immunity to malaria and yellow fever, see Kiple, The Caribbean Slave: A Biological History, pp. 14–20.

death rates were comparatively lower because of inherited immunities along with the other factors previously noted. Additionally, for reasons that are not entirely clear, birth rates among African female slaves were much lower than those among their American-born counterparts.[13] Thus, among slave populations with large numbers of African-born slaves, as was the case in Cuba and Brazil because of the ongoing slave trade, there were both lower birth rates and higher death rates.

Another variable that was been linked to differing mortality rates among slave populations is occupation and the work rhythms associated with particular crops and products produced by slave labor. Tropical sugar plantation agriculture has long been associated with the highest death rates of all of the slave-based economic activities. The Brazilian northeast was the first of these plantation systems in the Americas, and high mortality rates among slaves was a fundamental characteristic of slave demography there during the late sixteenth and seventeenth centuries and after. High death rates meant that continued African imports were essential for ongoing sugar production. This same pattern was found in nearly all regions where sugar was produced.[14] The British and French Caribbean colonies experienced the same kinds of high mortality rates among slaves working on sugar plantations during the eighteenth-century, and Cuba, which had become the largest sugar exporter in the world by the 1820s, repeated the experience of these other regions. High mortality rates also were found among slaves working in the Louisiana sugar plantations that developed during the 1820s and after.[15]

The inability of slaves to reproduce in sugar plantation zones was related to a combination of factors. These included tropical disease environments in unhealthy lowland districts, a skewed ratio of males

---

[13]   Herbert S. Klein and Stanley L. Engerman, in "Fertility Differentials between Slaves in the United States and the British West Indies: A Note on Lactation Practices," *William & Mary Quarterly*, Vol. 35, No. 2 (April 1978), pp. 357–74, have suggested that one explanation for lower birth rates among African females was the African cultural tradition of refraining from sexual intercourse while females were lactating, a practice that was not generally followed by American-born slaves.

[14]   See the masterful study by Stuart B. Schwartz, *Sugar Plantations in the Formation of Brazilian Society,: Bahia, 1550–1835* (New York: Cambridge University Press, 1985).

[15]   See Michael Tadman, "The Demographic Cost of Sugar: Debates on Slave Societies and Natural Increase in the Americas," *American Historical Review*, Vol. 105, No. 5 (December 2000), pp. 1534–75.

to females because plantation owners preferred male laborers for the grueling work of sugar cane harvesting, and possibly mistreatment and overwork by slave owners. Relatively small numbers of female slaves in relation to males would naturally result in a lower number of births compared to regions or local economies where sex ratios (the number of males per females) were more nearly equal. If diseases caused higher death rates in sugar plantation zones, and birth rates were lower in these regions, slave populations could not possibly increase naturally.

Subjecting slaves to horrendous living conditions and excruciatingly long work days during harvest season, as has been noted in studies of sugar plantation economies, were additional factors accounting for higher death rates. Mistreatment of slaves may appear to have been economically irrational. But if slaves were constantly available at reasonable prices from Africa – or, in the case of the Louisiana sugar districts, from the interregional slave trade – it may have been per-versely logical from a strictly economic point of view for masters to literally work slaves to death because of the high short-term profit possibilities, and then to replace them with fresh imports. While this has not been empirically proven, it may have been one of the factors accounting for the overall high death rates and the inability of slaves to reproduce in sugar plantation zones. This dynamic tragically underlines the ultimate barbarity of the slave system.

Distorted sex ratios (an overwhelming number of male slaves) were also typical of mining economies, which were usually located in inhospitable highland regions where humidity and the bone-chilling cold of the winter months resulted in a stark environment for humans. The most notable of these was in the Brazilian region of Minas Gerais, where gold and diamonds were discovered during the late seventeenth century. A large-scale slave trade developed to this interior region of Brazil before mineral reserves began to wane in the 1730s and 1740s, and in most population settlements and mining camps there could be as many as six or seven male slaves for every female.[16] This alone

---

[16]   See Charles Boxer, *The Golden Age of Brazil, 1695–1750* (Berkeley: University of California Press, 1962); A. J. R. Russell Wood, *The Black Man in Slavery and Freedom in Colonial Brazil* (New York: St. Martin's Press, 1982); and Laird W. Bergad, *Slavery and the Economic and Demographic History of Minas Gerais, Brazil, 1720–1888* (New York: Cambridge University Press, 1999).

precluded the possibility of natural slave population expansion because of the low overall number of births. We don't know enough about mortality rates in the mining regions to draw definitive conclusions, but they were probably quite high, and perhaps comparable to or even higher than those found in sugar plantation districts.

Another factor contributing to naturally declining slave populations in Cuba and Brazil may have been fairly significant manumission rates. Although this factor should not be exaggerated, scholars have recognized that it was more common for slaves to be freed by masters in Spanish and Portuguese Latin America and the Caribbean than in the British and French colonies and in the independent United States. A long tradition, originating in Roman juridical codes and continuing as part of Iberian medieval legal systems, theoretically permitted slaves to accumulate and own property as well as giving them the right to earn cash or specie in certain contexts. These traditions were carried over to Latin America, where slaves also had generally recognized rights to purchase their freedom outright or in installments.[17] This process of self-purchase was of extraordinary importance to slaves themselves, although access to cash, or securing respect for these traditions by slave owners, could never be guaranteed. Additionally, no scholar has been able to determine from surviving documents the actual numbers involved or the overall rate of self-purchase or manumission for any time period.

Slave owners voluntarily freed slaves in Cuba, Brazil, and elsewhere in Latin America much more frequently than was the case in the United States although once again precise manumission rates are unknown. Manumitted slaves were found in all age, sex, and birth origin categories and were not, as once thought, old, infirm, and unproductive slaves. It was more common for owners to free female slaves and domestic workers as opposed to males or field slaves working in agriculture. There were also significantly greater rates of manumission among urban slaves. Many voluntary grants of freedom made to slaves were written in last wills and testaments when owners were sick or dying. This was perhaps a reflection of a predominantly Catholic religious and cultural milieu in which final divine judgment

---

[17]   For a discussion of these legal codes, see Herbert S. Klein, *Slavery in the Americas: A Comparative Study of Cuba and Virginia* (London: Oxford University Press, 1967), pp. 37–85.

was expected, and in which slave owners implicitly recognized the immorality of slavery.[18]

How significant is the acquisition of freedom by slaves in helping to explain the overall net decline of slavery in Cuba and Brazil? Until scholars explore this important aspect of these slave societies in detailed studies with reliable statistical data, no real conclusions may be drawn on the influence of manumissions on long-term demographic patterns among Cuban and Brazilian slave populations. However, it is conspicuous that in both Cuba and Brazil, the free black and mulatto populations dwarfed those of the United States, although impressive rates of natural reproduction among free peoples of color rather than a constant influx of ex-slaves may have been the principal explanation for this.

Another factor that may have had some significance for declining slave populations in Cuba and Brazil is the comparatively greater number of slaves fleeing captivity for remote rural areas or for the anonymity afforded by large free black and mulatto communities. Slaves ran away in the United States as well, and in every other American slave society. However, as in the case of manumissions, we don't have accurate data on the number of successful runaways, so it is impossible to calculate the long-term demographic impact of slave flight on overall slave populations.

One final question that scholars have considered in attempting to explain the radically contrasting population patterns found in

[18]   Frank Tannenbaum, *Slave and Citizen: The Negro in the Americas* (New York: Vintage Books, 1946), underlined the importance of Catholicism and its impact on the behavior patterns of slave owners. For studies that have examined the profiles of manumitted slaves in Brazil and Cuba, see Stuart B. Schwartz, "The Manumission of Slaves in Colonial Brazil: Bahia, 1684–1745," *Hispanic American Historical Review*, Vol. 54, No. 4 (1974), pp. 603–35; Mieko Nishida, "Manumission and Ethnicity in Urban Slavery: Salvador, Brazil 1808–1888," *Hispanic American Historical Review*, Vol. 73, No. 3 (1993), pp. 61–91; James Patrick Kernan, "The Manumission of Slaves in Paraty, Brazil, 1789–1822" (Ph.D. thesis, New York University, 1976); Mary Karasch, *Slave Life in Rio de Janeiro, 1808–1850* (Princeton, NJ: Princeton University Press, 1987); Kathleen J. Higgins, *"Licentious Liberty" in a Brazilian Gold-Mining Region: Slavery, Gender, and Social Control in Eighteenth-Century Sabará, Minas Gerais* (University Park: Pennsylvania State University Press, 1999); and Laird Bergad et. al., *The Cuban Slave Market, 1790–1880*, pp. 122–42.

American slave societies is whether there was purposeful slave breeding on the part of masters in the United States but not in Latin America or the Caribbean. Did slave owners interfere in the lives of slaves in some way to create conditions that would encourage slave reproduction in the United States? There has been no definitive consensus on the part of scholars. Proponents of the slave "breeding thesis" have argued that rational economic motivations led southern U.S. slave owners to purposefully breed slaves, and that there may have been plantations where this was the primary economic activity. This would permit an increase in slave labor forces without incurring the purchase costs of new slaves, although there was considerable expense involved in raising a slave to maturity. Additionally, there were significant profit possibilities if slaves born in captivity reached working age and then were sold at prices that rose steadily, especially during the 1850s.[19] One of the problems with this interpretation is the implicit assumption that for some reason, cultural or otherwise, Latin American and Caribbean slave owners were economically irrational in their apparent lack of encouragement or attention to slave reproduction, although this comparative aspect of slave systems has never been systematically explored by scholars.

Those arguing against the idea of systematic slave breeding in the United States have pointed to the factors outlined previously to

---

[19]   The debates on slave breeding, like debates on most of the issues related to the economics or demography of slavery in the United States, were highlighted by the publication of Fogel and Engerman, *Time on the Cross: The Economics of American Negro Slavery*, which argued that systematic slave breeding was a myth, although the authors noted that there were certainly masters who encouraged reproduction. See "The Myth of Slave Breeding," pp. 78–86. Also see the technical arguments in "The Slave Breeding Thesis," in Fogel and Engerman, editors, *Without Consent or Contract, Technical Papers, Volume 2*, pp. 455–72.

Arguments in support of slave breeding are found in Richard Sutch, "The Breeding of Slaves for Sale and the Westward Expansion of Slavery, 1850–1860," in Stanley L. Engerman and Eugene D. Genovese, editors, *Race and Slavery in the Western Hemisphere: Quantitative Studies* (Princeton, NJ: Princeton University Press, 1975), pp. 173–210 and in Herbert Gutman and Richard Sutch, "Victorians All? The Sexual Mores and Conduct of Slaves and Their Masters," in David et al., *Reckoning with Slavery: A Critical Study in the Quantitative History of American Negro Slavery*, pp. 134–64, especially pp. 154–61.

explain the dynamic natural expansion of the U.S. slave population – comparatively better slave diets, higher birth rates, and lower death rates.[20] Without question, the encouragement of reproduction for economic reasons existed among some slave owners within the large and diversified slave society of the antebellum United States. However, these owners were probably exceptional rather than typical. If masters interfered in some way to stimulate reproduction, it was by ensuring an adequate diet and sometimes by providing slaves with small parcels of land to cultivate crops or raise animals to supplement their diets. In this way slave owners acted out of self-interest and economic rationality, since a healthier slave population with a decent diet would be more productive and reproduce more readily. This is something very different from purposeful breeding.

Comparative data on the total number of slaves imported to each country compared to the number of slaves present, at the onset of the Civil War, in the United States or at the beginning of the abolition processes in Brazil and Cuba, clearly indicate the general inability of Cuban and Brazilian slave populations to increase through reproduction. However, there were regions and time periods during the long 350-year history of slavery in Brazil in which slaves reproduced naturally at rates which may have been similar to those found in the United States.

Brazil's geographical vastness, immense resource base, and the fact that there were dispersed centers of settlement quite distant from each other led to the development of numerous regional slave-based economic cycles of expansion and decline from the sixteenth century until slavery was abolished in 1888.[21] In some ways, this same statement may be made about the United States. However, in the United States there was a greater degree of infrastructural linkage between regions by river, road, and eventually railroads. There was also integration of regional slave-based economic activities into a national economic system. Brazil's regional economic structures and cycles were often tenuously linked to one other and in many cases developed without significant connection to any coherent national economy.

[20]   See the citations in the previous footnote. The issue of slave family encouragement as a strategy of stimulating population growth will be explored in Chapter 5.
[21]   These economic cycles will be considered in Chapter 5.

Transportation infrastructures connecting the various Brazilian regions ranged from poor to nonexistent until railroad construction began on a significant scale in the 1860s.[22] There was no national banking system. Unlike the situation in the United States, there was no viable merchant marine that carried products to and from the nation or the various regions. Political structures were strongest and most developed at the provincial rather than the national level, despite the existence of a fairly stable national government.[23] All of this, among other factors, led to the creation of regional cultures, economies, societies, and even slave systems that in many respects were often very different from one another.

During nearly every period of regional economic growth until the abolition of the African slave trade to Brazil during the early 1850s – in the sugar, mining, coffee, ranching, and food-crop production industries, as well as in other sectors – slaves were imported to meet labor demands.[24] In most cases these slaves were newly-arrived Africans and not Brazilian-born slaves sold from stagnant or contracting local economies to areas of growth.[25] When cycles of expansion in regional economic systems ended, African imports almost always ceased,

[22]   See Richard Graham, *Britain and the Onset of Modernization in Brazil, 1850–1914* (New York: Cambridge University Press, 1972), especially Chapter 2, "Coffee and Rails," pp. 51–72. Also see William Summerhill, "Transport Improvements and Economic Growth in Brazil and Mexico," in Stephen Haber, editor, *How Latin America Fell Behind: Essays on the Economic Histories of Brazil and Mexico, 1800–1914* (Stanford, CA: Stanford University Press, 1997), pp. 93–117. A history of Brazilian railroads by Ivanil Numes, "História das Ferrovias," may be found on the internet at <http://www.angelfire.com/ar/ufa/ferrovia.html>.

[23]   See Roderick J. Barman, *Brazil: The Forging of a Nation, 1798–1852* (Stanford, CA: Stanford University Press, 1988), and his *Citizen Emperor: Pedro II and the Making of Brazil, 1825–9* (Stanford, CA: Stanford University Press, 1999.

[24]   See the study of the São Paulo coffee district by Warren Dean, *Rio Claro: A Brazilian Plantation System, 1820–1920* (Stanford, CA: Stanford University Press, 1976), and the classic study of a Rio de Janeiro coffee region by Stanley Stein, *Vassouras: A Brazilian Coffee County, 1850–1890* (Cambridge, MA: Harvard University Press, 1957).

[25]   After the end of the African slave trade a different situation emerged, and an interregional slave trade began on an important scale. See Robert Slenes, "The Demography and Economics of Brazilian Slavery: 1850–1888" (Ph.D. thesis, Stanford University, 1976), especially Chapter 3, "The Volume and Organization of the Inter-regional Slave Trade: 1850–1888," pp. 120–78.

although nuclei of slave populations remained to labor in a variety of endeavors after the end of export-led economic growth cycles.

Evidence from local-level studies of slavery in Brazil suggests that when African slave imports ended, slave populations usually declined in the short term. However, after a period of time that could be decades, they began to grow naturally at varying rates of expansion, some even suggestive of U.S. slave population growth rates. The most studied case has been that of the province of Minas Gerais, which became Brazil's largest slave-holding region during the early eighteenth-century mining boom. With the definitive end of mining expansion around 1750, African imports declined precipitously, and accordingly the slave population contracted steadily between the 1780s and about 1808. However, thereafter the slave population began to increase gradually because of natural reproduction. Throughout the nineteenth century, Minas Gerais had a greater slave population than any other province, and most slaves were born in Brazil.[26] This regional demographic pattern resembled the United States slave system. The kinds of detailed fertility and mortality data available for U.S. slave populations have not been found in documentary collections for Brazilian slaves. It is certain, however, that there were large numbers of Brazilian-born slave children in Minas Gerais in relation to women of child-bearing age throughout the nineteenth century until slavery was abolished. This evidence strongly suggests both the high birth rates and childhood survival rates that made the U.S. slave system so distinctive in its population history.

There are a number of fundamental factors explaining natural slave population expansion in Minas Gerais. First and foremost, the sex ratio gradually moved toward a more even distribution of male, and female slaves with the decline in African slave imports. The African slave trade to Minas was heavily male, and the result was a predominantly male slave population in the principal mining centers during the early eighteenth-century boom years. Female slaves, African- or Brazilian-born, had children to be sure, but not in sufficient numbers for the slave population to increase naturally. With the virtual end of African slave imports, the number of female slaves gradually increased, both numerically and as a share of the total slave population. This was because older African males slowly died off, and since the slave trade to

---

[26]   See Laird W. Bergad, *Slavery and the Demographic and Economic History of Minas Gerais, Brazil, 1720–1888* (New York: Cambridge University Press, 1999).

the province had ceased at any significant level, the slave population became increasingly Brazilian-born. By the late 1790s, there were more Brazilian-born slaves in Minas Gerais than Africans, and their relative portion of the overall provincial slave population increased continuously until abolition in 1888. Accordingly, since roughly equal numbers of male and female slaves were born in Brazil, the sex ratio gradually moved toward parity. This fact alone meant that over time the number of female slaves reaching the child-bearing years grew, and this created the preconditions for slave population expansion.

Second, because the number of Brazilian-born slaves in Minas Gerais constantly increased during the nineteenth century, and the number of Africans was reduced because of death and declining imports, there was a generalized decline in slave death rates. This occurred because death rates for African-born slaves were generally higher than those for American-born slaves, probably because of the differential in inherited disease immunities, among other factors. Thus, as the Brazilian-born slave population grew in Minas both in absolute terms and in relation to the number of surviving Africans, not only did birth rates increase because there were numerically more females, but death rates declined as well. At some point during the early nineteenth century, birth rates exceeded death rates, and the slave population began to grow naturally.

This pattern of natural slave reproduction in Brazil after African imports to regional economies ended has been confirmed by other local-level studies of Brazilian slave demography.[27] Conversely, there were areas in Brazil in which relatively small slave populations labored in a variety of endeavors, where sex ratios were fairly equal, and where populations were apparently expanding because of natural reproduction. However, when African imports began to arrive in significant numbers, these population dynamics changed decisively. This is a general profile of the Bananal region of eastern São Paulo during the early nineteenth century – a mixed agricultural economy not heavily involved in export-oriented activities at the close of the eighteenth century. Bananal is contiguous to the state of Rio de Janeiro, where coffee cultivation was spreading from north to south in the Paraiba valley system. On the margins of the coffee economy at the turn of the

---

[27]   See the study of Paraná in southern Brazil by Horacio Gutiérrez, "Demografia Escrava Numa Economia Não Exportadora: Paraná," *Estudos Econômicos*, Vol. 17, No. 2 (1987), pp. 297–314, and his "Crioulos e Africanos no Paraná, 1798–1830," *Revista Brasileira de História*, Vol. 8 No. 16 (1988), pp. 161–88.

nineteenth century, Bananal was gradually converted into a region of coffee production and one of the many destinations of the African slave trade to Brazil. Not surprisingly, the demography of the slave population was entirely transformed by the heavily male African imports, and the pattern of slave reproduction observed prior to the area's integration into the export coffee economy came to an end.[28]

The situation found in Bananal may have been found more generally throughout the province of São Paulo before coffee spread into the western regions of the province during the nineteenth century. One study that examined provincial-level census data found that in 1798, when the first detailed count of slaves is available, the sex ratio was only slightly skewed toward males – 117 male for every 100 female slaves. This is highly suggestive of a slave population that was largely the product of natural reproduction rather than one heavily impacted by African imports. In 1828, after coffee had begun its expansion into the region, the sex ratio stood at 154 males for every 100 females, a marked transformation from 30 years earlier. This is evidence that there were significant African slave imports into São Paulo, and that conditions for net natural reproduction among slaves were eroded because of the ensuing sex imbalance.[29]

It is clear that a critical variable determining the demographic dynamics of regional Brazilian slave systems was the volume of the African slave trade and all of the accompanying factors surrounding the presence of large African-born slave populations. These included distorted male to female sex ratios, lower birth rates, and higher death rates. The volume of the African slave trade, in turn, was linked to labor demands spawned by regional economic cycles. It must be kept in mind that during the nineteenth century the African slave trade to Brazil remained quite active long after slaving to the United States and to the British and French Caribbean had virtually ceased. Brazil was the destination of over 1.7 million African slaves from 1801 until 1850, when the slave trade was finally ended, and this represented some 55 percent of all slaves disembarking in the Americas during the first half of the

---

[28] See José Flavio Motta, "A Família Escrava e a Penetração do Café em Bananal (1801–1829)," *Revista Brasileira de Estudos Populacionais*, Vol. 6 (1988), pp. 71–101, and his *Corpos Escravos, Vontades Livres: Posse de Cativos e Família Escrava em Bananal (1801–1829)* (São Paulo: Annablume, 1999).

[29] Maria Luiza Marcílio, *Crescimento Demográfico e Evolução Agrária Paulista, 1700–1836* (São Paulo: Editora Hucitec, 2000), p. 78.

nineteenth century.[30] During periods when export crops such as sugar, coffee, and cotton, among others, expanded to new areas, labor demands were largely met through the importation of African slaves. The imbalance between African-born and Brazilian-born slaves in these regions meant that net natural slave population expansion was virtually impossible.

The Cuban case during the nineteenth century was quite different, because economic diversification and the cycles in slave-based activities in Cuba may not be compared to those in Brazil or in the United States. There were no large-scale regional slave systems in Cuba analogous to those in Minas Gerais. Although slaves worked in a variety of economic sectors, urban and rural, gradually Cuba became a classical Caribbean plantation economy during the first half of the nineteenth century. Coffee exports were important to the colonial economy during the 1790s and through the early 1840s. However, after steady growth starting in the 1740s, by the 1820s Cuba had become the leading exporter of sugar to the world market. Sugar and slavery defined the Cuban economy and society thereafter until the abolition of slavery in 1886. Throughout sugar's development in Cuba, African slaves were continually imported to meet sugar's labor demands, in much the same way as in the eighteenth-century English and French Caribbean, and in Brazil. Cuba was the last great destination of the transatlantic slave trade, which was not ended until 1867. Between 1790 and 1867, some 780,000 slaves were imported to the island.[31]

While there was clearly no net increase in the number of slaves because of natural reproduction, as was the case in the United States and in Minas Gerais, one scholar has argued that indeed Cuban slaves were reproducing, but that death rates among Africans were so high that in effect this reproduction was "masked" by demographic indicators as reflected in the general statistical data on slave populations that historians have perused, mainly published census materials.[32] Another

---

[30]   Eltis, "The Volume and Structure of the Transatlantic Slave Trade: A Reassessment."

[31]   See the data in David Eltis, *Economic Growth and the Ending of the Transatlantic Slave Trade* (New York: Oxford University Press, 1987), p. 245.

[32]   See the technical discussion on this in Jack Ericson Eblen, "On the Natural Increase of Slave Populations: The Example of the Cuban Black Population, 1775–1900," in Stanley L. Engerman and Eugene D. Genovese, editors, *Race and Slavery in the Western Hemisphere: Quantitative Studies* (Princeton, NJ: Princeton University Press, 1975), pp. 211–48.

noted Cuban historian has found a major change in the conditions of slaves during the decade of the 1840s, which may have led to higher fertility rates and lower death rates, as well as to conscious attempts by planters to encourage reproduction through better treatment.[33] These conclusions have not been explored in subsequent studies of Cuban slavery, but they are suggestive for the Brazilian slave system as well, with its huge numbers of African imports during the nineteenth century. It may be that in Brazilian areas that received large African slave imports, the extant population was reproducing despite demographic indicators, such as high death rates among Africans, that seem to indicate natural decline. Yet regardless of the fact that there may have been exceptions in certain geographical regions in Brazil during particular time periods, or that Cuban slave reproduction during the nineteenth century may have been obscured by the large and continuing importation of Africans, the U.S. slave system was the only case in which the number of slaves at abolition was greater than the number of slaves imported.

One of the fundamental differences that distinguished the United States slave system from the Brazilian and Cuban variants was that slaves were a relatively small percentage of the overall U.S. population. Additionally, they lived and labored within a society containing a relatively small free black and mulatto population. The 1790 census of the United States indicated that slaves made up about 18 percent of the total population, with free blacks and mulattos accounting for a mere 1.5 percent of all U.S. residents. The percentage of slaves in the overall U.S. population gradually declined to nearly 13 percent of the total on the eve of the Civil War in 1860, despite the steady increase in the absolute number of slaves. The free population increased during the nineteenth century at faster rates than the slave population. Conspicuously, free people of color still accounted for only 1.5 percent of total inhabitants in 1860. Thus, U.S. society was over 80 percent racially white, and enslaved blacks and mulattos were the overwhelming majority of the total population of color.[34]

Slavery was a dynamic and mobile labor system in the United States, Brazil, and Cuba. As a labor institution it was closely connected to

---

[33]   Manuel Moreno Fraginals, *El Ingenio: Complejo Económico Social Cubano del Azúcar* (Havana: Editorial de Ciencias Sociales, 1978), vol. 2, pp. 83–90.

[34]   There were marked regional differences in racial structures, and these will be considered later in this chapter.

overall patterns of internal migration and population expansion within each country, as well as to economic cycles that unfolded over time in different geographical regions.[35] In 1790, nearly all U.S. slaves, and most of the population, were concentrated in southeastern seaboard states.[36] Of slightly more than 697,000 slaves, more than 600,000 lived and labored in Maryland, Virginia, North Carolina, and South Carolina. Virginia alone had a slave population of more than 290,000, over 40 percent of all U.S. slaves, and it would remain the single largest slaveholding state in absolute terms until the outbreak of the Civil War in 1861. Slaves accounted for a significant percentage of the overall population in these key slave states in 1790: 39 percent of Virginia's population, 43 percent of South Carolina's, 32 percent of Maryland's, and about 25 percent of North Carolina's. By way of contrast, there were relatively few slaves in the northern states. New York, primarily the city itself, (22,000 slaves) and New Jersey (11,000 slaves) had the largest slave populations, although they made up only around 6 percent of the total population in each state. Free people of color in the key slave states made up only a very small share of the overall population in each: 1.7 percent in Virginia, 0.7 percent in South Carolina, 2.5 percent in Maryland, and 1.3 percent in North Carolina.[37]

The westward movement of slavery in the United States became a fundamental characteristic of the institution until the Civil War halted the process, and this reflected the general movement of the overall U.S. population into frontier regions with fertile land for agricultural development. The eastern seaboard states noted earlier, along with Georgia, have generally been referred to as the "Old South" by historians, while the inland states, some bordering the Gulf of Mexico, have been designated the "New South." (See Map 4.1.) Slavery expanded steadily into the states of the New South as the general

---

[35] These economic cycles and slavery's linkages to them will be considered in Chapter 5.

[36] For a map of the United States in 1790 see the web site <http://xroads. virginia.edu/~MAP/TERRITORY/1790map.html> maintained by the Perry-Castañeda Library Map Collection at the University of Texas.

[37] Census of the United States, 1790, located on the internet on the United States Historical Census Data Browser at <http://fisher.lib.virginia.edu/ census/>, and Richard H. Steckel, "The African American Population of the United States, 1790–1920," in Michael R. Haines and Richard H. Steckel, A Population History of North America (New York and London: Cambridge University Press, 2000), pp. 433–82.

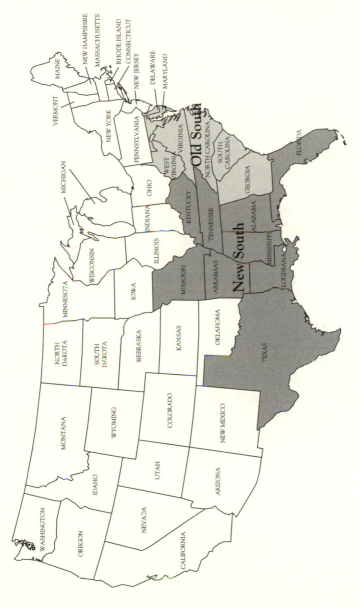

Map 4.1. U.S. Old South and New South states.

population increased and moved westward during the first half of the nineteenth century, and as particular economic activities such as cotton cultivation took hold in these frontier regions. Yet it must be kept in mind that slavery did not wane in the Old South, and that it was only in 1860 that the slave population of the New South finally eclipsed that of the older slave states. Table 4.1 indicates the slave populations of the Old and New South between 1790 and 1860.

If we examine each of these regions in its entirety, it is conspicuous that slaves made up similar proportions of the overall populations just prior to the Civil War, although there were marked variations by state. In 1860, slightly over a third of the population was enslaved in the "Old South," while in the "New South" nearly 31 percent of all inhabitants were slaves. Yet, as indicated in Table 4.2, in particular states slaves made up a much greater proportion of the total population. In South Carolina and Mississippi they comprised well over half of all inhabitants, while in Georgia, Alabama, Florida, and Louisiana, more than 40 percent of total populations were enslaved.

However, there were fairly significant differences in the numbers of free people of color found in the Old and New South prior to the Civil War. In the Old South, just over 4 percent of all inhabitants were free blacks and mulattos, although there were very marked regional differences. In Maryland, the free colored population nearly equaled the number of slaves, while in the nation's capital there were nearly four times as many free people of color as slaves. The general migration of people, and the forced movement of slaves into the New South, was not accompanied by the emergence of a sizeable free black and mulatto population in these states. Only 0.6 percent of the New South's overall population was composed of free people of color before the outbreak of the Civil War. (See Table 4.2.)

Comparative data on the Brazilian slave population are not as systematic, because few national-level census counts were conducted during the nineteenth century.[38] However, historians have considered

---

[38]   General sources for data on slave populations are found in Nina Rodrigues, *Os Africanos no Brasil* (São Paulo: Editora Nacional, 1982); Felix Contreiras Rodrigues, *Traços da Economia Social e Politica do Brasil Colonial* (Rio de Janeiro: Ariel Editora, 1935); Dauril Alden, "The Population of Brazil in the Late Eighteenth Century: A Preliminary Study," *Hispanic American Historical Review*, Vol. 43, No. 2, (May 1963), pp. 173–205; Francisco José Oliveira Vianna, "Resumo Histórico dos Inquéritos Censitários Realizados no Brasil," Brazil, Diretoria Geral de Estatística, *Recenseamento do Brasil, 1920,*

Table 4.1. *Slave populations of Old and New South, 1790–1860*

Year	"Old South" Slave Population	Percentage of Total Slaves	"New South" Slave Population	Percentage of Total Slaves
1790	642,280	97.7	15,247	2.3
1800	799,679	93.3	57,416	6.7
1810	983,999	84.5	179,855	15.5
1820	1,156,582	76.1	362,435	23.9
1830	1,360,695	67.8	644,780	32.2
1840	1,399,922	56.3	1,086,404	43.7
1850	1,624,087	50.7	1,579,964	49.3
1860	1,778,700	45.0	2,174,996	55.0

Note: The "Old South" states included here are Delaware, Maryland, District of Columbia, Virginia, North Carolina, South Carolina, and Georgia; the "New South" states include Kentucky, Tennessee, Missouri, Florida, Alabama, Mississippi, Arkansas, Louisiana, and Texas.
Source: Richard H. Steckel, "The African American Population of the United States, 1790–1920," in Michael R. Haines and Richard H. Steckel, *A Population History of North America* (New York and London: Cambridge University Press, 2000), pp. 433–82.

data amassed from a variety of sources for 1819, as well as those presented in the first Brazilian national census of 1872, to be fairly reliable. These indicate quite clearly that the pattern of slave and general population migration found in the United States was echoed in Brazil. Northeastern Brazil was the New World's first real slave society because of the labor demands paralleling the development of sugar production in the northeastern *capitanias* of Bahia and Pernambuco during the late sixteenth century. Although the mining cycle initiated by the discovery of gold and diamonds in Minas Gerais during the late seventeenth century resulted in the rapid spread of slavery toward this vast region in the center of Brazil during the first half of the eighteenth century, the north of Brazil remained the most important matrix of Brazilian slavery even at the beginning of the nineteenth century. In 1819, nearly 55 percent of the total Brazilian slave population was found in the northern regions of the country.

Vol. 1: Introdução (Rio de Janeiro, 1922); Giorgio Mortara, "Estudos Sobre a Utilização do Censo Demográfico para a Reconstituição das Estatísticas do Movimento da População do Brasil," *Revista Brasileira de Estatística*, Vol. 3, No. 5 (January–March), pp. 41–3; Roberto C. Simonsen, *História Econômica do Brasil (1500–1820)*, 6th ed. (São Paulo, Editora Nacional, 1969), (Coleção Brasiliana, Série Grande Formato, v. 10).

Table 4.2. *Total, slave, and free colored populations of the Old and New South, 1860*

	Total Population	Slave Population	Percentage of Population Enslaved	Free Colored Population	Percentage of Population Free Colored	Percentage of Population Slave and Free Colored
Old South						
Delaware	112,216	1,798	1.6	19,829	17.7	19.3
Virginia	1,596,318	490,865	30.7	58,042	3.6	34.4
Maryland	687,049	87,189	12.7	83,942	12.2	24.9
North Carolina	992,622	331,059	33.4	30,463	3.1	36.4
South Carolina	703,708	402,406	57.2	9,914	1.4	58.6
Georgia	1,057,286	462,198	43.7	3,500	0.3	44.0
District of Columbia	61,122	3,185	5.2	11,131	18.2	23.4
TOTAL	5,210,321	1,778,700	34.1	216,821	4.2	38.3
New South						
Alabama	964,201	435,080	45.1	2,690	0.3	45.4
Arkansas	435,450	111,115	25.5	144	0.0	25.6
Florida	140,424	61,745	44.0	932	0.7	44.6
Kentucky	1,155,684	225,483	19.5	10,684	0.9	20.4
Louisiana	708,002	331,726	46.9	18,647	2.6	49.5
Mississippi	791,305	436,631	55.2	773	0.1	55.3
Missouri	1,182,012	114,931	9.7	3,572	0.3	10.0
Tennessee	1,109,801	275,719	24.8	7,300	0.7	25.5
Texas	604,215	182,566	30.2	355	0.1	30.3
TOTAL	7,091,094	2,174,996	30.7	45,097	0.6	31.3

Source: U.S. census of 1860.

However, the arrival of the Portuguese crown in Rio de Janeiro in 1808, and the development of a variety of agricultural activities anchored by sugar and coffee production in central and southern Brazil during the first half of the nineteenth century, had the same kind of impact on the geography of slavery as the westward movement of slaves toward the New South cotton frontier in the United States. Slavery remained in northern Brazil, to be sure, in the same way that it persisted in the U.S. Old South, but it moved systematically toward the south of the country over the course of the nineteenth century. By the time of the national census of 1872, not only had the absolute number of slaves declined in northern Brazil – unlike the situation in the U.S. Old South, where the slave population expanded in absolute terms despite the westward movement of slaves – but nearly two-thirds of all Brazilian slaves lived and labored in the center (50 percent) and south (17 percent) of the country, as indicated in Tables 4.3 and 4.4. (See Map 4.2.)

One of the fundamental differences between the U.S. and Brazilian slave systems was that in Brazil there were no regions analogous to the northern United States, where slavery was of marginal importance or had been gradually abolished by the early nineteenth century. Slavery was found throughout the country, and in general slaves made up a larger percentage of the total population in Brazil in the early nineteenth century than in the United States. The 1819 Brazilian data indicate that about 31 percent of the total population was enslaved. Yet, while the 1820 U.S. census revealed that about 15 percent of the total population was enslaved, slaves were 35 percent of all inhabitants in the southern slave states. This was similar to the proportion of slaves found in the total Brazilian population.

By the time of the 1872 census, the Brazilian free population had grown faster than the population of Brazilian slaves, even though the number of slaves had increased in absolute terms. The abolition process had not yet begun in earnest in Brazil, yet slaves had fallen to about 15 percent of the total population, although there were sharp regional variations. Especially notable is the fact that in the north of the country the slave population had fallen from 33 percent to 10 percent of the total population between 1819 and 1872.

It is also conspicuous that the slave population in the southern United States did not decline in relation to the total population, as was the case in Brazil. Nearly 32 percent of the U.S. South's inhabitants were enslaved in 1860, only a slight decline from the 35 percent of 1820.

Table 4.3. *Total, slave, and free colored population's of Brazil by province, 1819 and 1872*

	1819			1872					
	Total Population	Slave Population	Percentage of Population Enslaved	Total Population	Slave Population	Percentage of Population Enslaved	Free Colored	Percentage of Population Free Colored	Percentage of Population Slave and Free Colored
North									
Bahia	477,912	147,263	30.8	1,379,616	167,824	12.2	830,431	60.2	72.4
Maranhão	200,000	133,332	66.7	359,040	74,939	20.9	169,645	47.2	68.1
Pernambuco	368,465	97,633	26.5	841,539	89,028	10.6	449,547	53.4	64.0
Alagoas	111,973	69,094	61.7	348,009	35,741	10.3	217,106	62.4	72.7
Ceará	201,170	55,439	27.6	721,686	31,913	4.4	368,100	51.0	55.4
Pará	123,901	33,000	26.6	275,237	27,458	10.0	110,556	40.2	50.1
Sergipe	114,996	26,213	22.8	176,243	22,623	12.8	100,755	57.2	70.0
Paraíba	96,448	16,723	17.3	376,226	21,526	5.7	200,412	53.3	59.0
Piauí	61,226	12,405	20.3	202,222	23,795	11.8	121,527	60.1	71.9
Rio Grande do Norte	70,921	9,109	12.8	233,979	13,020	5.6	107,455	45.9	51.5
Amazonas	19,350	6,040	31.2	57,610	979	1.7	8,592	14.9	16.6
Total North	**1,846,362**	**606,251**	**32.8**	**4,971,407**	**508,846**	**10.2**	**2,684,126**	**54.0**	**64.2**

Center

Minas Gerais	631,885	26.7	2,039,735	370,459	18.2	805,967	39.5	57.7
Rio de Janeiro[a]	510,000	28.6	1,057,696	341,576	32.3	252,271	23.9	56.1
Goiás	63,168	42.4	160,395	10,652	6.6	103,564	64.6	71.2
Espírito Santo	72,845	27.8	82,137	22,659	27.6	27,367	33.3	60.9
Mato Grosso	37,396	37.9	60,417	6,667	11.0	27,989	46.3	57.4
Total Center	1,315,294	28.6	3,400,380	752,013	22.1	1,217,158	35.8	57.9

South

São Paulo	238,323	32.6	837,354	156,612	18.7	207,845	24.8	43.5
Rio Grande do Sul	92,180	30.6	434,813	67,791	15.6	82,938	19.1	34.7
Paraná	59,942	17.0	126,722	10,560	8.3	37,377	29.5	37.8
Santa Catarina	44,031	20.8	159,802	14,984	9.4	15,984	10.0	19.4
Total South	434,476	28.8	1,558,691	249,947	16.0	344,144	22.1	38.1
Total Brazil	3,596,132	30.8	9,930,478	1,510,806	15.2	4,245,428	42.8	58.0

[a] For 1872, data are for the province and the city, which was designated as the "Corte."

Source: Brazilian census of 1819 and 1872.

121

Table 4.4. *Percentage of total Brazilian slave population by region*

	1819	1872
North	54.7%	33.7%
Center	33.9%	49.8%
South	11.3%	16.5%

Source: Brazilian census of 1819 and 1872.

Map 4.2. North, center, and south states in Brazil.

Quite clearly, the slave population of the United States increased at rates that were similar to those of the free population between 1820 and 1860 in the South, while the rate of increase among Brazilian slaves did not keep pace with that of free men and women, despite an African slave trade that was not curbed until the early 1850s.

While there were clear differences in the overall percentages of slaves found in the populations of Brazil and the United States during the nineteenth century, the most striking demographic difference between the two societies was in the comparative numbers of free blacks and mulattos. In 1872, when fairly reliable statistical data are available, nearly 43 percent of the total Brazilian population was composed of free blacks and mulattos, compared to a mere 1.5 percent in the United States in 1860. Additionally, Brazil was a nation in which people of color, slave and free, comprised the vast majority (58 percent) of all inhabitants. One more extraordinarily important comparative point should be stressed. In the United States, 89 percent of all people of African descent were enslaved in 1860. In Brazil, 74 percent of all people of color were free in 1872. Thus, not only was Brazil a society in which those of African descent were dominant, but to be black or mulatto was unequivocally not synonymous with slavery, as it was in the United States. This had profound comparative cultural consequences for both slaves and free people of color, and these will be considered in Chapter 6.

It also ought to be noted that as slavery moved from north to south in Brazil, important demographic differentiations emerged with respect to the relative number of free people of color in each region. As the proportion of slaves in the overall population declined in the north, the percentage of free blacks and mulattos soared. By 1872, when about 10 percent of the northern region's population was enslaved, some 54 percent of the total population was composed of free peoples of color. Nearly two-third of the Brazilian north's population were blacks and mulattos, enslaved or free, in 1872.

The center and south of the country present distinctive profiles. Slaves made up 22 percent of the center region's overall population, and free blacks and mulattos accounted for nearly 36 percent of all inhabitants in 1872. Thus, as in the north, the vast majority of all people (58 percent) were blacks and mulattos, and free peoples of color made up 62 percent of the total black and mulatto population. In the southern regions of Brazil, some 16 percent of the population was enslaved, and 22 percent were free blacks and mulattos. Thus, although the south had a sizeable enslaved and free population of color (38 percent of the total population), it was the only region in Brazil where the white population comprised the majority. Yet among all peoples of African descent, the free outnumbered slaves and made up 58 percent of all blacks and mulattos in southern Brazil in 1872. In all regions of Brazil, to be black or mulatto was emphatically not automatically associated with being enslaved, as was the case in the United States.

Cuban census data from 1792 through 1862 permit a series of comparisons with the demographic histories of slavery in the United States and Brazil, with special attention to the movement of slaves into frontier regions. First and foremost, it is conspicuous that in 1792 the slave population of Cuba accounted for a percentage of all inhabitants (31 percent) similar to that observed in the slave states of the United States in the census of 1790 (35 percent). Although there are no reliable data for Brazil as a whole until 1819, it is conspicuous that the slave population in that year represented 31 percent of all inhabitants, the same percentage found in Cuba in the early 1790s. Historians have considered the U.S. South, Brazil, and Cuba to be "slave societies."[39] It appears, at least for the late eighteenth and early nineteenth centuries, that one quantitative criterion defining these American slave societies was that roughly a third of the population was enslaved.[40]

Cuba, like Brazil, and in contrast to the United States, had a large free black and mulatto population that grew in absolute terms through the nineteenth century. Free peoples of color accounted for 20 percent of the total Cuban population in 1792 and, when considered along with the slave population, 51 percent of all inhabitants were of African descent. The growth of the Cuban slave trade because of a rapidly expanding sugar and coffee economy in the early nineteenth century led to a substantial increase in the slave population. The 1827 census indicated that the slave population had risen to 41 percent of the overall population, although this percentage declined to 36 percent in 1846, and 27 percent in 1862, despite slave population increases in absolute numbers. The population of African-descended peoples, slave and free, rose to 56 percent of all Cuban inhabitants in 1827, declined slightly to 53 percent in 1846, and in 1862 had declined to 43 percent of the total population, largely because of a fast-growing white population. This is precisely the same kind of change in the racial configuration of the population found in Brazil during the nineteenth century.

[39]   Moses I. Finley, *Ancient Slavery and Modern Ideology* (London: Chatto & Windus, 1980).

[40]   This observation is supported by precise quantitative data from Brazil's largest slaveholding province in 1808, Minas Gerais, where roughly 36 percent of the population was enslaved. See Bergad, *Slavery and the Demographic and Economic History of Minas Gerais, Brazil, 1720–1888*.

The free black and mulatto population remained relatively stable as a percentage of the total population: 15 percent in 1827 and 17 percent in both 1846 and 1862, underlining the fact that, as in Brazil, to be black and mulatto in nineteenth-century Cuba was not synonymous with being a slave. Indeed, if we examine both slave and free peoples of African descent together, it is notable that the population of freed men and women increased from 27 percent of all blacks and mulattos in 1827 to 39 percent in 1862.

The expansion of slavery into frontier regions was a fundamental characteristic of the Cuban slave system, and this was strikingly similar to the patterns of geographically mobile slave labor systems found in the United States and Brazil. In the early 1790s, slavery in Cuba was a highly diversified institution; slaves were found laboring in all economic sectors, urban and rural. Slightly over one-fifth of the entire Cuban slave population lived in the city of Havana itself, and another 27 percent were found in the rural areas surrounding the colonial capital. Accordingly, it is not surprising to find that approximately 48 percent of all Cuban slaves lived and labored in the Havana region in the late eighteenth century. It also should be noted that about 34 percent of the total population in western Cuba was enslaved.

By 1827, western Cuba had been transformed by the slave trade to the island and the meteoric rise of sugar and coffee production, processes that were not mirrored in the center and eastern regions of the colony. The slave population increased from around 52,000 in 1792 to nearly 200,000 in 1827 in the Cuban western districts, and slaves accounted for over 48 percent of the total population, a sharp increase from roughly a third of all people in 1792. About half of all these slaves still lived in the city of Havana and its outlying rural districts, although the spread of sugar cultivation south toward the Güines Valley and east toward the plains of Matanzas resulted in the rapid growth of slave populations along the routes of sugar's expansion into these frontier regions.

Cuba's 1846 population census underscores the clear movement of the slave population to the sugar cane–growing regions that developed during the 1830s and early 1840s, especially toward the eastern and southern frontiers within western Cuba. The matrices of western Cuba's slave population shifted away from Havana and toward the vast districts of Güines, Matanzas, and Cárdenas, which in 1846 had more slaves (over 90,000) than the colonial capital (67,000). The process of slave movement into these regions continued through the

Table 4.5. *Total, slave, and free colored populations of Cuba by municipal district, 1792*

	Total Population	Slaves	Percentage of Population Enslaved	Free Colored	Percentage of Population Free Colored	Percentage of Population Slave and Free Colored
West						
Havana and Arabales	51,307	17,970	35.0	9,800	19.1	54.1
Santiago de las Vegas	4,739	2,255	47.6	201	4.2	51.8
San Felipe y Santiago	1,953	739	37.8	116	5.9	43.8
Filipinas	4,192	650	15.5	1,154	27.5	43.0
Isla de Pinos	82	20	24.4	4	4.9	29.3
Santa María del Rosario	3,898	817	21.0	533	13.7	34.6
Guanabacoa	11,725	3,935	33.6	1,253	10.7	44.2
Jaruco	1,164	209	18.0	27	2.3	20.3
Matanzas	6,216	1,900	30.6	898	14.4	45.0
Partidos del Campo	65,854	23,530	35.7	6,818	10.4	46.1
Total West	**151,130**	**52,025**	**34.4**	**20,804**	**13.8**	**48.2**
Center						
Remedios	12,303	2,212	18.0	5,528	44.9	62.9
Santa Clara	10,475	1,442	13.8	2,247	21.5	35.2
Trinidad	11,611	2,676	23.0	4,049	34.9	57.9
Santi-Espírito	10,496	2,393	22.8	3,673	35.0	57.8
Príncipe	27,518	9,658	35.1	3,244	11.8	46.9
Total Center	**72,403**	**18,381**	**25.4**	**18,741**	**25.9**	**51.3**

East						
Bayamo	19,804	7,228	36.5	5,725	28.9	65.4
Baracoa	2,366	166	7.0	1,314	55.5	62.6
Holguin	5,837	753	12.9	1,056	18.1	31.0
Cuba (Santiago)	20,761	6,037	29.1	6,512	31.4	60.4
Total East	**48,768**	**14,184**	**29.1**	**14,607**	**30.0**	**59.0**
TOTAL	272,301	84,590	31.1	54,152	19.9	51.0

Source: Cuban census of 1792.

Table 4.6. *Total, slave, and free colored populations of Cuba by municipal district, 1862*

	Total Population	Slaves	Percentage of Population Enslaved	Free Colored	Percentage of Population Free Colored	Percentage of Population Slave and Free Colored
West						
Bahía Honda	11,081	5,890	53.2	839	7.6	60.7
Bejucal	24,659	7,052	28.6	2,191	8.9	37.5
Cárdenas	57,987	27,418	47.3	2,214	3.8	51.1
Cienfuegos	54,511	16,985	31.2	7,812	14.3	45.5
Colón	62,881	33,699	53.6	2,706	4.3	57.9
Guanabacoa	27,051	4,775	17.7	5,998	22.2	39.8
Gujanajay	40,359	17,708	43.9	3,653	9.1	52.9
Güines	61,920	24,817	40.1	4,473	7.2	47.3
Havana	205,676	29,013	14.1	37,768	18.4	32.5
Isla de Pinos	2,067	480	23.2	221	10.7	33.9
Jaruco	37,697	11,309	30.0	3,303	8.8	38.8
Matanzas	87,810	32,181	36.6	7,952	9.1	45.7
Nuevitas	6,278	1,608	25.6	505	8.0	33.7
Pinar del Río	66,307	14,590	22.0	10,251	15.5	37.5
Santa María del Rosario	8,559	2,307	27.0	884	10.3	37.3
San Cristóbal	28,938	7,760	26.8	3,290	11.4	38.2
San Antonio	33,328	11,189	33.6	2,491	7.5	41.0
Total West	**817,109**	**248,781**	**30.4**	**96,551**	**11.8**	**42.3**

Center

Puerto Príncipe	66,516	12,875	19.4	11,398	17.1	36.5
Remedios	40,689	7,182	17.7	5,652	13.9	31.5
Sagua la Grande	51,986	19,150	36.8	2,416	4.6	41.5
Sancti-Espíritus	45,844	8,828	19.3	7,318	16.0	35.2
Villa Clara	53,223	6,921	13.0	10,847	20.4	33.4
Santiago	18,678	4,897	26.2	2,555	13.7	39.9
Trinidad	37,965	10,141	26.7	9,353	24.6	51.3
Total Center	**314,901**	**69,994**	**22.2**	**49,539**	**15.7**	**38.0**

East

Baracoa	11,285	1,576	14.0	4,804	42.6	56.5
Bayamo	33,673	2,727	8.1	13,900	41.3	49.4
Cuba	96,028	32,255	33.6	36,030	37.5	71.1
Guantanamo	19,619	8,561	43.6	5,727	29.2	72.8
Holguin	53,026	4,391	8.3	7,243	13.7	21.9
Jiguaní	17,827	620	3.5	4,734	26.6	30.0
Manzanillo	25,355	1,184	4.7	11,271	44.5	49.1
Tunas	7,707	464	6.0	2,694	35.0	41.0
Total East	**264,520**	**51,778**	**19.6**	**86,403**	**32.7**	**52.2**
TOTAL	**1,396,530**	**370,553**	**26.5**	**232,493**	**16.6**	**43.2**

Source: Cuban census of 1862.

Map 4.3. West, center, and east in Cuba.

1850s, a decade during which the African slave trade to Cuba increased sharply and sugar production expanded impressively. The 1862 census revealed that while western Cuba accounted for nearly 60 percent of Cuba's total slave population, there had been a definitive movement of slaves from Havana toward these sugar-producing regions, whose slave population had increased to 118,000 while Havana's had declined to nearly 30,000.

These processes parallel those found in both the United States and Brazil. Slavery was a dynamic and highly mobile labor system in all three societies and developed in frontier regions as populations migrated and economic activities flourished, especially the production of export-oriented commodities such as sugar, coffee, and cotton. In Cuba, as in Brazil, sharp distinctions may be found in the racial compositions of regional populations, as well as in the importance of slavery to local social structures. Slaves were present in the central and eastern regions of the island, but their relative importance in those regions was always much smaller than in western Cuba. The 1862 census revealed that about 30 percent of western Cuba's total population was enslaved, while 22 percent were enslaved in the center and 20 percent in the east. There were also fundamental regional differences in the proportion of free blacks and mulattos. By 1862, about 12 percent of western Cuba's inhabitants were free peoples of color; 16 percent in central Cuba; and nearly a third of the population were free peoples of color in eastern Cuba. It is evident that Cuban free peoples of color migrated to regions where slavery was relatively less significant to demographic, social, and economic structures. The demographic structures of the Cuban population by region in 1792 and 1862 are indicated in Tables 4.5 and 4.6. (See Map 4.3.)

Slave systems in all three countries were dynamic in that over the course of the nineteenth century slave labor moved to frontier regions that experienced export-oriented economic expansion centered on agricultural staple products such as cotton, sugar, and coffee. This does not mean that slaves labored exclusively in these economic sectors, for slaves were found laboring in all occupations, urban and rural. However, slavery's mobility as a labor system was tied to frontier expansion into regions that were almost always settled and developed because of the profit possibilities tied to these export activities. The next chapter will focus upon the economic dynamics of slave labor in each country and will further illustrate the mobility of the slave system in the nineteenth-century Americas.

Preparing Thanksgiving turkey. *Down South*; pictures by Rudolf Eickemeyer, Jr.,
with a preface by Joel Chandler Harris.

Laundry day at "Volusia," a farm off Duke Street near Holmes Run, 1860s. Alexandria, Virginia, death records, 1863–68 (the Gladwin record) and 1869–96, complied by Wesley E. Pippenger.

Plantation well. *Down South*; pictures by Rudolf Eickemeyer, Jr., with a preface by Joel Chandler Harris.

Returning from the fields. *Down South*; pictures by Rudolf Eickemeyer, Jr., with a preface by Joel Chandler Harris.

Richmond, Virginia, slaves.

Stripping sugar cane. *Down South*; pictures by Rudolf Eickemeyer, Jr., with a preface by Joel Chandler Harris.

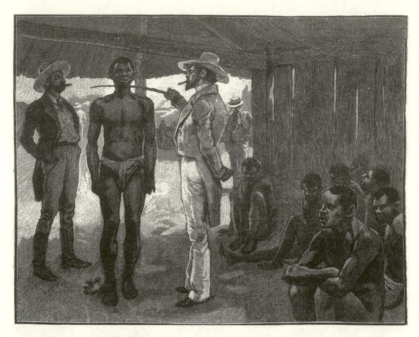

Buying slaves in Havana, Cuba.

Punishing slaves in Cuba.

Preparing manioc root. *Malerishe Reise in Brasilien* von Moritz Rugendas. Imprint Paris, Engelmann & Cie; Mülhausen (Ober-Rheinisches Dept.), 1835.

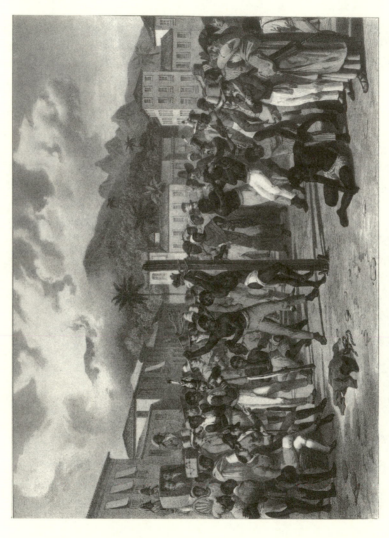

Public whipping of slaves. *Malerishe Reise in Brasilien von Moritz Rugendas. Imprint Paris, Engelmann & Cie; Mülhausen (Ober–Rheinisches Dept.), 1835.

Slave bounty hunter. *Malerishe Reise in Brasilien* von Moritz Rugendas. Imprint
Paris, Engelmann & Cie; Mülhausen (Ober–Rheinisches Dept.), 1835.

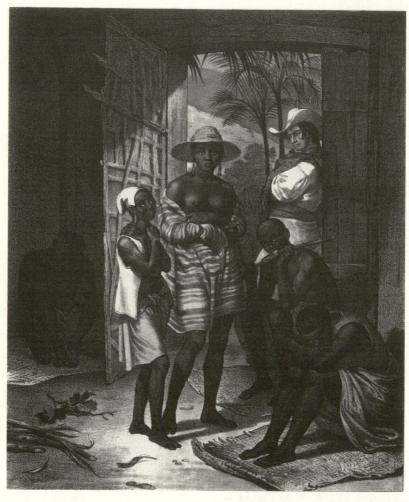

Recently imported slaves. *Malerishe Reise in Brasilien* von Moritz Rugendas.
Imprint Paris, Engelmann & Cie; Mülhausen (Ober–Rheinisches Dept.), 1835.

Slave couple, Brazil. *Malerishe Reise in Brasilien* von Moritz Rugendas. Imprint Paris, Engelmann & Cie; Mülhausen (Ober–Rheinisches Dept.), 1835.

CHAPTER FIVE

ECONOMIC ASPECTS

At its most basic analytical level, slavery must be understood as a labor system. Regardless of society, culture, or historical period, slave owners utilized slaves as workers to accomplish a wide variety of economic tasks. Slaves, however, were not simply laborers but were also valuable assets, since they were legally or customarily regarded as chattel to be bought and sold in the same way as land, animals, tools, and other forms of property. Thus, slaves filled two fundamental economic functions for their owners: as laborers for the production of goods and services, and as investments in property that could be bought, sold, rented, or used as collateral to secure credit from lenders.

Unlike systems such as wage labor, slaves rarely earned monetary or other compensation and had few choices as to occupation or owner/ employer, since ultimately the entire slave labor system was based upon coercion and often a great deal of brutality. Accordingly, the geographical mobility of slavery considered in the previous chapter, as well as the occupations and economic sectors in which slaves labored, were determined solely by the slave owners, whose motivations were almost always governed by the general economic principal of perceived profit maximization.

It is certain that the quest for a perverse form of social prestige may have also been a motive for owning slaves in the cultural context of some slave societies, or societies with slaves that "assigned" status to slave owners. However, all aspiring masters, regardless of motive, had to purchase slaves in the marketplace, sometimes at extraordinary prices. Slaves also had to be fed, clothed, and cared for, if only at the most rudimentary level, if their survival as valuable investments and as productive laborers were to be guaranteed. This meant monetary expenditures to maintain as well as to acquire slaves. Regardless of social and cultural value systems that conferred noneconomic rewards to slave owners, slaveholding almost always implied important and ongoing economic expenditures.

A fundamental question that historians have addressed revolves around why this barbaric system of forced labor, in which the laborers were also considered to be property, is found in almost all cultures and time periods throughout recorded human history. One very general conclusion that most scholars agree upon is that slavery developed because of the generalized absence of alternative voluntary labor systems such as wage labor, as well as the availability of potential slave labor. Forced labor in one form or another, including slavery, first emerged in predominantly agricultural societies with relatively small populations in relation to available land areas. Free people, if they had opportunity and choice, almost always sought to work their own land if it was available as opposed to working for others. In this context – abundant land and relatively small populations – land owners with the need for labor beyond their immediate or extended families almost always had to turn to some form of forced labor in order to acquire workers, and often this meant enslavement. Thus, the use of enslaved labor may have developed for lack of alternative labor systems, among other factors.[1] This is part of the explanation that helps us understand slavery's emergence and development in Cuba, Brazil, and the United States.

This explanation for the rise of slavery is very different from the sometimes-repeated misconception that slave labor was desirable because it was somehow "cheaper" to use slaves than to pay wages to salaried workers. Whether slave labor was more economical or expensive than wage labour or other forms of labor is a complex question requiring a vast amount of technical data to measure scientifically. Knowledge of slave prices, maintenance costs, free-labor wage rates, rent rates, and other economic variables are required to make precise calculations on the advantage of one labor system in comparison to another, and these data have often been unavailable to historians who have considered the various slave systems found throughout world cultures. But whether "cheaper" or not, clearly slave owning was in the economic best interests of masters, for if this had not been the case, the slave system would not have persisted for so long.

---

[1]   Clearly, another factor was the absolute control over labor power endowed to slave owners.

Mechanisms of enslavement varied by culture and time period, but almost always warfare was a means utilized to secure captives, who were often enslaved whether they were civilians or opposing soldiers. These captives then entered slave markets where they were sold, bartered, or rented. It is apparent that few societies enslaved their own members, and that almost always slaves were "outsiders" with different cultural, social, ethnic, or racial characteristics from those enslaving them. In the Americas, where the world's first extensive multiracial societies emerged in the sixteenth century, blending Caucasians, Africans, and Amerindians, race came to define social and legal status and eventually became the sole criterion utilized to determine who could or could not be enslaved.

The long history of Iberian contact with Africa dating from Portuguese exploration during the fourteenth century resulted in the development of an Africa-to-Europe slave trade, and eventually the Portuguese and Spanish word "*negro*" came to be synonymous with "slave." Gradually, because of legal intervention or custom, other racial and ethnic groups gradually ceased being enslaved, and the concept of African-origin racially based slavery emerged in Iberia and in the island possessions of Spain and Portugal off the African coast.

Yet before the development of African-based slave labor systems in the Americas, Iberian conquerors enslaved Amerindians during the period of conquest and colonization initiated by the Columbus voyages of the 1490s. This continued a long Iberian tradition of enslaving captives taken in war as well as defeated peoples who were regarded as heathens or nonbelievers in Christianity, for the most part Islamic peoples subjugated during the period of the Spanish *reconquista* of Iberia. The motivations of early conquerors and colonizers in the Americas are hardly difficult to discern. Extant civilizations had varying levels of resources and accumulated wealth, and Europeans sought to acquire these, especially precious minerals and stones. The one critical variable needed to accomplish this was labor power. Since there were no indigenous labor markets that Europeans fully understood or could tap into during the early phases of conquest and colonization, one way to secure labor was to enslave conquered peoples and force the transfer of extant wealth to the victorious conquerors. In regions where strong centralized states existed, such as the Aztec and Inca empires, Europeans could acquire wealth by using conquered indigenous elite social classes and preexisting political structures to mobilize labor.

It has long been recognized that enslavement of Amerindians by Europeans was fairly widespread in the early sixteenth century, well before African slavery developed on a significant scale. This process underlines the fact that European-controlled slave labor in the Americas first emerged when dominant social and political groups – conquerors and colonizers – had the potential for accumulating extant wealth, but no labor system other than coerced labor was available to effectively acquire it. Indigenous peoples would rarely work voluntarily, and among those who journeyed across the Atlantic during the early phases of American settlement there were few laborers other than personal servants and small numbers of African slaves.

By the middle of the sixteenth century, the Spanish crown and religious authorities ended the legality, if not the practice, of indigenous slavery for a variety of reasons. New institutional mechanisms were established to harness the labor power of Amerindian communities in the Spanish colonies, such as *encomienda* and *repartimiento*, and indigenous enslavement was no longer necessary. By the second half of the sixteenth century, slavery was legally limited by codes and edicts to those of African descent, although Indian slavery continued in areas where colonial authority was weak.

When the looting of pre-conquest mineral wealth in the Spanish colonies finally ended sometime in the first half of the sixteenth century, primarily because of its exhaustion, European elite groups faced a different set of labor problems. These revolved around how to create a labor force for the production of sustenance and potential wealth, as opposed to the confiscation of resources that had previously been accumulated by now-conquered indigenous peoples. In the densely populated pre-conquest imperial regions of Mesoamerica and Andean America, it was logical to turn to surviving indigenous populations to harness labor power. In regions with fewer native peoples, but with potentially valuable resources in the form of unexploited mineral resources or fertile agricultural land that could produce food and valuable marketable commodities such as sugar, cacao, indigo, tobacco, and other tropical staples, the problem of labor was more complex.

With abundant landed resources and small populations, elite groups in these areas were forced to turn to external sources of labor, and the choices were quite stark. Free Europeans could possibly be induced to journey across the Atlantic if compensation in the form of wages or land was high enough. Indeed, many efforts at attracting indentured servants were undertaken, and some were even successful in the short term.

But gradually rising European wage rates meant a reluctance to accept servile-like conditions in the New World. Free peoples who set off to cross the Atlantic usually sought to maintain their independence as small landowners, miners, artisans, and so forth, as opposed to laboring for others. In this milieu, elite groups often had few choices if they needed laborers. The African slave trade to Europe, São Tomé, Madeira, and the Canary and Cape Verde islands had created an infrastructure for the securing and transportation of slaves from Africa's west coast, and it is hardly surprising that this system of labor procurement was transferred to the New World very early in the sixteenth century.

The development of African slavery in Cuba, Brazil, and the United States was conditioned precisely by the sparse population, abundant land, and labor shortage scenario just described. While there were relatively large indigenous populations in each of these regions, there were no preexisting large-scale centralized states with sophisticated labor mobilization systems prior to conquest by Europeans. In the Cuban case, the rapid demographic collapse of indigenous populations in the early sixteenth century created labor shortages that induced elite groups to turn fairly quickly to African slaves for their labor needs. In the Portuguese-settled regions of early sixteenth-century Brazil, indigenous slavery rapidly took hold, but this system of labor was doomed to failure by rampant disease and high mortality rates among Indian slaves, as well as the flight into the vast Brazilian internal frontier by those who survived repeated epidemics. This same set of dynamics was found in the seventeenth-century British colonies that became the United States.

It is appropriate to first consider economic aspects of slavery in Cuba, because African slavery was entrenched there as a labor system for nearly a century before the first Europeans settled the future United States, and well before Africans began disembarking in Brazil in significant numbers toward the end of the sixteenth century. The Spanish conquest and occupation of the Caribbean in the late fifteenth and early sixteenth centuries was quickly followed by the discovery of placer gold deposits on the major islands of Hispaniola, Puerto Rico, and Cuba. By the time Cuba, the last of the three islands to be occupied by Spain, was invaded in 1511, a methodology for the exploitation of gold had been in effect for nearly two decades. Arawak indigenous peoples were enslaved, or their chieftains required to supply laborers under dire threats, and Spanish-controlled placer gold mining was able to thrive using the forced labor of native populations.

But by the 1520s not only had gold deposits started to wane, but epidemics and extreme working conditions had catastrophically reduced indigenous populations to the point of extinction.[2] Accordingly, by the 1530s the system of exploiting Arawak labor had virtually collapsed. Coinciding with this, explorers and conquerors using Cuba as a base of operations pushed westward and toward the south, discovering and conquering first the Aztec imperial system of Mesoamerica (1521) and later the Inca empire of the Andes (1532). The wealth and population density of these extraordinary civilizations acted as magnets for Europeans already settled in the Caribbean and for those crossing the Atlantic. Cuba, with the exhaustion of gold and the depletion of its indigenous population, was virtually abandoned. Cattle and pigs, introduced in the aftermath of conquest, reproduced in prodigious quantities, and those settlers remaining on the island periodically slaughtered these animals for hides, tallow, and meat. They also cultivated small quantities of sugar cane, mainly to produce *aguardiente* or cane brandy. Tobacco, an indigenous crop that Europeans learned to smoke in imitation of native customs, was also grown, harvested, cured, and marketed.

By the 1530s labor demands were minimal due to the small-scale subsistence-oriented economy prevailing in the aftermath of the gold boom and the colonization of Mesoamerica and Andean America. African slaves had been imported to the island in small numbers during the first two decades of colonization, but few residents could afford them in the economically destitute environment that engulfed the island thereafter.[3] If the Cuban economic panorama was bleak, the political situation was catastrophic. By the 1530s non-Iberian European powers, aware of the gold and silver trade from Mexico and Peru, began to attack Spanish shipping in the Caribbean. Undefended and nearly unoccupied, Cuba became an objective. The French sacked and burned Havana in 1537 and periodically attacked the other small population centers on the island's coast through the 1540s and 1550s, occupying Havana once again in 1555. Dutch and English marauders appeared as well, threatening Spanish shipping and

---

[2] Epidemics, probably of smallpox, swept through Cuba in 1519 and again in 1528. Klein, *Slavery in the Americas*, p. 131.

[3] Irene Wright estimated that some 700 African slaves had been imported to the island by 1530, and very few during the 1530s and 1540s. Irene Wright, *The Early History of Cuba, 1492–1586* (New York: Macmillan, 1916).

demanding defensive measures from Madrid if the constantly rising silver output of Mexico and Peru was to be securely transported back to Spain.

Spain's reaction to these threats shaped the economic development of colonial Cuba from the late sixteenth century onward, and directly impacted the growth of African slavery on the island. To protect its shipping to and from the New World, an armed convoy system was established during the 1540s that sailed twice yearly from the Spanish port of Cádiz. Once in the Caribbean, the fleet would divide and sail toward its ultimate destinations of Vera Cruz, Mexico, the portal to Mesoamerica, and Nombre de Dios, Panama, to service the South American colonies. With its naturally protected port and poised on the Florida straits at the gateway to the northeasterly currents that carried ships back to Europe, Havana became the point where military escort ships waited for the two fleets to return in preparation for the Atlantic crossing back to Spain. By the 1560s this system was officially institutionalized, and Havana became the critical rendezvous point for both fleets and their armed escorts.

The ease of the French seizures in 1537 and 1555 graphically underlined the fact that Havana had to be protected if it was to serve as a strategic point in Spain's transatlantic trading system. By the late 1550s an ambitious construction project to erect fortifications at the entrance to Havana harbor was begun, financed by substantial and ongoing infusions of Mexican silver. The fleets spent a considerable portion of each year in the harbor and thus pumped additional capital resources into the city, since crews and ships had to be provisioned and maintained while in the port. Havana, once resource-exhausted and with a miniscule population, was transformed during the second half of the sixteenth century because of its geographical location and strategic importance to the Spanish colonial commercial system. Arguably, it became the most important hub of colonial trade, and because of the influx of resources the economy grew rapidly and labor demands soared.

In the popular imagination, Cuban slavery is inevitably associated with sugar, despite the fact that it was not until the middle of the nineteenth century that the majority of Cuban slaves worked directly in the sugar economy. From its sixteenth-century origins, slavery in Cuba was a labor system of extraordinary diversity, and this mirrored an evolving economy with strong labor demands in a number of economic sectors, urban and rural. All of these were linked to the city and port of Havana and its critical role in servicing the fleet, beginning in the late sixteenth and continuing through the seventeenth and early eighteenth centuries. Workers building fortifications and the growing urban population had to be provisioned with food, a variety of consumer goods, entertainment, and the kinds of supporting services that cities must have in order to function. Food-producing and cattle farms spread in Havana's rural environs because of the growing urban market for dietary staples as well as hides and tallow for candles, wax, and other needs. A market for timber developed because of the construction of urban homes and shops, hotels to lodge transients, warehouses to store products, and the need for wood to repair and prepare ships for the Atlantic crossing. Every imaginable type of artisan shop emerged where carpenters, foundry workers, blacksmiths, and sail makers and menders all labored to service the fleet and the Havana population. Bars, taverns, and hotels appeared, and prostitution was widespread. Elites were served by domestic servants – cooks, laundresses, butlers, drivers, and nannies. The transportation services offered by the fleet also stimulated the development of rural commercial endeavors, especially tobacco farming and ranching. Tobacco for snuff, hides, and cured meats were produced to fill the vacant holds of ships destined for the great European consumer markets. Sugar and *aguardiente* were produced on small-scale *ingenios*. Import/export merchants, slave traders, and creditors emerged to service consumer, slave, and capital markets. Havana became the third-largest city in the Americas, behind Mexico and Lima.

African slaves labored in every occupation, urban and rural. The economic expansion resulting from Havana's critical role in the colonial trading system generated the capital needed to purchase slave labor, although care needs to be exercised here. Slavery became entrenched in the city of Havana and its contiguous rural regions, but Cuba may not be considered a slave society until the nineteenth century. Slaves were one component of a complex labor system in which most workers, urban and rural, were free people, and these included blacks and mulattos. Some worked for wages, others by contract for specific tasks. In rural areas, sharecropping, renting, or some exchange of labor for land was widespread among free people, regardless of race. Cuba was clearly a society with slaves, and although they played an important role in the colonial economy in western Cuba near Havana, the eastern regions of the island, with the exception of the city of Santiago, had few slaves owing to the low level of economic activity and accumulated capital. It is hardly surprising that when the first Cuban census was taken in 1774, over half of the island's slave population resided in the city of Havana, and a great many more in the rural regions surrounding the colonial capital.

Slaves, especially those in cities and towns, labored in material conditions that were not very different, by and large, from those found among free workers in the sixteenth and seventeenth centuries, and indeed Caribbean slavery in general was of a relatively small-scale nature until the British occupied Barbados in the 1620s and Jamaica during the 1650s. Slave labor in the Caribbean was gradually transformed during the latter half of the seventeenth century as English colonists, after unsuccessfully experimenting with European indentured servants on Barbados, turned to slave labor to produce tobacco and, more importantly, sugar.[4] Imitating the experience of the Brazilian northeast under Portuguese and then Dutch rule (1630–54), large-scale sugar plantations were established, first in Barbados during the 1640s and later in Jamaica, using extensive numbers of slaves working as gang laborers. This highly profitable model of production was followed by the French after their seizure of the western regions of Hispaniola and the establishment of the St. Domingue colony in 1700. The Caribbean sugar/slave plantation complex emerged in full force during the eighteenth century. Along with this economic system a slave-trading infrastructure was established linking European merchants and shipping, coastal African slave traders, and slave markets in the French and British Caribbean.

Cuban slavery was initially immune to these transformations occurring in economies and societies so close by. By the early eighteenth century there were Cuban-born and Spanish colonial elites who were well aware of the economic expansion and opportunities to create wealth around slave-based sugar production found in the British and French islands. But Cuba's economy still revolved around the functional role that Havana continued to play in the colonial system because of its strategic location and fortified harbor. Accordingly, the fundamental characteristics of Cuban slavery – occupationally diverse, heavily urban, small-scale, and only one part of a multiracial labor force that was predominantly free – were not transformed in any major way.

[4] See David Eltis, *The Rise of African Slavery in the Americas* (New York: Cambridge University Press, 2000).

Yet economic change occurred through the first half of the eighteenth century, and new directions were charted that eventually led to rising demands for forced labor. The agricultural export sector expanded significantly because of the spread of smallholder tobacco cultivation in western Cuba. Increasing production, legal trade, and smuggling to foreign merchants induced the Spanish crown to impose a tobacco monopoly in 1717, although it was resisted by the local populace and abolished temporarily in 1724. A privately financed monopoly company, the Real Compañía de Comercio de la Habana, replaced the state monopoly in the early 1740s, although the colonial authorities reimposed control in the early 1760s. Yet, despite tobacco's spread, no large plantations emerged, and slaveholding was marginal or very small-scale at best. However, tobacco's rise during the first half of the eighteenth century indicated that significant profits could be derived from the development of export crops. Elite groups, many of them noble families with formal titles granted by the crown who had been awarded huge extensions of land in the sixteenth and seventeenth centuries, took notice and gradually turned to sugar cane cultivation and sugar manufacture. There is no doubt that the British and French Caribbean models were sources of emulation.

There was no linear development of Cuba's slave/sugar economy until the last decades of the eighteenth century. Cane had always been grown in small quantities, and there were viable *ingenios* found in all periods dating from the sixteenth century. But the industry as a whole moved forward in fits and starts. Most mills were unsuccessful and functioned only for limited periods, often reverting to producing *aguardiente* rather than sugar or closing altogether because of the difficulty of generating profits. Changes began in earnest during the 1740s, when a genuine sugar-export industry slowly developed in the Havana region. This was characterized by a gradual increase in the number of mills and the utilization of slave labor on a scale previously not found in rural Cuba. It is conspicuous, of course, that all this followed the implementation of successful British and French colonial sugar production models, the expansion of European export markets, and the creation by the British and French of a slave-trading infrastructure that could efficiently transport large numbers of slaves from Africa to the Caribbean, even if Cuba was theoretically forbidden from trading with foreign nations.

The English seizure of Havana in 1762, which shattered the illusion that massive fortification projects had created invincible Spanish defenses, is usually noted as the point of departure for Cuba's plantation development.[5] But in fact the brief English occupation only intensified the transition to an agricultural export economy, a process that had begun earlier in the century with the growth of tobacco cultivation and in the 1740s with the successful establishment of slave-based *ingenios* in the Havana region. However, once again the role of sugar, although important to be sure, should be placed in comparative perspective along with other Cuban colonial economic activities. The sugar plantation economy grew dynamically during the late eighteenth century, moving toward the southern Güines Valley and slowly creeping eastward along valley systems outside of Havana. But small-scale tobacco cultivation thrived in Matanzas to the east until the 1840s, and coffee cultivation also became extremely important during the late eighteenth and early nineteenth centuries in western Cuba. Even as "late" as 1830, well after sugar had been expanding dynamically, it has been estimated that investments in coffee were about equal to those in sugar.[6] Urban trades, professions, and small-scale manufacturing continued in Havana, absorbing significant numbers of slaves and other laborers.

Thus, while slavery and sugar were inexorably linked in the British and French Caribbean during the eighteenth century, this generalization may not be made for Cuba by any means. Cuban nineteenth-century census data underline this. The 1827 census suggests that about one-quarter of the total Cuban slave population worked on sugar *ingenios*, although many more may have labored in rural and urban ancillary industries producing food, raising cattle, and laboring as transport workers and stevedores. But an equal number of Cuban slaves, 25 percent of the total, were found laboring on coffee farms, with another quarter in the island's cities. The remaining 25 percent were found on small-scale food crop farms (*sitios de labor*) and cattle ranches. Nearly twenty years later, in 1846, about one-third of Cuba's over 320,000 slaves worked on sugar plantations, an increase in relative terms from 1827, but still not a sufficient percentage to equate slavery solely with sugar, as has often been the case in popular imagery.

During the 1850s, however, the sugar economy not only expanded rapidly but also came to employ a significantly greater percentage of

---

[5] See Manuel Moreno Fraginals, *El Ingenio: Complejo Económico Social Cubano del Azúcar* (Havana: Editorial de Ciencias Sociales, 1978).

[6] Francisco Pérez de la Riva, *El Café: Historia de su Cultivo y Explotación en Cuba* (Havana: Jesús Montero, 1944).

Cuban slaves. The 1862 census found that about 47 percent of the Cuban slave population resided on sugar plantations, and it is certain that many more slaves were tied to the sugar export economy in a number of supporting urban and rural sectors. This was at the apex of the slave-based sugar plantation in Cuba, just six years prior to the outbreak of the Ten Years' War (1868–78), which began the gradual dismantling of slavery in the colony. Even then, it would be difficult to categorize nineteenth-century Cuba as a slave/sugar society on the order of the British and French Caribbean in the eighteenth century. Slavery began its trajectory in sixteenth-century Cuba as an extraordinarily diversified institution, and it remained that way through the final abolition law of 1880, despite the fact that sugar came to play such a dominant and driving role in the Cuban export economy by the mid nineteenth century. Most studies, however, have ignored the diversity of slave occupations and residential patterns, preferring to focus upon the sugar plantation economy.

The economic profitability of slave labor has been a theme of considerable importance to scholars who have sought to explain the rise, abolition, and impact of slavery in the Americas and on the world economy from the sixteenth century onward. One of the most influential works was Eric Williams' *Capitalism and Slavery*, which was published in 1944. Among his many important conclusions, Williams argued that the capital derived from the slave trade and slavery in the Americas helped to finance Europe's industrial revolution, and that slavery was eventually abolished because its profitability declined as the industrial revolution advanced during the nineteenth century. For Williams and for other subsequent scholars who subscribed to these ideas, slavery was an obstacle to the full development of capitalism and the free labor markets upon which capitalist relations of production relied.[7]

The prominent Cuban historian Manuel Moreno Fraginals, author of the acclaimed and pioneering *El Ingenio*, also argued that technological innovation in the sugar economy during the second half of the nineteenth century was incompatible with slave labor. In his view, in order for productive forces in the sugar economy to efficiently utilize

[7] Eric Williams, *Capitalism and Slavery* (Chapel Hill: University of North Carolina Press, 1944). See the debates on Williams in Barbara L. Solow and Stanley L. Engerman, editors, *British Capitalism and Caribbean Slavery: The Legacy of Eric Williams* (New York: Cambridge University Press, 1987).

new technologies, slavery had to be abolished.[8] Thus, slavery was ended in Cuba, and indeed in the rest of the Americas, primarily for rational economic rather than humanistic, moral, or even fundamentally political reasons.

It did not occur to these scholars that the utilization of slave labor in sugar production, however barbarous and inhumane, may have been extraordinarily efficient and highly profitable to plantation and slave owners in strictly economic terms, even with the rapid march of industrialization in the nineteenth century. The conclusions of Williams, Moreno Fraginals, and others on the incompatibility of technological innovation and slave labor, as well as the argument that slavery was becoming economically inefficient, were largely based on theoretical models of economic development rather than empirical evidence. During the 1970s and after, scholars studying slavery in the Americas began to examine hard economic data such as prices for slaves, sugar, and machinery; comparative wage labor costs; plantation account books; census materials, and a whole range of other information. The resulting conclusions, although surprising and contentious, indicated that in fact slave labor was highly profitable from a strictly economic point of view right up until abolition in the three largest slave societies of the Americas – Cuba, Brazil, and the United States.

The implications of these conclusions were monumental. Not only did they challenge theoretical models of capitalism that held that free wage labor was the most economically efficient way to produce goods and services, they also suggested that the causes of abolition were in all likelihood not connected to economic variables. Internal political struggles within each slave society, international politics, and even humanistic and moral motives – discounted by Williams in his 1944 treatise – may have been the principal factors behind the rise of an international abolitionist movement and the eventual abolition of slavery.[9]

As technological change accelerated during the nineteenth century, the efficiency and increasing profitability of the slave-based Cuban sugar economy is revealed by empirical data. The most important transformations took place in transportation and in the refining of sugar

---

[8]   Moreno Fraginals, *El Ingenio*. He also argued that the capital invested in slaves could have been more efficiently invested in technological innovation.
[9]   Chapter 8 will consider these themes.

from sugar cane. Mill owners were constantly seeking ways to transport cane from fields to mills more efficiently and to increase the yield of sugar from the cane brought to the *ingenios* at harvest time. The construction of vast and expensive railroad systems throughout western Cuba in the cane producing regions of Havana, Matanzas, and Las Villas provinces took place during the 1840s and 1850s.[10] These systems were of two general types. The first was internal to the plantations and linked the fields where cane was cut to the mills where it was refined into sugar. These railroad systems were portable at first, meaning that track was not fixed but could be moved quickly from one location to another. Wealthier plantation owners eventually constructed fixed lines to their most productive cane fields. Cane begins to lose its sucrose content very quickly about twenty hours after it is cut, so the more quickly it is transported to mills for processing, the higher the actual sugar yield, which is of critical economic importance.

The second type of railroad system linked the cities and major ports of colonial Cuba to the cane-growing regions and resulted in an extraordinarily efficient internal transportation system. By the mid-1850s, Cuba had the most extensive internal rail system in all of Latin America and the Caribbean, and this meant a drastic reduction in transportation costs for sugar plantation owners. They could ship their sugar to ports at a fraction of the price paid to move bulky sugar boxes and sacks overland on mules or ox-drawn carts, the way sugar had been transported from the sixteenth century until railroad construction began after 1837. The lowering of transportation costs increased overall profitability.

Plantation owners were also constantly adopting new, and often costly, technologies at the mill itself to increase the yield of sugar in relation to sugar cane processed. In the eighteenth century these techniques were quite simple and involved converting the rolling devices that ground the sugar cane as it arrived at the mill from two-roller vertical wood devices to copper-covered wood and then to three-roller horizontal cast-iron cane-crushing machines. Then there was the adaptation of the seventeenth-century "Jamaican Train" in Cuba, a mechanism invented in the British Caribbean colonies to more efficiently utilize wood, fire, and the distribution of heat in the

[10]   See Oscar Zanetti and Alejandro García, *Sugar and Railroads: A Cuban History 1837–1959* (Chapel Hill: University of North Carolina Press, 1998).

crystallization process.[11] During the 1830s, the French inventor Derosne developed a system for refining sugar using vacuum evaporators based on steam power, and these were eventually adopted by the largest Cuban planters. By the late 1840s and through the 1850s, Cuban plantation owners were starting to install more sophisticated vacuum pan evaporators at the mill, an innovation perfected by the mulatto New Orleans inventor Norberto Rillieux.[12] Later, centrifuges were adopted, which made processing more efficient still.

The point to be made is that these new technologies were very expensive and required extraordinary capital investment. By the 1850s these costly technological innovations were accompanied by a steep increase in the cost of labor in the form of rising slave prices.[13] Yet during the 1850s, despite a sharp escalation in slave costs, Cuban sugar planters imported more slaves and were willing to pay the higher prices. There was only one fundamental economic reason for this: not only did slave-based sugar production continue to be highly profitable, its efficiency was increasing notwithstanding the higher costs of both technological innovations and slave labor. This finding is in stark contrast to the interpretation that technological progress and slavery were economically incompatible. In fact, slavery became more profitable to planters with the resources to utilize new technologies.

Empirical economic data reveal this quite clearly. It is possible to provide a rough estimate of the gross income generated per slave laborer on the sugar plantations of Matanzas province, the heart of the Cuban sugar industry from the late 1850s through the mid-1870s, based upon detailed archival census materials found in the Cuban National

[11] The juice, or *guarapo*, extracted by crushing sugar cane by passing it through compressing rollers must be crystallized through the application of heat to produce sugar. Heat was derived by burning wood until the utilization of coal during the mid nineteenth century. A major problem facing producers was how to produce maximum heat with minimal utilization of vanishing wood reserves. During the mid to late seventeenth century, British sugar producers in Jamaica developed a system whereby the heat from one fire could be transferred to several "furnaces" that essentially boiled the cane juice in large cauldrons until it crystallized into raw sugar.

[12] See "Details of Rillieux's Inventions" at <http://www.princeton.edu/~ mcbrown/display/rillieux_biography.html#Evaporator>.

[13] Bergad et al., *The Cuban Slave Market*.

Archives.[14] In the Colón district between 1859 and 1878, the gross income produced per slave laborer working on sugar plantations increased 34 percent, from about 275 pesos to 369 pesos per slave. This was during the period when slave labor was, according to the traditional interpretation, becoming less efficient and a barrier to modernization. In fact, the technological transformations in the sugar industry described previously were having precisely the opposite effect: slave labor was becoming more economically productive during the very epoch in which slavery was being dismantled. In 1870 the Moret Law, promulgated in Spain for Cuba, stipulated that children born of slave mothers would be considered free, and that slaves sixty years old and older would be granted freedom. This law, which began the process of abolishing slavery, came about not in response to economic inefficiency but rather because of the political pressures created by the explosion of the Cuban insurrection in 1868 and the evolving abolitionist nature of the independence movement.

The relative efficiency and economic profitability of slave labor in the United States South right up to the outbreak of the Civil War in 1861 has generally been accepted by most scholars owing to the appearance of numerous detailed empirical studies on slave economics from the 1970s on. Yet, while slavery was a pervasive and fairly diversified labor system in Cuba and Brazil, and existed in all geographical regions, it was gradually abolished in the northern states of the United States after independence was consolidated in the late eighteenth century. In these states slaves generally made up a much smaller portion of overall populations, no more than 5 percent in most regions, and were economically not as important as was the case in the southern states,

---

[14] These documents are for the municipal district of Colón, where Cuba's largest sugar estates were located, and for contiguous Cárdenas, part of the most productive slave-based sugar plantation region in Cuba. They may be found at the Archivo Nacional de Cuba, Miscelanea de Expedientes, leg. 4120, no. M, "Repartos municipals de la jurisdicción de Colón, 1859"; Gobierno General, leg. 405, no. 19209, "Padrón de fincas rústicas de la jurisdicción de Colón, 1865"; Gobierno General, leg. 270, no. 13563, "Padrón general de fincas rústicas de este distrito, año de 1875 a 1876"; Gobierno General, leg. 945, no. 16724, "Padrón general de la riqueza rústica para regir en los años economicos de 1866 a 1867"; and Gobierno General, leg. 269, no. 13554, "Jurisdicción de Cárdenas. Padrón general de la riqueza rústica de esta ciudad y su jurisdicción para los años económicos de 1875 a 1876." These data are considered in detail in Bergad, *Cuban Rural Society*, pp. 217–28.

where they were a substantial portion of both the population and the labor force. Slave labor during the nineteenth century existed in the U.S. southern states only where tropical and semitropical export staples such as tobacco, rice, and cotton were the mainstays of local export-oriented economies, and where it was difficult to attract free laborers.

During the early colonial period roughly to the 1690s, colonists in the tobacco growing regions of the Virginia and Chesapeake littoral relied upon indentured laborers who worked alongside a relatively small number of slaves. But during the late seventeenth and early eighteenth centuries, indentured labor declined for a variety of reasons, including better working conditions and increasing wage rates in the expanding English economy, and slaves became the principal labor force that sustained the ever-expanding colonial tobacco plantation economy. During roughly the same period, rice cultivation began in earnest in South Carolina, and in the second half of the eighteenth century in Georgia, along with sea-island cotton. These activities relied upon slave labor from their onset, as it was difficult for planters to attract alternative labor systems.[15]

Thus, on the eve of the American Revolution, full-blown plantation economies based upon slave labor had been established in the various regions where tropical export products were produced. The reliance upon slaves was related to the absence of alternative labor supplies, to be sure. But it is unquestionable that the use of slave labor was highly profitable to plantation owners, or these activities could not have been sustained. While there have been no economic studies that have measured the relative profitability of free and slave labor during the eighteenth century, it is likely that slaves were economically more advantageous than free men and women. First, due to coercion and absence of choice, slaves constituted a reliable labor supply, and this was an important factor on plantations and farms of any size. Second, slaves were efficient and productive workers whose output may even have been greater than that of free laborers, in part because of long hours of labor forced on them by masters during peak seasons. Third, rising wage

---

[15]   For studies on the colonial tobacco economy, see Allan Kulikoff, *Tobacco and Slaves: The Development of Southern Cultures in the Chesapeake, 1680–1800* (Chapel Hill: University of North Carolina Press, 1986), and Philip D. Morgan, *Slave Counterpoint: Black Culture in the Eighteenth-Century Chesapeake & Lowcountry* (Chapel Hill: University of North Carolina Press, 1998). For the rice economy, see William Dusinberre, *Them Dark Days: Slavery in the American Rice Swamps* (New York: Oxford University Press, 1996).

rates for free labor over the course of the eighteenth century made the cost of slave labor comparable to, or even lower than, that of free workers, despite the relatively high purchase prices of slaves.

Slavery emerged from the American Revolution jarred but intact in the southern states, despite the ambiguities and paradoxes of a national revolution made in the name of liberty that ultimately sanctioned human bondage. But like the United States itself, slavery was confined to the eastern seaboard of the newly established nation. It was the cultivation of short-staple cotton that was most responsible for the spread of slavery to southern interior frontier regions in the early nineteenth century, and this was linked to technological innovation. The sea-island or long-staple cotton cultivated in South Carolina and Georgia coastal regions and islands during the colonial period could not be cultivated successfully inland for a variety of reasons, primarily because it required the particular climatic conditions of the semi-tropical lowlands to thrive. Another variety, short-staple cotton, could be grown at higher interior elevations, but unlike the long-staple variety this cotton was densely honeycombed with seeds that were difficult to separate from the fiber. The long labor hours mandated to extract the seeds made production costs extremely high, so the crop was only marginally profitable.

This had changed by the early nineteenth century. In the 1790s, Eli Whitney invented the cotton gin, a machine that mechanized the process of separating seeds from the cotton fiber, thus making cotton economically viable to grow and process because of reduced labor costs. In short, the spatial movement of cotton production and slavery to the southern interior was made possible by Whitney's revolutionary invention. Other technological improvements facilitating cotton's penetration into western frontier regions included better transportation systems along rivers made possible by the appearance of steam-driven riverboats, the construction of canals, and eventually the development of interior railroad systems.[16] Thus, as was the case in Cuba because of the boom in railroad construction from the late 1830s on, technological innovation was a primary factor in the expansion of slave-based economic activities – sugar in Cuba and cotton in the southern United States.

[16] For a description of cotton's expansion, see Gavin Wright, *The Political Economy of the Cotton South: Households, Markets, and Wealth in the Nineteenth Century* (New York: Norton, 1978), especially the map on pp. 20–1.

Cotton's expansion into what was called the Deep South, or New South, was ongoing and sometimes dramatic, fueled by the steady demand in the factories of England and New England for raw cotton and periodic booms in prices, especially during the 1830s and 1850s. Alabama, Mississippi, Louisiana, Arkansas, Texas, and Florida, all part of the New South, became the major cotton-producing states during the antebellum period, along with the older producing states of Georgia and South and North Carolina. By the eve of the Civil War, it is estimated that about half of all slaves in the United States worked on cotton farms and plantations in these regions. Additionally, many more slaves worked in ancillary activities, such as transportation and food production, that supported the cotton economy.

Slaves also continued to labor in the tobacco sector, which had moved westward, especially to the state of Kentucky, although the older colonial era tobacco-growing regions in Virginia and Maryland remained as important centers of production and of slavery. Slave-based rice cultivation remained an economic activity until the Civil War in coastal Georgia and South Carolina. Louisiana, acquired from the French in 1803, became a center of a slave-based sugar economy, in some ways reflecting to the structures of production found in Cuba and Northeast Brazil. Although about 90 percent of all slaves worked in agricultural activities or their supporting rural economic sectors, southern slavery also had an urban component. In Charleston, South Carolina, slaves outnumbered whites and worked in nearly every sector of the urban economy. New Orleans, Savannah, Richmond, Baltimore, Louisville, and St. Louis were important southern cities where slave labor was critical to the functioning of urban economic systems.[17]

Slavery as a labor system in the rural southern United States prior to the Civil War developed in the absence of any real free labor market, although southern plantations may have been unable or unwilling to develop free labor systems precisely because free workers were loath to work within the context of labor relations defined by coercion, intimidation, and brutality. This was similar in some ways to the labor structures found in the British and French West Indies in the sense that there was no internal free labor market. The latter situation was one of choice, however, since in those islands the dominant social classes who controlled decision making, political and economic, had made

[17]   See Richard C. Wade, *Slavery in the Cities: The South 1820–1960* (New York: Oxford University Press, 1964).

a decision to import only slaves after a brief experimentation with indentured servitude in the early seventeenth century.

However, the southern United States was very different from the Cuban and Brazilian slave systems. There were exclusive slave-based plantations and other economic activities found in each country, to be sure. But in Brazil and Cuba it was common to find free wage labor working on the same plantations or in smaller-scale rural or urban enterprises alongside slaves. This was not generally found on large-scale plantations in the nineteenth-century U.S. South. This exclusivity of slave labor in the U.S. South in the major export sectors requires that two fundamental economic questions be posed and answered. Did slavery develop as a labor system in the southern United States because there were no options? If so, does this mean that the use of free labor would have been more economically advantageous for plantation and smaller farm owners?

The first question is easy to answer. There were few alternatives to slavery because of the absence of internal labor markets in the southern states and the general inability of southern entrepreneurs to attract free labor from other regions of the United States or from abroad as migrants or indentured servants. This, however, does not mean that from a strictly economic point of view free labor would have been more lucrative to plantation owners than slave labor. In fact, historians have concluded not only that slavery was extraordinarily profitable, but also that the efficiency of southern slave-based plantations was probably greater than that of farms located in the nonslave states utilizing free wage labor. Rather than acting as a restraint on productivity, slave labor seems to have been highly efficient and extraordinarily lucrative to slave owners, and this accounts for the willingness of slave purchasers to pay ever-escalating prices for slaves, especially in the 1850s until the outbreak of the Civil War. These conclusions are similar to those reached about slavery in Cuba and Brazil, and later in this chapter the issue of slave labor's viability even as the purchase price of slaves soared will be examined in comparative perspective.

Slavery's development in Brazil followed the trajectory of export sectors, much as in the United States and Cuba, although slaves worked extensively in nonexport rural activities and were pervasive in urban economies as well. By the late eighteenth century there had been two great cycles in slavery's development with distinct, but connected, geographical poles that left lasting impacts on Brazilian economy, society, and culture. The sugar cycle of the northeastern *capitanias* of

Bahia and Pernambuco began in the late sixteenth century, when this region of Brazil became the New World's first slave-based sugar plantation society and the model upon which the eighteenth- and nineteenth-century French, British, and Spanish Caribbean sugar colonies were based. The near impossibility of attracting European free labor left few alternative ways, other than slavery, to produce sugar. After the generalized failure of indigenous slavery to provide a stable work force during the sixteenth century, Portuguese entrepreneurs turned to the same African sources of slave labor that had sustained their São Tomé and Madeira Island sugar colonies off of the African coast. By the early seventeenth century, an African slave–based plantation system had been consolidated, and slave labor became the bedrock upon which the Portuguese colonial economy rested. This meant the northeastern region – there were no other areas of the continent-sized colony of any real economic importance.

Sugar production in northeastern Brazil continued through the eighteenth and nineteenth centuries based upon slave labor, although the dominant position in world sugar markets established during the seventeenth century was ended by the British and French West Indian producers during the eighteenth century. As in all economic activities, there were short- and long-term economic cycles in the sugar sector, with periods of great prosperity as well as times of acute crisis depending on world market conditions for sugar, among other factors. But through these cycles sugar remained, and there was never any real success in weaning the industry from its dependence upon slave labor and continuing imports from Africa until the slave trade was curbed in the early 1850s and slavery finally abolished in the 1880s.

It also ought to be noted that slave labor was found in numerous ancillary rural and urban economic enterprises that supported the export-oriented sugar economy.[18] Slaves labored extensively in the production of food crops, cattle, raising, transportation, urban services, domestic labor, and shipping, among other activities, although it was common to find free laborers working alongside slaves in all of these sectors.

The second great cycle was of extraordinary importance to slavery's development in Brazil, for it lead to the large-scale geographical transfer

[18]   See B. J. Barickman, A *Bahian Counterpoint: Sugar, Tobacco, Cassava, and Slavery in the Recôncavo, 1780–1860* (Stanford, CA: Stanford University Press, 1998).

of slavery toward the interior and south of the colony. Placer gold deposits were discovered in the interior region of Minas Gerais in the 1690s, and there followed a veritable gold rush toward the newly discovered gold fields in the early eighteenth century. Along a mountainous corridor running roughly along a north-south axis in the center of the *capitania*, gold camps were established, giving rise to towns that serviced the mines and later became administrative centers for the Portuguese colonial government.[19] Colonization of the interior emanated from southern Brazil and the São Paulo region as well as from the economic and political center of the colony, Bahia and the colonial capital city of Salvador. The São Francisco River, which originates in Minas Gerais and empties into the Atlantic Ocean to the north of Salvador, became a major transportation artery linking the coastal northeast to the interior gold districts.

It was impossible to work the deposits without importing slave labor, for prior to the gold boom there had been scant population settlement and the complete absence of a potential labor force in the interior mountainous regions where gold was discovered. Those who made successful strikes became purchasers of slaves from slavery's principal center in Brazil – the city of Salvador and its surrounding sugar-based economy. Prices for slave labor and nearly all other commodities soared during the early years of the eighteenth century, and this served as a powerful incentive for slave owners on the northeastern Brazilian littoral to sell off their slaves to the mining camps. It was often more advantageous to sell slaves, often at extraordinary profits, than to produce sugar or other commodities. Accordingly, the sugar economy and its supporting urban and rural sectors began to suffer from labor shortages. Portuguese officials in Salvador issued edict after edict to halt the exodus of slave labor to the interior. But until the slave trade from Africa was able increase slave supplies, thus creating an equilibrium between slave supply and demand, prices remained high, and slave labor was transferred from the traditional areas previously identified with Brazilian colonial slavery – Bahia and Pernambuco – to the dynamic and expanding interior mining regions.

Not only was slavery as a large-scale labor institution developed in the interior because of the early eighteenth-century mining boom, but

[19]   The major centers were Mariana, Ouro Preto, Serro, São João del Rei, São José del Rei, and later Diamantina after diamonds were discovered there in the early eighteenth century.

the port of Rio de Janeiro, a small and relatively insignificant population center during the sixteenth and seventeenth centuries, gradually replaced Salvador as the major entrepôt linking the interior gold mining regions with European and African import and export markets. Gold was legally exported from the growing city, or smuggled to the many transit points to the north and south of Rio near Cabo Frio and Angra dos Reis. Rio de Janeiro came to rival and then move ahead of Salvador as the colony's center of slave imports, while the African slave trade increased to serve the seemingly insatiable labor demands of the interior gold and diamond regions.[20] Rio de Janeiro also surpassed Bahia in another economic activity that was always closely connected with slavery in Brazilian history. By the second half of the eighteenth century it became the leading producer of sugar in the colony, a fact not always recognized in the general histories of Brazil. The rapid expansion of African slavery was thus inevitable.

The city became a major economic center in its own right, and, as was the case in all of Brazil's important population centers, African slaves supplied the labor that drove most economic enterprises. In 1763, Rio was made Brazil's capital, symbolically completing the shift in power from the northeast to the south-center of the colony. Thus, during the gold boom, which began to wane during the 1740s and was definitively over by the 1760s and 1770s, African slavery as an institution was transferred from its original focal point, in the northeast of the colony, to the center and south of Brazil.

Slavery also developed on a significant scale further south, in the frontier *capitania* of São Paulo from which the great expeditions had been launched leading to the discovery of gold in Minas Gerais in the 1690s. São Paulo's African slave population was relatively small on the eve of the mining boom, and its economy was largely subsistence in nature. Accordingly, no significant internal slave trade developed between São Paulo and Minas Gerais as was the case with the

---

[20]   David Eltis has shown that in the first quarter of the eighteenth century, between 1701 and 1725, some 122,000 slaves were imported to southeastern Brazil, mainly through Rio de Janeiro, while nearly 200,000 slaves were imported to Bahia. But after 1725 more slaves were imported through the southeast. Between 1726 and 1750, nearly 214,000 slaves entered the colony via Rio and its environs, while slaves imported to Bahia numbered about 105,000. See David Eltis, "The Volume and Structure of the Transatlantic Slave Trade: A Reassessment," *William & Mary Quarterly*, 3rd series, Vol. 63, No. 1 (January 2001), p. 46, Table 3.

pre-mining northeastern slave-holding zones. However, São Paulo's traditional agricultural system was deeply affected by the mining boom and its reverberating impact on Rio de Janeiro.

First, it took some time for the mining regions to develop supporting industries such as food-crop production and cattle ranching. São Paulo's farmers were thus provided with emerging commercial markets for the foodstuffs that they had always produced for local consumption. The northern mining regions, from Ouro Preto and Mariana through Serro and Diamantina, were quite distant and usually provisioned from Bahia. But the southern mining zones, around São João and São José del Rei, became market areas for *Paulista* smaller farmers and larger plantation owners who produced dietary staples such as *mandioca* or hides, tallow, and dried meat from cattle ranching. All of this increased labor needs in the Paulista hinterland, and inevitably this meant the growth of slavery.

Second, the growth of Rio de Janeiro city and *capitania* provided even greater markets for food products. The city's rapid pace of economic development resulted in the accumulation of capital for investment by entrepreneurs in the city and in contiguous regions, as well as the most sophisticated slave-trading infrastructure in Brazil during the second half of the eighteenth century. Profits by *Paulista* entrepreneurs derived from trade with Minas and Rio, along with investment capital flowing into the region from these areas, led to the spread of sugar production in the Paraíba valley in eastern São Paulo contiguous to Rio de Janeiro. This, of course, meant rising labor demands and the importation of large slave contingents. Finally, long before coffee became important in the nineteenth century, sugar cane cultivation also penetrated the sparsely populated forested frontier in western São Paulo, with its flat lands and extraordinarily fertile soils. Slavery on a large scale spread there as well, providing the labor foundation for the later nineteenth-century development of coffee planting. It ought to be noted that unlike the sugar plantations of northeastern Brazil, *Paulista fazendas* produced a wide range of agricultural products in addition to sugar. Surpluses of dietary staples fed the local and regional slave populations and often were exported to Minas Gerais and Rio de Janeiro when local production could not meet the demand for food.[21]

[21] For the best consideration of the economic and social development of São Paulo, see Francisco Vidal Luna and Herbert S. Klein, *Slavery and the Economy of São Paulo 1750–1850* (Stanford, CA: Stanford University Press, 2003).

The gold cycle, then, had multiple effects upon the Brazilian economy, and society and on Brazilian slavery. It pulled the locus of Portuguese colonization toward the interior and south of the country and transferred the fundamental institutions of colonial society into these former frontier regions. The mining economy was responsible in many ways for the growth of the city of Rio de Janeiro; the dramatic increase in the African slave trade through the port; and urban slavery's development in the city, which became the colony's new capital in 1763. The investment capital generated by mining was also in many ways closely linked to the process of agricultural commercialization in rural São Paulo.

The overall development of regional economic systems, which included the growth of slave-based sugar cultivation in rural Rio de Janeiro and São Paulo, set the stage for the next great cycle in Brazil's economic development, that of coffee, which gradually came to define the independent nation during the nineteenth century. Coffee exports did not surpass sugar in value until the 1830s, and both sectors depended heavily upon new infusions of slave labor. This meant the African slave trade prior to the 1850s and the internal slave trade from northeastern Brazil after the successful closure of the African trade by the British in 1851 and 1852.

Coffee growing as a large-scale commercial endeavor did not begin until very late in the eighteenth century and gradually took hold in the Paraíba valley system to the north of Rio de Janeiro. With the sharp rise in coffee prices on world markets during the 1790s, in the aftermath of the Haitian slave revolt, coffee spread throughout the valley. As with the cultivation of sugar cane, there was never an alternative labor source available to planters other than slaves. One difference, however, was that coffee could be grown on smaller farms and large plantations alike because of relatively modest capital investment demands. Coffee did not need to be processed by expensive industrial equipment for marketing, as was the case with sugar cane, which had to be converted into sugar at mills. This meant that small-scale coffee farms with relatively few slaves were found, although extensive plantations, on the same scale as the sugar *fazendas*, with larger slave populations were also found.

Coffee cultivation spread southwest along the Paraíba valley into the eastern regions of São Paulo, part of the same valley system, and then into the western Paulista plains, following roughly the same spatial expansion patterns as sugar had previously. There were still relatively low population densities and the availability of virgin forest land that could be cleared and planted in coffee and other crops. Family labor could meet the demands of very small farms, but on larger estates it was impossible to mobilize enough labor for economic viability without the purchase of slaves. When coffee surpassed sugar exports from São Paulo in the 1850s, the province's productive capacity was entirely dependent upon the number of slaves laboring on plantations. Since the slave trade from Africa had ended after midcentury, imports from the northeast ensued, and without them production levels could simply not be sustained or increased. A third major region of Brazilian slave-based coffee development was the southeastern frontier region of Minas Gerais known as the Zona da Mata. Far removed from the mining region and closer geographically to the Paraíba valley and Rio de Janeiro, this densely forested region was gradually colonized during the 1830s in much the same way that the São Paulo coffee districts were.

In Brazil, then, slavery moved spatially in much the same way that the institution was transferred from the eastern seaboard of the United States to the internal cotton frontier during the first half of the nineteenth century, or in the way that it spread south and eastward from Havana during the early nineteenth century as sugar colonized the plains of Matanzas and then Santa Clara in Cuba. In all three countries slavery was flexible, highly mobile, and spread along with the geographical movement of export-driven economic activities. Slavery was an elastic institution as a labor system, and contrary to older theoretical constructs that interpreted slave labor as an impediment to capitalist development, slavery in these three major American slaveholding societies played a fundamental part in the growth of very dynamic capitalist economies. These were the last great slave societies in the Americas, and it is instructive that slave labor stubbornly persisted well into the second half of the nineteenth century, a period during which the industrial revolution and capitalist relations of production advanced steadily and dynamically.

The decade of the 1850s offers an opportunity to examine the issue of slavery's economic viability using comparative perspectives buttressed by hard economic data.[22] This was the last decade of slavery in the

[22] The following section of this chapter is based upon, and first appeared in, Laird W. Bergad, "American Slave Markets in the 1850s: Slave Price Rises in the U.S., Brazil, and Cuba in Comparative Perspective," in David Eltis, Frank Lewis, and Kenneth Sokoloff, editors, *Slavery in the Development of the Americas* (New York and London: Cambridge University Press, 2004).

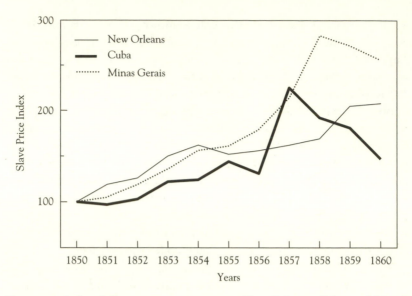

Figure 5.1. Indexed slave price movements in New Orleans, Cuba, and Minas Gerais, Brazil, 1850–1860, for male slaves ages 21–38, in nominal prices (1850 = 100).

United States, and it was a period during which there were few indicators of imminent abolition in all three nations. It was also a decade during which slave prices increased dramatically in all three countries. Yet, irrespective of these price rises, slave owners continued actively purchasing slaves. The reaction of businesspeople to changes in prices of commodities or labor is an important indictor of future expectations. The very fact that slave owners continued to buy slaves during periods of steep price increases in all three countries suggests an expectation that their slave-based economic activities would be profitable in the future.

Figures 5.1 and 5.2 depict the price rises for working-age male slaves between 1850 and 1860, a period that corresponded to increases in the production of major crops – cotton, sugar, and coffee – in each country, as indicated in Figure 5.3. These slaves were the core slave work force on plantations, and although female slaves engaged in labor in every rural and urban occupation, these male slave price trends may be used as indicators of the way in which overall working-age slave prices evolved.[23]

[23]   These data are based upon the systematic slave price data found in Laurence J. Kotlikoff, "Quantitative Description of the New Orleans Slave Market,

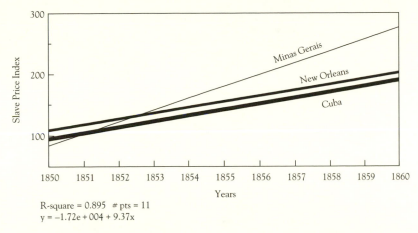

R-square = 0.895   # pts = 11
y = −1.72e + 004 + 9.37x

Figure 5.2. Trend lines for indexed slave price movements in New Orleans, Cuba, and Minas Gerais, Brazil, 1850–1860, for male slaves ages 21–38, in current prices (1850 = 100).

It ought to be emphasized that slave labor provided the core work force in the production of all three major export crops in each of these countries. A fundamental question revolves around the comparative aspects of the impressive economic expansion taking place in each country and the relation of slave markets to these processes of economic growth. There were five marked similarities that may be identified when comparing the three slave-based economies:

1. In all three nations, the agricultural expansion of principal crops – cotton in the United States, sugar in Cuba, and coffee in southern Brazil – was based on the spatial movement of production into high-yielding soils in previously underpopulated frontier regions before and during the 1850s. These processes have been described previously in this chapter.
2. Absolute increases in production in the principal crop linked to slave labor in each of the three nations, cotton, sugar, and coffee, demonstrate similar trends and are depicted by decade from the 1820s through the 1850s in Figure 5.3.

1804–1862," in Robert William Fogel and Stanley L. Engerman, editors, *Without Consent or Contract: Markets and Production, Technical Papers (Volume 1)* (New York: Norton, 1992), pp. 31–53; Bergad et al., *The Cuban Slave Market, 1790–1880*; and Bergad, *Slavery and the Demographic and Economic History of Minas Gerais, Brazil, 1720–1880*.

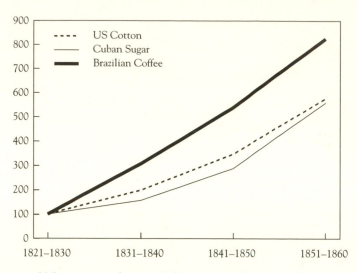

Figure 5.3. U.S. cotton production, Cuban sugar production, and Brazilian coffee exports by volume, 1821–1860 (indexed, 1821–30 = 100).
Source: B. R. Mitchell, *International Historical Statistics, The Americas 1750–1988* (New York: Stockton Press, 1993), pp. 205, 281, 294–5; Manuel Moreno Fraginals, *E1 Ingenio* (Havana: Editorial de Ciencias Sociales, 1978), vol III, pp. 35–6.

3. Productive expansion was paralleled by, and related to, important technological transformations in the U.S. and Cuban cases, although these were less critical to the growth of the Brazilian coffee economy during the 1850s. These included transportation innovations, especially the construction of railroads and the development of steamship service along rivers and to seaports. There were also marked improvements in communications heralded by the increased utilization of telegraph lines, which put producers in touch with local, regional, national, and international market conditions very quickly. The application of new technologies in the processing of sugar cane into sugar, and in the drying and hulling of coffee, were of great importance in increasing the efficiency of Cuban and Brazilian slave-based production.

4. A fourth similarity was found in the upward trend in prices for coffee, sugar, and cotton during the second half of the 1850s. This followed a long period of downward pressure on prices for these commodities. Although the general trend in cotton prices over the course of the decade was still downward, the surge in

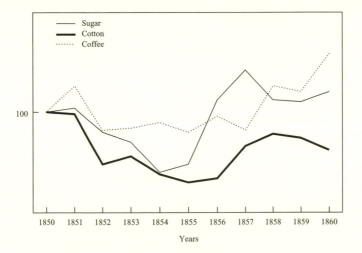

Figure 5.4. Indexed sugar, cotton, and coffee prices in the United States, 1850–1860, in real prices using U.S. "deflators" (1850 = 100).
Source: U.S. Department of Commerce, Bureau of the Cenus, *Historical Statistics of the United States, Colonial Times to 1970* (Washington: Government Printing Office, 1975), Part 1, p. 209; Part 2, p. 902.

prices after 1856 stimulated the impressive expansion of production in the U.S. South after 1857. This indicates the rapid response of slave-based cotton production to changes in market conditions. Coffee and sugar prices moved significantly upward in the second half of the decade, and although the timing was different for each crop, there is no question that labor cost increases in the form of higher real slave prices were made more tolerable by increased income linked to higher product prices. These price movements are depicted in Figure 5.4.

5. A fifth similarity was bound with respect to the efficient reallocation of slave labor toward the dynamic activities of cotton, sugar, and coffee production as market demand, profitability, and prices increased.

This fifth similarity is a critical indicator of slave labor's economic viability in all three nations. The reallocation of slave labor westward in the U.S. South is considered to be a major indicator of the flexibility, efficiency, and profitability of the southern U.S. slave-based economy.[24]

---

[24]   See Fogel, *Without Consent or Contract,* pp. 90–1.

The same processes of slave labor reallocation were found in Cuba and in the coffee-producing zones of southern Brazil.

The Cuban case is quite graphic. During the 1850s, as sugar cultivation was transformed technologically and spatially, there was a significant reallocation of slave labor toward sugar estates in regions where the most technologically advanced mills were located. The Cuban census of 1846 indicated that approximately 33 percent of all slaves resided on *ingenios*, an increase from about 25 percent in 1827. But by the next population count in 1862, nearly 50 percent of all Cuban slaves lived and worked on sugar plantations, and nearly two-thirds of all male Cuban slaves were found in the sugar sector.[25] This is only part of the labor reallocation process in Cuba, for these labor transfers must also be seen in the context of an escalating African slave trade during the decade and the large-scale importation of Chinese contract laborers, who were mainly destined for the sugar zones. Between 1850 and 1860, some 124,000 African slaves were imported to Cuba, as were over 58,000 Chinese laborers.[26] It may be assumed that a significant portion of imported slaves and nearly all of the Chinese workers were destined for the sugar sector given the 1862 census data just mentioned. If the United States reallocated resources in part because of the internal interregional slave trade, Cuba did so through the shifting of extant slaves and the channeling of newly imported slaves and Chinese workers to sugar plantation zones.

The gradual reallocation of resources toward southern coffee zones during the 1850s was also a fundamental aspect of mid nineteenth-century Brazilian economic history, although it should be kept in mind that cotton and sugar exports in other geographical regions were still important components of the Brazilian export trade.[27] With the closing of the Brazilian slave trade during the early 1850s, slave-based coffee

[25]   See the discussion in Bergad et al., *The Cuban Slave Market*, pp. 29–32. Many slaves also worked on cattle ranches and food-producing farms in the sugar zones, which supported the *ingenios*.

[26]   For data on Cuban slave imports, see David Eltis, *Economic Growth and the Ending of the Transatlantic Slave Trade* (New York: Oxford University Press, 1987), p. 245. Data on the Chinese are found in Bergad, *Cuban Rural Society in the Nineteenth Century*, p. 250, and were derived from documentation in the Public Records Office (London), ZHCI/3831, p. 6, "Report of the British Consulate General, Havana, September 1, 1873."

[27]   Between 1851 and 1860, coffee accounted for about two-thirds of Brazilian exports by value, sugar for one-quarter, and cotton for about 8 percent.

plantations depended upon extant populations or the transfer of slaves from other regions of the country if they were to expand their work forces.[28] It ought to be stressed that data for the interregional and intraregional Brazilian slave trade are scarce owing to the absence of regional, provincial, or national population counts until the census of 1872.[29] However, studies of internal Brazilian slave movements during the 1850s have concluded that indeed there were clear indications of slave imports to the *Paulista* coffee frontier during the 1850s, although these were not nearly as voluminous as those that occurred during the 1870s, when more accurate data are available.[30] Additionally, rising real prices for slaves did not act to inhibit increases in coffee production or slave purchases. This, of course, is a clear indicator of the coffee economy's ability to grow profitably regardless of changes in the slave market.

Thus, there were striking similarities in the development of slave-based export economic activities in the three countries under consideration. The abundance of economic data for the United States has led historians to nearly uncontestable conclusions on the rising profitability and efficiency of slave labor in the southern cotton-producing zones prior to the Civil War. Although these kinds of data are not available in such detail for Cuba and Brazil, the fact that similar slave price curves were found in all three nations suggests that the Cuban and Brazilian slave systems were as rational and profitable as the southern U.S. economy. The strong positive correlation between increased real slave prices in all three nations during the 1850s and the rising output of major slave-based export crops is one indicator that the economics of slavery were extraordinarily similar in all three countries.

[28] As in the southern United States, a large number of slaves were transferred to dynamic regions of growth because they were brought by their owners, rather than being imported through purchase.

[29] Klein has discounted the importance of the interregional slave trade during the early 1850s. See Herbert S. Klein, "The Internal Slave Trade in Nineteenth-Century Brazil: A Study of Slave Importations into Rio de Janeiro in 1852," *Hispanic American Historical Review*, Vol. 51, No. 4 (1971), pp. 567–85.

[30] Slenes has established a close statistical correlation between São Paulo's coffee exports, for which data are available, and its slave population, which expanded gradually during the decade. See Robert Slenes, "The Demography and Economics of Brazilian Slavery: 1850–1888" (Ph.D. thesis, Stanford University, 1976), Chapter 3, "The Volume and Organization of the Interregional Slave Trade: 1850–1888," pp. 120–78.

The economics of Brazilian slavery during the 1850s have not been closely examined by scholars owing to a lack of documentary materials. Studies on the 1870s and after, when abundant documentation has been located, however, have reached the same conclusions concerning the continued high profitability and efficiency of slave labor right up to abolition.[31] Coffee cultivation expanded regardless of price rises in real terms for slaves, who constituted nearly all of the laborers in the coffee economy until the late 1880s, when large-scale migration and abolition shifted the labor foundations of coffee plantations.

With respect to the economic aspects of slave labor, the striking similarities in American slave systems must be stressed. The connections between technological innovations, increased production, and the economic viability of slavery, even during periods of sharp price increases for slaves, were prevalent in all three nations and indicate marked economic parallels between the U.S., Brazilian, and Cuban slave systems.

[31]   See the works of Pedro Carvalho de Mello, "Expectation of Abolition and Sanguinity of Coffee Planters in Brazil, 1871–1881" in Robert William Fogel and Stanley L. Engerman, editors, *Without Consent or Contract: Conditions of Slave Life and the Transition to Freedom, Technical Papers* (New York: Norton, 1992), Vol. 2, pp. 629–46, and "Rates of Return on Slave Capital in Brazilian Coffee Plantations, 1871–1881," in Fogel and Engerman, editors, *Without Consent or Contract*, vol. 1, pp. 63–79. Also see his doctoral dissertation, "The Economics of Labor in Brazilian Coffee Plantations, 1850–1888" (Ph.D. thesis, University of Chicago, 1977).

Slenes has reached similar conclusions. See Slenes, "The Demography and Economics of Brazilian Slavery: 1850–1888," Chapter 5, "The Rational Planter and the Threat of Abolition: Changes in the Sanguinity of Slaveholders over Time," pp. 234–69.

CHAPTER SIX

Making Space

From the moment of enslavement, and throughout the entire tragic history of slavery, the one driving aspiration shaping the life experiences of slaves was the desire to be free men and women. Irrespective of where and when they lived as slaves, the dream of freedom for themselves and their families, however difficult or unlikely that may have been, was at the forefront of their objectives as human beings. When the real possibilities of acquiring freedom were remote and improbable, slaves asserted their humanity and insisted upon being treated with respect and dignity in the most adverse of all human conditions. Despite their dreadful positions as chattel, slaves struggled to negotiate the terms of their daily lives, even within the confines of slavery. They were not passive victims of oppression but sought to exert as much control as possible over their lives in a wide variety of ways. This aspect of the slave experience should not be glamorized or romanticized. In most cases, despite their efforts, intentions, and hopes, slaves were cruelly treated, separated from family members, abused in a variety of ways, and were unable to mitigate the basic conditions of brutality that governed their lives.

That, however, does not mean that they simply accepted perpetual servitude and the inevitable abuse and degradation that accompanied enslavement. Slaves sought to shape their lives to the greatest degree possible and demanded as much respect as could be extracted from masters, overseers, free workers who sometimes labored alongside them, and their fellow slaves. The ways in which they pursued these objectives were extraordinarily diverse, and their degree of success depended on a multitude of factors. These included the character of the individual masters, who ranged from the extremes of sensitive humanitarians to sadistic abusers. Most slave owners were neither and fell somewhere between these exaggerated poles of good and evil.

Nearly all masters and mistresses were concerned about ultimate economic issues, since slaves were very expensive to purchase and extraordinarily valuable as a source of labor power and private property. In the end, the use of their labor power had to be economically viable for most slave owners; if not, they had to be sold off. That meant two things. First, masters sought to maximize the exploitation of their slave populations in order to produce profits in their economic endeavors. Second, there were limits to the kinds of pressures that could be placed on slaves to perform their duties.

Slaves may have been regarded by their masters as property, but they were human beings with all of the idiosyncrasies, motivations, and abilities to cooperate (or not) with their masters' grand schemes for making money and turning profits. They could feign illness, slow down work rhythms individually or collectively, sabotage equipment, lose valuable tools, or "discover" fires in various fields or broken carts and other transportation vehicles. Slaves had the potential ability to disrupt and even hinder in a serious way the functioning of any economic enterprise, large or small, urban or rural. Of course, a great deal of cleverness and caution was needed if slaves were to exert pressure by disrupting or subtly threatening to disrupt production, since masters could unleash terribly harsh punishments if sabotage or outright disobedience was suspected. But masters knew very well that while they regarded their slaves as chattel, they were indeed human beings and had to be negotiated with at many different levels in order for economic enterprises to run smoothly. Too often the image of master/slave relations invokes an absolute power, one that existed at the ultimate level, to be sure, but that was mitigated to varying degrees by slaves through their ingenuity, intelligence, and insistence upon certain prerogatives as human beings. Again, this element of the slave experience – acting as their own "agents" – ought not to be exaggerated, for in the end the master class held a monopoly on power over the slaves they owned. A slave who pushed too far in seeking to assert more control over his or her life could be sold off at a moment's notice, the worst possible fate if he or she had close family members nearby. Thus, the ability of slaves to negotiate the terms of their lives existed within particular parameters and required much skill, diplomacy, finesse, and a carefully calculated knowledge of how much room for negotiation was available in any given circumstance.

It is difficult to generalize about the negotiating power of slaves in the three slave societies, as they showed distinctive regional variations in the way the institution of slavery evolved and constant change through time during the eighteenth and nineteenth centuries. Master/slave relations were always in flux and varied according to whether slaves lived and worked in urban or rural areas; the particular economic sector slaves labored in; the size of the enterprise and the number of slaves employed; whether slaves were of African origin or born in the Americas; the character and proclivities of their owners; and a long and complex series of other variables. But regardless of the huge variation in the slave experience, it can be stated unequivocally that all slaves, like all other human beings, wanted to have as much control over their lives as possible and that they constantly strove for this unlikely and difficult-to-attain goal.

This could mean many things. Above all, it meant demanding respect for family and extended kinship networks that were of critical importance and that were woven sometimes beyond the control or even knowledge of masters. Slaves married, lived together in consensual unions, had children, and valued multigenerational family structures that included grandparents, aunts and uncles, cousins, nieces, and nephews. Sometimes these extended over large geographical areas, with families spread out on distant farms, plantations, cities, and towns. The ability to visit, to convene family gatherings at holiday time, and to get together to celebrate marriages, births, and funerals were of utmost importance to slaves everywhere. Slave owners were aware of the broad contours of these relations, and if they wanted peace and smooth labor relations on their estates, they knew very well that prohibiting slaves from these normal human activities could be an invitation to disaster. By the same token, masters cleverly made use of these aspects of slave existence to exert pressures upon slaves to work efficiently and obediently. The threat of withholding permission to travel from the estate to visit wives, children, or parents was an effective means of social control. Thus, accommodation and compromise, as opposed to authoritarian methods and brutality, could be an effective way of accomplishing the goals of masters. By the same token, slaves could extract all kinds of concessions from masters by working effectively and obediently, even if there was seething anger and resentment at their constant degradation and the ultimate and arbitrary power held over them. Yet caution must be exercised here, for slave owners often cared little for the realities of slave family life, and it was very common for families to be broken apart through the sale of children or parents to locales so distant that they would never be reunited.

Visions of slave family life have shifted considerably over the last forty years.[1] Early in the twentieth century, the dominant view of slave family life in the United States was that the process of enslavement and slavery itself was so destructive to pre-slavery African social and cultural structures that the formation of nuclear and extended families among forcibly transplanted Africans was all but impossible. Even though most slaves were born in the United States rather than in Africa, by the early nineteenth century, the slave family was interpreted as having been destroyed so effectively during the first generations of slavery that the institution was unable to recover in any meaningful way. Plantation slave life, in particular, was conceived of as one of rampant promiscuity and little inclination toward forming stable families, especially among men, who often accepted no responsibility for their offspring.[2] In many ways these interpretations of the slave family conceived of slaves as passive victims of masters

---

[1]   For a concise account of the evolving historiography of the slave family in the United States, see Robert William Fogel, *Without Consent or Contract: The Rise and Fall of American Slavery* (New York: Norton, 1989), pp. 162–8. Two more broadly based summaries that examine Brazilian historiography on the slave family and compare it to U.S. studies are Robert W. Slenes, *Na Senzala Uma Flor: Esperanças e Recordações na Formação da Família Escrava, Brasil Sudeste, Século XIX* (Rio de Janeiro: Editora Nova Fronteira, 1999), pp. 27–68, and José Flávio Motta, *Corpos Escravos, Vontades Livres: Posse de Cativos e Família escrava em Bananal (1801–1829)* (São Paulo: Annablume, 1999), pp. 179–226. Also see Slenes's essay, "Black Homes, White Homilies: Perceptions of Slave Family and of Slave Women in Nineteenth-Century Brazil," in David Barry Gaspar and Darlene Clark Hine, editors, *More than Chattel: Black Women and Slavery in the Americas* (Bloomington and Indianapolis: Indiana University Press, 1996), pp. 126–46.

[2]   An example is found in Ulrich Bonnell Phillips, *American Negro Slavery: A Survey of the Supply, Employment and Control of Negro Labor as Determined by the Plantation Regime* (New York: Appleton, 1918). For a rebuttal of Phillips, but one that still agreed with the difficulty of slave family formation, see W. E. B. Dubois, *The Negro American Family* (Cambridge, MA: MIT Press, 1970), reprint of the 1908 edition). The classic studies of slavery in the United States that addressed and revised various notions of slave family life are E. Franklin Frazier, *The Negro Family in the United States* (Chicago: University of Chicago Press, 1939); Kenneth M. Stampp, *The Peculiar Institution: Slavery in the Antebellum South* (New York: Knopf, 1956); and Stanley M. Elkins, *Slavery: A Problem in American Institutional and Intellectual Life* (Chicago: University of Chicago Press, 1959).

who did not permit marriage and the formation of families; who encouraged licentious behavior so that slaves would reproduce, thereby adding to the owner's work force and property values; and who in effect destroyed the possibility of family formation and stability. They were heavily laden with racist attitudes, since those of African descent were seen as people with uncontrolled libidos who were hopelessly irresponsible about obligations toward children, and who placed little premium upon family relations and interactions. Additionally, slave family life and the ability of slaves to marry or form stable relationships were seen as dependent upon master/slave relations. The possibility of independent behavior on the part of slaves in forming their own institutions and cultural forms was not conceived of. Although these were extreme views, they became part of the erroneous interpretation of family development among U.S. slaves during the antebellum period, and this analysis was extended and applied to post-emancipation African-American culture.

In the decade of the 1970s scholars began to present a diametrically opposite interpretation of the slave family. Unlike the situation in the major Latin American and Caribbean slave societies, it was noted that there were nearly equal numbers of enslaved men and women in the U.S. slave South because of the impressive process of natural slave reproduction. This sex parity provided the underlying demographic conditions for the formation of couples and eventually families. Contrary to the image of rampant promiscuity and irresponsibility, slaves were found to have consistently formed close family bonds within immediate families headed by married or cohabitating partners, and these were nurtured within the context of multigenerational extended families or kinship networks.[3] The institution of co-parenthood was also extremely important, and this led to the creation of social networks linking families who were not blood relatives. These dynamics were

---

[3] The most influential study was Herbert G. Gutman, *The Black Family in Slavery and Freedom, 1750–1925* (New York: Pantheon Press, 1976). Also see John W. Blassingame, *The Slave Community: Plantation Life in the Antebellum South* (New York: Oxford University Press, 1972), especially Chapter 3, "The Slave Family," pp. 77–103; Eugene D. Genovese, *Roll, Jordan, Roll: The World the Slaves Made* (New York: Pantheon Press, 1974); Jacqueline Jones, *Labor of Love, Labor of Sorrow: Black Women, Work and the Family from Slavery to the Present* (New York: Basic Books, 1985); and Elizabeth Fox-Genovese, *Within the Plantation Household: Black and White Women of the Old South* (Chapel Hill: University of North Carolina Press, 1988).

found equally in cities, among house servants, and even on large plantations among field slaves.

For slaves, this was a strategy of affirming bonds to one another, to past and future generations, and of struggling against the depersonalization and objectification by slave owners and southern white society in general. Although the legal rights of slaves to marry were not necessarily recognized by law, many masters permitted or even encouraged marriage as a way to create stability among their slave populations, as well as to placate religious leaders who were concerned with issues of "morality" among slaves. Permitting marriage and family structures to flourish was an important means of exerting social control, for masters could use the mere threat of selling off wives, husbands, parents, or children to assure obedience, stability, and efficient work rhythms. Often spouses lived apart, on nearby plantations or farms, and legal permission had to be secured for visitation rights. If slaves caused few difficulties and fulfilled their labor obligations, then there was little point in causing discontent by denying these privileges. By the same token, the threat of withholding such permission to visit their kin could effectively be manipulated by slave owners to assure obedience and discipline.

Irrespective of the motivations or actions of slave owners, family ties were highly valued and were as central to the lives of slaves as they were to free southern men and women. The great difference, of course, was that the threat of family destruction was always present and in fact often imminent, especially as the geography of slavery shifted westward with the spread of cotton into the frontier. A central question addressed by historians has been how the interregional slave trade from the coastal Old South to the interior New South affected slave families.[4] Or, phrased another way, how often did masters break up families by selling off husbands, wives, or children in order to reap economic rewards? The answer, according to recent studies, is that families and communities of slaves were devastated by the internal nineteenth-century U.S. slave trade. Although some of the westward movement of slaves was composed of owners moving with their families and slaves seeking opportunities in frontier regions, it is likely that over 50 percent of the slaves exported from the older slave

---

[4]   This movement westward has been called the "second Middle Passage" by Ira Berlin, in his *Generations of Captivity: A History of African-American Slaves* (Cambridge, MA.: The Belknap Press of Harvard University Press, 2003).

states were simply sold off irrespective of their family and community bonds.[5] There was little guaranteed stability in family structures because of this overwhelming and arbitrary power wielded by the master class. Keeping families together was a constant struggle, and even the most compliant slaves, those who went to great extremes to accommodate their owners in an effort to keep family structures intact, ran the risk of being marketed to speculators who would march them toward the frontier for sale in distant locales. If this was their fate, in all likelihood they would never see their original families again.

There also seems to have been a considerable difference in the ability of slaves to maintain family structures according to the size of slave-holding on farms and plantations. One recent study has emphasized the fact that slaves on larger plantations were more likely to preserve family ties than slaves residing on smaller farms with fewer slaves. Presumably, each individual slave on smaller holdings represented a larger portion of the total capital investment to owners, so that when slave prices rose, the likelihood of a master selling off a slave to capitalize on rising values was greater than on larger plantations, irrespective of family bonds.[6] Another study of the Piedmont area of Virginia has found that a minority of slave children lived in families headed by both parents, and that female-headed families were much more commonly found. Additionally, nuclear families were few and far between, with multigenerational extended families providing a greater source of comfort and stability than immediate families.[7] Similar findings were generated by a study of Louisiana slave family structures in the nineteenth century. As in

[5] See Walter Johnson, *Soul by Soul: Life Inside the Antebellum Slave Market* (Cambridge, MA: Harvard University Press, 1999), and Michael Tadman, *Speculators and Slaves: Masters, Traders, and Slaves in the Old South* (Madison: University of Wisconsin Press, 1989). For a critical evaluation of these studies, and especially of Tadman's estimates, which are seen as exaggerated, see Jonathan B. Pritchett, "Quantitative Estimates of the United States Interregional Slave Trade, 1820–1860," unpublished paper available on the internet at <http://www.tulane.edu/~pritchet/personal/trade.pdf>.

[6] See the study of the "mountain south" by Wilma A. Dunaway, *The African-American Family in Slavery and Emancipation* (New York: Cambridge University Press, 2003), and the accompanying web site, <http://scholar.lib.vt.edu/vtpubs/mountain_slavery/index.htm>.

[7] Brenda E. Stevenson, *Life in Black & White: Family and Community in the Slave South* (New York: Oxford University Press, 1996).

northern Virginia, less than half of children lived in households with two parents present.[8]

Yet, despite the terrible and arbitrary power wielded by masters, it is clear that the family, nuclear or extended, was of critical importance to the culture of slaves in the southern United States and that with or without the consent of owners, or legal sanction by state laws, extensive family bonds were formed and carefully nurtured. This does not mean that families were not ruthlessly and tragically broken apart by inhumane owners to whom slave family structures were meaningless or of little concern compared to the prospect of monetary gain. Yet there were also owners who respected slave family life and in fact encouraged and sanctioned legal marriage. There were also many slaves, male and female, who were irresponsible and to whom familial responsibility, parenthood, and kinship networks were of marginal or no importance. But these variations in attitudes and behavior patterns toward the family among both masters and slaves were in all likelihood not very different from those found within the free population, white or of African descent. The diversity of the human experience with respect to behavior and attitudes toward such institutions as the family was manifest among all peoples, regardless of their race or legal status. For slaves, however, the power to ultimately control family structures was tragically vested in their owners. All too often, without much notice, family members were sold off irrespective of the deep pain and sorrow caused to their kin.

Following the debates about the slave family in the United States, Brazilian scholars have produced an extraordinary literature on the same themes and in many ways have arrived at conclusions similar to those discovered for slave families in the U.S. South. As in the United States, a fundamentally racist interpretation of the possibilities for slaves to form families developed in the early twentieth century among Brazilian intellectuals. Familiar themes were invoked, and stereotypical images of slaves were generated that depicted them as uncontrollably libidinous, irresponsible about the rearing of children, and incapable of nurturing and sustaining families. But whereas in the United States male slaves were seen as the principal culprits because of their inability to control sexual urges, in Brazil slave women were

---

[8]   Ann Patton Malone, *Sweet Chariot: Slave Family and Household Structure in Nineteenth-Century Louisiana* (Chapel Hill: University of North Carolina Press, 1992).

labeled in the same way. A supposed instinctual promiscuity among both male and female slaves was seen as one of the principal factors inhabiting family formation.[9] Thus, an unrestricted sexuality among those of African descent was interpreted as standing in the way of any real ability to nurture stable families within slavery.

Yet, contrary to legal codes in the United States, formal marriage was sanctioned by law within Brazilian slave society, and it was rare that masters intervened to preclude marriage or consensual cohabitation among slaves or even between slaves and free blacks and mulattos. This does not mean that the Catholic Church performed marriage rites among slaves in Brazil more frequently than Protestant churches did for slaves in the United States, or that the prevalence of family formation was any greater in Brazil. In fact, the evidence uncovered by recent research suggests similar patterns with respect to the extent of nuclear and extended families as well as kinship networks. Additionally, *compadrio*, or co-parenthood, may have been more important in Brazil in creating bonds between non-blood-related slaves, which resulted in wider social linkages among families.[10]

One of the fundamental differences between Brazil and the United States with respect to the comparative dimensions of family formation and the persistence of ongoing kinship networks among slaves was the constant arrival of Africans via the transatlantic slave trade to Brazil. In the United States the trade had ended in 1808, and this meant a fairly balanced sex ratio among slaves, demographic structures that were relatively undisturbed by outside arrivals, and a slave population that had largely been born into slavery by the beginning of the nineteenth century. For these reasons and despite the internal slave trade toward the New South, United States slave populations were much more demographically stable than their Brazilian and Cuban counterparts,

[9] These interpretations are found in Gilberto Freyre, *The Masters and the Slaves: A Study in the Development of Brazilian Civilization* (Berkeley: University of California Press, 1986); Roger Bastide, *As Religiões Africanas no Brasil* (2 vols.) (São Paulo: Livrearia Pioneira Editôra, 1971); Raymundo Nina Rodrigues, *Os Africanos no Brasil* (São Paulo: Companhia Editora Nacional, 1932); Florestan Fernandes, *A Integração do Negro na Sociedade de Classe* (São Paulo: EDUSP, 1965); and Emilia Viotti da Costa, *Da Senzala à Colônia* (São Paulo: Difusão Européia do Livro, 1966).

[10] See Stuart B. Schwartz, "Opening the Family Circle: Godparentage in Brazilian Slavery," in his *Slaves, Peasants, and Rebels: Reconsidering Brazilian Slavery* (Urbana and Chicago: University of Illinois Press, 1992), pp. 137–60.

which experienced the continual arrival of Africans through the middle of the nineteenth century. About two-thirds of Africans arriving were men, which created a sex imbalance that left many men unable to find stable partners, at least in the short term. While slaves who had been in Brazil for long periods of time or who had been born there had established family ties with other slaves, and sometimes with free men and women, newly arrived Africans seldom were connected to slaves other than those with whom they had shared the tragic journey from African ports, who were called *malungos*. Cuban slave society experienced similar dynamics. Yet empirical studies have found that over time, marriage rates and consensual unions seem to have been as significant among African-born slaves as they were among couples who were Brazilian-born. Additionally, intermarriage between Africans and Brazilian slaves was common, as was marriage between slaves and free blacks and mulattos, especially in urban areas.

Since the mid-1970s, an extraordinary outpouring of regional-level studies has been produced on the Brazilian slave family, based on the utilization of widely available manuscript census reports and postmortem inventories discovered in provincial and municipal archival collections. These have helped produce a very precise quantitative profile of marriage and family connections among local slave populations, although many of the qualitative elements of slave family life remain unknown, in large part because of the general absence of slave narratives or testimonies.[11] In general, these studies, and the

---

[11]   For two of the earliest studies, see Donald Ramos, "Marriage and the Family in Colonial Vila Rica," *Hispanic American Historical Review*, Vol. 55, No. 2 (1975), pp. 200–25, and Richard Graham, "Slave Families of a Rural Estate in Colonial Brazil," *Journal of Social History*, Vol. 9 (1976), pp. 382–402. See the detailed quantitative studies on São Paulo: José Flávio Motta, *Corpos Escravos, Vontades Livres: Posse de Cativos e Família escrava em Bananal (1801– 1829)*; Robert W. Slenes, *Na Senzala Uma Flor: Esperanças e Recordações na Formação da Família Escrava, Brasil Sudeste, Século XIX*; and Francisco Vidal Luna, "Casamento de Escravos em São Paulo: 1776, 1804, 1829," in Sérgio Odilon Nadalin et al., editors, *História e População: Estudos Sobre a América Latina* (São Paulo: Fundação Sistema Estatual de Análise de Dados, 1990), pp. 226–37. Also see Alida Metcalf, "Searching for the Slave Family in Colonial Brazil," *Journal of Family History*, Vol. 16, No. 3 (1991), pp. 283–97, and Katia de Queirós Mattoso "Slave, Free and Freed Family Structures in Nineteenth Century Salvador, Bahia," *Luso-Brazilian Review*, Vol. 25 (1988), pp. 69–84. For Bahia, see Stuart B. Schwartz, "The Slave Family and the Limitations of Slavery," in his, *Sugar Plantations in the Formation of Brazilian*

documentation on which they have been based, reveal slave marriage and family connections to have been pervasive in all regions of Brazil. Africans seem to have married in formal ceremonies more frequently as a percentage of their overall numbers than Brazilian-born slaves, and perhaps this reflected priorities placed on legally sanctioned family bonds within the different African ethnic groups. This finding alone is in sharp contrast with an earlier literature that saw African cultural forms as having been destroyed by the enslavement process and trans-atlantic crossing. Postmortem documentation on slaves makes reference to extensive family linkages by labeling slaves as parents, grandparents, sons, daughters, husbands, wives, cousins, and even godparents. That these designations are systematically found in all regions of Brazil, and in all time periods, indicates that these family connections were critical to slaves and that they were widely recognized not only by slave owners, but also by secular authorities recording these notations.

After 1850 and the effective closing of the transatlantic slave trade to Brazil, a significant internal transfer of slaves from the northern regions to southern Brazil took place, largely to the Rio de Janeiro and São Paulo coffee districts. The greatest volume of this internal slave trade took place during the 1870s and 1880s, when the coffee economy of São Paulo expanded rapidly. In some ways this transfer of slaves from north to south is comparable to the east-to-west internal movement of slaves in the United States, although the latter process was initiated earlier in the nineteenth century. A fundamental question is whether the impact on slave families in Brazil paralleled the U.S. experience.

Previously it was indicated that a significant percentage of slaves forced westward in the United States were sold off by masters, resulting in the breakup of families. Yet in the U.S. interregional slave trade perhaps half or more of all slaves were moved because their owners relocated toward the west-ward-moving frontier in search of new opportunities. In the Brazilian case there is almost no evidence of slave owners relocating from the north to the south of the country. This means that nearly all slaves were sold away from their primary places of residence, and surely this implies that a significant number of slave families from the north of the country were effectively broken up by the

Society Bahia, 1550–1835 (New York: Cambridge University Press, 1985), pp. 379–412. For Rio de Janeiro, see Manolo Florentino and José Roberto Góes, *A Paz das Senzalas: Famílias Escravas e Tráfico Atlântico, Rio de Janeiro, c. 1790–c. 1850* (Rio de Janeiro: Civilização Brasileira, 1997).

interregional traffic.[12] It is unfortunate that there has been almost no scholarly consideration of this important theme.

In the case of Cuba, surprisingly, there has been very little research into the dynamics of slave family life.[13] Because of the heavily urban component of slavery in the eighteenth and early nineteenth centuries, whereby slaves had more flexibility and leeway, it is very likely that nuclear and extended families as well as kinship networks were a fundamental part of the slave experience in much the same way as in Brazil and the United States. Large slave-based plantations developed on a significant scale only during the first half of the nineteenth century, long after slave cultural norms and institutions such as the family had been established and consolidated. The slave family was surely impacted by the large-scale African slave trade to Cuba during the nineteenth century in much the same way as in Brazil. Sex disequilibrium in favor of adult males meant that many newly arrived African males probably had difficulty finding marriageable female slaves. This does not mean, however, that the sex imbalance precluded family formation or that the same kinds of mixed arrangements found in Brazil were not also present in Cuba. It is likely that African male and female slaves married or lived together in consensual unions and that there were cases of African and Cuban-born slaves marrying one another. Additionally, intermarriage with free blacks and mulattos was probably significant, especially in urban areas such as Havana, where both populations had maintained large and continuous communities from the sixteenth century.

Brazilian slave studies have produced precise quantitative profiles of these kinds of unions, formal and informal. There are no such data on Cuban slave families. However, Cuban slave legal codes are the most precise in the Western Hemisphere with respect to protections for slave families. In 1842, Spanish colonial authorities proclaimed a series of laws explicitly designed to regulate a number of aspects of master/slave

[12] For a fairly comprehensive profile of this interregional slave traffic in Brazil, see Robert Wayne Slenes, "The Demography and Economics of Brazilian Slavery: 1850–1888" (Ph.D. dissertation, Stanford University, 1976), Chapter 3, "The Volume and Organization of the Interregional Slave Trade," pp. 120–78.

[13] A recent book, María del Carmen Barcia Zequeira, La Otra Familia (Parientes, Redes y Descendencia de los Esclavos en Cuba) (Havana: Casa de las Américas, 2003), is fundamentally a transcription of historical documents rather than an analytical or even narrative treatment of the theme of the slave family.

relations in Cuba, among them marriage and family life.[14] Stipulations and restrictions were imposed upon slave owners. It was explicitly stated that masters could not impede the formal marriage of their slaves to those of other owners, and that they were obligated to give these married slaves a dwelling place. Additionally, the sale of one married slave could not be undertaken without the sale of the wife or the husband to the same purchaser, who was also obligated to purchase all of the children of the slave couple in order to keep the family together. It is not known how extensively these laws were applied in practice, but there were no such specific legal codes designed to protect the integrity of slave family life in Brazil or the United States.

One great contrast between Cuban slavery and the Brazilian and U.S. institutions is that there was no interregional slave trade of any major significance in Cuba that could have had the same kind of devastating impact on families. There was a transfer of slaves from other economic sectors to sugar plantations during the 1860s and 1870s, but this did not involve the kinds of expansive geographical distances that marked the internal slave trades of both Brazil and the United States, although it is certain that some families were inevitably divided.

Family life was critical to slaves in the creation of space to assert the most basic elements of their humanity. There were multitudes of other ways. Rituals of all kinds were important to slaves everywhere.[15] The celebration of births, weddings, funerals, birthdays, religious holidays, and secular holidays such as New Year's were as important to slave populations as to free men and women. Slaves insisted upon organizing and participating in these and other collective celebrations where they wore their best clothes, prepared elaborate meals, played festive music, danced, drank, and carried on like all human beings at celebratory events. More often than not, these kinds of gatherings were sanctioned and permitted by masters, although once again the

---

[14]   See "El Bando de Gobernación y Policia del Gerneal Valdés. El Reglamento de Esclavos. Su Analisis," in Fernando Ortíz, *Los Negros Esclavos* (Havana: Editorial de Ciencias Sociales, 1987), pp. 339–43. This is available in English in Robert L. Paquette, *Sugar Is Made with Blood: The Conspiracy of La Escalera and the Conflict between Empires over Slavery in Cuba* (Middletown, CT: Wesleyan University Press, 1988), pp. 267–72, reprinted in Stanley L. Engerman, Seymour Drescher, and Robert L. Paquette, editors, *Slavery* (New York: Oxford University Press, 2001), pp. 134–7.

[15]   See Leslie Howard Owens, *This Species of Property: Slave Life and Culture in the Old South* (New York: Oxford University Press, 1976).

not-so-subtle aspects of power relations between slave owners and slaves were manifest. As long as work was accomplished expediently and tasks were completed, and there were no disruptions to discipline and general harmony, it would have been foolish of masters to cause rancor and discontent by forbidding celebrations. On the other hand, slave populations knew quite well that these important events could be cancelled or forbidden if there were any problems between them and their owners. The relations of power could be stark, and lines of authority were clearly drawn. It was generally better for those on both sides of those lines to avoid confrontation and arrive at implicitly, and sometimes explicitly, negotiated compromises so that the priorities of each could be maintained.

Slaves were usually very religious, and this had many meanings. The influence of African religious beliefs was in all likelihood fairly pervasive among the first generations of slaves imported to the English colonies that became the United States. Yet this was mitigated by the fact that many slaves in seventeenth-century Virginia, the largest of the slave colonies, arrived from the Caribbean rather than directly from Africa. These slaves had been somewhat acculturated into English-inspired Protestant religious systems, initially forced upon them by their owners but later embraced to varying degrees. Those slaves born in the Caribbean and then transported to the United States were less impacted by African religious influence, although there were always manifestations of African religious traditions even among nominally Christian/ Protestant slaves. Such customs as the clapping of hands, call-and-response preaching, and much of the tradition of singing and dancing among slaves during religious ceremonies, weddings, baptisms, and burials, even in the context of slave-embraced Protestantism, are rooted in African religious forms and customs.

Among British colonial and religious authorities debates over the efficacy of baptizing slaves ebbed and flowed until the 1740s. One concern was that baptism was an explicit admission of basic humanity and the right to ultimate freedom and liberty. But a generalized process of religious revival, the "Great Awakening," swept through the English colonies in the mid eighteenth century. This gradually led to the proliferation of evangelical missionaries among the general population and an embracing of the concept among masters that slave baptism was desirable.

From the religious revivalism of the mid eighteenth century on, the importance of Christianity among slaves in the southern United

States is something that has been emphatically noted by scholars studying slave religion.[16] Slaves usually adhered to the same Protestant denominations as their masters, and this almost always meant that they were Baptists or Methodists. Both denominations preached a message that centered on the spiritual aspects of human existence and the importance of inner peace, freedom, and ultimately salvation. The appeal of this message to slaves was widespread. There was also an attractive element of egalitarianism in evangelical Protestantism, since all human beings, slave or free, were seen as equal before the Almighty. Additionally, these Protestant sects focused upon proselytizing and conversion, and for this to occur there was the need for preachers who carried the message of God to their brethren. This opened space for the emergence of slave preachers who could spread the word and help the organized church secure converts among the enslaved population.

In the late eighteenth century it is estimated that about one-quarter of the total members of the Methodist Church were of African descent, slave and free. At times these congregations were integrated, with slave and free blacks and mulattos sitting at the back of the church during services. But as church membership grew among people of color, separate black churches were established, although many had restrictions imposed by authorities or were closely supervised. On large plantations, Sunday was a special day for convening of informal or formal congregations complete with celebration, worshipping, and social interchange. Sometimes slaves came together for religious services, with the approval of their masters, although meetings might also be more furtive or even clandestinely organized. These gatherings offered the opportunity for slaves to interact, sing, pray, and commiserate about the world around them, and they gave a special status to the preachers who emerged among them embodying the word of God.

At times slave interpretations of Christianity could be influenced by African religions, and all kinds of non-Christian rituals, usually grouped under the term "magic," were sometimes manifest. This could mean the use of various remedies for illness – potions, ceremonies, invocations of deities and superstitions – that had their origins in African practices.

---

[16] For a complete survey, see Albert J. Raboteau, *Slave Religion: The "Invisible Institution" in the Antebellum South* (New York: Oxford University Press, 1978).

Yet without the constant arrival of Africans, who brought with them their particular ethnic deities, rituals, and organizational structures, as was the case in Cuba and Brazil, organized African religious forms receded in importance to slaves after the closing of the slave trade in 1808.

Slaves created their own religious institutions parallel to, and sometimes separate from, those of their masters. They insisted on participation in the meetings, ceremonies, and rituals, which they themselves aspired to control as much as possible. For slave owners, to prohibit these important social and religious gatherings among the slave population could produce much unneeded discontent. If slaves accomplished their work tasks expediently, it was pointless to try to interfere in these slave-created forms of social and cultural interaction. At the same time, such gatherings were so important to slaves in their affirmation of bonds to each other and to a conception of God that they created and embraced, that it was better to do what the master wanted, within reason, than threaten participation in these community-affirming religious-oriented activities.

In Cuba and Brazil, where the slave trade was ongoing until the middle of the nineteenth century, the influence of African religions was much more profound than in the United States, since African cultural infusions continued to influence extant slave populations until several decades prior to abolition. Additionally, in these Catholic countries evangelical Protestantism did not exist. Thus, slave religious systems emerged with little resemblance to those found in the United States. African deities continued to be worshipped through the epoch of slavery, often in forms that incorporated Catholic saints, and that legacy remained strong after abolition and even down to the present. Not only were African gods worshipped, often openly, in these nominally Catholic countries, but elites in both nations were forced to recognize the rights of Africans to convene all kinds of social, political, cultural, and religious organizations that represented particular African ethnic groups. The Cuban *cabildos de nación* (African ethnic congregations or associations) were a fixture in Cuban colonial society and a focal point of both slave life and the lives of the free colored population, especially in urban areas. These had thrived in medieval Spain and developed along with *cofradías* (religious brotherhoods, confraternities, or mutual aid societies) in most areas of Spanish and Portuguese colonization. Often these institutions were imported from African cultural centers in Iberia rather than directly from Africa, although many of the ideas and beliefs that guided them were African in origin.[17]

By way of comparison, it also ought to be noted that African-based ethnic organizations such as *cabildos*, *cofradías*, and *irmandades* in Brazil (to be discussed later) were not sanctioned and generally did not exist among United States slaves, especially in the nineteenth century after the closing of the slave trade. Thus, slaves in the United States did not have institutional forms that could have been used to preserve particular African ethnic-based and religious belief systems as was the case in Cuba and Brazil. This made the transmission of these African beliefs to future generations more difficult in the United States.

A distinction should be made between these *cabildos de nación* and the many secret societies prevalent in Cuba that worshipped various African religious cults. *Cabildos* were usually legally sanctioned and recognized by authorities and slave owners, in large part because free men and women of color were the prime organizers and participants. They functioned as sophisticated mutual aid societies that provided a wide range of support to members and their families, and were a critical nongovernmental institution for the support of African-origin Cubans, free and enslaved. They were also "spaces" where free and enslaved peoples of color of various African ethnic groups met and interacted, especially in urban areas.

Secret societies were more sinister in the eyes of elite groups, and usually corresponded to particular ethnic groups that existed within broader cultural parameters. The most famous in Cuba was the Abakuá secret society, although there were many others.[18] Part of Yoruba culture, the Abakuá peoples maintained a separate cultural identity, as did other Yoruba ethnic groups such as the Lucumí, Carabalí, and Ogboni. In many cases these ethnic groups were synthesized over time, with several distinctive groups merging together under one umbrella organization such as the Abakuá. It also ought to be noted that the secret

[17] The terms *nación* in Spanish and *nacão* in Portuguese translate literally into the word "nation." When ascribed to African-origin populations, slave or free, the words are used to indicate different ethnic groups in Africa that Europeans understood as "nations." These ethnic groups, especially first-generation slaves from Africa, did not see themselves as "African." Their concepts of identity revolved around broadly defined cultural groups. Thus, there were many different organizations, such as the Cuban *cabildos de nación*, representing distinct African ethnicities.

[18] The Abakuá society was sometimes called Ñañingo.

societies almost always were exclusively male, and that women were usually prohibited from participation in rites and rituals.

In the contemporary world these ethnic and religious forms of organization are all grouped together under the generic term *santería* which literally means "saint worship." *Santería* is of Yoruba origin, an overarching African culture encompassing many different ethnic and linguistic groups and corresponding roughly to the region of contemporary Nigeria and Benin. Original practitioners of *santería* in Cuba adhered to a set of guidelines called the *regla de ocha*. The term *regla* derives from the Spanish *reglamentos* or rules, and these refer to the *reglamentos* constructed to govern the African-origin *cabildos de nación*. The term *ocha* derives from the word *orisha*, which is an African conceptualization of deity. In Brazil the word is *orixá*, which is pronounced the same way and is used in a similar manner by *candomblé* religious sects.

Although the concept of a creationist god was present in most African religions and within both *santería* and *candomblé*, no monotheistic concepts of an exclusive Almighty were found in non-Islamic African religious beliefs, and there were many *orishas* that had various powers to be invoked in different situations.[19] There are seven principal *orishas*, known as the "seven powers," and they were organized hierarchically, although there were additional minor *orishas* as well. Each of these *orishas* came to be identified with Catholic saints in both Cuba and Brazil, and over time a complex cultural merging took place that blended African and Catholic religious beliefs into a new form of religious ritual practiced by slaves, free blacks and mulattos, and even by sectors of the white population who incorporated these ever-evolving *santería* or *candomblé* beliefs into their religious systems.[20]

[19]   An exception to this is found among those West African slaves who had been influenced by, and often converted to, Islam, which is a monotheistic religious system in much the same way as Catholicism. Islamic influence seems to have been of very marginal importance in the United States slave states and of some importance in Cuba. In Brazil, especially in the northeastern states of Bahia and Pernambuco, Islamic influence was fairly widespread, although *candomblé* was more prevalent.

[20]   Olurun, sometimes known as Olodumare, the "owner of the sky," was conceived of as the god who created the world. Obatalá, one of the sons of Olurun, is the father of all humanity and was feminized as Our Lady of Mercy; Eleggúa, who stands at the crossroads between humanity and the divine, became Saint Anthony; Changó, a warrior or god of thunder and lightning, became a female saint, Saint Barbara; Ogun, the god of iron, war,

These African-derived religious forms and their accompanying organizations, *cabildos* or secret societies, played an important cultural role among urban free black and mulatto populations in Cuba, and to a great extent among slaves there as well. Yet the dimensions of adherence or participation within different geographical, economic, and employment sectors of Cuban slave society in the eighteenth and nineteenth centuries is largely unknown. That these practices were of critical importance to many slaves in carving out their identities is without question, especially in urban areas where they interacted regularly with free peoples of color. However, the exact mechanisms by which they were preserved, and the negotiations that went on between slaves, masters, and secular and Catholic religious authorities so that space could be created for the flourishing of African religious beliefs, *cabildos*, and secret societies are not generally known. These groups in all likelihood conducted an ongoing struggle to survive and flourish, and this involved a constant testing of the limits of what they could and could not do. But clearly they not only managed to maintain an active presence in Cuban society through the eighteenth and nineteenth centuries, they were also critical institutions in the preservation of African cultural forms and in the transmission of these to future generations.

In Brazil, the preservation of African religious beliefs is usually linked to the spread of *candomblé*, a nineteenth-century term bestowed upon multifaceted West African religious forms that were practiced among distinct ethnic groups during the epoch of slavery and after, in free and slave communities alike.[21] There is a clear parallel between the development of *candomblé* in Brazil and *santería* in Cuba as almost all of the deities are similar and the principal origin of both religious systems

and work, became Saint Peter; Oshún, who rules over rivers, lakes, and streams, became the patron saint of Cuba, Our Lady of Charity (*Nuestra Señora de la Caridad*); Yemaya, the goddess of the seas, became Our Lady of Regla; and Oya, the goddess of the winds, became Saint Teresa.

[21] *Candomblé* is a word of *bantu* origin, and it means "ritual drum music." This word was most commonly used during the nineteenth century and after to refer to the complex African-based religious systems described later in this chapter. Prior to the use of the word *candomblé*, these African religions were referred to as *batuque*, which is thought to be another *bantu* word with the same meaning. For some idiosyncratic reason the word *batuque* is used in contemporary Rio Grande do Sul, the southernmost Brazilian state, rather than *candomblé*.

was among Yoruba slaves. However, Brazilian *candomblé* is emphatically not a replication or imitation of Cuban *santería* by any means and developed independently.

In some ways the evolution of *candomblé* religious practices was tied to the formation of *irmandades* or religious brotherhoods within the context of the Catholic Church. The brotherhoods were nominally mutual aid societies, although their functions were multifaceted. For the African-born slave and free populations they functioned much like the Cuban *cabildos de nación*. The *irmandades*, like the *cabildos*, were medieval European institutions and developed in the Americas in the same way as guilds and confraternities. They were dedicated to helping their members and families in times of illness, death, incapacitation, or if some other disaster or emergency befell them. Long before the "discovery" of Brazil in 1500, Lisbon had a large African-origin population that incorporated the European traditions of forming these kinds of collective mutual aid societies, and these organizations were transferred to Brazil.[22]

The *irmandades* were sometimes based upon race and class, and there were often separate organizations for whites, blacks, and mulattos, although within urban contexts this pattern of segregation often broke down. Sometimes, in fact, the brotherhoods were completely integrated, and this reflected an interesting acculturation process whereby even whites became adherents of African religious or semireligious rituals.[23] Additionally, there were often specific brotherhoods for particular African ethnic groups, slave and free.

These organizations were pervasive throughout Brazil.[24] Wherever slavery developed because of the various economic cycles described in the previous chapter, brotherhoods were established quickly by slave populations or incipient free black and mulatto communities.

---

[22] A. C. de C. M. Saunders, *A Social History of Black Slaves and Freedmen in Portugal, 1441–1555* (Cambridge and New York: Cambridge University Press, 1982).

[23] See A. J. R. Russell-Wood, *Slavery and Freedom in Colonial Brazil* (Oxford: Oneworld Press, 2002), Chapter 8, "Collective Behavior: the Brotherhoods," pp. 128–60.

[24] For studies on Minas Gerais, see Julita Scarano, *Devoção e escravidão: a Irmandade de Nossa Senhora do Rosário dos Pretos no distrito Diamantino no século XVIII* (São Paulo: Companhia Editora Nacional, 1976), and Caio César Boschi, *Os Leigos e o Poder (Irmandades Leigas e Política Colonizadora em Minas Gerais)* (São Paulo: Atica, 1986).

That these organizations were founded at the initiative of slaves and free people of color is testimony to the critical importance of their role within these communities as semiautonomous institutions. Their formation also underscores the inability of secular or religious authorities, or of slaveholders themselves, to control every aspect of the lives of slaves. Wherever possibilities were found for independent forms of human activity that created collective bonds, slaves did not hesitate to act in their own self-defined interests. The formation of brotherhoods in Brazil and *cabildos* in Cuba is a prime example of this, and it ought to be noted that these kinds of organizations did not exist in the slaveholding United States.

The Catholic Church often saw the Brazilian brotherhoods in a different way – as organizations through which Christianity could be taught to linguistically diverse African slave populations, and perhaps as institutions through which some measure of social control could be exercised. Thus, from a religious and cultural point of view, the *irmandades* became dual-purpose organizations, although they were probably not intended to function in this way. Slaves and free blacks and mulattos could practice their religious beliefs utilizing their own deities, surreptitiously and sometimes openly. But a nominal façade of Catholicism had to be carefully maintained so that there was a legitimacy bestowed by church and state authorities. In short, the *irmandades* were the perfect place for religious syncretism to be developed. Inevitably, as in Cuba, Yoruba deities became interchangeable with Catholic saints, at least nominally. It is apparent that participation rates in these brotherhoods, especially among African free men and women, were extraordinarily high. A recent study examining postmortem probate records in Bahia between 1790 and 1830 found that about 80 percent of deceased free Africans had been members of *irmandades*.[25]

Another important impact of the brotherhoods over time was gradual acquiescence, if not outright acceptance, on the part of the white population and within the structures of religious and governmental power. It was recognized that Africans, enslaved or free, had their own religious beliefs, deities, and institutions that needed to be respected and sanctioned. Through the establishment of the *irmadades*, Africans were able to carve out a space for themselves in the religious, spiritual, and corporate realm which could not, under any circumstances, be

---

[25] João José Reis, *Death Is a Festival: Funeral Rites and Rebellion in Nineteenth-Century Brazil* (Chapel Hill: University of North Carolina Press, 2003), p. 45.

taken away. In this regard it should be emphatically recognized that religious syncretism is not a one-directional process. Africans may have incorporated Catholic saints into their religious systems, but it is also clear that many practicing Catholics unwittingly, or overtly, came to accept and even embrace African deities, and these eventually became an integral part of Brazilian and Cuban cultures.[26] This does not mean that there were not many slaves who were practicing Catholics or believers in many of the central tenets of Catholicism. The fact that baptism was a common ritual found throughout slave communities in Brazil as well as in Cuba indicates at least a nominal acceptance of Catholic rituals.

The impact of *condomblé*, or blends of African-based religion and Catholicism, on slave populations was widespread. There are three distinctive but related strains of *candomblé* in Brazil, and these reflect the extraordinary diverse African ethnic origins of the Brazilian slave population. The most important is *candomblé ketu*, which is perhaps most similar to the Cuban variant of *santería* as it was developed by Yoruba slaves largely during the nineteenth century in the northeastern Brazil regions of Bahia and Pernambuco.[27]

The second largest *candomblé* group was the *candomblé bantu*. The *bantu* linguistic group is one of West Africa's largest and extends from the Congo basin south through Angola, present-day Namibia, and South Africa and is found in many of the East African nation-states. Thus, it is located considerably south of the center of Yoruba culture. There are many similarities between the deities of the Yoruba and Bantu peoples, although all of the principal gods have different names and in some instances different functions. Yet the concept of

---

[26]   The yearly celebration of pre-Lenten carnival throughout Brazil is rife with subtle and sometimes overt references to African deities. On New Year's Eve, at all of the major beaches in every urban area of Brazil, homage to the goddess Iemanjá, the goddess of the seas, is paid by Brazilians of all races. The fact that the African deities worshipped by the brotherhoods have become an integral part of Brazilian culture, regardless of race, is indicated by the fact that the names of all of the major Yoruba *orixas* and their definitions are found in nearly all Brazilian dictionaries of the Portuguese language. See *Novo Dicionário Aurélio da Língua Portuguesa* (Rio de Janeiro: Editora Nova Fronteira, 1986).

[27]   *Ketu* was one of the major ethnic groups of the Yoruba along with *nagô*, *ijexá*, *egbá*, and others. See Roger Bastide, *As Religiões Africanas no Brasil* (São Paulo: Livraria Pioneira Editora, 1971), vol. 1, p. 67, and his *O Candomblé da Bahia: Rito Nagó* (São Paulo: Companhia das Letras, 2001).

an all-powerful creator god, Zambi in *candomblé bantu*, and many *orixas*, or *inkices* in the *bantu* language variant, are quite similar to *ketu*.

The third major *candomblé* variant was the *candomblé jeje*, whose African origins are closer geographically to the Yoruba. *Jeje* originated among Fon and Ewe ethnic groups of the Dahomey region of Africa, roughly corresponding to the contemporary nation of Benin. The name itself means "stranger" in Yoruba, indicating both proximity and distance from Yoruba culture. Again, as is the case with the *candomblé bantu*, the *jeje* utilized a different vocabulary. Rather than *orixas*, their gods were referred to as *vodum* (*vodun* in Spanish and "voodoo" in English). But the similarities in myth and function of these gods make this variant close enough to the *bantu* and *ketu* variants to consider all three part of an overarching *candomblé* religious system.

Candomblé is often confused with *macumba*, but this is a different set of religious beliefs and more superstitious in nature. *Macumba* developed and was centered specifically in Rio de Janeiro rather than spread all over Brazil. Finally, in Brazil the African-based religion *umbanda* is also sometimes confused with *candomblé* and *macumba*. But *umbanda* was a post-abolition twentieth-century religious movement that blended *espiritismo*, or the worship of spirits, with elements of African religion as well as Christianity and is entirely different from the Yorbua-Bantu-Jeje based *candomblé*.

It is always tempting to suggest some kind of solidarity among those who were enslaved, or who had managed to acquire their freedom in one way or another. But the evidence on the *irmandades*, from Cuban *cabildos de nación*, and indeed from the different *candomblé* sects that were organized around ethnicities suggests fierce conflicts between different ethnic groups that mirrored the kinds of strife found in Africa itself. Additionally, there was often a great gulf between African-born and Brazilian-born free and enslaved blacks and mulattos.[28] Thus, African religious forms such as *candomblé* may have looked rather homogeneous to outsiders – that is, to free whites and the religious and secular authorities. But the internal view was one of extraordinary differentiation and thus very different meanings of *candomblé* and the different brotherhoods to the slave and free participants themselves.

Despite rivalries, differences, and conflicts, in these formal or informal organizations slave populations created their own separate connections with one another and with free blacks and mulattos, as well

[28] See Reis, *Death Is a Festival*, p. 48.

as individual and collective identities that were of critical importance to them as human beings. Free men and women may have seen those who were legally enslaved as an undifferentiated mass, but for themselves as individuals they were able to carve out particular social and cultural realities of which masters, religious, and governmental authorities often had little understanding. If these associations, formal or informal, were nonthreatening, masters generally left them alone. If work was accomplished and discipline maintained, if no threat was posed to security and order, then there was little purpose in causing discontent and unrest through prohibition of collective activities that were religious and sometimes secular in nature. Slaves were very much aware of the limitations upon forming associations of any kind, and cleverly carved out as much space as possible for themselves by adhering to a set of rules that were well known to master and slave alike, but that were unwritten and often unstated.

Like all human beings, slaves sought as much independence and control over their own lives as they could possibly claim. For rural slaves this meant securing rights to pieces of land they could cultivate on their own, and areas within farms and plantations where they could raise chickens, goats, pigs, and cattle for themselves. Slaves even were sometimes permitted to hunt wild game to supplement their diets. This offered advantages to slaveholders and slaves alike. If slaves produced a significant portion of their own food supplies, then expenditures of capital by slave owners to feed them could be reduced or eliminated. Some historians have even referred to the emergence of a proto-peasantry among the Brazilian slave population, a broad-based class of smallholders who were (paradoxically) legally enslaved.[29] For slaves, access to what were called "provision grounds" in the United States and the British Caribbean, *conucos* in Cuba, and *roças* in Brazil afforded important possibilities in three different, but related, realms.

First, and most obviously, it permitted slaves a certain level of control over the ability to feed themselves and their families that rested upon their own efforts. Producing some portion or even all of their own food reduced dependence upon masters. After the work day was completed, or on Sundays, slaves took pride in working their own plots or caring for animals that were generally recognized as their own property.

---

[29] See Schwartz, *Slaves, Peasants, and Rebels: Reconsidering Brazilian Slavery*, Chapter 3, "Peasants and Slavery: Feeding Brazil in the Late Colonial Period," pp. 65–102.

Second, and perhaps just as important, the independent production of food or live animals permitted slaves to enter the broader world of local market economies for dietary staples. This opened up opportunities for the acquisition of a variety of consumer goods through barter, or through purchase using the accumulated cash derived from the sale of their independently produced commodities. The acquisition of cash through small-scale trade dramatically increased the options for slaves and was much more commonplace than the traditional view of slaves as completely dependent upon masters suggests.

Third, permitting slaves access to garden plots and the ability to raise their own animals could be utilized by masters as an important manipulative tool of social control. Granting these kinds of privileges to slaves who were cooperative, obedient, and who caused little difficulty could be a much more effective means of maintaining discipline and the smooth functioning of farms and plantations than the threat or actual use of force or punishment. By the same token, the threat of taking away these privileges could keep slaves from being disruptive to their owners in any way.

It is difficult to generalize about the degree of slave access to provision grounds in rural areas, not only because of the enormous diversity in the slave experience in the three countries, but also because rural economic conditions varied both by region within each country and over time as product mixes and land use patterns changed. An important factor determining access to land by rural slaves was the size of the enterprise on which they lived and labored. Most slave owners in all three nations owned relatively few slaves. Over half of the slaveholding class owned five or fewer slaves. Without romanticizing master/slave relations or invoking an older paternalistic interpretation of these, on small rural farms and ranches slaves were often an integral part of small-scale family enterprises. This does not by any means imply that they were part of the master's nuclear or extended family, that their labor was not exploited, or that they were not often cruelly mistreated or even sold away arbitrarily. But on a day-to-day basis their material living conditions were not unlike those of their master's family, especially with respect to diet and access to small areas to cultivate their own food or raise their own animals.

On larger plantations, where gangs of slaves labored in a completely different ambience, conditions varied widely depending upon the principal crop. Some 50 percent of all slaves lived and worked on farms and plantations with twenty or more other slaves in each of the three slaveholding societies. Cotton farming in the U.S. South was so productive and utilized relatively so little land – it has been estimated that only 6 percent of all cultivated acreage was planted in cotton – that providing land for slaves to farm their own provision grounds was rarely problematic, at least in the dominant cotton economy of the nineteenth century. In the sugar economies of Cuba and Brazil there were great variations depending on the size of the plantation, its degree of specialization, and the accessibility of local markets for food to provision slaves. In general, it was counterproductive not to permit slaves access to small plots, not only because of defrayed food costs to masters, but also because providing *conucos* or *roças* was an important positive incentive for slaves to cooperate in the general functioning of the master's enterprise. Yet many highly specialized plantations were also found, especially in Cuba after the 1850s, in which every bit of arable land was planted in cane for profit maximization, where food was purchased to provision slaves who lived in barracks-like conditions, and where independent land use by slaves was heavily restricted. These plantations, however, were atypical in the experience of most rural slaves, who usually were afforded the ability to engage in independent production to supplement their diets and to provide opportunities to engage in small-scale commerce.

It should also be noted that while slave barracks with rigid controls clearly existed on some large specialized plantations, the reality on most farms, large and small, was that slaves lived in their own modest houses in nuclear or extended families, which were usually clustered together some distance from their owners' residences. This permitted them a measure of privacy and space to tend to their own affairs and conduct their own activities out of sight of and beyond the control of their owners. It also meant that they could leave their estates or farms more or less when they pleased to meet with other slaves or free men and women in public gathering places, even though it was generally illegal to do so without permission. Part of these interactions with the broader population involved marketing the crops they raised or meat and hides derived from the animals they tended or hunted. This description applies to U.S., Cuban, and Brazilian rural slaves, although sweeping generalizations about every slave in all rural areas are not possible.

Yet caution should be exercised. An image of slaves living without restrictions, or with the kinds of freedoms enjoyed by free men and women, should not be evoked. Nevertheless, slavery was a complex system with both rigid controls and built-in flexibilities. Where there were possibilities for slaves to assert themselves and make space for their own independent activities, they took advantage of these without hesitation. There were limitations, to be sure, and slaves knew the rules and who was ultimately in charge. Boundaries that could not be crossed clearly existed, and every slave knew precisely where those were. They cleverly approached them and were smart enough not to push beyond the limits imposed by masters for fear of losing prerogatives, such as access to land, that were by no means guaranteed.

The relative autonomy afforded slaves in rural areas after hours or on weekends, and their ability to and insistence upon carving out a culture and rhythms of life beyond the view of their owners, is important to notice if the complexity of the slave experience is to be appreciated. Often slaves are written about or described in general terms as if they constituted an undifferentiated mass of people who were similar enough because of their legal bondage to make differences among them of minor importance. In fact, within slave quarters and small communities significant and sometimes extraordinary distinctions were made, which may not have been perceived by outsiders and especially by their masters. There was clearly a social structure within slave populations, with positions determined by skill level, linguistic ability, ethnic or national origin, sex, formal religious training – African or Christian – and many other variables that were determined by slave populations themselves.

Creole slaves, those born in the country of servitude, almost always were higher up in these structures than African-born slaves. This was an especially important variable in determining the internal hierarchies of slave populations in Cuba and Brazil because of the ongoing African slave trade. In the United States, a slave's origin, African or native-born, was a factor in a similar way in the eighteenth century, but with the closing of the slave trade in the early nineteenth century and the rapid natural reproductive process that led to explosive slave population growth, most U.S. southern slaves were born in the Americas by the 1830s.

There was great respect for slave elders, especially those who had long-developed skills or an acquired authority based on their religious or intellectual knowledge. Slaves who knew how to read and write and who could better negotiate with the outside world, or who were conduits for news derived from reading newspapers, were also greatly respected and held in esteem. Midwives who brought forth life, and nurses with special knowledge of cures and the use of herbs and other natural medicines, commanded great respect and held high-ranking positions within slave hierarchies. Many other such distinctions were made among slave populations, most of them beyond the knowledge of their masters or the general populace. These were critical parts of a culture of servitude that was created by slaves themselves, yet within the framework of their enslavement.

The importance of these "spaces" to slaves should not be underestimated, for they permitted them carefully, and sometimes surreptitiously, to carve out certain semiautonomous, albeit restricted, aspects of their lives. Through bartering or marketing the commodities they produced, their diets could be diversified and enriched, the clothes and shoes they wore could be ameliorated, and rudimentary consumer goods or tools could be acquired. Near plantations and farms there were always towns, and if not, taverns and small stores were usually found close by where slaves congregated, drank, told stories, socialized, formed bonds and connections with family and friends, and where they could sometimes sell the products they had produced or acquired through barter. Sometimes this behavior was sanctioned by masters, sometimes masters "looked the other way." And even if such activities were specifically forbidden, slaves were generally not locked down and had the ability to steal away to engage in these most normal of human behaviors. There was a fine line that had to be maintained by masters and slaves alike in these situations. In the end, as long as work was completed, orders followed, responsibilities fulfilled, and discipline maintained, there was little point in master interference in these activities. Slaves pushed the boundaries of their servitude whenever possible, to be sure, and this is an area of master/slave relations in which the quest to secure some degree of control over their existences was largely fulfilled by rural slaves.

For slaves employed in the great mining economies of the interior of Brazil, there was even more leeway and flexibility than has previously been imagined by scholars.[30] The mining camps, situated in the harsh rugged mountainous interior of Minas Gerais, or even farther inland in Goiás or Mato Grosso, were by their very nature places where control and discipline by government officials and slave owners was always a question less of absolute power than of constant negotiation. This does

---

[30]   See Kathleen J. Higgins, *"Licentious Liberty" in a Brazilian Gold-Mining Region: Slavery, Gender, and Social Control in Eighteenth-Century Sabará, Minas Gerais* (University Park: Pennsylvania State University Press, 1999).

not mean that discipline was not periodically imposed, or that slaves were not often arbitrarily abused or poorly treated. But the remoteness of the interior, and the difficulty of developing any kind of absolute authority because of the extreme distance from the coastal centers of power, facilitated possibilities for slaves to simply vanish into the vast frontier if terribly mistreated. Through time, a culture of master/slave relations gradually emerged where slaves were often left alone panning rivers and streams for gold or diamonds, and as long as they periodically delivered an agreed-upon satisfactory amount to their owners, they were largely permitted an enormous amount of flexibility in their day-to-day lives. This included the accumulation of their own capital through the appropriation of gold dust or small diamonds, which could easily be hidden, and these resources in turn permitted participation in local market economies and even the possibility of purchasing freedom. This was especially true among slave *faiscadores* (prospectors) who were simply sent out by their masters to work deposits distant from towns or camps. Slaves working on fixed *lavras*, or areas demarcated by government authorities where owners were granted official permission to mine, were supervised more closely and had less leeway in their day-to-day behavior.

Not all slaves, of course, were afforded this kind of flexibility. Labor conditions in mining zones could be extraordinarily harsh, life expectancy limited, and early death commonplace, especially among slaves forced to work in frigid mountain streams during the cold, humid winter months. Many slaves were obligated to work long hours under the constant vigilance of overseers, foreman, or owners themselves. These dreadful conditions notwithstanding, slavery in the mining economy was complex, and the experiences of slave men and women ranged from extraordinary exploitation and abuse at one extreme to a great deal of latitude for human behavior at the other. There was not one slave experience but many, and these were determined by a broad range of difficult-to-measure variables.

There is no question that urban slavery afforded slave populations the most flexible and varied possibilities for carving out prerogatives for themselves. In part this was because of the occupational diversity found among slaves living in cities, since a significantly greater portion of the urban slave population worked in skilled trades and in domestic service. Slaves living in rural areas worked in skilled occupations, to be sure – as carpenters, iron smiths, drivers, mechanics, domestic servants, and in many more trades. But most slaves living in rural areas worked in agriculture. Working conditions for skilled slaves were very different in cities, because most labored in small workshops and because their value was so great to masters that often they worked in semiautonomous situations. Others labored on public works maintaining streets, collecting garbage, or cleaning public facilities. There was always the presence of slaves working as stevedores loading ships in ports, and in some cases, such as in Havana, slaves dominated the dock-working profession. As long as work obligations were met, these slaves had a great deal of leeway in their activities; especially important was the ability to earn small amounts of cash through moonlighting or taking on tasks for small fees after hours. This was, in some ways, analogous to rural slaves marketing some of the commodities produced on provision grounds.

In Cuban and Brazilian cities, which had long and extensive traditions of urban slavery, a major share of city commerce was conducted by slave populations in the employ of their masters. In Havana, Santiago de Cuba, Rio de Janeiro, Salvador, Recife, São Paulo, Ouro Preto, and other cities and towns, much of the open-air food and retail market activity was dominated by female slaves. In the United States, New Orleans, Mobile, Savananah, Charleston, Richmond, Baltimore, Louisville, and St. Louis were cities with similar dynamics in the earlier part of the nineteenth century. Traveling sales people – that is, women and men who sold merchandise from carts moving through the city streets or from house to house – were more commonly slaves than not.

Slaves involved in these retail trade activities had an enormous amount of flexibility in how they conducted their businesses, and there was always room for a little extra padding of prices, or pilfering of profits, as long as their owners were provided what they expected each day or week for the merchandise being sold or consigned. There are even examples of masters dividing profits with their slaves as an incentive for efficient service, or even paying them nominal salaries for their labor by the day, week, or month. The point to be made is that slaves involved in the retail trade in urban commercial systems, largely women, actively sought every possible advantage and potential to personally benefit from their activities. Some were successful to varying degrees, while others were not, as in all realms of human behavior.

One of the most common practices found in Cuban and Brazilian cities was the hiring out of slaves by their masters. Although there are no reliable quantitative profiles available that permit a calculation of how many or what percentage of the slave population was rented, contemporary accounts and historical studies suggest this practice was carried out on a very significant scale. Although this was less common in the United States, the practice of renting out slaves in the major southern cities was important as well. Slaves who were rented out were usually highly skilled and often received compensation in the way of cash or a small salary for their labor. Skilled slaves knew their value, both to owners and to those hiring them, and also were aware of exactly how to extract as much advantage and benefit as possible in return for their services. This of course does not imply that all slaves who were hired out were skilled, or that they were always able to extract cash from their employers. But the practice was widespread enough to provide yet another important avenue for participation in market activities by urban slaves.

It is conspicuous that in all three slave societies female slaves were always more numerous than male slaves in urban areas. In part this may have been the result of strong occupational demands for domestic servants – cooks, maids, ironers, washers, wet nurses, and nannies. Additionally, there were greater demands for male slaves in agriculture. Whatever the particular reasons in any region or local economic system, the impact of slave women on urban slave society, because they were demographically dominant among the slave population, was much more profound than in rural areas.

It is likely that slave women in cities had greater opportunities for access to cash and to the broader world of the marketplace than their contemporaries in the countryside. Their prominent role in urban commerce has already been noted, and there was nothing of comparable dimensions in rural areas. It was also common to find slave women working in urban bordellos or as freelance prostitutes, sometimes for their masters, oftentimes after hours as independent sex workers. This was another mechanism to gain access to cash and participation in market activities that helped increase the material possibilities for urban slave populations. All of these factors taken together help explain the generally recognized fact that urban slaves lived in conditions that were much better materially than those of their rural counterparts.

The greater degree of fluidity and flexibility in urban environments was also made possible by the fact the cities were places with fairly large and diverse free black and mulatto populations. In Havana, Santiago, Rio de Janeiro, Salvador, São Paulo, and many other smaller Cuban and Brazilian cities and towns – people of color, slave and free, were a majority or near-majority of the population. This was in great contrast with U.S. cities, although in Charleston, South Carolina, the majority of the population was of African origin in the 1820s. In most other southern U.S. cities whites were demographically dominant. In the Brazilian and Cuban urban contexts, this meant not only that there were constant interactions between slaves and the free population of color, but also that whites could never be certain who was enslaved and who was not. This permitted an extraordinary degree of spatial mobility among slaves in urban areas as they could "blend in" with the free colored population and not be automatically targeted or identified as slaves. By way of contrast, in southern United States cities there was a free black and mulatto population, to be sure, but the general assumption was usually that if a person was of African origin, he or she was a slave and thus the object of vigilance and subject to being stopped, searched, and asked for identification and an explanation as to why they were on their own.

Access to cash increased the options for slaves with respect to their participation in market activities and offered the possibility of a better standard of living compared to slaves who had limited possibilities of acquiring money or participating in local or regional barter economies. But these aspects were dwarfed by one of the major motivating factors for securing cash – the possibility of purchasing one's freedom or freedom for children or other family members. Of the three slave societies, the institution of gradual selfpurchase, or *coartación* in Spanish, was most developed in Cuba, where it had been established by custom from the earliest period of colonization and importation of African slaves in the sixteenth century. This custom and judicial practice derived from a medieval tradition in Spain during the middle of the thirteenth century in a highly developed legal code based on Roman law known as the *Siete Partidas*. The term *coartado* was specifically used for slaves in Spanish legal codes from 1712 on and was written into the Cuban slave laws of 1842, which guaranteed slaves the right to initiate and consummate the purchase of their freedom.[31]

---

[31]   For the text, see *Las siete partidas del rey Alfonso el sabio, cotejadas con various codices antiguos, por la Real Academia de la Historia*, 3 vols. (Madrid: Imprenta Real, 1807). See Ortíz, *Los Negros Esclavos*, pp. 283–90, and Paquette, *Sugar Is Made with Blood*, pp. 267–72, for the 1842 Cuban slave code. For a discussion of this, see Alejandro de la Fuente, "Slave Law and Claims-Making in Cuba: The Tannenbaum Debate Revisted," *Law and History Review*, Vol. 22, No. 2 (Summer 2004), pp. 340–69.

These laws, which ratified what was custom and practice, specifically permitted slaves to own property, to accumulate and possess cash, and to legally initiate the process of purchasing their freedom by placing a down payment on ultimate liberty and making piecemeal payments at a price agreed upon with their owners. Freedom could be purchased outright if the individual slave had enough capital, but the periodic payment method was the most common mechanism for slaves to become *coartados*. In Cuba, once a slave had made a down payment on his or her freedom, their legal status changed from slave to *coartado*. This meant several, perhaps astonishing, things. First, the final price of freedom was frozen and could not be arbitrarily altered by masters. Second, the *coartado* acquired a series of rights and privileges guaranteed by law that were not available to slaves. Although still under the legal jurisdiction of their owners, *coartados* could not be sold to another master without their express permission, and if this occurred their *coartado* status and contract had to be honored at the stipulated final price for freedom. Additionally, if a *coartado* was rented out, he or she had the right to revenues earned equal to the percentage that had been paid on his or her freedom. For example, if a slave had paid 50 percent of the final price of freedom, he or she had the right to 50 percent of the income derived from being rented out by the owner.

The institution of slave self-purchase was nearly nonexistent in the British, French, and Dutch colonial possessions, whose legal codes were not based upon Roman law as was the case in Spain's colonies. When the United States became independent in the 1780s, no such institution of self-purchase was written into U.S. law or slave codes, and although there may have been many cases of slaves able to acquire their freedom in this manner, this was not a generalized practice or custom. Historians of Brazilian slavery have noted that self-purchase existed, particularly in urban areas, but the institution does not seem to have been as prevalent, widespread, or to have had the same parameters as was the case in eighteenth- and nineteenth-century Cuban slave society. It was more common for slaves to somehow accumulate the capital needed to buy their freedom outright and at that moment to be granted a *carta de alforria* or letter of freedom, as opposed to self-purchase by making periodic payments.[32]

---

[32] The document in Spanish America was the *carta de libertad*. See Russell-Wood, *Slavery and Freedom in Colonial Brazil*, "Paths to Freedom," pp. 27–49, for a discussion of strategies to acquire cash and freedom.

Additionally, there were no formal legal guarantees provided in Brazil for slave self-purchase until 1871. Archival documentary evidence on the role played by slave self-purchase in Brazil is not as systematic or extensive as it is the historical record for Cuban slaves, and less is known about how this institution functioned in practice. For example, it is uncertain whether the price of final freedom was frozen in Brazil the moment self-purchase was initiated, or whether *quartados* (the Portuguese equivalent of *coartados*) had legal rights and privileges different from those of slaves. It also is generally unknown whether slaves, had the right to initiate the process of self purchase in Brazil, as was clearly the case among Cuban slaves. The historical evidence suggests that slaves in Brazil could become *quartados*, but that the process had to be granted at the initiative and prerogative of slave owners, a significantly different situation than that afforded Cuban slaves, who had this privilege as a customary and legal right. In many cases Brazilian *quartados* acquired this designation in the last wills and testaments of their owners, who stipulated that a particular slave or slaves should be freed after an additional period of time in bondage, and after designated yearly payments were forthcoming.[33]

Two critical questions may be posed about *coartados* in Cuba, where the institution was widespread, and in Brazil, where it was apparently less integral to the slave experience. First, what percentage of the slave population was actually able to begin the process of self-purchase and become *coartados*? Second, how many *coartados* were able to complete the process of self-purchase and become free men and women? It is unfortunate that historians do not have answers to these questions, largely because of the lack of documentary evidence discovered to date in Cuban or Brazilian historical archives. It is likely that scholars will never be able to determine this with precision. A detailed study of the Cuban slave market, however, is suggestive. In an examination of over 23,000 slave sales between 1790 and 1880, it was found that about 13 percent of the total were in fact *coartados*. It is unknown whether this means that roughly this percentage of the Cuban slave population had at least been able to initiate the process of self-purchase. The evidence suggests that the process was important to some slaves, and that it may have held out hope to others. It is clear, however, that the vast majority of slaves were not able to begin the process of

[33]   See the discussion of this in Bergad et al., *The Cuban Slave Market, 1790–1880*, pp. 134–6.

purchasing their freedom in Cuba or Brazil, despite the existence of this important institution.

There is another extraordinary aspect of the *coartado* population found in Cuba between 1790 and 1880. Of over 3,400 *coartados* noted in historical documentation, 68 percent were female. In all likelihood this reflected the fact that female slaves, especially those working in urban areas, had greater access to cash than male slaves and thus relatively better opportunities to begin the process of self-purchase. Also, there was not any built-in bias against slaves born in Africa as opposed to Cuban-born slaves. The sample found that 51 percent of the Cuban *coartado* population was born in Africa, while the other 49 percent were Cuban-born slaves. There were relatively few children or older slaves who had become *coartados*, as 84 percent of the total were working-age slaves between fifteen and forty years of age. This suggests that few parents felt compelled to begin the process of purchasing freedom for their children. These data are all suggestive rather than conclusive, and it is impossible to determine whether the profile of Brazilian *quartados* was similar.[34]

Slaves could also acquire their freedmen through voluntary manumission by masters. This also took place on a limited scale in Brazil and Cuba, and less often in the slave states of the United States during the nineteenth century, where manumitting slaves was often illegal. There have been a number of important empirical studies that have produced fairly precise demographic profiles of slaves who were freed through manumission. The most striking feature of these grants of freedom is that slave women were manumitted more frequently than men. In nearly every Brazilian and Cuban case study of manumission, female slaves made up at least 60 percent of those who were granted freedom. Additionally, adult slaves over fifteen years of age comprised the great majority of slaves who were freed, usually somewhere between 70 and 80 percent of totals. However, unlike in the case of Cuban *coartados*, Creole slaves tended to be voluntarily freed by their masters more frequently than African-born slaves – about 60 percent of all cases in Cuba and Brazil. The data also suggest that urban slaves tended to be freed by their masters more frequently than rural slaves. What is generally unknown is the percentage of the total slave population who were granted freedom by their masters during any given period of time.

---

[34]   These data are derived from Bergad et al., *The Cuban Slave Market, 1790–1880*, pp. 122–5.

The preponderance of women in voluntary manumissions by masters in Cuba and Brazil was in all likelihood tied to several interrelated factors. First, urban slaves were manumitted more frequently than rural slaves, and as indicated previously, female slaves were a significant majority of urban slaves. Second, slave women who labored in household occupations in both rural and urban areas – cooks, washers, wet nurses, laundresses – tended to have a greater degree of personal contact with their owners, male and female, than nonhousehold slaves. This does not suggest that they were integrated into their owners' family structures, but personal relationships were inevitably formed in many cases. This often translated into grants of freedom being made in the last wills and testaments of masters. Third, the nature of these relationships often went beyond the casual. Slave women sometimes became the concubines or mistresses of their masters, overtly or surreptitiously, and many even bore their masters' children. These "favored" slave women, and sometimes their children, were often granted freedom upon the death of their owners. Fourth, urban slave women often worked in occupations that generated enough cash that they could compensate their masters for their value, who in turn freed them. This was analogous to self-purchase, although in many instances the grant of freedom did not stipulate that this was the case.[35]

In so many areas of their existence, slaves in Cuba, Brazil, and the United States struggled continuously to carve out space to assert their basic humanity. Yet they did so within the context of the worst form of human oppression, and in the end they had no ultimate power to determine their own destinies, even in the most favorable contexts. While some slaves were able to accommodate their lives to perpetual

---

[35] For Brazilian studies on manumission patterns, see Stuart B. Schwartz, "The Manumission of Slaves in Colonial Brazil: Bahia, 1684–1745," *Hispanic American Historical Review*, Vol. 54, No. 4, (1974) pp. 603–35; Mieko Nishida, "Manumission and Ethnicity in Urban Slavery: Salvador, Brazil 1808–1888," *Hispanic American Historical Review*, Vol. 73, No. 3, (1993), pp. 361–91; James Patrick Kiernan, "The Manumission of Slaves in Colonial Brazil, Paraty, 1789–1822" (Ph.D. thesis, New York University, 1976); Hebe Maria Mattos, *Das Cores do Silêncio: Os Significados da Liberdade no Sudeste Escravista, Brasil, Eéc. XIX* (Rio de Janeiro: Editora Nova Fronteira, 1998); and Higgins, *"Licentious Liberty" in a Brazilian Gold-Mining Region: Slavery, Gender, and Social Control in Eighteenth-Century Sabará, Minas Gerais*, pp. 145–74. An important study of manumission in Cuba is Bergad et al., *The Cuban Slave Market, 1790–1880*, pp. 137–42.

servitude and make the best of dreadful situations, others just could not tolerate the degradation and continual abuse of slavery. Most slaves never lost sight of and hope for freedom. Others actively sought it for themselves, their families, and their fellow slaves through conspiracy, generalized resistance, running away, and, most extremely, through violent rebellion.

CHAPTER SEVEN

Resistance and Rebellions

The ability of slaves to carve out prerogatives for themselves, while a real and important aspect of the slave experience, ought not to be exaggerated. Despite the fact that space sometimes existed for negotiating some of the terms of servitude, the power of masters could be arbitrary, capricious, and ultimately abusive and degrading. Slaves were sometimes punished for imagined offenses and could suffer terrible consequences for indiscretions perceived or real. They could be whipped, manacled, confined in horrifying physical conditions, and deprived of contact with loved ones. Wives, daughters, mothers, lovers could be sexually abused by masters or their sons, and there was little recourse for slaves to act or protest without risking the worst consequences. In the end, slaves had little power over the most basic elements of their lives and were subject to the absolute and total control of their owners and the governmental powers that stood behind the slaveholding class. Desperation at the inability to determine the most basic aspects of existence often led to varied forms of resistance to servitude and sometimes spontaneous or organized rebellions and conspiracies to achieve freedom.

Resistance was ongoing and fundamental to the slave experience in Brazil, Cuba, and the United States. The most common form was simply to run away – individually, with family members, or with co-conspirators. This was a common occurrence, although men were overwhelmingly the great majority of slaves who ran away.[1] Newspapers

---

[1] See the full-length study of runaways in the United States by John Hope Franklin and Loren Schweninger, *Runaway Slaves: Rebels on Plantations* (New York: Oxford University Press, 1999). In most states studied, well over

in slaveholding regions of the United States, Cuba, and Brazil were filled with advertisements in nearly every issue that offered rewards for the capture of slaves who had fled.[2] Running away was sometimes well planned but often a spontaneous reaction to systematic abuse. The destination was usually a remote frontier area where it was rumored or known that other slaves had successfully established maroon communities far from the reach of authorities. In these often well-organized communities, runaways were sometimes able to produce their own food supplies and organize elaborate armed defenses against potential attacks by government authorities or mercenary armies recruited by slave-holders seeking the return of their property.[3] Runaways had a greater possibility of success if they were able to make it to these havens. Often slaves fled to cities where there were free black and mulatto communities into which they could potentially "disappear." In the United States, the lure was always the free states of the North, especially to slaves who lived close to them.

This gave rise to the professional slave bounty hunter who pursued runaways, often traveling in groups with bloodhounds, horses, and a large array of weapons. Spontaneous flight usually ended in recapture rather quickly, and the ensuing punishment could be devastating, acting as an effective deterrent to future attempts at escape. The whip was used liberally, and flogging was often a sadistic public ceremony to "set an example" to other slaves. Binding slaves in manacles, in wooden stocks, clamping irons tightly around ankles for extended periods, imprisonment in sweltering boxes without ventilation or adequate food or water, and sometimes even the arbitrary severing of limbs were some of the horrific punishments meted out for seeking freedom.

80 percent of all runaways were males (see pp. 211–2). For an earlier study of Virginia, see Gerald W. Mullin, *Flight and Rebellion: Slave Resistance in Eighteenth-Century Virginia* (New York: Oxford University Press, 1972).

[2] See Daniel E. Meanders, editor, *Advertisements for Runaway Slaves in Virginia, 1801–1820* (New York: Garland Publishing, 1997); and for Brazil, "Newspaper Advertisements Offer Rewards for the Return of Runaways," in Robert Edgar Conrad, *Children of God's Fire: A Documentary History of Black Slavery in Brazil* (Princeton, NJ: Princeton University Press, 1983), pp. 362–6. Also see Lathan A. Windley, editor, *Runaway Slave Advertisements: A Documentary History from the 1730s to 1790* (Westport, CT: Greenwood Press, 1983).

[3] In Cuba the slave bounty hunter was known as the *rancheador*, while in Brazil he was called the *capitão do mato* or *capitão do campo*. Maroon communities were known as *palenques* in Cuba and elsewhere in Spanish America, and as *mocambos* or *quilombos* in Brazil.

Slaves ran away continually, to be sure, and many more sought to escape slavery in this manner rather than participate in rebellion. But of the millions of slaves found throughout the centuries over the long history of slavery in the three countries considered, only a small portion ever attempted to flee, and a smaller number were successful at acquiring freedom in this way. Flight was a valiant, perhaps heroic, form of resistance. But the realities should not be exaggerated. Although they may have admired and even hoped to emulate their fellow men and women who did so, most slaves did not run away, nor did they participate in rebellions, for the possibilities of success were extremely remote and the consequences of failure were traumatic and destructive to individuals and families.

The most graphic form of resistance was to rise up against masters in violent rebellion. This happened time and again in an organized fashion through elaborate conspiracies, or as spontaneous reactions to repeated abuse. Conspiracies to rebel were often discovered before slaves were able to put into practice detailed plans, and in these cases severe repression followed and many slaves were executed, flogged, jailed, shackled for extended periods, tortured in other dreadful ways, or punished by having family members sold away never to be seen again. The decision to rebel or participate in a conspiracy was not an easy one because of the awful consequences that failure meant; the graphic forms of retribution by masters were well known to all slaves. In reality, although there were repeated conspiracies and rebellions, most slaves through the long history of slavery in the Americas did not participate in these and found other ways to resist oppression and carve out space for themselves and their families within the slave system.

Slave rebellions in Cuba date from the very early sixteenth century and continued in nearly every region of the island where slave concentrations were found through the seventeenth and eighteenth centuries. Most of these insurrections were small-scale, spontaneous, and doomed to failure. Sparked by abuse or desperation, small groups of slaves rose up and sometimes killed their masters, set fire to fields, destroyed equipment, and fled to the immediately surrounding countryside, where they were usually discovered by local authorities fairly quickly. If murder was involved, those found responsible were inevitably executed, although if damage to property occurred without loss of life, it was rare that a slave would be put to death. Punishment, however, was usually drastic and extreme. Such punishments as whipping, incarceration, and chaining and shackling were brutal public ceremonies, in the hope that this would act as a deterrent to other slaves contemplating similar actions.

Small *palenques* (maroon communities) could exist for some time, but they had difficulty establishing food-producing infrastructures to sustain themselves and were inevitably forced to raid nearby farms or plantations for provisions. This was usually a fatal mistake, for authorities were thereby alerted to their presence, and campaigns were organized to destroy the communities and recapture runaways. Without adequate self-defense capabilities, these smaller communities inevitably succumbed. It was possible for small groups of runaways to forage for food in remote mountain areas, but survival over the long haul was exceedingly difficult. The fact the *rancheadores* were paid lucrative bounties for capturing runaways also lead to a constant state of pursuit. If small groups of runaways were to hold out for any substantial period of time, they had to be well hidden and have little contact with the outside world.

Although spontaneous rebellions and flight were common, it must be underlined that Cuban slavery was heavily urban prior to the eighteenth century and that large-scale imports from Africa did not begin in earnest until late in the eighteenth century. It is not surprising that when large slave contingents arrived from West African ports with men and women who had once lived in freedom, incidences of conspiracy, rebellion, and repression increased significantly. These were inevitably tied to the epoch of revolution and its aftermath during the late eighteenth and early nineteenth centuries. The effects of the revolutions for freedom and liberty in the United States that exploded in 1775, and the French Revolution of 1789, were extraordinary throughout the Caribbean and directly lead to the large-scale slave uprising in the French colony of St. Domingue in 1791. This revolt, known as the Haitian Revolution, was the only successful slave rebellion in the history of the Americas. It resulted in the establishment of the independent nation of Haiti and provided a model and example for slaves throughout the Caribbean and the rest of the Americas. It also was a graphic indicator to the slaveholding class of the dangers they confronted and the need for increased vigilance and security to guarantee their interests and safety.

Thus, the Haitian Revolution acted both as a beacon of liberty to Cuban slaves and as an example to masters of what could happen if discipline and security were not tightened dramatically, especially in light of the large influx of Africans arriving in Cuba during the first quarter of the nineteenth century. Isolated rebellions occurred in sugar districts in western Cuba; flights to the countryside by *cimarrones* (the word used for runaways in Cuba) continued on a steady basis; and notices of small-scale *palenques* were common in the early nineteenth century. However, the vigilance of colonial authorities and the security measures adopted by slave owners precluded the development of any large-scale rebellions or conspiracies until 1812. In that year, the Aponte conspiracy was "discovered" by colonial authorities and a large wave of repression was unleashed upon free people of color and slaves alike, the usual response to perceived threats to the slave system.

The Aponte conspiracy reveals the intersection between free people of color, slaves, the *cabildos de nación*, and revolutionary abolitionism in early nineteenth-century Cuba. José Antonio Aponte was a free man who had served in the free colored militia of Havana.[4] He was the nominal leader of the *Cabildo Shangó Tedum*, a Yoruba *cabildo* with close ties to other *cabildos* representing various African ethnic groups that were powerful and respected in Havana's free black and mulatto communities. The nature of their ties to the slave population is not fully known, but without doubt there were contacts, ongoing connections, and active plotting for a full-blown anti-Spanish rebellion on the order of the revolutions that had exploded from Mexico through most of South America beginning in 1810. The abolition of slavery in a projected independent Cuba was a clear objective.

In fact, this was the template for most of the ambitious conspiracies in Cuba. Germination did not usually take place on plantations or among slaves themselves, although there is no question that rebellious sentiment was widespread, especially where there were large numbers of Africans in rural plantation districts. But most organization and plotting took place among free blacks and mulattos, and this was inevitably within the secret structures of the *cabildos de nación*, often unseen and poorly comprehended by secular and religious authorities. It was common to find slaves, especially urban skilled slaves, as members of these societies, and this provided a bridge to slave populations throughout

---

[4]   The classic account is José Luciano Franco, *La Conspiración de Aponte de 1812* (Havana: Publicaciones del Archivo Nacional, 1963). It is retold in many places, most succinctly by Phillip A. Howard, in *Changing History: Afro-Cuban Cabildos and Societies of Color in the Nineteenth Century* (Baton Rouge: Louisiana State University Press, 1998), pp. 73–9. Also see Matt D. Childs, *The 1812 Aponte Rebellion in Cuba and the Struggle against Atlantic Slavery* (Chapel Hill: University of North Carolina Press, 2006), published after this book was written.

the island. Another important point to note about the large-scale conspiracies such as the Aponte events of 1812, and later the more famous *La Escalera* conspiracy of 1844, is that they were anticolonial nationalist movements in which slaves would play a leading role and would be freed if success were won. Cuban nationhood and slave-initiated abolitionism were thus bound together early in the nineteenth century, and not simply as a byproduct of the Ten Years' War fought between 1868 and 1878.

Aponte himself was not an aloof leader who remotely directed affairs, but was intimately involved in organizing every aspect of the conspiracy. Through his service in the free colored militia, he had a network of friends and associates with access to weaponry. He even had documented contacts with independent Haiti, where support was actively sought. When authorities became alarmed that something was being planned in Havana very early in 1812, Aponte traveled clandestinely through the island to rural areas. He also sent his representatives to plantation districts far from Havana to organize support for the planned uprising, which was postponed several times. The problem with secret conspiracies that involved large numbers of supporters was that they could not remain secret for very long. Indeed, colonial authorities began to arrest potential participants and were able to extract information on the chilling, to them, dimensions of the plot.

After postponing the date of the uprising until early March 1812, Aponte's followers struck. They rose on the Peñas Altas and Trinidad sugar estates near Havana, destroying most of the equipment and setting fires to the fields. However, a planned simultaneous uprising in Havana had been previously discovered, and the conspirators were arrested before they could act. To make matters worse, slaves on plantations near Peñas Altas and Trinidad did not join the revolt, and those who had acted fled in a disorganized way into the countryside in the aftermath of the uprising. These slaves were rounded up in short order by Spanish militias; Aponte and his fellow conspirators who had not fled the island were arrested; and in early April 1812 the major leaders of his and other *cabildos* were publicly hanged.

Despite elaborate planning by dedicated, extraordinarily skilled, and careful revolutionaries, the revolt turned into little more than a spontaneous rebellion by slaves in rural areas who were quickly routed by the authorities. This underscores the incredible difficulty of effectively organizing slave uprisings on a scale that could give them even a remote possibility for anything but ephemeral success. The violence and destruction of rebellion may have provided participants with a sense of controlling their own destinies, if only for a brief period. But slaves who witnessed the aftermath and the barbarous and horrific punishments meted out by authorities were often effectively deterred from participating in such conspiracies in the future. When the dimensions of conspiracies such as the 1812 Aponte uprising were discovered, Cuban colonial authorities and planters put into practice long-term security measures designed to stave off such incidents in the future. In large measure these were successful at precluding major uprisings, although sporadic episodes of slave violence against abusive foreman or plantation owners took place on a periodic basis throughout the island, especially in western Cuba, where the slave population was concentrated.

The large-scale importation of Africans after 1800 and the movement of sugar cane cultivation eastward from Havana toward the plains of Matanzas changed the western Cuban countryside in every possible way.[5] The natural environment was transformed as forest and pasture were colonized by cane and cattle. Along with this ecological change, the demographic composition of the eastward-moving frontier was heavily impacted by the importation of a largely African-born slave population to work on the newly established *ingenios* and their supporting rural endeavors, such as cattle ranches and food-producing farms. In many districts, demographic structures resembled those of eighteenth-century Jamaica and Haiti. Rather than the diversified racial mixture that was typical of Cuba prior to the nineteenth century, where whites, slaves born in Cuba or Africa, and large free black and mulatto populations lived in proximity to one another, rural districts of Matanzas and later Cárdenas and Las Villas further east were in effect "Africanized" because of the slave trade and sugar's colonization. In many districts well over 70 percent of populations were enslaved, and most of these slaves were Africans recently imported to Cuba.

This is the demographic background to the wave of slave rebellions and conspiracies that swept through Matanzas province from the 1820s through the early 1840s and that culminated in a massive wave of

---

[5]   While some 57,000 Africans were estimated to have been imported to Cuba between 1775 and 1800, between 1801 and 1825 about 270,000 slaves were forcibly brought to the island. Nearly 300,000 slaves were imported between 1826 and 1850, and 153,000 between 1851 and 1867, when the Cuban slave trade was ended. See David Eltis, "The Volume and Structure of the Transatlantic Slave Trade: A Reassessment," *William & Mary Quarterly*, 3rd series, Vol. 58, No. 1 (January 2001), p. 46, Table 3.

repression against slaves and free blacks and mulattos launched by the colonial government in 1844, known as the conspiracy of *La Escalera*.[6] There has long been a direct association between the presence of African-born slaves, who had been born in and known freedom, and slave revolts. The fact that slave rebellions in Cuba were centered in rural Matanzas, which was the destination of newly imported Africans, is not coincidental.

In 1825 there was a widespread rebellion in the rural Matanzas district of Guamacaro, where 90 percent of the total population was enslaved, a large number of them Africans. Over twenty farms were ransacked and burned and a number of whites were killed by the rebels, who fled into the surrounding countryside afterward. It is not known whether this was an elaborately planned rebellion or a spontaneous revolt sparked by the dreadful conditions found on recently established plantations. It ended quickly and was followed by extraordinary repression, massive security precautions on the part of planters and the colonial state, and the effective garrisoning of rural Matanzas by Spanish militiamen. The specter of the successful Haitian slave revolt reverberated through Cuba, and elite groups were determined not to permit what they referred to repeatedly as an "*otro Santo Domingo*."[7]

An enforced "peace" was imposed for some time, but in 1835 another slave uprising took place on a large sugar plantation, the Ingenio Carolina, and it spread quickly to surrounding farms. The pattern of the revolt and its aftermath recalls the 1825 rebellion and suggests a spontaneous reaction by slaves to repeated abuse rather than an elaborate conspiracy. Rebel slaves tried to find refuge in the countryside, but they were rounded up by the Spanish militia or *rancheadores*, and tight security measures were imposed throughout the region yet again. These were successful only in the short term.

Then there was the infamous *Amistad* incident of 1839, in which slaves on a ship bound to Puerto Príncipe from Havana staged a successful mutiny and seized control of the vessel. The captain and several crewmen were killed, and there was an unsuccessful attempt to sail the ship to Africa. The prevailing winds took them north, and they were

[6] *Escalera* means "ladder" in Spanish. Slaves who were punished by repeated whippings were often tied to ladders while being whipped.

[7] Haiti, or St. Domingue, was referred to as Santo Domingo in the Spanish-speaking Caribbean.

picked up by U.S. authorities off the Long Island, New York, coast and were tried and exonerated in a Connecticut court.

In 1841 there was a violent incident in Havana during the construction of the home of one of Cuba's wealthiest planters, Domingo Aldama. Slaves, purportedly members of the Lucumí secret society, refused to work because of mistreatment and their unfulfilled demands for some type of monetary compensation. Although not a rebellion in the classic sense, the incident was alarming to Spanish authorities because of its audacity, and a full-scale attack on the unarmed slaves was ordered by nervous officials. Many were killed and wounded.

The largest slave rebellion ever launched in Matanzas, which was now the center of Cuba's slave-based sugar economy, exploded in March 1843. The revolt which seems to have been well planned, spread over a fairly large geographical area in both Matanzas and contiguous Cárdenas. It was centered in rural areas where slaves were vast majorities of populations, of whom large numbers of recently imported Africans made up a substantial portion of the slave population. Some of the largest and most productive mills in the area were burned, and the revolt spread to such an extent that local authorities could not contain it. Military units had to be sent by ship from Havana to aid in the repression of the uprising. The British consul present in Matanzas sent a lengthy report on the rebellion and reported that nearly 1,000 slaves had participated, and that of these, about half had been killed by authorities. Most were hanged after being captured, and those who survived were viciously flogged in public. Remarkably, despite the concerted repression and security measures, eight months later slaves rebelled again on two large sugar estates, but the revolt was contained quickly.[8] Additionally, the legendary slave "bandit" José Dolores roamed the Matanzas countryside with his *cuadrilla* or gang between February 1843 and March 1844, attacking mills and robbing farms of all types. To underscore the limitations of even the most stringent security measures, he was never captured.

All of these events set the stage for the great wave of repression unleashed in 1844 throughout western Cuba, and particularly in Matanzas, known as the conspiracy of *La Escalera*. Three major factors precipitated the massive unleashing of colonial state power against

---

[8]   The slave rebellion of March 1843 is described in a letter of April 18, 1843, by the British consul, Joseph Crawford, found in the Public Record Office, FO 72/ 634, pp. 59 – 60 (London). See Bergad, *Cuban Rural Society*, pp. 240 – 1.

slaves and free blacks and mulattos suspected of plotting an uprising. The first was the recent history of fairly large-scale slave insurrections throughout Matanzas, especially the events of 1843. These were interpreted as warning signs to planters and colonial officials alike that something bigger was being planned, and they may have been correct in their assessment. The repeated invocation of *otro Santo Domingo* struck fear into elite social groups, and there was a resolute determination to strike first to prevent the development of any more conspiracies or insurrections.

Second were the abolitionist activities of the English in Cuba, personified by the British consul in Havana, David Turnbull, who was intent on seeing the British–Spanish treaties of 1817 and 1835 banning the slave trade to Cuba enforced. Turnbull was a member of the British and Foreign Anti-Slavery Society, and there is no question that he was militantly against slavery. The Spanish authorities were certain that, in addition to Turnbull's official charges and public activities, he was actively involved in drawing up conspiratorial plans with other British abolitionists residing on the island. They were suspected of working with free blacks and mulattos as well as slaves to begin a rebellion on the dimensions of the Haitian slave revolt. In fact, there was a substantial community of English diplomats, merchants, and mechanics who serviced modern milling equipment in Cuba, and there was certainly abolitionist sentiment among them. Many of these mechanics resided on the largest sugar estates of Matanzas.[9] Colonial officials were convinced that there had to be a connection between British abolitionist meddling and the repeated incidents of slave rebellions described previously.

Third, Cuba's sugar-producing elite was investing huge sums of capital during the early 1840s in two general and related endeavors. The first was the importation and installation of the most modern and costly new technologies for processing sugar cane into sugar from English and United States manufacturers. Matanzas province was the site of the most technologically sophisticated mills for the production of sugar in the world by the early 1840s. Second, these same elites were

---

[9] Turnbull's activities have been written about in most treatments of early nineteenth-century Cuban history. See Robert L. Paquette, *Sugar Is Made with Blood: The Conspiracy of La Escalera and the Conflict between Empires over Slavery in Cuba* (Middletown, CT: Wesleyan University Press, 1988), Chapter 5, "David Turnbull and the Crusade against Slavery in Cuba," pp. 131–57.

constructing a sophisticated network of railroad lines linking the sugar-producing districts of the interior with the port cities of Havana, Matanzas, Cárdenas, and Cienfuegos on Cuba's southern coast. Additionally, they were beginning to install railroad lines within their estates to move cut cane quickly from field to mill, which would dramatically increase sucrose content and profitability.[10] These massive capital investments were clearly threatened by the graphic instability created by the slave rebellions of the 1830s and early 1840s, as well as by meddling British abolitionists. The entire system of sugar production rested upon the foundation of slave labor, and this meant the need for continued slave imports from Africa as well as the compelling requirement of stability among the slave population if the system was to run smoothly.

The elites had had enough of the instability caused by slave rebellions by the end of 1843. Accordingly, early in 1844 the captain-general of Cuba ordered the Spanish military to investigate the nearly endless rumors of an impending insurrectionary conspiracy linking British abolitionists, slaves, and prominent free blacks and mulattos and to take decisive action. It is unknown whether these rumors were in any way true, simply the product of fear, or a pretense to move against the British abolitionists. Troops were mobilized and began an ongoing campaign of large-scale repression against suspected conspirators in western Cuba lasting for several months. Thousands of free blacks and mulattos were arrested, and those born outside of Cuba were deported along with many British residents, mostly skilled workers laboring on sugar estates. Slaves suspected of plotting rebellion were methodically arrested and tortured, and "confessions" were extracted. Many slaves and free people of color, including the famous mulatto poet Plácido, were executed, although the precise number murdered by the colonial state remains unknown. More were publicly flogged, incarcerated for long periods of time, or punished in other dreadful ways. Whether or not there was a conspiracy remains unknown. But the repression was so thorough, and the security measures established afterward so stringent, that the colonial regime and the great sugar planters achieved their objectives. Until the outbreak of the Ten Years' War in eastern Cuba in 1868, there would be little slave instability other than isolated incidents in the western Cuban sugar

[10] On Cuban railroad building, see Oscar Zanetti and Alejandro García, *Sugar and Railroads: A Cuban History, 1837–1959* (Chapel Hill: University of North Carolina Press, 1998).

districts. Notices of slave rebellions all but disappear from the historical record after *La Escalara* of 1844. The preemptive strike against real or imagined conspirators was a smashing success from the point of view of elite groups. Slaves had to fall back on other methods of resistance and accommodation to try to establish some element of control over their lives, in an environment of relentless repression, harsh security measures, and constant vigilance. The era of Cuban slave revolts was virtually over until slaves began abandoning plantations in small numbers to join the independence forces in eastern Cuba after 1868.

Slave resistance in Brazil was very different from that found in Cuba for one fundamental reason. The vast Brazilian interior offered extra-ordinary opportunities for refuge and the establishment of remote runaway slave communities, *mocambos* or *quilombos*, and these became the principal manifestations of slave rebelliousness.[11] This does not mean that there were not violent rebellions, spontaneous or planned, or conspiracies with elaborate and well thought-out objectives. But compared to the limited possibilities for forming maroon communities with some degree of permanence in Cuba, because of the island's comparatively smaller geographical area and fewer isolated and impenetrable regions, Brazil offered nearly unlimited internal frontier regions so remote that it was often too difficult for authorities to mount successful raids to dismantle them. Thus, the principal form of slave resistance in Brazil revolved around escaping from slavery rather than overthrowing the slave system.

The most famous of all the *mocambos* and perhaps the model upon which historians have based their interpretations of the maroon communities of Brazil was the conglomeration of villages known as Palmares. One account enumerated ten separate population centers, with one, Macaco, functioning as the capital of a federation of smaller *mocambos*. Located in an inhospitable interior region of the captaincy of

---

[11]   Although in contemporary Brazil the word *quilombo* is used to refer to these communities, in fact during the epoch of slavery the more common word was *mocambo*. See the discussion of the meanings of these terms in Stuart B. Schwartz, "Rethinking Palmares: Slave Resistance in Colonial Brazil," in his, *Slaves, Peasants, and Rebels*, pp. 122 – 8. The word *quilombo* is in fact derived from a word utilized by the Mbundo ethnic group, one of many inhabiting what is today Angola. The word was *ki-lombo*, and it referred to a warrior society within Mbundo culture. The word *mocambo* was also a Mbundo word that translates into "hiding place." See R. K. Kent, "Palmares: An African State in Brazil," *Journal of African History*, Vol. 1 (1965), pp. 161 – 75.

Alagoas, northwest of the coastal city of Maceió, Palmares emerged sometime in the early seventeenth century and lasted in one form or another until 1694, when it finally succumbed after a brutal two-year military campaign conducted by a mercenary army in the employ of Portuguese colonial authorities.[12] Through its long history some of the villages were periodically destroyed only to be rebuilt by new slave arrivals or by older residents who had fled the fighting. Originally established by slaves who had abandoned the sugar plantations of Pernambuco, especially during the Dutch occupation of the region between 1630 and 1654, the villages making up Palmares became racially and ethnically diverse over time. African and Brazilian-born slaves, indigenous peoples, mestiços, free blacks and mulattos, and even some whites came to inhabit and interact in this extraordinarily eclectic and ever-changing community. Although some of the more glorified interpretations of Palmares have portrayed it as a re-creation of African political, social, and cultural structures in Brazil, the mocambo was the product of very diverse Brazilian colonial as well as clear African influences. Paradoxically, slavery existed within Palmares. The various communities and villages that made up Palmares engaged in extended periods of war with outsiders, as well as raids on neighboring settlements, and captives taken in battle were subject to enslavement.[13] This was an old custom within Africa, where warring ethnic groups had enslaved one another long before Europeans arrived on African shores, and it was also a medieval European custom to enslave captives taken in war.

[12]   Palmares is mentioned in every work on Brazilian slavery and has been studied by a number of scholars. The oldest work is by Edison Carneiro, O Quilombo dos Palmares (São Paulo: Companhia Editora Nacional, 1958). Also see Délcio Freitas, Palmares: a Guerra dos Escravos (Porto Alegre: Editora Movimento, 1973). The article by R. K. Kent, "Palmares: An African State in Brazil," is informative. It is reprinted in Richard Price, editor, Maroon Societies: Rebel Slave Communities in the Americas (Baltimore: Johns Hopkins University Press, 1979), pp. 170–90. A full-length fictional film about Palmares titled Quilombo (1986) was made by the famous Brazilian filmmaker Carlos Diegues.

[13]   See Pedro Paulo de Abreu Funari, "A Arqueologia de Palmares: Sua Contribuição para o Conhecimento da História da Cultura Afro-americana," in João José Reis and Flávio dos Santos Gomes, editors, Liberdade por um fio: História dos Quilombos no Brasil (São Paulo: Companhia das Letras, 1996), p. 31. This article provides a series of maps and figures that locate the various villages of the mocambo.

At its peak sometime in the middle of the seventeenth century Palmares may have had a population of between 10,000 and 20,000 people, but it impossible to determine the exact number. How many of these were either runaway slaves or their descendants is unknown, but in all likelihood most of the population had its origins in slavery. It is also certain that the area was a magnet for slaves seeking freedom for as long as it survived, and that its existence was well known among the slave populations of nearby regions in Alagoas and, more importantly, among slaves on the sugar plantations of Pernambuco. This is why there were long, generally unsuccessful military campaigns undertaken against the *mocambo* throughout the seventeenth century.

Palmares survived as an agricultural community whose residents cultivated food crops, raised animals, engaged in trade with nearby and sometimes distant regions, and on occasion raided other areas to secure supplies that could not be acquired through commerce. In this sense the *mocambo* was not very different from other subsistence communities found throughout Brazil's vast interior. But because it was always under threat of attack, the dynamics of daily life also revolved around constant vigilance and defensive measures. Not only was there a class of men who trained as professional warriors – a standing army – but the larger villages were fortified in various ways with moats, palisades, lookout towers, and even sharp pikes to ward off potential attacks.

Palmares was unique in that its independent political structure resembled and was clearly based on African administrative models. Reports written by the heads of the many military missions that waged campaigns against Palmares in the mid seventeenth century indicated that the inhabitants of the many *mocambos* swore allegiance to a powerful king, Ganga Zumba (Great Lord), who resided in the royal village of Macacos. Despite its diverse ethnic composition, it is evident that those of African origin, probably from ethnic groups originating in Angola, constituted the political elite of Palmares.[14] Ganga Zumba was an effective administrator and military leader who managed to successfully defend Palmares from repeated incursions. But he was also a shrewd diplomat who maintained lines of communication with Portuguese colonial authorities and negotiated with them at appropriate moments in order to try to secure peace as well as official

[14] Stuart Schwartz points out that Palmares was called *Angola janga*, which means "little Angola," by its residents. See Schwartz, "Slave Resistance in Colonial Brazil," p. 125.

recognition of the community's autonomy. Peace treaties were often actually signed but never adhered to, since ultimately Portuguese authorities refused to recognize the autonomy of any Brazilian region because of the dangerous precedent that doing so would establish.

In the aftermath of a treaty made during the late 1670s, there was a revolt led by Ganga Zumba's nephew Zumbi, who succeeded in killing his uncle and taking control of Palmares. Whether this coup d'etat was the result of a power struggle within the royal family, or stemmed from disagreements about policy, strategies, and tactics for preserving the *mocambo* will never be known. Zumbi would be the last king of Palmares.[15] Some six military expeditions targeted Palmares during the 1680s. They were all beaten back, and the *mocambo* under Zumbi's leadership was able to survive. Perhaps it is coincidental that the discovery of gold in Minas Gerais became known in the early 1690s, at precisely the same time that the authorities in Pernambuco decided to hire *Paulista* mercenaries to mount an attack on Palmares with the objective of destroying the *mocambo* once and for all. These were rugged frontiersmen, many of mixed European/Amerindian lineage, and some were battle-hardened indigenous warriors accustomed to life and war in difficult terrain and circumstances. They marched the extraordinary distance from São Paulo in search of the substantial bounty offered for the destruction of Palmares. It took them two years of nearly constant warfare, and in the end they had to call on some 3,000 regular militiamen from Pernambuco to help in the final assault. By early 1694 they had reduced Palmares to a single village, and when they launched their all-out attack in early February they confronted only the remnants of the once powerful *mocambo*. Hundreds of defenders were massacred, and those captured were transported to the coast to be sold into slavery. Zumbi was taken alive and publicly beheaded in November 1695.[16] Palmares passed into myth and legend.

The large-scale transfer of slavery toward the gold-mining and diamond-producing centers of Minas Gerais in the early eighteenth century was accompanied by every institutional manifestation of slavery present in Bahia and Pernambuco during the seventeenth century.

---

[15] In the more romanticized interpretations Ganga Zumba is viewed as an accomodationist "sell-out," while Zumbi is seen as the embodiment of African revolutionary zeal. There is no evidence whatsoever to support these claims.
[16] See Kent's account in Kent, "Palmares," pp. 186–7.

This included the constant quest for freedom on the part of slaves by running away to remote areas and the formation of small-scale *mocambos* in every district where large slave populations lived and worked. None would ever parallel Palmares in geographical extension, population size, or longevity. But many lasted for extended periods and were difficult, if not impossible, for authorities to dismantle.[17] The danger of permitting "another Palmares" to emerge as a beacon of liberty for slaves was noted over and again by colonial officials in Minas from the very onset of colonization in the early eighteenth century. Large numbers of speculators, wealth-seeking adventurers, and Portuguese bureaucrats made their way to the mining regions from the northeast, usually along the Rio São Francisco, which runs north of Salvador and just to the south of the location where Palmares once stood. Palmares was not simply an abstract memory, especially to Portuguese colonial officials, but a very vivid and real presence.

The extraordinary dimensions of the mineral wealth discovered in the 1690s were quickly understood by government authorities. The ensuing large-scale importation of slaves to the mining districts, a large number of them of African origin, created very real security concerns from the vantage point of officials and entrepreneurial elites. In most mining camps slaves were a majority of the population, sometimes overwhelmingly so. Rumors and fears of slave rebellions permeated the communiqués flowing from the interior mining zones to colonial officials in Salvador during the early eighteenth century, and the formation of another Palmares stood front and center as a principal preoccupation. This was fully justified. From the very onset of the heavily male importation of slaves, marched to Minas along the banks of the São Francisco River, or from São Paulo, slaves ran away continuously and formed small-scale *quilombos* that threatened gold production, tax collection, and the transportation of wealth to the coast, from which it was exported to Lisbon.[18]

These early *quilombos* were always located fairly close to the mining camps in areas where it was difficult or impossible to produce food

[17] For an early full-length study, see Waldemar de Almeida Barbosa, *Negros e Quilombos em Minas Gerais* (Belo Horizonte: Imprensa oficial, 1972). Also see Carlos Magno Guimarães, *Uma Negação da Ordem Escravista: Quilombos em Minas Gerais no Século XVIII* (São Paulo: Ícone, 1988).

[18] Although the word *mocambo* prevailed in seventeenth-century Bahia and Pernambuco, in eighteenth-century Minas Gerais the word *quilombo* was almost always used to refer to runaway slave communities.

because of poor soils and generally inhospitable conditions for short-term agricultural development. To survive, runaways raided established farms or attacked settlements, isolated prospectors, or caravans trans-porting consumer goods, cattle, and sometimes even gold itself. Thus, for elite groups security was a fundamental concern. If Cuban planters and colonial administrators were perennially preoccupied with the fear of "*otro Santo Domingo*" during the nineteenth century, in Brazil the specter of "*outro Palmares*" haunted elites in the same way during the eighteenth century, especially in Minas Gerais during the mining boom. The threat was so grave that the government of the *capitania* created a special, if loosely organized, military unit specifically dedicated to hunting and capturing runaways and destroying *quilombos*. This was called the Regimento dos Capitães do Mato, or the slave hunter's regiment. It has been estimated that about 15 percent of the troops recruited were ex-slaves.[19]

At best, efforts to destroy the Minas *quilombos* may be described as a holding action. The *capitania* was so vast, with so many difficult-to-penetrate remote mountain areas and impenetrable forests, that it was virtually impossible to destroy the dozens of *quilombos* that were formed and sometimes disintegrated for various reasons, only to be recon-stituted over and again during the eighteenth and early nineteenth centuries. Well over one hundred Minas *quilombos* have been identified in historical documents, although most of these were small-scale set-tlements containing a few dozen inhabitants or less. The very largest may have had several hundred people during various periods, for these villages were always in flux, with people coming and going con-tinuously. Many settlements labeled as *quilombos* by authorities were racially mixed, as was the case in the Brazilian northeast, with indi-genous peoples, *mestiços*, legally free blacks and mulattos, runaway slaves, and even whites who had fled the confines and controls of Portuguese-administered centers all residing together. In some ways these were independent communities of peoples who had fled colonial restrictions of one sort or another, whether slave or free, and of African origin or not. Other Minas *quilombos* had clear African-inspired

[19] During the eighteenth century the word *quilombo* began to replace *mocambo* in official historical documentation, and the residents of these were referred to as *quilombolas*. For a description of these, see Carlos Magno Guimarães, "Mineração, Quilombos e Palmares: Minas Gerais no Século XVII," in Reis and Santos Gomes, *Libertade por um Fio*, p. 144.

organizational schemes and were mainly inhabited by runaway slaves, but on a smaller scale than Palmares. This meant kings, princes, royal families, a bureaucracy modeled upon those of various African ethnic groups, and functioning agricultural and cattle-raising economic structures.[20] But there are no examples in Minas Gerais of leaders who attained the stature of Ganga Zumba or Zumbi of Palmares.

Governmental authorities could never dismantle the many *quilombos* of the *capitania* despite repeated efforts. Many were established in such remote regions, and in terrain that made defensive measures so effective, that it was too costly and difficult to destroy them. However, periodic military campaigns precluded the formation of any large-scale communities such as Palmares in Minas Gerais. Essentially, colonial authorities led a war of attrition with the objective of containment, not victory, for they were well aware that it was impossible to dismantle all of the fairly small *quilombos* existing in so many regions of the *capitania*. In some ways these communities became a marginalized part of colonial society and one more cost of empire in Brazil. As long as no direct threats were posed to settled communities and *quilombolas* lived relatively peacefully, it was a waste of resources to mount large-scale military campaigns against them that would fail more often than not. Yet when rumors of imminent slave rebellion swept through the major mining areas, which occurred periodically, even small-scale *quilombos* could be targeted for elimination.[21] If settled communities, mining camps, or *tropeiros* were attacked in any region, there was a fairly quick response to root out those responsible, who were sometimes common bandits roaming the countryside and often *quilombolas* struggling for survival.

Although Pernambuco, Bahia, and Minas Gerais were the principal centers of Brazilian slavery through the mid eighteenth century, slavery spread to every region of the colony where economic activities created labor demands of varied dimensions. The gold rush to Minas in the early eighteenth century led to extensive explorations further west in Goiás and Mato Grosso, and placer deposits of varied sizes were discovered in

[20]   See the essay by Roger Bastide, "The Other Quilombo," in Price, editor, *Maroon Societies*, pp. 191–201.

[21]   See Carla Maria Junho Anastasia, *Vassalos Rebeldes: Violência Coletiva nas Minas na Primeira Metade do Século XVIII* (Belo Horizonte: Editora C/Arte, 1998), pp. 125–36, for a discussion of slave plots and reactions to them. Also see Donald Ramos, "O Quilombo e o Sistema Escravista em Minas Gerais do Século XVIII," in Reis and Santos Gomes, *Liberdade por um Fio*, pp. 164–92.

numerous regions. These resulted in both the enslavement of local indigenous populations and the inevitable importation of African-origin slaves from Brazil's major slave centers farther east. According to a census conducted in Goiás in 1779, between 45 and 80 percent of local populations were categorized as *pretos* (blacks), and in all likelihood the great majority were enslaved.[22]

These vast, sparsely populated regions had served as destinations for small groups of indigenous and African slave runaways from as far away as Bahia during the seventeenth century, and there were small *mocambos* found scattered through areas that were usually remote and impenetrable. *Bandeiras* from São Paulo were sometimes organized to attack and destroy these communities and to apprehend runaways, but these were usually private endeavors looking for the financial gain to be derived from selling captured slaves or collecting rewards for them, as opposed to colonial state-sponsored missions that had security issues as their main concern. This changed with the discovery of gold deposits, the influx of significant numbers of slaves through the eighteenth century, and the development of colonial state power charged with overseeing security, tax collection, and the shipment of valuable minerals from the interior to coastal ports. As the number of slaves increased so did the number of runaways, and this resulted in the growth of established *mocambos* or the formation of new ones. Older communities may have had elaborate agricultural and stock-raising infrastructures to provision them with basic food supplies. But more recently formed *quilombos* relied on banditry and repeatedly attacked settled areas, farms, mining camps, and the mule trains that brought supplies to the distant frontier and left with gold or other minerals for the coast.

These threats, of course, were not something unique to frontier regions such as Goiás and Mato Grosso. Escalating slave imports to any Brazilian region were always accompanied by increased numbers of runaways, the formation of *mocambos*, and threats to security that inevitably led to state-sponsored repression. The colonial state sanctioned *bandeiras*, official *capitães do mato*, and in interior regions such as Goiás and elsewhere indigenous peoples with long warrior traditions, who often considered *quilombos* and slaves in general as

---

[22]   Mary Karasch, "Os Quilombos do Ouro Na Capitania de Goiás," in Reis and Santos Gomes, *Liberdade por um Fio*, p. 242. For Mato Grosso, see Luiza Rios Ricci Volpato, "Quilombos em Mato Grosso: Resistência Negra em área de Frontiera, in Reis and Santos Gomes, *Liberdade por um Fio*, pp. 213 – 39.

their enemies, were mobilized and officially sanctioned by local authorities. All were part of generalized efforts to destroy runaway communities, to capture as many escaped slaves as possible, or at the very minimum to push runaways toward more remote regions and away from centers of economic activity.[23] Yet the complete security of towns, farms, mining camps, and mule convoys was impossible to guarantee, for slaves continued to seek freedom by running away. The imperative of survival in the absence of stable food-producing systems inevitably led to foraging raids on settlements of all types as well as on the *tropeiros* who provisioned the interior and transported gold to the coast. At best, colonial authorities could keep these threats in check, but they could never completely control the ability of slaves to run away and form *mocambos*, nor could they totally guarantee security.

Maranhão, in the Brazilian north, was another focus of economic development and slave population growth in the late eighteenth century. This was largely because of colonial economic policies and the establishment of joint capital companies with Portuguese state backing. In the late 1750s, as gold production waned in the mining areas, the reformist Marquis de Pombal, who in essence ran the Portuguese government, sought to stimulate agricultural diversification and economic development in Brazilian regions that had not previously attracted settlement and investment. The Grão Pará and Maranhão Commercial Company (1755–77) imported some 12,000 slaves who worked on cotton, rice, and sugar *fazendas* in areas along river systems flowing into the bay anchored by the capital, São Luis. These zones of development were fairly close to the littoral. The interior jungles were vast, impenetrable, and beyond the control by the colonial state, and offered all of the conditions for slave runaways to establish small-scale *mocambos*, which were found by the early nineteenth century in numerous regions. These were impossible to suppress completely, as was the case in other Brazilian regions.

Maranhão was wracked with political upheaval and conflict in the 1820s and 1830s as local elites with competing interests sought control

---

[23] See Karasch, "Os Quilombos do Ouro Na Capitania de Goiás," pp. 253–8. João José Reis notes that it was quite common for colonial authorities to make extensive use of indigenous peoples in various regions of Brazil to combat *quilombos*, whom they usually saw as invaders of their semiautonomous territories. He discusses the extensive use of *cariris* peoples in the campaigns against the Oitizeiro *quilombo* in southern Bahia. See João José Reis, "Escravos e Coiteiros no Quilombo do Oitizeiro," pp. 341–3.

of the province in the absence of any strong central government in the aftermath of Brazilian quasi-independence in 1822. *Mocambos* and slave runaways in general were inevitably drawn into the various struggles by elite groups who sought to utilize and manipulate their potential military value, or as objects of repression because they were seen as symbols of instability or because they represented real threats to the established order. This was especially the case during the civil war in Maranhão known as the *Balaiada*, which took place between 1838 and 1841, although the participation of *mocambeiros* on an extensive scale is not certain. *Mocambos* were targets for destruction because they were clearly outside of elite group and government control, although Maranhão was no different in this regard than the rest of country.[24]

Another peripheral area where slavery, runaways, and *mocambos* developed was the southernmost region of the colony, Rio Grande do Sul, although these dynamics occurred much later than in other Brazilian areas, since significant economic and population growth developed only in the late eighteenth and early nineteenth centuries, anchored by a predominantly ranching economy. Yet the dynamics of slave resistance were similar to those found in previously settled regions. The relative proximity of the border with Uruguay and Argentina, where runaway slaves would be considered free men and women, was one motivating factor, although it was not easy to reach the border. More significant were the mountainous regions close to settled areas as well as small islands in the vast lake systems to the south of contemporary Porto Alegre, which offered possibilities for forming small-scale *quilombos*.[25]

The region surrounding Guanabara Bay and the port city of Rio de Janeiro, which was designated as the capital of the colony in 1763, experienced extraordinary economic expansion, slave imports, and the establishment of *mocambos* during the eighteenth and nineteenth centuries. The process of economic growth, the development of slavery, and slave resistance were initially linked to the Minas gold cycle during the first half of the eighteenth century. Rio gradually emerged as the principal entrepôt for the import/export trade, including the African slave trade, because it was located closer to the mining districts than

---

[24] See Matthias Rohrig Assunção, "Quilombos Maranhenses," in Reis and Santos Gomes, *Liberdade por um Fio*, pp. 433–66.

[25] See Mário Maestri, "Pampa Negro: Quilombos no Rio Grande do Sul," in Reis and Santos Gomes, *Liberdade por um Fio*, pp. 291–331.

Salvador, the old capital. Additionally, coastal regions to the west of Rio, such as Angra dos Reis and Paratí, served as major smuggling centers for illegal gold exports. But by the early nineteenth century and the arrival of the Portuguese *corte* in 1808, the capital city itself became a large urban market for foodstuffs and cattle by-products. This stimulated the economic expansion of farms and ranches surrounding the bay that helped provision the city. Additionally, during the first half of the nineteenth century slave-based coffee cultivation grew rapidly in the Paraiba valley region, which divided the province with Minas Gerais. All of these economic activities resulted in extraordinary slave population growth in the city itself and in the province's rural areas. Inevitably, this meant more and more runaways and the development of *mocambos* and their persecution by authorities.

The major region of *mocambo* development was along the Iguaçu and Sarapuí Rivers, which emptied into the northwestern region of the bay. The area itself had a majority slave population from the late eighteenth century, and possessed all of the geographical and ecological preconditions for the establishment of small runaway communities.[26] Remote and impenetrable forests, isolated mangrove swamps, and numerous caves and other hiding places made total destruction of the *quilombos* that took hold there all but impossible. Indeed, the river basins in this region provided refuge for slave runaways from the late eighteenth century through the mid nineteenth century, and they were impossible to eradicate completely. As elsewhere in Brazil, authorities mounted repeated campaigns when attacks on settled communities or *tropeiros* posed major threats to economic activities or public order. Many *quilombos* were periodically destroyed, but others inevitably took their place after campaigns of repression, sometimes in exactly the same geographical locales. The costs of mounting campaigns against small-scale runaway communities were high, and once they were withdrawn it was a major undertaking to organize repressive forces once again. Thus, it was absolutely impossible to eliminate these small-scale runaway communities permanently, and they persisted nearly to the end of Brazilian slavery in the 1880s, even so geographically close to the center of power in Rio de Janeiro.

[26] See Flávio dos Santos Gomes, "Quilombos do Rio de Janeiro no Século XIX," in Reis and Santos Gomes, *Liberdade por um Fio*, pp. 263–90. In the Iguaçu region, about 55 percent of the population was enslaved in the 1780s; nearly 60 percent in 1821; and as late as 1850, over 50 percent were slaves.

Among the many forms of slave resistance it is clear that flight and the formation of *quilombos* were the major strategies utilized by slaves to seize some measure of control over their lives and destinies. Until very late in the eighteenth century it is conspicuous that organized conspiracies geared toward violent rebellion were almost nonexistent in all major Brazilian regions where slavery became an integral part of the economy, culture, and society. There were innumerable instances of spontaneous violence directed at abusive foreman, government officials, and even masters on occasion. But there are very few documented actual rebellions that exploded, or conspiracies such as those uncovered in Cuba and the United States. Perhaps this was linked to the possibility of flight into the vast Brazilian interior and the existence of so many *quilombos* in every region. These offered real possibilities of at least temporary freedom and safe haven to slaves seeking liberty. Running away was apparently a viable alternative to rebellion, and this may explain the absence of slave revolts in the nation that received the greatest number of Africans in the history of the transatlantic slave trade.

However, beginning in the 1790s and ending in the late 1830s, there was a series of unprecedented slave rebellions and conspiracies in Brazil. Nearly all of them were centered in Bahia, and most in the province's capital city of Salvador. A fundamental question addressed by historians is why, after more than two centuries of slavery in Brazil, did slaves come together during this particular historical period to plan or participate in organized revolts?[27] A number of factors may help to explain this period of slave rebellion, which concluded with the large scale Muslim-led uprising of 1835.

Bahia in the 1790s experienced an economic revival based around its traditional export staple product, sugar, although tobacco, cotton, and staple crop production, mainly *mandioca* or manioc root, also expanded. The virtual destruction of the Haitian sugar industry during the slave rebellion there, which began in 1791, stimulated planters in the Caribbean, Brazil, and elsewhere to increase production because of

---

[27]   For the two most thorough considerations, see Schwartz, *Sugar Plantations in the Formation of Brazilian Society*, Chapter 17, "Important Occasions: The War to End Bahian Slavery," pp. 468–88, and João José Reis, *Slave Rebellion in Brazil: The Muslim Uprising of 1835 in Bahia* (Baltimore: Johns Hopkins University Press, 1993), Chapter 3, "The Rebellious Tradition: Slave Revolts Prior to 1835," pp. 40–69.

rising prices in the major European consuming markets. This led to a revival of slave imports from Africa as labor demands escalated; indeed, unlike the case of Minas Gerais, where the vast majority of slaves were Brazilian-born by 1800, over 60 percent of Bahian slaves were of African origin by the early nineteenth century. This is of critical importance in understanding the slave rebellions of the period for several reasons. First, almost all conspiracies and rebellions were led by African-origin slaves, and nearly all participants in these uprisings were Africans as well. Not only did Brazilian-born slaves generally not join rebellions in significant numbers, but unlike the situation in Cuba, the free black and mulatto communities of Bahia did not participate in any significant way in slave conspiracies or revolts. Additionally, the armed forces of repression mobilized against *quilombos*, and used to suppress the uprisings of the early nineteenth century, were usually composed of free black and mulatto soldiers.

The most important conspiracies and rebellions of the early nineteenth century reveal much about the complexity of Brazilian slavery, the African slave trade, the notion that slaves in general and free peoples of African origin constituted an undifferentiated mass of people because of a common racial heritage, and the belief that these peoples had a unified set of interests and aspirations. The term "African" was utilized to some extent by slaveholders, traders, government officials, and outside observers with little understanding of the ethnic complexities of Africa itself. Slaves born in Africa rarely considered themselves "Africans" but identified themselves by their ethnic groups and religious affinities. Race played almost no role in the way slaves from Africa viewed themselves in relation to one another, although over time it defined their place in American slave societies from the vantage points of elites. Additionally, the ethnic composition of slave populations arriving in Brazil from Africa was in large part determined by internal African politics. Slaves entering the Atlantic slave trade were generally composed of captives taken in warfare between different African nation states, which were often organized along religious or ethnic lines. Victorious armies shipped captives to the coast for marketing by African merchants and eventual absorption into the slave trade to the Americas. Thus, the ethic makeup of slaves arriving in Bahia during any period was connected to the constantly shifting dynamics of internal African political strife, power struggles, and warfare.

The changing African ethnicity of Bahian slaves is important to note in the context of the slave rebellions and conspiracies of the early nineteenth century, because most of these were organized by specific African ethnic groups rather than by a pan-African slave population. This underscores the lack of trust and confidence of particular African-born slave ethnic groups in relation to ethnic and religious groups who had been their mortal enemies in Africa, and whose deep-rooted enmities survived the Atlantic crossing and enslavement in Brazil or elsewhere. Race itself, and even the common legal status as slaves, produced little solidarity in the context of continued African arrivals. Although the Brazilian slave trade was dominated by West and Central African slaves in the seventeenth and eighteenth centuries, during the early nineteenth century slaves were increasingly shipped from the Bight of Benin, an area wracked by warfare. This increased the volume of *bantu*-speaking slaves arriving in Bahia from Angolan ports. Many were military men captured during repeated campaigns launched against them by Muslims from the north, who had a long-standing tradition of slaving across the Sahara and to the Atlantic ports for transshipment to Brazil and elsewhere. Additionally, strife in the region resulted in the gradual dismantling of various Yoruba states, and their defeat also led to enslavement and transshipment to the coast and then to the Americas. After 1815, Yoruban-origin slaves (known as Nagôs in Bahia) captured in the ongoing warfare were increasingly shipped to Bahia, and became an important component of the slave population of the city of Salvador thereafter.[28]

Renewed economic expansion, increased slave imports, and a shift in the ethnic composition of the African-born slave population of Bahia were important factors in creating the environment in which the slave revolts and conspiracies of the early nineteenth century germinated and then exploded. Additionally, there is evidence that the social situation and material conditions of slaves deteriorated in a number of ways, especially during the 1820s and 1830s, although this ought not to be exaggerated as slaves were always the most exploited sector of Bahian society. Nevertheless, rising prices for commodities, economic pressures upon the slaveholding class, and the political instability surrounding Brazilian independence in the early 1820s may have led to increased exploitation of slaves and other laborers who sustained the Bahian economy.[29]

---

[28]   See Schwartz, "Important Occasions," pp. 474–5.
[29]   See Reis, *Slave Rebellion in Brazil*, "Hard Times," pp. 3–20, for a description of this situation.

The overall political situation in Bahia from the late 1790s through the 1830s may be described as one of cyclical unrest and periodic instability. Conspiracies and rebellions by sectors of the free population, as well as among slaves, were rife, especially during the 1820s, when competing forces struggled to reap the rewards of the end of the colonial system. The slave revolts of the epoch must be seen within this context of political upheaval. In 1798, a conspiracy centered in Salvador was put in motion to launch an insurrection for Brazilian independence known as the Tailors' Rebellion. The influences of the French and American Revolutions were evident as the posters hung throughout the capital before dawn on August 12 of that year called for equality, free commerce, and other revolutionary demands reflecting Enlightenment philosophies emanating from the North Atlantic world.[30] This was the only major incident in which Brazilian-born slaves, free blacks and mulattos, and sectors of the white population from the lower echelons of the social order came together in an attempt to forge political alliances with common, if vaguely defined, objectives. Thereafter, political movements of free peoples, white and of color, and those of slaves would be completely separate, unlike the many conspiracies found in Cuba during the same epoch.

The cycle of slave conspiracies and revolts that ended with the great Muslim-led uprising of 1835 began in 1807 with the discovery of a fairly extensive slave conspiracy in Salvador, purportedly led by Hausa slaves. Their plans were fairly elaborate and included diversionary fires to be set in key locations, attacks upon whites designed to create panic, the hope that rural slaves on the sugar estates of the *Recôncavo* would join the rebellion, and purportedly a plan to seize ships with the objective of returning to Africa. The plotters were betrayed by a fellow slave, and after extensive inquiry government officials confirmed that indeed the conspiracy was widespread. A large wave of repression was launched, and concerted military campaigns against the many small-scale *quilombos* near Salvador were undertaken.[31]

This repression was not new in the context of the 1807 conspiracy. In fact, the plot itself may have been a reaction by slaves to the fierce attacks against *quilombos* launched in 1805 by the strident new governor of Bahia, João Saldanha da Gama, who was intent on imposing stringent controls on the quasi-independent activities of some slaves. Many

[30] See Schwartz, "Important Occasions," pp. 476 – 7.
[31] See Reis, *Slave Revolt in Brazil*, pp. 42 – 3.

quilombos functioned as refuges of sorts where slaves fled on weekends or holidays to escape the drudgery of servitude, only to return to their masters after living beyond their control for a short time. While they were certainly not viewed as innocuous retreats by Bahian colonial authorities, most bureaucrats were so overwhelmed with other issues and problems that *quilombos* were sometimes simply left alone provided they posed no direct threat to order because of banditry or other attacks on established settlements. Saldanha felt this was a grave mistake and mobilized military forces, often militias composed of free blacks and mulattos, to launch repeated attacks on the Bahian *quilombos* shortly after assuming office.

Perhaps because of these repressive measures, imposed curfews on slaves, as well as prohibitions on gatherings and celebrations of all types, *quilombos* near Salvador and in the *Recôncavo* played central roles in almost all of the conspiracies and rebellions that took place during the early nineteenth century. In late 1808, Hausa slaves stormed the town of Nazaré in the heart of the *Recôncavo*, using a recently formed *quilombo* there as a base of operations. They were beaten back in defeat, but immediately thereafter, in early January 1809, several hundred African-born slaves from Salvador, also purportedly led by Hausas, deserted their masters and headed to join the insurrection. They were also decisively defeated by military forces, largely composed of free black and mulatto militiamen. Yet another wave of repression ensued, but ultimately conspiracies and rebellions could not be stopped or curbed as slaves, especially the African-born, never lost sight of, or hope for, freedom.

In February 1814 the cycle of rebellion began anew, again in Salvador. This time several hundred slaves left the city and headed north toward an older established *quilombo*. From there they launched attacks on a small village, killing many whites, and then made their way toward the *Recôncavo* to rally support. In route they were met by organized militiamen and soundly defeated. It was reported that one of their battle cries was "Death to whites and mulattos!"[32] This reflects the complex state of race relations in Bahia and the obstacles to success faced by rebellious slaves. African slaves sometimes considered free peoples of color as well as many Brazilian-born slaves as their enemies in the same way that they conceived of whites. This was quite logical. When they rose in rebellion – and almost all of the slaves participating

[32]   See ibid., pp. 45 – 7, and Schwartz, "Important Occasions," pp. 482 – 3.

in the 1814 revolt were African-born (purportedly Hausas once again) – they faced largely free black and mulatto troops who killed them in battle as ruthlessly as soldiers of any race would have in the same circumstances. Not only did they face free peoples of color in pitched battles, but there was little overt support among the free black and mulatto population of Bahia for their struggles for freedom, a situation in marked contrast with the Cuban conspiracies and rebellions.

Yet a month later, in March 1814, Hausa slaves once again rebelled in one of the largest sugar districts in the Bahian *Recôncavo*. The results were the same, but did not deter the continuation of valiant attempts at freedom. In March 1816 there was another large-scale rising in the major sugar-producing zones, again purportedly led by Hausas. Plantations were burned, whites were murdered, and the rebellion was ruthlessly destroyed by the militia. There were reports that even loyal slaves, in all probability Brazilian-born, participated in the repression.

For the Bahian elite, and especially for the planters of the *Recôncavo*, where in some sugar districts slaves could account for 80 percent or more of total populations, instability threatened every aspect of life. Demands were made upon government officials for tightened security. Privately financed security forces were organized to try to destroy *quilombos* and preempt any possible threats. Petitions for actions to guarantee security were taken as far away as the *corte* in Rio de Janeiro. But ultimately it was impossible to stop slaves from running away, and it was difficult for security forces to penetrate the world of African-born slaves who spoke their own languages, kept their plans secret from Brazilian-born slaves who could possibly betray them, and never lost sight of the possibilities for freedom, no matter how many defeats they suffered or how insurmountable the obstacles to success appeared. Slave resistance and rebellions continued, although there was a hiatus during the period surrounding Brazilian independence in the early 1820s when Bahia was turned into an armed camp by competing forces trying to prevent true political independence, or to reap the rewards of the formal separation from Portugal.

Bahia was the scene of civil war in late 1822 and 1823. The declaration of Brazilian independence in 1822 was followed by the occupation of Salvador by forces loyal to the departed Portuguese crown. The region became sharply divided between Brazilian forces led by the regional elite, who were almost always large-scale slaveholders, and the Portuguese military, backed by colonial officials and the powerful Portuguese import-export merchants. Although there were some disturbances among the slave population, by and large the cycle of rebellions was temporarily halted until the Portuguese were defeated and the overall political situation stabilized in 1824 with the consolidation of quasi-independence. Thereafter, slave revolts began anew.

In Ilhéus, far to the south of Salvador, slaves rose in 1824 and formed a fairly visible and viable *quilombo*, which lasted until 1828, when it was finally dismantled. Most of the participants were reported to be Brazilian-born slaves, an anomaly in the context of most Brazilian slave revolts. In 1826, slaves rose in Cachoeira, located in the heart of the *Recôncavo*. In the same year, African-origin slaves who had formed the *Urubu Quilombo* just outside of Salvador rebelled. In 1827 there were three more slave uprisings in various *Recôncavo* districts, and more followed in 1828. Although all were decisively defeated, the quest for freedom among the slave population could not be curbed. In 1830, for the first time, there was a large-scale uprising in the heart of Salvador itself. Slaves, apparently well organized and with elaborate plans, laid siege to a police station in the quest for arms. A massacre of the participants – almost all Africans, purportedly Nagôs – followed. It was reported that over fifty slaves were murdered. Security was tightened in the city, but to no avail. The greatest slave uprising in Bahian history would take place five years later in 1835, exploding in the heart of Salvador.[33]

The 1835 rebellion was meticulously planned by African-born Muslim slaves, known as Malês in Bahia.[34] Although Yorubas (Nagôs) were the majority of the African-born Muslim slave population in Bahia, almost all of the African ethnic groups, Muslim and non-Muslim, were represented in the conspiracy and in the revolt itself, although the Nagôs played the leading roles. It is difficult to calculate the percentage of the Bahian slave population that adhered to Islamic religious doctrine, although it is certain that it was a fairly small portion even among African slaves. In the city of Salvador followers were more numerous than in the countryside, and often Muslim practices were interwoven with *candomblé* and *orixa* worship. Brazilian-born slaves, both blacks and mulattos, were almost completely absent from the 1835 uprising, as had been the case in most of the Bahian revolts of the early nineteenth century. Many Muslim African-born freedmen, however,

---

[33]   See Reis, *Slave Revolt in Brazil*, pp. 55–69, for an account of the post-independence revolts.

[34]   This account of the 1835 revolt is based upon Reis, *Slave Revolt in Brazil*.

did participate both in the preparations for the rebellion and in the revolt itself. Because of their greater freedom of movement, they played a particularly important role in communications between the city of Salvador and the *Recôncavo* sugar districts, with their large African-born slave populations.

The rebellion was not a spontaneous uprising caused by any one incident of abuse by masters or government officials. It was a revolt designed to secure freedom for the slaves of Bahia, especially those of African birth, rather than to seek retribution or vengeance against any particular slaveholder or bureaucrat. Although most of the planning was secret, by the end of 1834 there were rumors within the African sectors of Salvador's slave population that something was going to occur in early 1835. The rising was projected for Sunday, January 25, 1835, at the end of Ramadan, and it is clear that the leaders utilized Islamic religious celebrations held in late 1834 to recruit followers, although no one was told when the revolt would explode or what the plans and objectives were.

The leaders of the revolt, almost all of them *mestres* or Islamic religious leaders, projected an uprising that would begin in Salvador, spread among the great masses of the African slave population in the city, and then move rapidly to the *Recôncavo* sugar districts where Bahian African-born slaves were heavily concentrated. While the Malês were strongest in Salvador, from its inception Islam had been a proselytizing religious system, and in Bahia the tradition of spreading the faith in order to convert nonbelievers was an important part of Muslim activities in the city itself and in surrounding rural areas. Muslim African-born freedmen played an important role in the spread of Islamic religious doctrine into the rural sugar-producing zones, and the leaders of the conspiracy counted upon the support of converts and other African-born slaves who they felt would be prompted to action by Malê leaders once the revolt began to spread. Little effort was made to appeal to Brazilian-born slaves, who were highly distrusted by Africans and were not expected to support the uprising. Free blacks and mulattos for the most part were conceived of as enemies just as whites were, unlike the situation in Cuba.

Elaborate conspiracies involving large numbers of people are difficult to keep secret for long. By early 1835 there was generalized knowledge among Salvador's slaves that something important was going to occur, and rumors, innuendo, and gossip were rife. The danger of this for the conspirators was that there was no unity among Bahian slaves. Not only were there sharp divisions and animosities between African and Brazilian-born slaves, but among Brazilian slaves there was often a perverse loyalty to masters and authorities in general. The greatest threat to the conspirators was that they would betrayed by enemies among them – Brazilian-born slaves, who were carefully excluded from any awareness that an uprising was planned. Too many slaves became privy to the generalized knowledge that something was going to occur, and in the end the conspirators were forced into action prematurely because of betrayal by Brazilian-born slaves, and this realized their greatest fear.

The uprising had been planned for dawn on Sunday, January 25, but on Saturday the city was awash with rumors, and these, through betrayal, reached the ears of the authorities by Saturday evening. The reports were alarming, and very quickly the armed forces of the city, from police to militia men, were mobilized in every district. Houses were raided and searched, and in one of the homes targeted by the police a large group of African participants had congregated expecting to attack the authorities in the morning. They were forced into action prematurely and spread into different city districts calling fellow Africans to action. At one of the main squares, in front of the governor's palace, the city jail was attacked to release African prisoners and to secure arms. But this group of slaves was subject to withering fire from the mobilized armed forces, and they were forced to disperse to other districts of the city in search of supporters and to try to secure weapons. Numerous attacks were launched by the rebels against government positions throughout the city. Various police barracks were attacked, one by a group of nearly 200 poorly armed slaves attempting to secure weaponry. They were beaten back after a fierce struggle and forced to retreat through the city's streets. The element of surprise had been lost and with it any hope of success against the well-armed and fully prepared forces of state authority. A decision was made to vacate the city and to try and find refuge and support in the sugar districts. But escape was impossible because a cavalry outpost stood between the rebels and the only route leading toward the *Recôncavo*. The rebels were met by mounted troops as well as soldiers who garrisoned the barracks, and they were subjected to murderous firepower. It was no contest. High casualties were suffered, and the rebellion then turned into a mad attempt by slaves to escape into the countryside with their lives, pursued by mounted troops. Some scattered groups continued resisting in some parts of the city, but by dawn, when it was to have begun, the rebellion was virtually over. Conflicting reports were offered on the number of casualties suffered. Some estimates indicated as many as seventy rebellious slaves had died in their heroic quest for freedom, with many more severely wounded.

In the aftermath of the rebellion, the repression directed at the African community of Salvador was ghastly, much like the assault on free peoples of color and slaves in Cuba during *La Escalera* in 1844. The homes of Africans were repeatedly searched and often ransacked. African slaves and freedmen were arrested en masse during the first half of 1835. Formal legal charges were lodged against captured insurgents. Slaves were flogged; freedmen were deported; several of the participants were executed. New edicts forbidding a wide range of slave activities, religious and secular, were promulgated. Even freedmen had their liberties severely curtailed and were subjected to curfews and prohibitions on gatherings and other independent activities.

In many ways the repression directed at Bahia's African slave population was similar to the aftermath of *La Escalera* in Cuba, although there were fundamental differences. In both nations the repression effectively ended threats of slave rebellion. Slaves rose spontaneously against abusive masters or overseers on occasion, but these were isolated incidents and, with the exception of a possible plot in 1845, no more organized conspiracies in Bahia are known to historians. However, the task of controlling the Bahian slave population may have been easier because of the fact that only Africans, slaves and free, had to be targeted for repression and vigilance. Brazilian-born slaves were considered to be loyal, and indeed they did not participate in any meaningful way in slave revolts. This dichotomy is not known to have existed in Cuba, as both African-born and Cuban-born slaves and freedmen and women participated in the conspiracies and uprisings that took place there. This meant that the entire slave population was suspect and had to be targeted to preclude the threat of conspiracy to foment rebellion. After 1835, slaves in Bahia and elsewhere seeking absolute freedom or temporary space to escape from the control of their masters reverted to flight, the most common form of resistance to the degradation of servitude. Conspiracies may have ended, but all over Brazil *quilombos* thrived until the end of slavery, and these communities of peoples who struggled to achieve some control over their lives could never be eradicated, along with the hope for and constant striving for freedom.

Slave resistance in the United States was fundamentally different from the experiences of slaves in Brazil, and to some extent in Cuba.

Although U.S. slaves deserted farms, plantations, and urban enclaves continuously in search of ultimate freedom, or at least a temporary respite from the harsh conditions of slave life, it was extraordinarily difficult for them to form viable maroon communities that could survive over extended periods of time. In part this was because of the very different demographic structures in the three slave societies. Although there were many regions where slaves constituted a substantial portion of the local population in the United States, in most areas slaves were a small minority of the population. The overwhelming preponderance through most historical periods of free people, almost all of them white, meant several things.

First, security was easier to impose and maintain because of numerical superiority. In many Cuban and Brazilian plantation and mining regions, slaves were the vast majority of inhabitants, and their sheer numbers made absolute control difficult and in some cases nearly impossible. Brazilian *quilombos* could never be eradicated completely, and even if they were temporarily destroyed new ones would usually be formed fairly quickly by slaves seeking freedom or temporary refuge. Because they were so few in relative numbers, slaveholders and government officials found it nearly impossible to impose controls that could prevent slaves from running away to safe havens. In the United States, slaves were more easily controlled because they were usually a small minority of the population.

Second, in Cuba and Brazil free blacks and mulattos constituted a significant population sector, and in many regions they were the largest demographic group, especially in the nineteenth century. This meant that blacks and mulattos appearing in public places, in both rural and urban areas, were not necessarily identified as slaves. With respect to supervision of slave populations this made matters fairly complex in Cuba and Brazil. White society was accustomed to seeing free people of color moving about on their own in urban and rural areas without supervision of any sort, and this could offer decisive advantages to slaves who ran away. They could blend in with, or find refuge among, free black and mulatto communities until they could make their way to the numerous safe havens established by other slave runaways in remote rural zones. This was utterly impossible in most U.S. slaveholding regions. To be black or mulatto was to be considered a slave, and people of color seen on their own, especially in rural areas, were automatically under suspicion and subject to questioning, search, and, if documentation was not proper and forthcoming, to seizure. Most rural areas were dominated by a multitude of small farms and ranches, and in most cases these were owned by whites who did not own slaves. The non-slaveholding white population constituted the vast majority of people, and blacks and mulattos not known to local populations were easily identified. All of this made flight to safe havens on established communications arteries almost impossible. Slaves had to flee through swamps, jungles, and other inhospitable terrain, which made their quests for freedom and the establishment of maroon communities much more difficult than was the case in Brazil and, to a lesser extent, in Cuba.

A third factor that resulted in better security from the point of view of the slaveholding class was that in the United States slaveholders in rural areas, large and small, were almost always resident on their small farms or large plantations. They took a direct role in supervision and management of their properties and in establishing security measures to control their slave populations. In Brazil and Cuba, the number of absentee estate owners was high. The slaveholding class that controlled most slaves resided in cities and towns and delegated operational responsibilities to foremen or overseers. These administrators did not necessarily share the same set of economic interests as their employers, and in many instances lax supervision created space for slaves to run away, temporarily or permanently, to maroon communities.

A fourth factor explaining the smaller number of maroon communities in the United States was related to internal slave demography. On the eve of the American Revolution, about 80 percent of the total slave population had been born into slavery in the United States. African-born slaves continued to decline in relative numbers even as the slave trade continued to 1808, and through the nineteenth century the percentage of Africans among the slave population fell to insignificance. This, of course, was in sharp contrast to both Brazil and Cuba, where the slave trade from Africa continued at high, if fluctuating, levels until 1851 in Brazil and until 1867 in Cuba. The constant influx of Africans, most of whom had been born into freedom, and who brought with them their own languages, cultures, and religions, reinforced general slave rebelliousness as has been graphically demonstrated in the Brazilian case.

Additionally, because the slave trade from Africa was heavily male, distorted sex ratios made family formation less likely in Cuba and Brazil than in the United States. By the early nineteenth century there were nearly as many females as males within the U.S. slave population, in sharp contrast to the extraordinarily high proportion of males in most regions of slaveholding Cuba and Brazil.[35] Younger males without family linkages had a greater tendency to flee from slavery, and a proportionally lower number of these African-born males were present in U.S. slave society.

A fifth factor was the relative absence in the United States of remote frontier regions offering environmental havens for the formation of maroon communities and possibilities for their long-term survival, especially when compared to Brazil. Maroon communities did take hold in the huge Dismal Swamp region in the Virginia and Carolina lowlands and in other isolated areas as well. But settlement patterns and the development of farms and plantations usually meant the wholesale clearing of land for the production of various crops and the disappearance of natural refuge areas that might allow runaway slaves to congregate in any significant numbers. These regions did exist in distant western areas, but vigilance on roads, rivers, and in the countryside made it difficult for runaways to reach these regions in significant numbers.

A final factor was the gradual evolution of the free states of the northern United States. The Revolutionary War resulted in the first real growth of a free black and mulatto population on a significant scale.[36] The English reached out to slaves offering freedom if they would fight against the rebellion, and many slaves naturally seized this opportunity. Others fought with the revolutionaries and were granted freedom for their military service. Slaves also took advantage of the wartime instability and chaos to flee to freedom. In the aftermath of the American victory the issue of slavery was debated throughout the new republic. The northern states promulgated laws gradually ending slavery. Not only did a free population of color grow on a significant scale during the early nineteenth century, but the free states of the North eventually emerged as beacons of liberty for southern slaves. Freedom was forthcoming if fleeing slaves were able to reach the Mason-Dixon Line dividing the free and slave states. The real possibility of acquiring liberty if runaways could reach the North, and the emergence of a network of antislavery sympathizers, white and African-American, which would be called the Underground Railroad, drew thousands of

[35]   The 1820 Census of the United States indicated about 783,000 male slaves and 745,000 female slaves.

[36]   There were about 60,000 free people of color in the United States in 1790 and about 186,000 in 1810, according to census data for those years.

slaves yearly, especially from the states of the upper South. All of this meant that the efforts of slaves to acquire freedom did not focus on carving out tenuous and highly vulnerable maroon communities, as was the case in Brazil, because there was another very real and viable opportunity for freedom in the North, at least until the Fugitive Slave Act of 1850. (See Chapter 8.)

Thus, although slaves in the United States probably deserted their masters at rates that were comparable to those found in Cuba and Brazil, the formation of maroon communities was not a major part of the slave experience in comparative perspective, especially when the centrality of *quilombo* formation in Brazil is considered. However, there were other forms of resistance that may have distinguished U.S. slaves from their counterparts in Brazil and Cuba, and these have been debated by historians. Broadly referred to as "day-to-day resistance," these modes covered a wide range of slave efforts both at bettering themselves within the slave system if possible, and at noncooperation with masters and overseers if demands upon them were deemed unreasonable. In other words, slaves sought to assert as much control over their own lives as possible within this horridly oppressive system. This was the case with Cuban and Brazilian slaves as well. But the strategy seems to have been more effective in the United States, perhaps because nearly all slaves had been born in the United States by the early nineteenth century, and because there were nearly equal numbers of males and females, which meant that the formation of families was relatively easier in the United States.[37]

Slaves, especially in urban areas, sought education and vocational training, recognizing that even within the confines of servitude there were distinct advantages to higher skill levels. Indeed, many slaves were literate and worked in occupations requiring literacy skills; other slave occupations demanded sophisticated mechanical aptitude obtained only by education or apprenticeship. This ought not to be exaggerated, but indeed one way of resisting the oppression of slavery was to improve life possibilities through the use of innate intelligence. Slaves assigned task work, and even those working as gang laborers, could work efficiently and quickly. This was not so much to please masters or overseers but rather to give them more opportunity to work on their own endeavors, such as gardening and raising animals, or to

[37] For a discussion of changing interpretations of "day-to-day" resistance, see Fogel, *Without Consent or Contract*, pp. 155–62.

spend time with their families in small huts or slave quarters beyond the sight of masters. Of course, the dimensions of these activities are largely unknown.

Slaves who perceived that masters were unbending in their labor demands or unwilling to create space for independent human behavior had the option of resorting to other forms of resistance that fell short of running away or rebelling. Tools could be lost and machinery broken; fires could be set deliberately in fields or buildings; animals could suffer crippling injuries; food supplies could be contaminated; and a whole range of other problems could occur to masters who were intransigent in their demands. In this way, slaves resisted by making it known that they were human beings with bargaining power that they would not hesitate to utilize to improve their immediate material and social conditions.

Slaves in the United States conspired and rebelled in the same way as their counterparts in Cuba and Brazil, although the frequency of rebellion seems to have been far lower in the United States. In broad terms, the lower incidence of slave revolt was linked to the fact that by the nineteenth century most slaves had been born in the United States. In Brazil, as has been graphically demonstrated in the case of Bahian slave revolts, and in Cuba as well, slave uprisings and conspiracies were closely associated with African-born slaves. The relative number of Africans within slave populations was directly linked with the level of the African slave trade, which was abolished in 1808 to the United States. Thus, while Africans continued to maintain a strong and sometimes rebellious presence in Cuba and Brazil because of the ongoing African trade, they became insignificant in numerical terms within U.S. slave society. Other factors explaining the lower frequency of slave revolt in the United States were the same as those precluding the formation of maroon communities. These included overwhelmingly white populations in most regions and the tighter security precautions extant in rural areas because of low levels of owner absenteeism.

There were numerous instances of spontaneous uprisings in American centers of slavery, especially in Virginia, during the late seventeenth and early eighteenth centuries.[38] But the first real planned conspiracy among slaves to launch a rebellion apparently took place in

---

[38]   In the Chesapeake region conspiracies to rebel were discovered in 1709, 1710, 1722, 1729, 1730, and 1731. Berlin, *Generations of Captivity*, p. 65.

New York City in 1712.[39] Slaves had been imported by the Dutch West India Company beginning in 1626. The British takeover in 1664 saw the continued arrival of slaves both from the Caribbean and directly from Africa. New York City became a major center of urban slavery in seventeenth-century colonial America as well as an important slave-trading hub. The growth of slavery in the city itself became a major security concern to authorities because of steadily increasing numbers of slaves. Accordingly, legislation designed to impose controls was continually enacted during the early eighteenth century, including a law forbidding congregations of three or more slaves in 1702.

In April 1712 a major revolt exploded, apparently led by African-born slaves in the city. It was a planned uprising, with arms secured and hidden on the outskirts of town. Over twenty conspirators met, and once armed they set fire to buildings. This was designed to attract the response of citizens to extinguish the blaze. When these arrived they were ambushed, and five whites were killed and many more wounded. The militia was quickly mobilized as well as all able-bodied free white men. The repression that ensued was ghastly. The leaders of the rebellion apparently committed suicide, but many captives were rounded up and held for trial. Of twenty-seven accused conspirators, twenty-one slaves were executed, some publicly in a grisly manner. Legislation designed to impose strict controls over the activities of slaves was continuously enacted and finally codified in a general slave code in 1731.

In 1741, near hysteria and fear of slave revolt swept through the city again because of a series of fires that were set, one in the governor's mansion itself.[40] There had been considerable racial tension within the city's working classes as the economic downturn of late 1740 and early 1741 was exacerbated by a bitter winter, with many people unable to afford firewood or even food. The white working classes harbored deep resentments against slaves, who were often rented out by owners at rates that were well below their salary levels. In brief, slaves became

[39] For the history of African-Americans in New York City, see Leslie M. Harris, *In the Shadow of Slavery: African Americans in New York City, 1626 – 1863* (Chicago: University of Chicago Press, 2002). Also see Graham Russell Hodges, *Root and Branch: African Americans in New York and East Jersey, 1613 – 1863* (Chapel Hill: University of North Carolina Press, 1999).

[40] For a recently published study, see Jill Lepore, *New York Burning: Liberty, Slavery, and Conspiracy in Eighteenth-Century Manhattan* (New York: Knopf, 2005).

scapegoats for widespread unemployment and deteriorating living conditions among a fairly significant sector of the free population. Fires continued to break out mysteriously throughout the city. A fort at Battery Park caught fire and was destroyed. Fires were set in warehouses and in homes in the more affluent sections of the city. The city council launched an investigation, and one of the potential witnesses testified that the fires had indeed been set by slaves along with some poor whites and had been designed to burn down the entire city. Formal legal charges were leveled against a large number of people, but fires continued to be set throughout the city, which exacerbated the hysteria. In the end, a conspiratorial slave uprising was never proved, but seventeen African-Americans were hanged and thirteen were executed by burning. More than seventy were exiled from the city and forbidden to return under threat of arrest. It is not known whether there was an actual conspiracy, but African-Americans, slave and free, suffered the brunt of the repression.

Perhaps the most extensive and violent rebellion of slaves prior to the Revolutionary War took place in Stono, South Carolina, in 1739 and is known as the Stono Rebellion. In many ways this revolt was connected to British–Spanish rivalries along the frontier separating Spanish Florida from the British colonies. The endemic European wars between Great Britain and Spain inevitably carried over to the Americas, with each side continually attacking or trying to destabilize the other. During the early 1730s, as part of these efforts, a Spanish royal decree declared that all fugitive slaves reaching Spanish territory in Florida would be freed.[41] With the outbreak of Anglo-Spanish war in Europe in 1739, Spanish authorities in Florida reiterated the decree and issued proclamations advising slaves in the British colonies that they were welcome and could live as free men and women if they reached Spanish territory.

This was a source of extraordinary alarm in the context of early colonial South Carolina, which had a demographic structure more similar to that of eighteenth-century Jamaica or Bahia than to the future state itself during the nineteenth century. In 1739, it has been estimated that about 80 percent of the total population of some 44,000 inhabitants were slaves, and many of these were of African origin.[42]

---

[41]   See the account in Herbert Aptheker, *American Negro Slave Revolts* (New York: International Publishers, 1993), pp. 184–91.

[42]   In 1820, slaves made up 51 percent of the state's total population.

Generalized unrest characterized South Carolina's slaves during the 1730s. Slaves continuously ran away, heading on the long and dangerous journey toward Florida and freedom. Rumors of a slave conspiracy swept through Charleston in 1738, and whites were even mandated by authorities to attend Sunday church services armed because of the generalized fear of an uprising. It indeed occurred in early September 1739. Some twenty slaves gathered near Stono and raided a store that sold weapons and ammunition. After arming themselves, they began to move southward and were joined by fellow slaves who may have been acting spontaneously. A significant number of whites, perhaps as many as twenty-five, were killed by the rebels, whose objective was clearly to reach Florida and liberty. Previously, slaves had run away individually or in groups with the same objective, but this time there was a decision by a fairly large number of slaves to use force of arms in the quest for freedom. Various estimates have indicated that more than seventy slaves were part of the rebellion. Authorities mobilized the local militia, which quickly put an end to the revolt. Poorly armed slaves were no match for mounted troops with superior firepower. It was reported that nearly fifteen slaves were killed in battle and that an undetermined number, perhaps as many as fifty, were hunted down, taken prisoner, and later murdered by shooting, hanging, or quartering. The repression did not dampen the quest for freedom. In June 1740 another conspiracy was discovered near Charleston, and it was reported that some fifty slaves were hanged in public as a deterrent.[43]

The Revolutionary War, which exploded after 1775, created a number of opportunities for slaves to act in their own interests and to seek freedom. In the northern states, where slavery was less entrenched, slaves took advantage of the fighting to flee to safe havens or to join the British and American armies. Virginia's colonial governor, Lord Dunmore, offered slaves freedom in 1775 if they joined the British cause and created the Ethiopian Regiment, which was later defeated in battle by American forces.[44] In the lower southern states the same processes unfolded, with slaves joining competing armies in return for freedom. Or they fled their owners when fighting created enough confusion and disorder for them to run away to cities controlled by the British such as Savannah, which fell to the colonial forces in 1778, and Charleston, which was seized in 1780. Another, older alternative was Spanish

---

[43]   Aptheker, *American Negro Slave Revolts*, p. 189.
[44]   Berlin, *Generations of Captivity*, pp. 111–12.

Florida and freedom if slaves could escape the British colonies. Perhaps because of these other options there were no large-scale slave revolts during the American Revolution. Additionally, the future United States was an armed camp, and any attempts by slaves to rebel would have been suicidal because there were garrisoned standing armies and militias everywhere on both sides of the conflict.

In the aftermath of the revolutionary victory of the early 1780s, the newly formed United States vigorously debated the meaning of liberty, freedom, and justice for all. In the end, slavery was sanctioned throughout the South and dismantled gradually in the North, and when the dust of revolutionary euphoria settled it was evident that the concept of all men being created equal applied only to white men. The hope of freedom engendered in slaves was crushed, and slavery was institutionalized and expanded. For a period of time the confusing spirit of liberty and democracy may have meant that a bit more leeway and autonomy was extended to slaves. In the 1780s and 1790s there were no major known conspiracies or rebellions in the new nation. This all changed suddenly and dramatically with the discovery of a massive conspiracy for freedom in Virginia in 1800, which historians have labeled Gabriel's Rebellion.[45]

Clearly, the undelivered promise of freedom for slaves in early revolutionary America was the single most important factor that led in the conspiracy. There was certainly awareness among slaves of Haiti's massive slave revolt, but while revolutionary Haiti may have been a source of inspiration, the causative factors were home grown. The free black and mulatto population of Virginia grew during and after the Revolutionary War, but the vast majority of peoples of color were enslaved and given little hope of freedom.[46] Gabriel Prosser was a highly skilled blacksmith who benefited from the post-revolutionary loosening of restrictions upon urban slaves, especially with respect to the practice of hiring out.[47] Essentially he made his own money contracting his services to various employers and paid the bulk of his earnings to his master. However, his share of cash wages was substantial,

---

[45] For a full-length study, see Douglas R. Egerton, *Gabriel's Rebellion: The Virginia Slave Conspiracies of 1800 and 1802* (Chapel Hill: University of North Carolina Press, 1993).

[46] In 1800, Virginia had a free colored population of 20,493, representing 2.3 percent of the total population. There were 346,671 slaves, representing 39.2 percent of the total population.

[47] Prosser was his master's surname.

and Gabriel Prosser was clearly a slave of privilege who lived and worked in conditions far superior to those of other slaves. His freedom of movement and access to cash did not make him free, but many aspects of his life were similar to those of free men until he was arrested and jailed on at least two occasions for petty theft.

While Gabriel's main motivation was freedom for himself, his family, and the oppressed slaves of the Virginia region, studies of the conspiracy indicate a highly developed political awareness and even notions of the importance of social class, especially in Richmond, where he lived and worked. His rebellion would not be directed against all whites, and unlike the Bahian slave revolts the mantra "death to whites" was never part of his revolutionary plans. Gabriel was an artisan, and he worked alongside many whites whose living and working conditions were similar to his own. He recognized that these people were not his enemies. Additionally, he was very much aware that there were many important figures in white society who were ardent abolitionists, many of them Quakers and Methodists, and in his thinking he clearly distinguished these sectors from the slaveholding class. But the bulk of his wrath was directed at Richmond's merchant class, who charged usurious interest rates and earned astronomical incomes because of the labor of artisans like Gabriel. Yet, despite the lack of animosity toward some sectors of Virginia's white society, Gabriel worked almost exclusively among the slave population to recruit followers, although some free blacks were approached. Unlike those participating in the Bahian conspiracies, the greater share of these slaves were not of African origin but had been born in the United States.

Gabriel recruited slaves in Virginia counties close to Richmond with a great degree of success. He was a charismatic figure, a gifted speaker, and a skilled organizer. His plans were sophisticated and included a full-scale assault on Richmond, with strategic points such as bridges and places with arms and ammunition as his initial objectives, to be followed by the seizure of the governor's mansion and the imprisonment of the Virginia governor, James Monroe. With the city under his control, negotiations for the freedom of Virginia's slaves would take place. There would be no wholesale murdering of whites or destruction of the city. He expected that once the revolt established momentum with its initial successes, there would be a general uprising of slaves throughout the city and in the surrounding rural counties. Gabriel and his followers organized supporters in the utmost secrecy, but the plot became so large that inevitably rumors spread in Richmond itself and throughout Virginia.

This was the paradoxical dilemma facing all leaders of slave conspiracies. There was little chance of success unless there were large
numbers of supporters among the slave population. But if knowledge of
a particular plot became too widespread, the danger of betrayal
increased enormously. This is what occurred time and again, and it was
precisely the fate of Gabriel's conspiracy.

Slave conspiracies were almost always betrayed by other slaves. In
the case of Brazil, there was a sharp cleavage between the African and
Brazilian-born slave populations; Africans looked upon Brazilian slaves
as their enemies just as they conceived of whites and free peoples of
color in general. But in the Virginia conspiracy of 1800 no such division
existed, and most of the leaders of the plot and followers of Gabriel were
American-born. They were betrayed by another slave who also had
been born in the United States. Motivations for betrayal could vary.
Some slaves perversely felt an allegiance to their owners, especially on
small farms or enterprises where master and slaves labored together at
the same tasks, which created personal bonds of sorts. Others were well
treated by their owners and afforded privileges and prerogatives that
assured loyalty. Still other slaves sought to curry favor with their masters
and the authorities in general, hoping that betrayal of conspiracies
could lead to freedom, or at least gain them more privileges, better
treatment, and some type of reward.

The plot's betrayal precluded the uprising. The governor was advised
before Gabriel's slave followers could be fully mobilized, and militias
were rapidly called out in Richmond and contiguous counties. They
conducted extensive searches in every district, and although the conspirators had begun to gather, instead of rebelling they were forced to
flee chaotically for their lives. Many were rounded up very quickly, but
some of the major leaders managed to escape, including Gabriel himself,
who eluded capture for several weeks. After finding temporary safe
haven on a schooner moored in the James River, he was betrayed by a
slave seeking the reward for his capture. After his seizure, he was tried
and ultimately hanged along with around twenty-five other slave participants in the conspiracy. Virginia's white society was shocked when
the dimensions of the rebel plans gradually become known through the
judicial process, during which many participants were offered clemency
for revealing details about the plot. Even after Gabriel's death there was
still an effort to foment revolt among slaves who had been in some way
connected with the 1800 conspiracy but had not been captured.
A conspiracy to rebel sometime around Easter in 1802 was instigated,

but it did not reach the dimensions of Gabriel's plot and was never consummated. Yet another heroic attempt at freedom was frustrated.

The largest conspiracy for freedom by slaves in the United States took place in Charleston, South Carolina, in 1822 and was led by an ex-slave who had acquired his freedom, Denmark Vesey.[48] Vesey was born either in Africa or in the West Indies, and it is likely that he labored for a short time in pre-revolutionary Haiti on a sugar plantation. Because he suffered from epilepsy he was an ineffective worker, and his owner, a ship captain named Joseph Vesey, employed him as his personal servant aboard a slave ship that he operated between Africa and the Caribbean. After two years of working in and observing the degradations and barbarities of the African slave trade, Vesey's owner decided to give up slaving. He settled in Charleston in 1783 after the revolutionary victory that created the independent United States.

As an urban slave who worked as a personal servant, Vesey was relatively privileged within Charleston slave society. Charleston County, South Carolina, had a demographic structure that resembled the British West Indies prior to abolition, or that of many of the sugar plantation zones in Cuba and Bahia, Brazil. In each U.S. census undertaken between 1790 and 1820, more than 70 percent of the total population of Charleston was enslaved. There was a minuscule free black and mulatto population, accounting for a little more than 4 percent of Charleston's population in 1820. Vesey was a very lucky man. In 1800, he won a substantial sum of money and was able to purchase his

---

[48] For considerations of the revolt, see Douglas R. Egerton, *He Shall Go Out Free: The Lives of Denmark Vesey* (Lanham, MD: Rowman & Littlefield, 2004); John Lofton, *Denmark Vesey's Revolt: The Slave Plot That Lit a Fuse to Fort Sumter* (Kent, OH: Kent State University Press, 1983); Edward A. Pearson, editor, *Designs Against Charleston: The Trial Record of the Denmark Vesey Slave Conspiracy of 1822* (Chapel Hill: University of North Carolina Press, 1999); David Robertson, *Denmark Vesey* (New York: Knopf, 1999); and Robert S. Starobin, editor, *Denmark Vesey: The Slave Conspiracy of 1822* (Englewood Cliffs, NJ: Prentice-Hall, 1970). See the *William & Mary Quarterly* January 2002 issue, 3rd series, Vol. 59, No. 1, for an academic debate on the Vesey conspiracy, and particularly Michael P. Johnson, "Denmark Vesey and His Co-Conspirators," *William & Mary Quarterly*, 3rd series, Volume 58, No. 4 (October 2001), pp. 915–76. Johnson examined evidence derived from the trial records and asserts that there was no plot at all. Johnson argues that the plot was invented by the mayor of Charleston to curry favor with the local white population by indicating his vigilance over security matters, and to sabotage his critics and political rivals.

freedom as well as to set up a lucrative carpentry business. His business prospered, and he became a man of considerable wealth. His position in the free black and mulatto community of Charleston was enhanced by his religious activities. He was one of the founders of and a minister in a Methodist church that was established in 1816. His activities there were an important part of his life, and when local authorities closed the church in 1820 as part of a campaign to curb independent African-American religious and cultural activities, Vesey may have been pushed beyond his tolerance. Because he was a wealthy and influential free person of color, this attack on independent religious worship and expression on the part of African-Americans was probably decisive in pushing him to plan for freedom for the slaves he lived, worked, and worshipped with. At the church, which had somewhere near 3,000 members, Vesey had railed against slavery using biblical incantations, and he was apparently quite familiar with abolitionist literature emanating from England and the United States, which was also used in his sermons. The use of the church in Charleston to rally antislavery supporters may have had some similarity to the way Muslim slaves used religion to build support for their 1835 uprising in Bahia.

Vesey was well acquainted with the Haitian Revolution, and having lived and worked in French St. Domingue for a short time, he probably followed events there closely. It was even rumored that he had made appeals to the independent black republic for assistance in his plot, although this may have been falsely asserted by authorities to justify the brutal repressive measures and mass arrests that occurred after the plot was betrayed. Regardless of its possible Haitian inspiration, Vesey's plot, unlike Gabriel Prosser's conspiracy in 1800 Richmond, included plans for the use of mass violence to kill as many whites as possible, purportedly a plan to raze the city of Charleston by setting massive fires, and a utopian scheme to seize ships and set sail for Haiti and freedom. How much of this was invented by the betrayers or by the authorities is unknown.

If indeed these reports are true, Vesey's conceptualization of slavery in South Carolina was very different from Gabriel Prosser's vision for Virginia. Prosser thought that he could force the abolition of slavery. Contemporary accounts of the Vesey conspiracy, which may have been grossly exaggerated, indicate that it was designed to wreak vengeance upon whites and to secure freedom for those who participated in the rebellion rather then to bring about a general ending of slavery. The stories released after the mass arrests and most of the histories of the events note as many as 9,000 participants or followers in the conspiracy, a number that was surely distorted for effect. But if the conspiracy indeed existed, and if only a fraction of those indicated as followers adhered to the plot, it would have been the largest slave uprising in the history of the United States. However, in many ways the Vesey incidents of 1822 were similar to the *La Escalera* conspiracy in Cuba of 1844. In Cuba, no hard evidence indicating a plot on the dimensions insisted upon by the Cuban authorities was ever uncovered, and this was in all likelihood the case in Charleston in 1822. Something was probably in the planning stage, but in South Carolina the repression unleashed may have been more a preemptive strike to assure that no real plot would unfold. This was exactly the scenario in Cuba, which helps to explain the repressive measures adopted there in 1844.

If a conspiracy existed, then it was betrayed in the usual manner. A fellow slave, loyal to his master, reported the plot long before any real uprising could take place. State and city armed forces were mobilized, and Vesey was arrested along with many of his followers. More than 130 people were charged with conspiracy; 35 slaves and free blacks, including Vesey, were hanged; and more than 40 were deported from the United States. As was always the case after such conspiracies, real or imagined, were discovered, a series of repressive laws limiting the movement and activities of slaves and free peoples of color were enacted. There would be no more conspiracies for freedom in Charleston until the Civil War.

The most famous, violent, and extensively chronicled slave revolt in U.S. history was the Nat Turner rebellion of 1831. The revolt took place in Southampton County, Virginia, located in the eastern part of the state contiguous to North Carolina, where Turner was born and raised. In 1830, nearly 50 percent of the county's population was enslaved. Turner was born in Southampton County and in all likelihood lived all of his life there. Historians know a great deal about the Turner slave revolt because of a detailed confession he made after his capture, which was subsequently published as a small pamphlet.[49]

The revolt itself seems to have been largely spontaneous, and there is no evidence of a generalized or well-planned conspiracy among Southampton County's slaves. There is little evidence of inspiration

---

[49]   Nat Turner, *The Confessions of Nat Turner, the Leader of the Late Insurrection in Southampton*, Va. (Baltimore: T. R. Gray, 1831). The full text may be found on the internet at <http://docsouth.unc.edu/turner/turner.html>.

from any previous slave rebellions in the United States or invocation of the Haitian slave revolt, as was the case with Vesey. Turner was a very religious man and a preacher who conceived of himself as a messianic figure. He affirmed that his motives were rooted in a series of religious visions he had had at various points in his adult life, which he interpreted as divine interventions instructing him to lead his people to freedom. His motives were not based upon personal abuse or affronts, and he stated in his confession that his master at the time of the rebellion was a good man who treated him well, although during the revolt he was murdered. The influence of the abolitionist movement elsewhere in the United States or even in Virginia, where there was some opposition to slavery, is unknown.

The events surrounding the uprising are well known and have been written about over and again. Turner claimed that his final vision, a total eclipse of the sun that took place on August 13, 1831, was in reality a divine signal for him to act to deliver his people into freedom. With no more than five followers at its outset, Turner's revolt began its mission of delivering death to whites and freedom to slaves. His master was murdered along with his entire family. As it moved through the South-ampton countryside, other slaves and a few free men spontaneously joined Turner's small army, which grew to somewhere around fifty men. There is little evidence of any planning. The rebels marched through the county over a period of about thirty-six hours, killing any and all whites they encountered, and before the revolt could be contained there were between fifty and sixty dead. There is little evidence of a mass uprising of slaves, and contemporary accounts indicate that the slave population was as terrified of the revolt as whites, although they would bear the brunt of the repressive measures after the rebellion was quelled.

As word of the revolt spread rapidly through the county, militias were mobilized in Virginia and neighboring North Carolina, and some 3,000 federal troops were dispatched from Washington. Upon attacking the town of Jerusalem, Virginia, Turner's poorly armed rebels were routed and scattered into the countryside. Then a rampage of violence and vengeance was undertaken by whites, who rounded up, tortured, and purportedly murdered hundreds of slaves, most of whom had no connection whatsoever to the rebellion. White hysteria spread to surrounding counties in both Virginia and North Carolina, where wide-spread atrocities against slaves took place. Turner himself was able to escape and hide out for several months, but he was eventually captured, and from his jail cell he dictated his infamous "confessions." All of the participants in the revolt were jailed, and after judicial proceedings more than fifty were hanged. Although slavery's future was debated in Virginia in the aftermath of the rebellion, there was little sentiment for abolition among the state's elite. As was almost always the case after conspiracies or rebellions were discovered or defeated, repressive laws against slaves and free peoples of color were enacted to impose tight control over meetings, religious or otherwise, and restricting freedom of movement. Nat Turner died for his valiant attempt at freedom, and there would be no more mass revolts for liberty among Virginia slaves up to the beginning of the Civil War in 1861.

In Brazil, Cuba, and the United States, slaves found overt and covert ways to assert their fundamental qualities as human beings and their desire to live with as few restrictions as possible within the abominable conditions of enslavement. Organized violence and rebellions exploded throughout the histories of slavery in all three countries, and frustrated and betrayed conspiracies were discovered over and again. Slaves never stopped running away in search of freedom, and particularly in Brazil they were successful at establishing maroon communities where at least a respite from oppression could be found, even if only on a temporary basis. Most slaves sought more subtle ways of resisting by trying to carve out prerogatives for themselves and the their families wherever this was possible.

In the end, however, freedom and emancipation would come largely because of a series of political factors, although not all historians agree on this explanation. Political conditions shifted dramatically in the slaveholding countries during the nineteenth century. The paradoxes of slavery and advancing liberal ideologies in Western Europe and throughout the Americas increasingly entered the public's consciousness. Beginning in the late eighteenth century, these new ideas underscored humanity's supposed progressive march toward greater liberty and freedom. The spread of industrial capitalism and its reliance upon wage labor shaped the thinking of elite groups everywhere, even though slave labor may have been as efficient and productive from a strictly economic point of view. The embracing of abolitionism by religious forces of all persuasions had an important impact on common people in every country. All of these factors, and many others, produced a growing consensus by the middle of the nineteenth century that the issue of slavery had to be confronted in the three remaining great slaveholding nations of the Western Hemisphere. Yet despite increasing awareness that the institution of racial slavery was indeed doomed, the slaveholders and their political supporters stubbornly held on. It would take a destructive Civil War to end slavery in the United States, and a rebellion for independence in Cuba; and when it was the last country in the Western Hemisphere in which slavery continued, Brazil was reluctantly forced to end the institution in 1888.

CHAPTER EIGHT

ABOLITION

The United States, Cuba, and Brazil were the last nations in the Americas to abolish slavery. The Civil War (1861–65) ended slavery in the United States. Spain had little choice but to begin the dismantling of slavery in Cuba in the aftermath of the Ten Years' War, a violent rebellion for independence that raged from 1868 to 1878 in which abolition became a major issue designed to attract slaves to the revolutionary cause. Brazil, which held out the longest, finally succumbed to abolitionism in 1888, largely because of extraordinary domestic and international political pressure but without any cataclysmic violence, as was the case in the United States and Cuba.

Prior to slavery's abolition, the transatlantic slave trade had been gradually dismantled, largely because of concerted British efforts to end first slaving and then slavery. A British-American treaty of 1807 ended the slave trade to the United States and the British colonies in 1808. Britain, which took the international lead in exerting pressure upon both Spanish Cuba and imperial Brazil, forced various accords to abolish the slave trade upon each country. These were largely ineffective. Spain signed treaties ending the Cuban trade in 1817 and again in 1835. In 1862, British naval patrols had been given free rein to search suspected slave ships flying any flag, including those of the United States, and this increased pressure upon the Cuban slave trade. However, slaving continued until 1867 and the aftermath of the U.S. Civil War. Prior to Brazilian independence in 1822, British pressure on Portugal had produced treaties in 1815 and 1817, first limiting the trade to Brazilian regions north of the equator and then supposedly abolishing the slave trade altogether. These were as ineffective as the Anglo-Spanish treaties. British pressure resulted in another antislaving treaty with independent Brazil in 1826 that was designed to ban the slave trade in 1830. In 1831, after the establishment of the Brazilian empire, yet another law was proclaimed supposedly freeing any slave entering the nation after that year. But the trade continued until extraordinary British diplomatic pressure, backed by British naval patrols off Rio de Janeiro's coast, forced Brazil to end the African slave trade in 1851.[1]

Historians have debated the factors that led to the rise and spread of abolitionism in Europe and the Americas and eventually to the curbing of the slave trade and to freedom for nearly all slaves over the course of the late eighteenth and nineteenth centuries. The publication of Eric Williams's seminal book *Capitalism and Slavery* in 1944 was a catalyst for an intensive debate on the causes for the abolition of both the slave trade and slavery.[2] Prior to what has become known as the "Williams thesis," which focused on economic explanations, the rise of antislavery sentiment was interpreted as part of broad changes in attitudes among philosophers, religious leaders, and eventually masses of people who succeeded in influencing political leaders to enact laws and exert international pressure leading to the end of the slave trade and slavery. Their motivations were said to have been conditioned by major shifts in ideas focusing upon humanistic and moral questions that paralleled the rise of rationalism and democratic political systems in Europe and the United States.

For millennia, slavery had existed in all cultures and was philosophically, ideologically, and politically accepted as part of a supposed natural order that governed the human experience. In the late seventeenth and early eighteenth centuries, however, outspoken condemnations of human bondage were forthcoming from religious figures, especially among Quakers in England and in the United States.[3] With the growth of rationalism, scientific knowledge, and the gradual spread of the Enlightenment's ideas on human liberty and freedom during the

---

[1]   See Leslie Bethell, *The Abolition of the Brazilian Slave Trade: Britain, Brazil and the Slave Trade Question 1807–1869* (New York and London: Cambridge University Press, 1970), and Arthur F. Corwin, *Spain and the Abolition of Slavery in Cuba, 1817–1886* (Austin: University of Texas Press, 1967).

[2]   Eric Williams, *Capitalism and Slavery* (Chapel Hill: University of North Carolina Press, 1944).

[3]   See David Brion Davis, *The Problem of Slavery in the Age of Revolution 1770–1823* (New York: Oxford University Press, 1999), Chapter 5, "The Quaker Ethic and the Antislavery International," pp. 213–54.

eighteenth century, the philosophical and religious justifications for racial slavery were undermined. England became the center of an antislavery mass movement during the late eighteenth century, and gradually abolitionism was embraced by British political elites who lead a militant international campaign to end both the slave trade and slavery.

The interpretation that a growing tide of humanism, morality, and rationality produced the antislavery movement was for the most part a self-congratulatory history written by the abolitionists themselves, but it was by and large accepted by most historians through the mid twentieth century.[4] Williams in his 1944 *Capitalism and Slavery* asserted that morality and humanism had little to do with the rise of abolitionism and argued that self-serving economic factors were behind Great Britain's antislavery policies during the nineteenth century. Williams maintained that slavery in the British West Indian colonies had become unprofitable after the successful American Revolution and that the dominant slave-based sugar economy was experiencing crisis and decline in the early nineteenth century. Slavery was an obsolete form of labor, no longer economically sustainable, and wage labor was clearly more productive and rational. Great Britain was the leading European economic and imperial political power as well as the unquestioned center of the industrial revolution and an expanding world capitalist system. It was in its economic interests not only to end slave labor in its own colonies, but also to force its European rivals as well as the United States to abolish slaving and slavery itself. If successful, this would lead to more rational and efficient labor systems everywhere and to greater productivity and profitability as industrial capitalism advanced, and these factors would help to consolidate Great Britain's position as the world's premier economic power and imperial center. Williams rejected the notion that moral and humanistic considerations had anything at all to do with the rise of British abolitionism. Economic self-interest was the driving factor behind the British antislavery campaigns of the nineteenth century.

---

[4]   The writings of Thomas Clarkson, who began to publish antislavery tracts in the 1780s, exemplify this. See Thomas Clarkson, *The History of the Rise, Progress, & Accomplishment of the Abolition of the African Slave Trade, by the British Parliament* (Philadelphia: Brown & Merritt, James P. Parke, No. 119, High Street, 1808).

The "Williams thesis" was attractive to scholars examining slavery and abolition in the aftermath of World War II, when economic interpretations of historical processes became widespread and highly influential. In many ways Williams's arguments were indeed logical as abolitionism's rise in Great Britain occurred precisely when the industrial revolution, capitalism, wage labor, and British imperial power were all expanding dynamically. However, if economic obsolescence and the declining profitability of slave labor were responsible for the rise of abolitionism, Williams presented little evidence to support his claims. By the late 1950s, historians began to subject the economic aspects of slave labor in the Americas during the epoch of abolition to close scrutiny. A body of literature on the internal economic dynamics of slavery gradually emerged that demonstrated that slave labor was extraordinarily efficient in most places and highly profitable from a purely economic point of view, the dreadful human barbarity of the slave system notwithstanding. With respect to the British colonies, it was convincingly demonstrated that Williams was wrong in stating that the West Indian sugar economies were contracting and confronting a crisis that led to the abolitionist movement. To the contrary, the colonial sugar economy was dynamic, expanding, and highly profitable precisely as abolitionism grew and was consolidated in Great Britain. It was the abolition of the slave trade in 1808 and then slavery in 1833 that caused a severe economic crisis in the Caribbean colonies. This finding was exactly opposite to the Williams conclusions on the economic aspects of slavery and abolition.[5] If slavery was indeed economically profitable right up until it was abolished, then a renewed examination and explanation of the rise of abolitionism had to be forthcoming. Indeed one was: there was a return, sometimes reluctantly, to the idea of a moral, humanistic, and religious imperative that the abolitionists themselves had originally popularized.

[5]   See Seymour Drescher, *Econocide: British Slavery in the Era of Abolition* (Pittsburgh: University of Pittsburgh Press, 1977), for the most emphatic evidence and arguments against the economic interpretations of Williams. For considerations of the Williams thesis, see Barbara Solow and Stanley L. Engerman, editors, *British Capitalism and Caribbean Slavery: The Legacy of Eric Williams* (New York and Cambridge: Cambridge University Press, 1987). For a summary of the competing interpretations of abolitionism, see Stanley L. Engerman, "Forward," in Seymour Drescher, *From Slavery to Freedom: Comparative Studies in the Rise and Fall of the Atlantic System* (New York: New York University Press, 1999), pp. xi–xxii.

British and American Quakers, a small Protestant sect that emerged during the seventeenth-century English civil wars, played the initial role in antislavery religious and political activism. In the mid eighteenth century, well before the American Revolution, Quakers in the future United States denounced both slavery and the slave trade. At their 1758 meeting in Philadelphia members were forbidden to own slaves or to participate in any way in slave trading; in 1774, English Quakers voted to expel any member who was in any way associated with the African trade. Although they were fairly isolated as political actors, Quakers slowly reached out to other Protestant religious denominations, particularly to Methodists, and gradually many religious leaders embraced abolitionism on strictly moral grounds. In 1783, the first formal petition to the British House of Commons was presented by Quaker activists calling for the abolition of the slave trade, and it was then that the organized political campaign to end slaving and slavery began. The British prime minister, as to be expected, expressed some sympathy but little else. In 1787, London Quakers formed an official antislavery organization, the London Abolition Committee, which included Anglican evangelicals.[6] By the early 1790s some representatives in Parliament were members or sympathizers of the Abolition Committee, which had undertaken a successful public campaign to spread anti–slave trade ideas. Pamphlets were published and distributed; sympathizers outside of London were approached, principally within Methodist churches with significant urban working-class members; antislavery preaching was pursued to build support; and a fairly impressive campaign of presenting petitions to Parliament asking for the slave trade's abolition was undertaken. Far from an elite movement of religious leaders, British anti–slave trade sentiment grew very quickly among common people associated with Protestant denominations, and abolitionism became a veritable mass social movement as Britain's role in the African trade became a widely discussed public issue throughout the nation.

In 1792, over 500 antislavery petitions were presented to the British Parliament, containing an astounding 400,000 signatures representing about 9 percent of the total British adult population.[7]

---

[6] See Fogel, *Without Consent or Contract*, pp. 211–18, for a succinct summary.
[7] See Seymour Drescher, "Two Variants of Anti-Slavery: Religious Organization and Social Mobilization in Britain and France, 1780–1870," in Drescher, *From Slavery to Freedom*, pp. 35–56.

The drafting of these petitions and the gathering of signatures were made possible with the cooperation of churches as well as provincial and city governments throughout the nation. This developing mass abolitionist movement had a profound impact upon British politicians. In the same year, the House of Commons passed a law gradually outlawing the slave trade, although it was not approved by the House of Lords. Within ten years the issue of slaving had been transformed from a peripheral concern championed by Quakers and other religious organizations into a social and political movement that carried over to the nation's centers of political power. Although the crisis induced by the French Revolution and the onset of the Napoleonic Wars temporarily reduced national attention to the issue of the African slave trade, in 1807 Britain, along with the United States, formally ended participation in slaving as of January 1, 1808.

A somewhat parallel process of building support for anti–slave trade measures developed in the future United States prior to the Revolutionary War. While the revolution interrupted antislaving religious activists, the founding of the republic based on the concept that all men were created equal led to a renewal. Abolition societies with Quaker leadership were formed in Pennsylvania, where a gradual emancipation law had been passed in 1780, and in New York City as well. Petitions were sent to the new Congress in 1783 to abolish the African slave trade. But the issue of slavery subsided in the context of a revolutionary government that was occupied with the monumental task of creating viable political structures for the new nation. The central issue faced by the United States was the need to form a strong national government in the face of insistence by individual states and sectional interests on maintaining independent power and authority. Antislavery sentiment was an aspect of the victorious American Revolution, but it was not one that produced a mass political movement focusing upon slaving or slavery, as was the case in Great Britain in the 1780s and 1790s. U.S. merchants and maritime interests played a marginal role in the African slave trade compared to the British, and perhaps because of this, the moral repugnance to slaving was not as intense in the United States. Additionally, while the new republic and its revolutionary Constitution protected the rights of slaveholders and sanctioned slavery, a 1794 law prohibited U.S. citizens from participating in the slave trade with foreign nations. By 1798, a full decade prior to 1808, when the Anglo-American treaty banning the slave trade took effect, all states had made it illegal to import foreign slaves.[8]

There was also a fundamentally different character to antislaving and antislavery issues in the United States compared to Great Britain.[9] In the United States, these issues were rapidly secularized after the revolutionary victory and independence. Religious leaders in Britain led a moral crusade, were successful at building a mass movement, and then enlisted political support in Parliament. The process in the United States was entirely different. Slaving and slavery quickly became political rather than religious or strictly moral issues in the independent United States and were debated by governmental officials at all levels, local, state, and national. Quakers who had raised these issues during the colonial period were delegitimized in the short term because they had not supported the Revolutionary War, and this very fact marginalized their activities and influence after independence.

Additionally, slavery was entrenched in the southern states, and this gave rise to a powerful pro-slavery lobby that counteracted the activities of abolitionists and weakened their mass appeal at the national level, despite strong support in the northern states, where slavery was gradually ended. The power of the southern states, in the national government was such that every attempt to pass legislation limiting slavery was decisively defeated in the first two decades of the republic's history. The 1808 ban on the slave trade effectively diminished slaving as a political or moral issue of widespread popular concern in the United States, and the question of slavery itself did not take hold on any significant scale among the general public in the early nineteenth century, despite the continued, but weakened, activities of abolitionists. The new republic had other concerns, and the territorial expansion westward produced heated political debates about whether slavery should be permitted in the new territories, soon to become states, rather than about whether slavery should be definitively abolished. Abolitionism would be a minor force in U.S. politics until the 1830s, when it was revived.

[8]   South Carolina reopened the slave trade from Africa in 1803. Additionally, it ought to be noted that the Constitution restricted the national government from proclaiming any law ending slaving until 1807. Thus it was up to the states to enact their own laws on the issue of the slave trade. Despite legal proscriptions, nearly 100,000 slaves were imported to the United States during the period between 1776 and the formal outlawing of the trade in 1808.

[9]   See Fogel, *Without Consent or Contract*, pp. 240–54.

No such pro-slavery political forces existed in Great Britain, and when the slave trade was abolished a sustained campaign was undertaken to end the African trade conducted by other nations. Using diplomatic pressure a series of treaties was negotiated or imposed upon Spain, Portugal, and Brazil, as indicated previously. The treaties not only aimed at forcing these nations to end participation in the slave trade, but also stipulated that British warships would be granted permission to stop and search suspected slave ships anywhere on the high seas. In 1819 the African Squadron of the British Navy was established to patrol the African coast in search of slave ships, which if discovered would be seized, their slaves freed, and their crews arrested. Special "admiralty courts" were established in British colonial Freetown in Sierra Leone, Havana, Rio de Janeiro, and in Dutch-controlled Paramaribo in Surinam. These became known as courts of "mixed commission," since they were to be composed of citizens of the nations that had signed anti–slave trade treaties – Spain, Portugal, and the Netherlands. Each of these countries was pressured to form its own antislaving naval squadron. Clearly controlled by the British, the mixed commissions were to adjudicate cases involving seized slave ships. Additionally, the British Foreign Office created a Slave Trade Department to oversee the enforcement of treaties, the activities of the African Squadron, and the mixed commission courts. Thus, the British led a broadside attack on the slave trade that was to play out in different phases over nearly fifty years, until Cuba was finally forced to halt African imports in 1867. Over the course of this period over 570 slave ships were seized by naval squadrons, and more than 150,000 slaves were freed.[10]

The attack on the slave trade in the first half of the nineteenth century was a British-led endeavor, although there were varying degrees of support in other European nations and in the United States. Since the United States had in fact abolished the trade in 1808, and was not dependent on the importation of Africans because of the impressive process of natural reproduction among its slave population, slaving receded as a political cause of great significance. The issue of the African slave trade was of critical political and economic importance in Spanish Cuba and in Portuguese and then (after 1822) independent Brazil. However, this was not because of any rising antislave trade

---

[10]   For a nuanced account of this long and costly campaign, see Eltis, *Economic Growth and the Ending of the Transatlantic Slave Trade*, Part III, "The Abolitionist Assault on the Slave Traffic, 1820–50," pp. 81–122.

sentiment, but rather quite the opposite. Far from opposing the slave trade, elites in both countries were dependent upon and in favor of continued slaving, and there were no popular-based expressions of antislavery sentiment of any significance. Brazil and Cuba experienced dynamic economic growth around slave-based economic sectors during the first half of the nineteenth century and needed the continued importation of Africans to maintain labor supplies, notwithstanding the theoretical illegality of the slave trade. While abolitionism was destined to become a powerful political force in the United States during the 1830s, it would take hold much later in the nineteenth century in Cuba and Brazil and would never become the religious, civic, and political movement that it became in the North Atlantic world. There were no Protestant denominations such as the Quakers or Methodists working to mobilize popular support for abolition in Cuba, Brazil, Portugal, or Spain. Nor was there widespread sympathy for abolition among political elites in colonial Cuba or imperial Brazil, since so many powerful public figures were slaveholders whose economic lifelines were linked directly or indirectly to slavery. Additionally, slavery was pervasive in nearly every region of Brazil and Cuba; there were no areas analogous to the northern free states of the United States where abolitionism could establish a base of support.

Paralleling the concerted attack on the slave trade, British anti-slavery activists turned to the issue of complete abolition in the West Indian colonies. In 1823, the London Antislavery Committee was formed, although there was little initial success at mobilizing mass public support for abolition. For a variety of complex reasons having to do with internal British politics, this situation changed quickly during the early 1830s.[11] A slave uprising in Jamaica in late 1831, its violent repression, and persecution launched against abolitionist missionaries resident on the island became public issues of importance within Great Britain. In the aftermath of the revolt, the Antislavery Committee's call for immediate emancipation found supporters within the nation's political elite, and by 1833 key politicians had begun to focus upon the abolition of slavery. The Emancipation Act, freeing all slaves in the British colonies, was passed by Parliament and signed into law by the king in August 1833. It called for immediate freedom for slaves,

[11] The committee's official name was the Society for the Mitigation and Gradual Abolition of Slavery. See Fogel, *Without Consent or Contract*, pp. 218–33, for a synopsis.

although an "apprenticeship" system was established that permitted slave owners to "use" the labor of their ex-slaves for six years while they were to be prepared for freedom.

With the secularization of abolition as a political issue in the United States, the ending of the slave trade in 1808, the pro-slavery offensive by southern politicians, and the resulting erosion of abolitionism as a potent political force by the second decade of the nineteenth century, antislavery activists readjusted their tactics and strategies. Evangelical Protestants and Quakers continued to preach against the evils and sins of slavery, but outside of churches and small groups of sympathizers their impact on the general public was minimal. Some focused upon strategies for manumitting slaves. Others developed colonization schemes for creating areas within the United States for freed slaves or even for developing colonies of manumitted slaves in Africa, particularly in Sierra Leone, where British abolitionists had established a colonization project. In 1817 the American Colonization Society was founded, advocating gradual emancipation and a return to Africa for freed men and women. There was some support from antislavery elements in the North and even in the slaveholding South, but it was marginal at best. It was only in the 1830s that abolitionism was revived in the United States.

This was preceded by a movement of religious revivalism that swept the nation, known as the Second Great Awakening. The First Great Awakening had taken place during the colonial period from the 1730s through the 1770s and was led by New England Baptists and Presbyterians in Pennsylvania and New Jersey. This movement of religious zeal also swept through Great Britain and other parts of northern Europe where Protestantism was entrenched. In some ways it was designed to counter the growing influence of rationalism and scientific reasoning and the threats that these Enlightenment ideas posed to religious doctrines, especially the fundamental notion of the need for salvation through allegiance to an omnipotent deity. While historians have debated the influence of this religious revivalism on the American Revolution, it is clear that the revolutionary period interrupted the movement of religious zeal sweeping the colonies. But after independence in the 1790s, there was a gradual renewal of evangelical Protestantism, especially of Calvinism, with its emphasis on salvation as determined more by inner faith and moral righteousness in one's life and less as a predetermined condition in the hands of an almighty God. These religious ideas made possible a reconciliation between the secular democratic political ideals that in part shaped the new United States and the religious piety of common people, who could conceive of a democratic ability to achieve salvation through their moral actions, life decisions, and free will. Although this revivalism began in New England, it gradually swept through the mid-Atlantic states, to the southern frontiers, and westward toward the new territories that were being wrenched violently from indigenous peoples. It also began to spread among newly arriving immigrant groups, who were courted by evangelicals.

Although abolitionism had never disappeared from the agendas of many religious and political leaders, it was emphatically reborn as a popular movement in the 1830s, in part because of the moral righteousness engendered by the religious revivalism of the early nineteenth century and the conviction that slavery was a sin standing in the way of personal and national salvation. Antislavery sentiment was revitalized as a powerful religious, social, and political movement that would shape American political debates until the outbreak of the Civil War in 1861. In 1831, the Boston journalist William Lloyd Garrison established a newspaper, the *Liberator*, dedicated to the immediate abolition of slavery, and the following year he helped found the New England Anti-Slavery Society. An antislavery society had been formed in New York in 1831, and in 1833 abolitionist groups came together in Philadelphia to organize the national-level American Anti-Slavery Society, which adopted the position that slavery should be abolished immediately. Abolitionists had previously endorsed gradual emancipation, and some supported the colonization schemes mentioned previously. Now the issue was framed in the moralistic and religious terms of revivalism and regeneration, but the objective was political as well. For the sake of nation's salvation, the sin of slavery had to be ended.

Using churches to spread their message to common people, organizing lecture tours organized to further their cause, and printing and mailing pamphlets, magazine articles, and journalistic pieces to be read by the increasingly literate public, the society had some 200,000 members and 2,000 local organizations by 1840. Free peoples of color in the northern states were active participants, and six African-Americans were on the organization's original board of managers. Ex-slaves who had acquired freedom in a number of ways also became important activists in the organization. The most famous was Frederick Douglass, the runaway slave who had acquired freedom in the North, and who galvanized the public with his eloquent testimony during the 1840s and 1850s on the barbarity of slavery in the South.[12] Yet the history of the Anti-Slavery Society was not a smooth one. There were schisms over strategy and tactics, splits between different religious denominations, and a pro-slavery backlash both in the North and especially in the South, where proselytizers attempted to spread the antislavery message in the heart of the slave states. Mobs were often organized to attack speakers violently. As was the case with any contentious issue, there was sharp polarization among the public in the ever-expanding United States. While there was no linear march of antislavery sentiment in the nation up to the eve of the Civil War, the issue was eventually adopted and addressed by all political parties.

In 1840 the abolitionists organized the Liberty Party, which was the first formal national-level political party, dedicated to ending slavery, and this was its single issue. It was a fringe party, drawing some 3 percent of the national vote in the 1844 presidential election, but its participation marks the formal entrance of abolitionism into national politics. In 1848, after the invasion of Mexico and the seizure of about one-half of Mexican national territory in the war known in the United States as the Mexican-American War, which raged from 1846 to 1848, a new political party was founded – the Free-Soil Party. Antislavery forces in the mainstream Democratic and Whig Parties, as well as members of the defunct Liberty Party, formed the Free-Soil Party, which called for the proscription of slavery in the newly acquired western territories transferred to the United States through the 1848 Treaty of Guadalupe Hidalgo, a treaty forced upon Mexico to end military occupation of that nation by the United States.

The issue of extending slavery into new territories and future states – which led to the secession of the southern states, the formation of the Confederacy, the cataclysmic Civil War, and the end of slavery in the United States – dated from the early years of the republic. Two general laws governing slavery in territories extending to the Mississippi River were passed by Congress in the 1780s: the Northwest Ordinance of 1784 prohibited the extension of slavery north of the Ohio River, and the Southwest Ordinance of 1787 permitted slavery in the territories south

[12]   There are many editions of Douglass's autobiography, first published in 1855. For a recent version, see Frederick Douglass, *Life and Times of Frederick Douglass: His Early Life as a Slave, His Escape from Bondage, and His Complete History: An Autobiography* (New York: Gramercy Books, 1993).

of the same river. These were attempts to resolve potential sectional rivalries even before slavery was abolished in all of the northern states.

The issue surfaced again after the unanticipated acquisition of all territory north and east of pre-1848 Mexico to the Pacific Ocean through the Louisiana Purchase of 1803 from Napoleonic France. Perhaps because these areas were so sparsely populated and because the future impact of the acquisition was not yet fully grasped, the question of slavery in the newly acquired west was not addressed or resolved. However, in 1819, when the Missouri Territory petitioned for statehood, slavery in the territories once again became a contentious political issue pitting southern and northern sectional interests against one another. Most of the Missouri settlers had originated in the southern slave states, and many had brought slaves with them. Yet when the statehood issue came up in Congress, the House of Representatives included the banning of future slave imports and gradual freedom for all slaves born in Missouri as conditions for entrance into the Union. The Senate refused to vote favorably on these stipulations, and after acrimonious debate a pact known as the Missouri Compromise of 1820 was finally reached. This permitted slavery in the state of Missouri but permanently banned slavery in all future states north of the southern Missouri boundary. Essentially a north/south line governing the future of U.S. slavery was extended westward from the Mississippi River, and this conformed to the ordinances of 1784 and 1787. However, most territory included in the Louisiana Purchase was in fact north of the southern Missouri boundary, and in many ways the compromise was interpreted in both the North and the South as a victory of the antislavery forces. Nevertheless, the issue of slavery's extension into the West nearly disappeared as a divisive national political concern until the annexation of Texas in 1845. The passionate antislavery rhetoric heard during the debates leading to the 1820 compromise had a lasting effect on southern politicians, who were concerned about the possibility of an eventual all-out northern-led campaign against slavery.

In the context of the antislavery religious revivalism sweeping through the northern states, the increasing polarization of southern proslavery and northern antislavery sectional interests, and the annexation of the western and southwestern regions of the continent, the issue of slavery was once again placed front and center in national political debates during the 1840s. Although the Missouri Compromise had theoretically settled the question of slavery's extension into new territories, the petition of Texas to be admitted into the union as a slave state resurrected the acrimonious conflict. Texas had been settled as part of the southern tier migration westward and became a major producer of cotton based upon slave labor. Nominally part of Mexican national territory, but sparsely populated and militarily indefensible, Texas won its independence from Mexico in 1836 and immediately petitioned for annexation to the United States as a slave state. For a variety of reasons, including fear of war with Mexico; an undefined western Texas frontier; the opposition of northern antislavery interests, who felt that the balance of power would shift to the slave states; and international pressures, Texas was not made part of the United States until 1845, when it was admitted to the union with slavery legally sanctioned. This was the first salvo in the renewed conflict over the extension of slavery in the territories, and it would eventually lead to the Civil War and the abolition of slavery.

The rapid settlement of California following of the discovery of gold in 1848, the adoption of that state's antislavery constitution, and an 1849 petition for California to be incorporated into the union as a free state continued to place the issue of slavery's role in the territories at the forefront of political contention. After the war with Mexico, southern sectional interests were clearly threatened because of an aggressive attempt by antislavery sectors of Congress to completely ban slavery from the huge western regions that were formally annexed in 1848. A crisis was avoided by yet another brokered deal, the Compromise of 1850. In a series of laws passed by Congress, California was admitted as a free state, but it was agreed that the issue of slavery in other, still sparsely populated territories would be decided at a later date when statehood was petitioned. Slavery was not specifically forbidden in these new territories in order to placate the South. As a further concession to southern interests, the Fugitive Slave Act of 1850 was enacted. This made northern federal authorities responsible for apprehending suspected runaway slaves and returning them to their rightful owners. Law enforcement officials were also obligated to cooperate with agents who had been dispatched to the North by southern slaveholders to recuperate runaways. For northern antislavery activists, these were grave blows. The southern pro-slavery interests had forced the federal government to make complicity with slavery in the free states obligatory by law under the terms of the Fugitive Slave Act.

Although the conflicts over slavery's extension into the western United States were secular and political, the antislavery movement's appeal to common people had for the most part been based on religious and moral arguments. The role of Protestant denominations, particularly Methodists, in spreading the abolitionist gospel had been central. Yet there had always been a secular strain to the antislavery movement, and with the conflicts of the late 1840s over the extension of slavery westward, political considerations among the abolitionists began to move to center stage in their campaign to build popular support. The United States had been transformed during the first half of the nineteenth century by migration westward, large-scale immigration from Europe, rapid industrialization in the North, urbanization, the growth of an urban working class, and dynamic population growth, among other factors. One faction of the abolitionist movement came to the realization that slavery would be ended only if the appeal of antislavery forces broadened and moved away from strictly religious principles. The debates about the extension of slavery into the territories were largely political, and if slavery was ever to be abolished a broad secular political base of support that could push the nation toward abolition would have to be constructed.

During the 1850s, the antislavery forces sought to build support through religious appeals and secular strategies that centered on moral and political indictments of southern society and culture. In a propaganda onslaught tinged with religious overtones, the South was depicted in near-diabolical terms as immoral, culturally bankrupt, and riddled with sin because of slavery. Additionally, southern politicians representing a newly labeled "Slave Power" were accused of conspiring politically and economically to subvert and dominate the United States through their insistence on extending slavery into the frontier. Finally, in a fundamental reconsideration of prior conceptualizations, the Constitution was reinterpreted as a document that permitted federal intervention in the states to abolish slavery.

Until the late 1830s, abolitionists and indeed most politicians in both the North and the South recognized that slavery was not regulated by federal law and that only the states had the right to determine the legality of human bondage. The abolitionists felt, perhaps naively, that moral and religious arguments as well as rational appeals would eventually convince southern slaveholders to abandon their stubborn defense of slavery and recognize that human progress mandated abolition. But by the mid-1840s the acrimonious conflicts over slavery's extension into the western frontier, coupled with the fierce defense of slavery by southern politicians, shattered any illusion that slavery would be voluntarily abandoned. Political arguments were advanced and disseminated calling for the national government to enforce a Constitution requiring federal intervention in the states over the issue of slavery. To the southern slave interests this was an ominous direction, and matters were made worse by the founding of the Republican Party in 1854, which embraced the position of the Free Soil Party that slavery should be banned from all territories and future states and that the Constitution gave the federal government the power to enforce this.[13]

The sectionalist acrimony over the issue of slavery and its extension into the territories was exacerbated in 1854 by yet another law passed by Congress governing the remaining unsettled territories within the Louisiana Purchase. The Kansas-Nebraska Act of 1854 abrogated the Missouri Compromise of 1820 by affirming the concept of popular sovereignty within each future state. The 1820 law had banned slavery north of the southern Missouri boundary. The 1854 act stated that the issue of slavery would be decided by the people of each territory upon petition for statehood. Thus, slavery could legally be extended to the northern future states in the West. The 1857 Dred Scott decision rendered by the Supreme Court made matters worse for the abolitionist movement. Scott had lived for many years on the legally free soil of Illinois and Minnesota, and had been granted freedom after a lawsuit filed on his behalf in his home state of Missouri, although this was reversed by the Missouri Supreme Court. The decision was appealed to the U.S. Supreme Court, which ruled not only that Scott remain a slave, but also that the Missouri Compromise of 1820 was emphatically unconstitutional and that the federal government had no power to exclude slavery from any existing or future territories. In another affront to those who believed in abolition and human freedom, the highest court of the land also ruled that African-Americans were not citizens of the United States even if they were free and that they had "no rights the white man was bound to respect."

The virulent attacks on southern culture and society by the abolitionists and their allies during the 1850s pushed leading politicians in the South to defensive positions, to be sure. But a more ominous line of reasoning was that southern slavery, the foundation of a prosperous and productive agrarian economy, would never be secure without political autonomy. This opened the road to possible formation of an

---

[13]   For a succinct summary of the secularization of antislavery sentiment in the 1840s and 1850s and the dynamics of the new abolitionism, see Fogel, *Without Consent or Contract*, pp. 322–54.

independent nation and secession. On the other side of the contentious divide, the victories by the southern pro-slavery interests in Congress and in the Supreme Court in 1854 and 1857 were self-fulfilling prophecies for the northern sectional interests and irrefutable evidence that the demonic southern "Slave Power" not only sought to take over the national government, but might already have done so.

Yet in the North it was one thing to rally public support for anti-Southern and antislavery positions or diatribes; it was another to build the political support and alliances needed to elect officials at all levels of government. This was the task facing the Republican Party after its founding in 1854. Although the party clearly represented northern sectional political interests that conceived of a southern conspiracy to take over the national government, it did not advocate the abolition of slavery despite the presence of militant abolitionists within the party. The party's major issue in seeking to rally popular support was reversing the national-level political power that the southern sectional interests had achieved and would consolidate if slavery were extended into the future western states through the concept of popular sovereignty as affirmed by the 1854 Kansas-Nebraska Act.

The reorganization of American political parties during the 1850s was closely linked to the issue of slavery's extension into the West. The northern United States was undergoing rapid economic and social transformation. Cities were expanding and immigrants were flocking to them from Europe, engendering an anti-immigrant backlash among native workers, who saw each wave of newcomers as competitors for jobs. An urban working class grew and increasingly participated in politics in its own independent organizations as well as within mainstream political parties. The national political party system that had prevailed from the 1830s, in which Whigs and Democrats disputed elections, began to collapse with the founding of the Free Soil Party in 1848 and the rise of the anti-immigrant and anti-Catholic American Party, dubbed the Know-Nothing Party by its opponents, during the early 1850s. The national Democratic Party was increasingly controlled by its southern wing, and northern Democrats, despite their vehement defense of the South's interests, soon found that the slaveholders' increasingly extreme demands outstripped their ability to comply. The Republican Party adopted an unambiguous position at its first party convention in 1856 declaring that Congress had the authority to, and should, ban slavery in the new territories. When the outcry over the Kansas-Nebraska Act revitalized antislavery sentiment throughout the

North, the Republican Party emerged to harness that sentiment. Between 1856 and 1860, the party was able to build and consolidate support from a diverse and disparate base of supporters, including anti-slavery Whigs and Democrats, Free Soil abolitionists, urban working-class organizations, and even from Know-Nothing Party supporters who had become disenchanted with the single-focus anti-Catholic and anti-immigrant positions of the party.

Abolitionism and Republicanism in the North were also aided by the Kansas crisis of 1856 and the violence known as "Bleeding Kansas" that exploded in the state. The federal government officially recognized the pro-slavery government and intervened to arrest the leaders of the abolitionist government in Lawrence, Kansas. Pro-slavery mobs went on a rampage, attacking antislavery leaders, and the infamous John Brown responded in kind by attacking pro-slavery colonists. A state of war exploded in eastern Kansas, and the violence subsided only after some 200 people had been killed on both sides of the struggle. The crisis was exacerbated when a Republican senator, Charles Sumner of Massachusetts, was beaten mercilessly by a South Carolina pro-slavery Democratic legislator after delivering a lengthy speech attacking the southern Democrats for their pro-slavery activities in Kansas.

The collapse of the old political party system, the rise of Republican power in the North, and the sectional split over the issue of slavery's future in the western frontier was graphically revealed in the 1856 presidential election, which took place while the civil war in Kansas raged. The Republicans narrowly lost the Electoral College vote, but they won eleven northern states. An alliance between remaining Whigs and the Know-Nothing Party diverted a substantial number of potential votes from the Republicans and permitted the Democrats to win the key northern states of New Jersey, Pennsylvania, Indiana, and Illinois, and thus the presidency. Not only was the election embittered by the issue of slavery in the territories, it was the first in which the sectional cleavage of the nation was so prominent in a presidential campaign. The task of the Republicans was clear in the aftermath of the election. If the party could siphon off enough moderate votes in 1860, they could win the presidency by focusing only upon the northern states, and this is exactly what propelled Abraham Lincoln to victory, although he won less than 40 percent of the popular vote. Equally important, the Democratic Party split apart in 1860, fielding separate candidates in the North and the South. In the border states, the remnants of the Whig Party nominated yet another candidate. In this four-way race, Lincoln could win the presidency even though he was not even on the ballot in nine southern states. In December 1860, South Carolina seceded from the United States and was joined by six other southern states. In April 1861, the Civil War that would end slavery began when the newly formed Confederacy attacked the federal Fort Sumter in Charleston harbor.

On the eve of the Civil War, political support for the Republican Party in the North was directly linked to the North's growing hostility to slavery. There were many radical abolitionists, white and African-American, who called for slavery's destruction in the South. But Lincoln himself was emphatically not an abolitionist even though he personally believed slavery to be morally wrong. In fact, he went to great lengths to acknowledge the Constitution's protection for slavery in the states where it already existed. Nor did he believe that African-Americans should be equal to whites before the law; for Lincoln, race and slavery were two separate issues. Blacks and whites were equally entitled to their freedom, to the fruits of their labor, Lincoln said, but that did not mean that they were equally entitled to vote or to marry one another. Nevertheless, he believed that "slavery is wrong and ought to be treated as such." That meant restricting slavery's expansion. Like most people, he believed that slavery needed to expand in order to survive, so that restricting it would put slavery "on the course of ultimate extinction."

Thus, the fundamental issue in 1860 was whether or not slavery would be allowed into the frontier. The lives of the peoples whose fates would be determined by these decisions, the slaves themselves, were not major or even important issues for most people at the onset of the fighting. Racism in the North was probably as virulent as racism in the South, but Lincoln and the Republicans were careful to argue that while slavery was immoral, racial segregation was not. They focused on the expansion of slavery not as a way to avoid the moral issue, but because slavery's expansion was where the issue of slavery arose in American politics. This was not a new issue. It extended back to the founding of the republic in the 1780s, but it had always been resolved by compromise. The war, unanticipated to be sure, changed everything, and Lincoln, his advisors, and even public opinion in the North moved to the position that the only way to defeat and subjugate the Confederacy and to make certain that the "Slave Power" could never be resurrected was to destroy slavery completely. The dismantling of slavery would present an opportunity to remake the South and the nation itself, perhaps realizing the stated aspirations of the late eighteenth-century revolutionaries who wanted to create a republic in which indeed all men were created equal (although nothing was said about women).

The reaction to the outbreak of war of the slaves themselves, and of the African-American population of the northern states, was critical in shaping and furthering the cause of freedom. African-Americans had been prevented from enlisting in the armed forces of the United States by a 1792 law, and this law was still in effect when the Civil War began. Lincoln's government moved with caution on the issue of black soldiers, since at the beginning of the war there was some hope that southern leaders would reverse course, call for an end to hostilities, and rejoin the union. More than that, Lincoln and the Republicans were afraid that if they moved too quickly on emancipation and the enlistment of black troops, support for the war among northern whites would collapse, making the defense of the Union impossible. But African-American leaders pressured the government to permit them to join the fight against the South. To them, the war was a struggle against slavery and for equality. As the determination of the Confederacy to press forward became apparent, the North's policy of excluding peoples of color from the armed forces changed. In July 1862, laws were enacted permitting African-Americans to enlist in the army, and after the preliminary Emancipation Proclamation of September 1862, the first African-American regiments were organized and entered the battle for freedom. The final Emancipation Proclamation became law on January 1, 1863, freeing all slaves in areas still in rebellion against the United States. In the border states that had not joined the Confederacy and where slavery was legal – Delaware, Maryland, Kentucky, and Missouri – slaves were not freed by the 1863 proclamation, since the president had no constitutional power to abolish slavery in states that were loyal to the Union. Nor were slaves freed in southern areas occupied by the Union army. But by then Lincoln had already drafted legislation to abolish slavery in the border states and ordered his army not to return slaves who escaped to Union lines – no matter what part of the South they came from. The objective of the war had now changed, but it would take a Thirteenth Amendment to the Constitution to guarantee that when the war ended slavery was abolished as well.

Given the opportunity to contribute to the struggle to end slavery in the South, African-Americans joined the Union army enthusiastically. It has been estimated that between 180,000 and 200,000 African-American soldiers fought in the Civil War and that some 38,000 died for the cause of freedom. By 1864, African-American soldiers were participating in nearly every military campaign of the war. Many were runaway slaves who had made it to the North and freedom. Others were southern slaves who had abandoned plantations and farms in the quest for freedom when the Union army neared. In keeping with the racism of the times, African-American soldiers were initially paid lower salaries than white soldiers, and many refused to accept their wages because of this indignity. But in 1864 Congress proclaimed equal pay for all soldiers regardless of race.

Although there was no general uprising of slaves in the South during the war itself, and despite the fact that some slaves were found in the Confederate army, usually impressed by their masters, hundreds of thousands took advantage of the chaos of war to flee toward the northern lines and freedom.[14] Others utilized the confusion to increase their bargaining power with masters and mistresses for better treatment and more prerogatives, especially if they found themselves distant from the front lines. Many slaves just stopped obeying orders that could not be enforced by their owners, who were often absent serving in the Confederate army. They went about the business of survival by looking after their own provision grounds and animals and biding their time until conditions favored flight and freedom. When the Union army approached, more often than not they simply abandoned servitude.

A war that had begun as a conflict over the political balance of power between northern and southern sectional interests turned into a war against slavery. There is no question that African-American political pressures from the North, the willingness to fight for the freedom of all slaves in the Union army, and the resistance by slaves in the South engendered by the war itself contributed to its transformation into one of liberation. As the war lengthened and the casualties mounted, the bitterness and hatred on both sides increased enormously. In the North, public opinion moved toward the position not only that the "Slave Power" should be permanently destroyed but that slavery should be ended as well. Lincoln was well ahead of northern public opinion on this, but he was careful to move against slavery in ways that would not undermine the Union war effort. Within weeks of the war's outbreak he

[14]   The role of southern slaves in their own liberation has been debated by scholars. See Ira et al., editors, *Freedom: A Documentary History of Emancipation, 1861–1867. Volume 1, Series 1: The Destruction of Slavery* (New York: Cambridge University Press, 1986).

let stand the military's decision to declare runaway slaves "contraband of war." In July he signed the first Confiscation Act, authorizing the confiscation of slaves owned by rebellious masters. And in December 1861 Lincoln quietly announced that contraband and confiscated slaves would be considered "liberated" by the federal government. The Emancipation Proclamation pushed the dismantling of slavery still further. And before the final surrender of the Confederate forces in April 1865, the Thirteenth Amendment to the U.S. Constitution, passed by Congress in January of that year, forever ended slavery in the United States, although it was not enacted until December. For African-Americans, this was only the beginning of a new struggle for racial equality, for to end slavery was one thing, to end racism and discrimination would prove to be something entirely different.

Abolitionism in the United States emerged and was consolidated because of diverse factors – moral, political, economic, religious, humanitarian, and purely pragmatic. Perhaps most importantly, however, it was a product of the very myths and symbols that had led to the founding of the republic. Theoretically the revolutionary nation of the late eighteenth century was to be based on the concept that all men are created equal, but the reality was something quite different. Nothing in the Declaration of Independence or the Constitution mentioned anything about women or equality for peoples of color. The concept of one man, one vote was supposed to reign supreme in this new democracy, but it was not realized. The most blatant manifestation of this was the barbarous and dehumanizing system of racial slavery, which completely marginalized slaves and even free peoples of color from democratic participation. Myths are sometimes more powerful than realities, and despite the paradoxes and contradictions highlighted by the absence of women's rights, racial slavery, and institutionalized racial discrimination, most citizens of the United States sincerely believed in democracy, freedom, and humanitarianism despite its application to white males exclusively.

Perhaps this, among many other factors, distinguished colonial Cuba and imperial Brazil from the United States. There were no democratic pretensions, especially among elites, and the theoretical concepts of equality and citizenship did not exist for most people across the social hierarchy. Democratic elections where issues were debated and ultimately decided by universal white male suffrage were nonexistent. Although there were humanitarian abolitionists in both societies during the nineteenth century, they were few and far between and were confined to intellectual elites and some religious figures. Racism toward peoples of color, slave or free, was virulent among whites in all three countries, probably to a similar degree. But in Cuba and Brazil there were few doubts about condescending and racist attitudes toward slaves and free peoples of color. There was fairly universal agreement among whites, especially the power elites, that peoples of African descent were inferior because of race and thus not deserving of full participation in political, economic, and social institutions. There was also the nearly complete absence of democratic myths and symbols that could have raised any doubt among elites who wielded power about their assumptions of a natural hierarchical social order in which all men were not created equal, especially those of color.

In contrast to the United States, slavery existed and was accepted in every area of both countries, despite regional social, economic, and political antagonisms that manifested themselves at times as struggles between regional elite groups. Slavery was not uniformly important in all areas of Brazil and Cuba, to be sure. But even in regions where slavery was unimportant to local economies, few people questioned its legality or desirability. Slavery was not a contentious regional issue that politically divided either nation or colony.

Protestant denominations that had popularized abolitionist sentiments in England and the United States, such as the Quakers and Methodists, had no influence in Brazil or Cuba. The Catholic Church was officially sanctioned as the exclusive religious authority in both countries, and attempts at evangelical Protestant penetration were countered by policies discouraging or forbidding their presence. Thus, abolitionism as an important political force did not exist on any significant scale in either Cuba or Brazil until the late 1860s and 1870s, and when it emerged it never developed as a popular political movement of any great consequence, as was the case in Britain and the United States. In the Brazilian case, abolitionism as a mass movement appeared in the 1880s, a few years before final abolition in 1888. In the Cuban case, there was no popular antislavery mobilization, although abolitionism was an important component of the anti-Spanish war for independence that raged from 1868 to 1878, the Ten Years' War that forced Spain to begin the gradual abolition process.

Antislavery sentiments in Cuba were of little importance among the island's Cuban-born or Spanish political class or intellectual elite during the early nineteenth century. Labor supplies to support the explosive growth in the sugar and coffee export economies were almost entirely dependent upon slavery and the African slave trade. The most powerful sectors of Cuban colonial society, as well as the Spanish merchant class and many political officials, were interconnected through marriage, and all were in some way linked to slavery. Sugar, coffee, slaves, and slave trading sustained nearly every sector of this Spanish-Cuban elite. Their prosperity, however, was threatened on two fronts. First, the British-U.S. abolition of the slave trade in 1808 was an ominous sign that the Cuban trade could be ended as well. Indeed, the 1817 antislave trade treaty imposed upon Spain was foreboding, although it would quickly be subverted after theoretically taking effect in 1820. The second was the fear of slave revolt produced by the successful Haitian rebellion so close to eastern Cuba, where many French planters settled and recounted horrifying tales of the uprising. The Cuban elite was plagued in the early nineteenth century by the predicament of having continually to import more Africans to sustain the expanding economy and the fear of a Haitian-style revolt.

One response, which is difficult to place within the context of the antislavery movement, was a desire to "whiten" and "civilize" the Cuban population, according to the verbiage of the epoch, by encouraging European immigration that would also reduce dependence upon slaves. In 1815, the intendant and captain-general of Cuba established a Junta de Población Blanca (Council for White Population) charged with encouraging white immigration, and in 1817 land was offered as an incentive to lure migrants. But most of those who arrived in the aftermath of the law were refugees from the Spanish-American wars of independence, and many were from elite social classes who saw opportunities in the expanding Cuban economy. Instead of diversifying the labor force, these commercially minded immigrants helped increase the market for slaves, for their investments were usually in slave-based economic sectors. The theme of "whitening" would be resurrected repeatedly during the nineteenth century as an alternative to slavery.

One of the progenitors of Creole, or native-born, patriotism in Cuba during the early nineteenth century, Father Félix Varela, saw the abolition of the Cuban slave trade as a way to reduce the threat of slave revolt. Varela, who had been chosen as a deputy to represent Cuba in the Spanish Cortes or parliament in the early 1820s, put forth the first formal proposal for gradual abolition, which would free slaves who had served for 15 years with the same master as well as those born after an emancipation law was proclaimed.[15] The Cuban elite attacked these ideas unanimously, and there was little public support for them among the free white population. Varela was also identified with Cuban liberalism, a subversive ideology, and he was exiled from Spain to New York in 1823 because of his progressive political positions.

The person most identified with Cuban anti–slave trade sentiment in the nineteenth century, José Antonio Saco, repeatedly condemned the slave trade in the 1820s and early 1830s. He had been a student of Varela's at the University of Havana and was clearly influenced by his mentor's views on slavery and colonialism. Despite being elected to the Spanish Estatuto Real, the successor to the Cortes, he was permanently exiled from Cuba in 1834, the exaggerated response to any potential threat to Spain's sovereignty.[16] The antislavery issue in Cuba was bound up with liberalism and Creole patriotism, both intolerable to the colonial regime, and Saco represented these subversive ideologies in the eyes of the Spanish government. Abolitionism was also considered a British-inspired ideology, and the meddling of British diplomats was despised by Cuban planters, merchants, and Spanish officials, especially those who served on the Havana mixed commission courts.

Saco condemned the slave trade for various reasons, and there is no question that humanitarian ideas and European-inspired liberalism and abolitionism influenced his thinking. However, he was most concerned with the complexion of a future Cuban nation as well as the danger of a slave revolt if Africans continued pouring into the island. Saco, like Varela, wanted to see the slave trade's abolition in order to halt the growth of a black population that he saw as inferior and detrimental to Cuban society. He also wanted to encourage "whitening" through European migration. Cuban liberals adhered to racist conceptualizations of Africans and their descendants, and these were bound together with anti–slave trade rhetoric. Indeed, racism was widespread among the white population of all social classes, and the fear of Africanization could be used to appeal to elites and masses alike. Ideas reflecting the British-led movement against slavery were circulated only among a small group of educated intellectuals and some progressive planters. The Spanish colonial regime did not permit public debate of any sort, and

---

[15] Corwin, *Spain and the Abolition of Slavery in Cuba*, pp. 37–8.
[16] Christopher Schmidt-Nowara, *Empire and Antislavery: Spain, Cuba, and Puerto Rico, 1833–1874* (Pittsburgh: University of Pittsburgh Press, 1999), pp. 18–19.

there were tight restrictions on the press. Most people were illiterate; there was no antislavery preaching in Catholic religious institutions; Protestant denominations were not permitted; and vocal opponents of the colonial system or any of its manifestations, such as slavery and the slave trade, were arrested and exiled. It is not surprising that little public support emerged for progressive ideas, and no political movement of any significance developed against slavery in Cuba.

The abolition of slavery in Jamaica by the British in 1833 did not help the few isolated Cuban voices calling for enforcement of the anti–slave trade treaties Spain had signed with Great Britain. In Spain itself, slavery was abolished in 1837 to placate the British, but there were very few slaves in the peninsula and the impact of antislavery sentiment on Spanish domestic politics was minimal. By the 1840s, Cuban abolitionism as a political force or social movement was moribund, and matters were made worse by the antislavery activities of the British on the island within the "mixed courts" as well as at the consulate. The repression against the *Escalara* conspiracy was launched in 1844 and marked the end of any abolitionist activities on the island until the mid-1860s, although many of the figures of Cuban anti–slave trade sentiment, such as Saco, were active in exile through publishing anti–slave trade tracts and public speaking against the trade.

However, even in exile from Cuba their situation was made more precarious by flirtation with the annexationist movement of the late 1840s, which advanced the idea that Cuba would be better off if the island were incorporated into the United States. Slavery could then be defended against British meddlers and the institution made more harmonious, as it supposedly was in the U.S. South in the eyes of Cuban slaveholders. The threat of slave revolt would be reduced considerably if the U.S. model of natural slave reproduction were emulated, reducing the need for imports from Africa, which continued at high levels to Cuba into the 1850s. The sector of the Cuban elite adhering to these ideas had little understanding of slavery or race relations in the United States, and their attitudes were shaped by a highly romanticized and distorted imagery projected by southern slaveholders. From afar, this southern slave society looked inviting, and the idea of a stable Cuban slave system protected by the American flag and free of Spain as well as Great Britain was intriguing. For Spain, this was one more justification for repression, arrest, and deportation of those who were perceived to be against Spanish colonialism, annexationists or not. Anti–slave trade advocates were caught up in the net of arrests that was cast, especially after a failed invasion attempt in 1851 launched by Cubans from the United States with the objective of annexation. Although he wrote extensively against annexation, Saco himself was implicated because he had married the widow of Narciso López, who was the leader of the invasion. Annexationist ideas had little chance of spreading in Cuba during the 1850s and abruptly died with the outbreak of the U.S. Civil War in 1861.

Abolition in the United States at the end of the Civil War led directly to the formation, in 1865, of the first abolitionist society in Spain, the Sociedad Abolicionista Española. Its founders were neither Spaniards nor Cubans, but rather Puerto Rican antislavery activists for whom abolitionism was part of a reformist political movement seeking to redefine Puerto Rico's and Cuba's colonial relationship with Spain. Slavery had supported Puerto Rico's sugar industry during the first half of the nineteenth century, as it had in Cuba, but while slave-based sugar production steadily expanded in Cuba, by the 1850s it was on the decline in Puerto Rico. The coffee sector, based on nonslave labor, was increasingly becoming more important to the Puerto Rican colonial economy by the 1860s. It was easier for Puerto Rican liberals to advocate ending slavery because slave labor was less important to Puerto Rico's elite social classes. There were only slightly more than 40,000 slaves in Puerto Rico by the early 1860s – less than 10 percent of the total population – compared to over 370,000 slaves in Cuba, who made up nearly 27 percent of all inhabitants.

Cuban intellectuals in exile now faced a critical quandary. In order for them to have any success at reforming the island's colonial relationship with Spain, which was bound together in some ways with anti–slave trade sentiment and liberal reformism, they needed the support of the Cuban elite. There was some sympathy among certain sectors of the island's powerful social classes for ending the slave trade to Cuba, even if it was muted because of the repressive policies of the Spanish colonial regime on the island. Support for curbing the African trade was based on the careful way in which Saco and his colleagues framed their position on slaving. They never condemned slavery, as was the case with abolitionists in the United States. The slave trade had to be ended, not because it was barbaric and destructive to human beings, but rather because of the danger to Cuban security posed by the possibility of a slave revolt if Africans continued arriving in Cuba and because of the racial implications for the future Cuban population.

This was the anti–slave trade position in the 1820s, and it continued into the 1860s. Cuba's antislaving leaders, all in exile, could never bring themselves to condemn slavery on moral, religious, humanitarian, or even political grounds for fear of completely alienating the Cuban elite, whose support they sought and needed. Their anti–slave trade politics were portrayed to Cubans and Spaniards as part of a long-term vision for stimulating European immigration – a way to resolve labor future labor problems and, perhaps more importantly, to create an increasingly white population through miscegenation. The idea that "whitening" would lead to a more civilized Cuban society in the future was perfectly acceptable to most of Cuba's racist colonial elite, Spanish and Cuban. As long as slavery itself was not attacked – for it was the labor foundation of the sugar economy, and slaves represented a huge portion of the sugar planters' investments and accumulated capital – anti–slave trade politics could be accepted to a limited degree. Although often subscribing to European liberal ideologies, the humanitarian, moral, and religious condemnations of slavery so common in Great Britain, the United States, and elsewhere are not found in the writings of the leading opponents of the Cuban slave trade.

The end of the U.S. Civil War abruptly removed slaving as an issue, since the Cuban trade was finally brought to a close in 1867, ending this tragic aspect of European, African, and American history. The exiled intelligentsia, progressive planters, colonial bureaucrats, and politicians in Madrid were reluctantly forced to confront slavery itself, and for those who stubbornly defended slave labor, the situation was ominous to be sure. The slave system of the United States had been dismantled, and slavery had been abolished everywhere in the Americas with the exception of Cuba, Puerto Rico, and Brazil. Investments in slaves were massive, and despite a period during which Chinese contract laborers were imported into Cuba after 1847 as an alternative to African slaves, the prosperous, ever-expanding, and highly efficient sugar economy was as dependent upon slave labor as ever. There was little political will to end slavery in Cuba on the part of the sugar-producing elite, the merchant class, or the Spanish colonial regime. This all changed dramatically with the explosion of revolution in eastern Cuba in October 1868 and the liberal revolution in Spain of the preceding month.

The Spanish liberal revolution of 1868 swept away the Bourbon dynasty in Spain, which had reigned since 1700, and brought to power a complex coalition of political parties dedicated to implementing political reforms. An extraordinarily progressive constitution was written in 1869, heavily influenced by European liberalism. It proclaimed universal male suffrage in Spain and provided for representation in the Spanish government for Puerto Rico and Cuba. The Spanish Abolitionist Society took advantage of new political freedoms and, along with allies in the liberal government, asked for immediate emancipation. The Puerto Rican abolitionists demanded freedom for slaves in both Cuba and Puerto Rico. However, the Cuban reformers hedged and vacillated. Saco, in Paris, supported a process of gradual abolition but was more concerned, as always, with protecting the property rights of slave owners for fear of alienating the Cuban slaveholding elite. Within Cuba, the separatist revolution that had exploded in the east initially hoped for the support of the powerful western planters who dominated the island's sugar industry and thus moved cautiously on the issue of abolition, since more than 80 percent of Cuba's slaves were found in the western and central sugar districts.

During the initial phases of the war there were calls from the rebel leadership for gradual freedom along with indemnification for slave owners, but these issues would be settled only after independence had triumphed. By 1869, however, the situation had been transformed by slaves and free blacks and mulattos, who supported the rebellion in the zones controlled by the rebels designated as the Republic of Cuba or *Cuba Libre*. In April of that year, the revolutionary government declared freedom for all slaves within the territory controlled by the republic, although the newly freedmen and women were obligated to continue working for their masters. With the growing recognition that the western sugar barons would not support the rebellion, the government of the republic in arms formally abolished slavery unconditionally in December 1870 and offered freedom to all slaves who deserted their masters and reached rebel territory. There was some hope that the rebellion would be aided by the United States if slavery were abolished. The revolution now stood for abolition as well as independence.

Despite its liberal posture the colonial government in Spain moved rapidly to repress the revolt, although they would be unsuccessful until 1878. However, the fear of a general slave uprising in the context of the rebellion's abolitionist objectives, along with international pressures, forced Spain to begin the dismantling of Cuban slavery. In 1870, the Spanish government proclaimed the Moret Law, or law of the free womb. Children of all slave women born after September 1868 would henceforth be free, as well as slaves reaching sixty years of age.

The chronological end of Cuban slavery was thus projected, although the process could take a half-century or more.

The Cuban anti–slave trade movement had produced very little since its first appearance in the 1820s and 1830s except for the marginal circulation of unpopular and unacceptable ideas in both Cuba and Spain. There was minimal elite or mass support among the white population for ending slavery before or after 1868 in Cuba. Time and again the Cuban exiled leaders who opposed the slave trade hedged on the issue of slavery, for, unlike the humanitarian strain of abolitionism found in Britain and the United States, the Cuban anti–slave trade activists demonstrated little concern for the slaves themselves and were beholden to the social class from which they hailed. Their principal priority was to avoid alienating Cuba's elite rather than to end the barbarous system of racial slavery. It was only the prospect of violent revolution and a slave uprising, the historical and sometimes hysterical fear of Cuba's sugar planters, that forced the hand of reluctant Spanish politicians. The Spanish Abolitionist Society managed to mobilize an important antislavery campaign in Spain, in part because of the new freedoms accompanying the 1868 liberal revolution. But the real Cuban abolitionists were the revolutionaries who fought for independence, many of them peoples of color both slave and free, and most of them had few ties to the exiled intelligentsia that purportedly stood for freedom.

As the war raged on and could not be contained by Spain or won by the insurgents, Cuba's slaveholding elite and Spanish political leaders had to recognize and prepare for the inevitable. Slavery's end was in sight after the 1870 Moret Law, but the insurrection had made slavery a political issue that had to be addressed in a more immediate way. The appeal of the insurgents to slaves would only offer more long-term danger to the colonial system, which both the powerful Cuban planters and the Spanish government were determined to maintain. As in the United States, the abolition of slavery in Cuba was above all a political issue and only marginally related to economic or humanitarian matters. If the political structures of colonial rule were to be maintained, slavery would have to be ended. If not, there was the risk of a slave uprising that had stoked the fears of the Cuban elite from the early nineteenth century, when the recurring nightmare of *otro Santo Domingo* (another Haitian slave revolt) was constantly alluded to. This is why the anti–slave trade activists and their plans for European immigration to "whiten" the population, with the objective of reducing the threat of slave rebellion, were tolerated.

The rebellion for nationhood and the abolition of slavery was ended by Spanish colonial forces in 1878, and peace was restored. The slave population of the western Cuban sugar districts had not rebelled, largely because of the tight security measures imposed by the government and planters to protect their estates. However, all Cuban slaves were now aware of the Moret Law as well as of the abolitionist nature of *Cuba Libre*. Peace between Spain and the insurrection was one thing, but for slaves to go back to the old parameters of their lives prior to the rebellion was impossible. Resistance to the absolute discipline imposed by masters before 1868 was widespread when the war ended. Slaves ran away more frequently, even if only temporarily. They often demanded wages for labor, or more provision grounds for their own use and extra time to work them. Masters had few options other than to negotiate with their slaves, who sensed that great changes had taken place and that more would be forthcoming.

In 1879 another short-lived war, *La Guerra Chiquita*, exploded, underlining the instability of the peace that had been imposed on the independence forces. Again, the specter of slave rebellion arose. If Cuban abolitionists were few and far between, as well as muted within the colony, the Spanish Abolitionist Society had worked during the Ten Years' War to mobilize public support for an end to Cuban and Puerto Rican slavery, which was closely tied to liberal reformism in Spain. Indeed, slavery had been abolished in Puerto Rico in 1873. The outbreak of yet another insurrection in Cuba so soon after the long and devastating war was perhaps the final signal to Spanish politicians. If colonialism was to survive, the slavery question in Cuba had to be resolved as a strategy for depriving future revolutionaries of a potential base of support. In 1880 an emancipation law was enacted, but it established an eight-year transition period called the *patronato* during which slaves, now referred to as *patrocinados*, would continue to labor for their masters, who now would be called *patronos*.[17]

Patrocinados could legally be bought and sold, although under the terms of the law the new *patronos* would be obligated to free one-quarter of their ex-slaves beginning in 1884, in descending ages beginning with the oldest. The end of the *patronato* was to come in 1888 with full freedom for all slaves. Although the *patronato* did not change master-slave relations in theory, there could never be a return to the absolute,

17   See Rebecca Scott, *Slave Emancipation in Cuba: The Transition to Free Labor, 1860–1899* (Princeton, NJ: Princeton University Press, 1985).

arbitrary, and often brutal domination of the past. The emancipation law established regional and local bureaucratic structures, the Juntas de Patronato or Patronato Boards, which could be used by slaves to file complaints about violations of the new law or grievances against their masters that could result in freedom being declared if the newly named *patronos* were found to be guilty. The law also required masters to pay a small wage to each slave.

The lines between masters and slaves, who had acquired new rights and a definitive chronological limit to their enslavement, were now clearly drawn. Masters sought to maintain the old system of labor discipline and arbitrary control. Slaves sought to resist every attempt at reestablishing the pre-1880 system of abuses, and they frequently took advantage of the provisions in the emancipation law to file complaints before the Juntas in every region of Cuba. In some cases masters began to recognize the inevitable and gradually began freeing their slaves, hoping that the good will they demonstrated would induce them to remain working on estates. With freedom in sight, slave resistance to continued domination made the *patronato* impossible to maintain, and this was recognized by both the colonial state and the slaveholding class in the early 1880s. By 1883, about half of all slaves had been legally freed, and finally in 1886 the *patronato* was suppressed and full freedom was declared for all slaves, nearly four centuries after the first African slaves had arrived in Cuba with Spanish explorers, conquerors, and settlers. As in the United States, abolition meant the beginning of a new struggle for racial equality.

Abolitionism in Brazil as a political movement was nearly nonexistent until the 1860s. In the Cuban case, anti–slave trade thinkers and the few abolitionists who dared to broach the subject of ending slavery were arrested and exiled by a repressive colonial state. There were no religious or secular institutions within colonial society advocating emancipation, which might have resulted in the development of a popular movement against slavery. Almost no sectors among elite social classes ascribed to the ideas of human freedom and slave emancipation. In this hierarchical social order, peoples of color were considered inferior and slavery perfectly acceptable on moral grounds, pervasive concepts that guided the thinking of elite social classes. There was no popular mobilization against slavery, since there were no institutions, such as Protestant denominations or abolitionist organizations, that pushed forth the idea of freedom for slaves. In the absence of public education in both Cuba and Brazil, most people were illiterate, slave

and free. The circulation of printed matter advocating abolition emanating from Europe or the United States was marginal at best and
confined to privileged social groups.

Brazil was not a colonial society, yet the attitudes toward slavery and
freedom among elites were remarkably similar to those found in Cuba.
There was little sympathy for, or even consideration of, emancipation
for slaves, except among a handful of intellectuals until this issue was
forced upon Brazilians by international pressures in the 1860s, especially the U.S. Civil War and the end of slavery in the American South.
Even then abolitionism did not become an important political force. It
was only in the 1880s, after slavery had been abolished in Cuba and
Brazil remained as the only nation in the Western Hemisphere where
slavery was legal, that abolitionism became important to national
politics. Joaquim Nabuco, the public figure most associated with abolitionism in Brazil, helped found the Sociedade Brasileira Contra a
Escravidão (Brazilian Anti-Slavery Society) in Rio de Janeiro only in
1880. This was well after the Rio Branco Law of 1871, which, like the
1870 Moret Law in Cuba, freed all children born to slave mothers. In
Brazil, however, older slaves were not freed until an 1885 law gave
liberty to slaves sixty five years of age and older.

The emergence of abolitionism in Brazil stands out because it was the
emperor himself, Dom Pedro II, who was sympathetic to both European
liberal ideas and the eventual abolition of slavery.[18] In the aftermath
of the U.S. Civil War, and before the conclusion of Brazil's war
with Paraguay, which raged between 1864 and 1870, Dom Pedro
came under increasing British and French abolitionist pressure to begin
dismantling the Brazilian slave system, and he was receptive to the idea.
Once he embraced the concept of gradual abolition, the political problem faced by the Brazilian emperor was how to convince representatives of the various Brazilian regional elites to back this vague idea.
Abolitionism began as a top-down movement from the center of the
imperial government in Brazil rather than as the result of any popular
mobilization or even elite group pressure, and this was very unlike the
case in both the United States and Cuba.

[18]   This section relies heavily upon Robert Conrad, *The Destruction of Brazilian
Slavery, 1850–1888* (Berkeley: University of California Press, 1972). Also see
Robert Brent Toplin, *The Abolition of Slavery in Brazil* (New York: Atheneum,
1972).

Dom Pedro gradually began to enact a series of decrees in the mid-1860s that unambiguously indicated his desire to move toward abolition. In 1864, he freed *emancipados*. These were slaves who had been seized by British patrols off the Brazilian coast and whose fate had been adjudicated by the British-Brazilian mixed commission court in Rio de Janeiro. They had been placed in the hands of the Brazilian government but in fact were never really freed and were often mistreated and worked as slaves by government bureaucrats and private entrepreneurs who were entrusted with them. In the same year a decree was issued that forbade the whipping of slaves, and in 1866 slaves were banned from employment on any government public works project. Under pressure from French abolitionists, Dom Pedro publicly stated that he was committed to gradual emancipation, a declaration that sent shock waves through the slaveholding class. This was followed by a decree freeing slaves who had served in the Brazilian armed forces, a law proclaimed in the middle of the war with Paraguay, and Dom Pedro himself freed his own slaves for service in the army. In 1867, a reformist bill was presented to the Council of State, but never enacted, that expressed the desire that slavery be abolished on December 31, 1899, with full compensation to slave owners.

The emperor then turned to the freeing of newborn slaves and gently applied pressure through his ministers for the acceptance of the idea. With the end of the U.S. Civil War and the Spanish proclamation of the free birth law in 1870, opposition to this proposal was difficult, especially because of the deference paid to Dom Pedro even by representatives of states with the greatest slave concentrations in the south-center of the country. Because of the interregional slave trade from north to south, slavery had declined dramatically in importance in the northern states, where there was less resistance among elites to emancipation. Liberalism and abolitionism had also made tentative inroads among a small group of Brazilian politicians throughout the country. They were not powerful enough to oppose the slaveholders, but with the emperor himself clearly backing the concept of free birth as well as gradual emancipation, the Rio Branco Law was proclaimed in 1871. As in Cuba, a chronological end to slavery was now assured, and time was provided for the slaveholding class to adjust to the inevitable realities of the future.

Abolitionism in Brazil was connected to liberal reformism, as it was in Spain and nearly everywhere else in Europe and the Americas. In the context of a nation ruled by an emperor, progressive though Dom Pedro was, political space was narrow and circumscribed. Nevertheless, liberal ideas spread among elites, and although there may not have been full acceptance of the concept that all citizens should be equal before the law, the issue of abolishing slavery was at the forefront of the liberal movement by the 1870s. The end of the Paraguayan war in 1870 and the proclamation of the free birth law in 1871 provided Brazilian liberals with expanded possibilities for spreading their ideas and building support for abolition. The debates preceding the proclamation of the Rio Branco Law had sharpened the regional divisions in Brazil over the issue of slavery.

Elites in Minas Gerais, Rio de Janeiro, and São Paulo – where over 850,000 slaves were found in 1872, or about 60 percent of all slaves in Brazil – generally opposed reforms, including the free birth law. The slave-based coffee economy was expanding rapidly in western São Paulo and in the southeastern Zona da Mata of Minas Gerais, and coffee was still being produced in the Paraiba valley extending through eastern São Paulo and Rio de Janeiro. These regions had been importing slaves from the north since the end of the transatlantic slave trade in the early 1850s. The elites in northern provinces were more sympathetic to abolition, since their labor systems were more diversified and less dependent upon slave labor. Yet the regional divisions in Brazil did not in any way resemble the sectionalism of the United States. There were no divisions between free and slave provinces, and a free black and mulatto population of considerable size existed in every Brazilian region and in many was the most numerous racial and legal category. Nevertheless, antislavery liberalism seems to have established a more solid foundation among elites in the northern and western Brazilian regions of the nation, where slavery was less important.

The Rio Branco Law of 1871 went much further in theory than the Moret Law in Cuba. Not only were slaves born to slave mothers after 1871 freed, but a series of other provisions indicated to slaveholders that full-scale abolition would be effected gradually in Brazil. The children of slave mothers were classified as *ingênuos*, or minors, and their owners had the option of using them as workers until they were twenty one years of age or accepting indemnification from the government. Thus, the *ingênuos* were only theoretically free at the discretion of their masters. If compensation was not elected, the *ingênuos* continued to live in the same conditions as if enslaved, in much the same way as Cuban children born to slave mothers after 1870. On a more positive note, the right of self-purchase, which had been a customary part of Brazilian slavery but never guaranteed, was now codified into law, and a public emancipation fund was established that would permit slaves to be freed upon payment of their assessed values to masters. Municipal councils were established to select slaves who would be freed. Older males and younger females as well as family members of freed slaves were prior-itized, leaving the core workforce intact. Although only slightly over 20,000 slaves were freed this in this way by 1885 – a small fraction of Brazil's slave population in 1872 of 1.5 million – the government-sponsored liberation of slaves contributed to stimulating the public debate on emancipation. And slaves with their own savings, guaranteed by law, had the right to purchase their freedom. Another stipulation of the law that furthered the developing national debate on slavery was the registration mandated for all slaves in the nation within a one-year period. Any slave not registered was to be freed. The not-so-subtle implication of this provision was that the national government, rather than individual slave owners or provincial governments, asserted jurisdiction over the fate of the country's slave population.

The issue of ultimate freedom for Brazilian slaves had been put before the public during the decade of the 1870s. However, the concept of "public" should be carefully delineated. Brazil was a nation without public education, and more than 80 percent of the population was illiterate. A popular movement for abolition developed in the decade of the 1880s, but it was led by a sector of the nation's literate elite, and its followers were primarily people in urban areas of the country, north and south, who could read and write. Yet the most important component of that popular movement for freedom was the slave population itself. Sensing freedom, and aware of every single nuance of the legal frame-work governing their enslavement, which had changed so radically during the 1870s, slaves began to shape their own destinies through large-scale resistance that was primarily nonviolent.

In 1880, the Brazilian Anti-Slavery Society was founded; it began publishing its monthly journal, O Abolicionista, in November of that year, with the objective of building support throughout the country for the end of slavery and applying pressure on the nation's political elite through mass mobilization. In the aftermath of the 1880 Cuban aboli-tion law, Brazil was the only nation in the Western Hemisphere where slavery was still legal, and perhaps sensing the tide of history, the abolitionist movement began to grow, especially in the north of the country where slavery had long ceased to be critical to local elites. Ceará took the lead by forming antislavery societies throughout the province, and there emerged a veritable popular movement that resulted in the complete abolition of slavery in Ceará in 1884. The province of Amazonas ended slavery in the same year. Goiás and Paraná followed shortly thereafter. Slaves in neighboring provinces were aware of these developments, and like southern slaves in the United States who fled toward the northern free states, many sought freedom through flight to the free provinces of the nation.

The march toward abolition was contentious, and in the coffee-growing south of the country the pro-slavery forces reacted to the rise of abolitionism with spirited defenses of slavery, attempting to stave off what was becoming inevitable. Abolitionists had formed organizations in the city of São Paulo, in the heart of the coffee-producing south, and in 1884 Rio de Janeiro saw for the first time the emergence of a mass abolitionist movement with the unsuccessful objective of declaring an end to slavery in the city. In Porto Alegre, the capital of the southern province of Rio Grande do Sul, slavery was abolished by the end of 1884, although it took until 1887 for abolition to be declared throughout the province. Finally, in perhaps the most dramatic developement of all, São Paulo's port of Santos was declared a slave-free region and became a destination for runaway slaves from surrounding areas. A huge *quilombo* called Jabaquara emerged on the outskirts of Santos, attracting as many as 20,000 runaways from surrounding districts.

With the passage of the law freeing slaves reaching sixty five years of age in 1885; the growth of the abolitionist movement in nearly every region of the country in the early 1880s, including the coffee-producing heartland of the south-center; the abolition of slavery in Ceará, Amazonas, Goiás, Paraná, and Rio Grande do Sul; the creation of a free zone for runaways in Santos; and the inescapable fact that abolition was only a question of time, slaves began to take matters into their own hands to force a definitive end to their suffering and oppression. Abolitionists were emboldened by the groundswell of support for emancipation sweeping through Brazil in the early 1880s, and the most militant and audacious among them began to encourage slaves to simply abandon plantations en masse. Some of these antislavery activists spread this message into the heart of the São Paulo coffee economy with surprising success. At the end of 1886, slaves began to leave farms and plantations in large numbers, and by early 1887 the abandonment the coffee estates in São Paulo had become so widespread that there was absolutely nothing that planters or local authorities could do to control the situation. By leaving their masters, slaves simply declared that they were free, and planters made desperate attempt to strike bargains with them by offering wages, conditional emancipation, or even small parcels of land if they would remain and labor. There were few attempts at the restoration of the arbitrary control that they had wielded for so long over so many people. By exercising mass civil disobedience, slaves themselves drove the final nail into the coffin of racial slavery in Brazil and the Americas. The *Paulista* planters capitulated by early 1888, when slavery was banned in the city of São Paulo and shortly thereafter throughout the state. In May 1888, slavery was abolished forever throughout Brazil through the proclamation of the Golden Law, which unconditionally ended racial slavery without compensation to owners.

The end of slavery in all three societies was closely connected to a series of political factors above all. The struggle over the issue of slavery's extension into the western territories and the implications of whether future states would be admitted to the Union as free or slave was the central issue around which abolitionism in the United States turned. It is certain that there was a broad range of other factors that shaped the anti-slavery struggle – moral, religious, humanitarian, as well as economic rivalries between sectional interests. But beyond the issue of slavery in the territories, there was little political will to actually abolish slavery, even in the northern states, on the eve of the Civil War. Had the South not seceded and formed the Confederacy, there is no telling how long racial slavery would have lasted.

The outcome of the U.S. Civil War hastened the end of Cuban slavery as well. The Cuban slave trade was abolished only because the United States permitted British antislaving naval patrols to stop and inspect all ships in the Caribbean regardless of the flag they were flying. With the slave trade closed, and with the demise of slavery in the United States, Cuban slaveholders surely knew their days were numbered. Yet it was only the political pressure exerted upon the colonial elite because of the abolitionist nature of the Cuban republic in arms during the Ten Years' War that forced Spain's hand. The threat of a slave insurrection, or of the massive abandonment of western Cuban plantations by slaves because of the offer of freedom if republican territory was reached, made abolition nearly mandatory to preserve Spanish colonialism. There was little favorable sentiment in Cuba among colonial power brokers, Cuban-born or Spanish, for the abolition of slavery, even on the eve of the Ten Years' War in 1868. To have even the slightest appeal, Cuban abolitionists were forced to weave their arguments for ending slavery around the need for a "whitened" future Cuba. Slaves were incidental to this process, and in fact Cuban abolitionists rarely invoked humanitarian images of their horrendous exploitation, the dreadful material conditions in which they lived, or the systematic abuses they suffered. Reluctantly, the slaveholding elite was forced to accept emancipation, not because of the economic obsolescence of slavery, or because there was a moral questioning of slavery. In the absence of democratic myths and symbols of equality, such as those associated with abolitionism in England and the United States in Cuba, there was almost no consideration among the Cuban colonial elite that peoples of color should have the same kinds of rights and privileges as whites. Of course, among the multiracial partisans of *Cuba Libre* and within the broad masses of slaves and free blacks and mulattos there was another history, but it is largely one that has not yet been written. Until the eve of emancipation, most Cuban elites were perfectly comfortable with an antiquated racist hierarchical conceptualization of the social order in which a supposed natural law reigned. This left slaves and peoples of color at the bottom of society. Had Spanish officials and Cuban elites not been forced by the political dangers to colonial rule posed by the insurrection to abandon slavery, the institution would have lasted well beyond 1886.

Similar comments may be made about Brazilian elites. There was little humanitarian sympathy with the plight of slaves themselves and a strong racist conviction that inequality based on race was part of a natural social hierarchy. Yet a sense of national shame came over those Brazilians with liberal persuasions, including the emperor himself, for by 1880 Brazil was the last nation in the Western Hemisphere where slavery was still virtually intact. The abolitionist movement in Brazil was a marginal political force until the 1880s, and in fact the emperor was the figure most responsible for spreading the message that slavery could not be sustained indefinitely. Had the U.S. Civil War and emancipation not obligated the Cubans to end the slave trade, or had the Ten Years' War not forced the issue of slave abolition in Cuba, there is little reason to believe that Brazilian elites would have begun dismantling the slave system on their own. A series of external political events and processes pushed the imperial government to initiate the process that led to the gradual end of slavery. This is not to say that sympathy for abolition did not exist in Brazil, below the level of elite social groups, and indeed a real popular abolitionist movement exploded in Brazil's major urban areas in the final years of slavery. But the end of slavery in the United States and Cuba weighed heavily on Dom Pedro and forced him to signal to the Brazilian political class that slavery could not be sustained. When the process began in the late 1860s, it gave energy and impetus to antislavery activists, who changed the parameters of abolitionism to focus upon internal Brazilian issues. In the very end, it was the slaves themselves who made it clear that slavery would no longer be accepted, and the *Paulista* elite was forced to accept the inevitable.

Racial slavery came to an end in the Americas in the 1880s, but racial discrimination emphatically did not. Without question, the descendants of slaves – Brazilians, Cubans, and African-Americans in the United States – still occupy the lowest socioeconomic positions within each society, even in purportedly egalitarian socialist Cuba. This does not mean that there has been no upward social mobility or opportunities created for peoples of color since slavery was abolished in the second half of the nineteenth century. Great strides have been made in each society in opening opportunities for those of African descent. But when income distribution, educational attainment, access to political power, and a host of other factors are subjected to scrutiny, peoples of color lag dramatically behind whites. A fundamental question is whether this lamentable situation is linked solely to the tragic legacy of slavery, or whether it is also connected to the fate of peoples of color since slavery was abolished. Clearly, both sets of factors must be examined to explain the systematic inequality by race that reigns in these three former slave societies of the Americas today.

Bibliography

Aguirre Beltrán, Gonzalo. *La Población Negra de México, 1519–1810: Estudio Etno-histórico*. México, D.F.: Ediciones Fuente Cultural, 1946.

Alden, Dauril. "The Population of Brazil in the Late Eighteenth Century: A Preliminary Study." *Hispanic American Historical Review*, Vol. 43, No. 2 (May 1963), pp. 173–205.

Anastasia, Carla Maria Junho. *Vassalos Rebeldes: Violência Coletiva nas Minas na Primeira Metade do Século XVIII*. Belo Horizonte: Editora C/Arte, 1998.

Andrews, George Reid. *Afro-Latin America, 1800–2000*. New York: Oxford University Press, 2004.

   The Afro-Argentines of Buenos Aires, 1800–1900. Madison: University of Wisconsin Press, 1980.

Aptheker, Herbert. *American Negro Slave Revolts*. New York: International Publishers, 1993.

Attman, Artur. *American Bullion in the European World Trade, 1600–1800*. Gotenberg: Kungl. Vetenskaps- och Vitterhets Samhället, 1986.

Bakewell, Peter J. *Miners of the Red Mountain: Indian Labor in Potosí, 1545–1650*. Albuquerque: University of New Mexico Press, 1984.

   Silver Mining and Society in Colonial Mexico: Zacatecas 1546–1700. New York: Cambridge University Press, 1971.

Baquaqua, Mahommah Gardo, *Biography Of Mahommah G. Baquaqua, A Native Of Zoogoo, In The Interior Of Africa. (A Convert To Christianity,) With A Description Of That Part Of The World; Including The Manners And Customs Of The Inhabitants, Their Religious Notions, Form Of Government, Laws, Appearance Of The Country, Buildings, Agriculture, Manufactures, Shepherds And Herdsmen, Domestic Animals, Marriage Ceremonials, Funeral Services, Styles Of Dress, Trade And Commerce, Modes Of Warfare, System Of Slavery, &C., &C. Mahommah's Early Life, His Education, His Capture And Slavery In Western Africa And Brazil, His*

Escape To The United States, From Thence To Hayti, (The City Of Port Au Prince,) His Reception By The Baptist Missionary There, The Rev. W. L. Judd; His Conversion To Christianity, Baptism, And Return To This Country, His Views, Objects And Aim. Written And Revised From His Own Words, By Samuel Moore, Esq. Detroit: Geo. E. Pomeroy & Co., Tribune Office, 1854.

Baronov, David. *The Abolition of Slavery in Brazil: The "Liberation" through the Emancipation of Capital.* Westport, CT: Greenwood Press, 2000.

Barbosa, Waldemar de Almeida. *Negros e Quilombos em Minas Gerais.* Belo Horizonte: Imprensa Oficial, 1972.

Barcia Zequeira, María del Carmen. *La Otra Familia (Parientes, Redes y Descendencia de los Esclavos en Cuba).* Havana: Casa de las Américas, 2003.

Barickman, B. J. *A Bahian Counterpoint: Sugar, Tobacco, Cassava, and Slavery in the Recôncavo, 1780–1860.* Stanford, CA: Stanford University Press, 1998.

Barman, Roderick J. *Brazil: The Forging of a Nation, 1798–1852.* Stanford, CA: Stanford University Press, 1988.

Citizen Emperor: Pedro II and the Making of Brazil, 1825–91. Stanford, CA: Stanford University Press, 1999.

Bastide, Roger. *As Religiões Africanas no Brasil* (2 vols). São Paulo: Livraria Pioneira Editôra, 1971.

O Candomblé da Bahia: Rito Nagó. São Paulo: Companhia das Letras, 2001.

The African Religions of Brazil: Toward a Sociology of the Interpenetration of Civilizations. Baltimore: Johns Hopkins University Press, 1978.

Beckles, Hilary McD. *White Servitude and Black Slavery in Barbados, 1727–1715.* Knoxville: University of Tennessee Press, 1989.

Bergad, Laird W. *Cuban Rural Society in the Nineteenth Century: The Social and Economic History of Monoculture in Matanzas.* Princeton, NJ: Princeton University Press, 1990.

Slavery and the Demographic and Economic History of Minas Gerais, Brazil, 1720–1888. New York: Cambridge University Press, 1999.

Bergad, Laird W., Fe Iglesias García, and María del Carmen Barcia. *The Cuban Slave Market, 1790–1880.* New York: Cambridge University Press, 1995.

Berlin, Ira. *Generations of Captivity: A History of African-American Slaves.* Cambridge, MA.: The Belknap Press of Harvard University Press, 2003.

Many Thousands Gone: The First Two Centuries of Slavery in North America. Cambridge, MA: The Belknap Press of Harvard University Press, 1998.

Berlin, Ira, Barbara J. Fields, Thavolia Glymph, Joseph P. Reidy, and Leslie S. Rowland, editors. *Freedom: A Documentary History of Emancipation, 1861–1867. Volume 1, Series 1: The Destruction of Slavery.* New York: Cambridge University Press, 1986.

Bethell, Leslie. *The Abolition of the Brazilian Slave Trade: Britain, Brazil and the Slave Trade Question 1807–1869.* New York and London: Cambridge University Press, 1970.

Blassingame, John W. *The Slave Community: Plantation Life in the Antebellum South.* New York: Oxford University Press, 1972.

Boschi, Caio César. *Os Leigos e o Poder (Irmandades Leigas e Política Colonizadora em Minas Gerais).* São Paulo: Atica, 1986.

Bowser, Frederick P. *The African Slave in Colonial Peru, 1524–1650.* Stanford, CA: Stanford University Press, 1974.

Boxer, Charles R. *The Dutch Seaborne Empire, 1600–1800.* New York: Knopf, 1965.

The Golden Age of Brazil, 1695–1750. Berkeley: University of California Press, 1962.

Carneiro, Edison. *O Quilombo do Palmares, 1630–1695.* São Paulo: Editora Brasiliense, 1947.

Carvalho de Mello, Pedro. "The Economics of Labor in Brazilian Coffee Plantations, 1850–1888." Ph.D. thesis, University of Chicago, 1977.

Childs, Matt D. *The 1812 Aponte Rebellion in Cuba and the Struggle against Atlantic Slavery.* Chapel Hill: University of North Carolina Press, 2006.

Clarkson, Thomas. *The History of the Rise, Progress, & Accomplishment of the Abolition of the African Slave Trade, by the British Parliament.* Philadelphia: Brown & Merritt, James P. Parke, No. 119, High Street, 1808.

Conrad, Robert. *The Destruction of Brazilian Slavery, 1850–1888.* Berkeley: University of California Press, 1972.

Contreiras Rodrigues, Felix. *Traços da Economia Social e Politica do Brasil Colonial.* Rio de Janeiro: Ariel Editora, 1935.

Cook, Noble David, and W. George Lovell, editors. *Born to Die: Disease and New World Conquest, 1492–1650.* New York: Cambridge University Press, 1998.

"Secret Judgments of God": Old World Disease in Colonial Spanish America. Norman: University of Oklahoma Press, 1991.

Corwin, Arthur F. *Spain and the Abolition of Slavery in Cuba, 1817–1886.* Austin: University of Texas Press, 1967.

Crosby, Alfred W., Jr. *Ecological Imperialism: The Biological Expansion of Europe, 900–1900.* New York: Cambridge University Press, 1986.

The Columbian Exchange: Biological and Cultural Consequences of 1492. Westport, CT: Greenwood Press, 1972.

Curtin, Philip D. *Death by Migration: Europe's Encounter with the Tropical World in the Nineteenth Century.* New York: Cambridge University Press, 1985.

The Atlantic Slave Trade: A Census. Madison: University of Wisconsin Press, 1969.

David, Paul A., Herbert G. Gutman, Richard Sutch, Peter Remin, and Gavin Wright. *Reckoning with Slavery: A Critical Study in the Quantitative History of American Negro Slavery*. New York: Oxford University Press, 1976.

Davis, David Brion. *The Problem of Slavery in the Age of Revolution 1770–1823*. New York: Oxford University Press, 1999.

De la Fuente, Alejandro. "Slave Law and Claims-Making in Cuba: The Tannenbaum Debate Revisted." *Law and History Review*, Vol. 22, No. 2 (Summer 2004), pp. 340–69.

Dean, Warren. *Rio Claro: A Brazilian Plantation System, 1820–1920*. Stanford, CA: Stanford University Press, 1976.

Debien, Gabriel. *Les Esclaves aux Antilles Françaises (XVIIe–XVIIIe Siècles)*. Basse-Terre: Société D'Histoire de la Guadeloupe and Fort-de-France: Société D'Histoire de la Martinique, 1974.

Douglass, Frederick. *Life and Times of Frederick Douglass: His Early Life as a Slave, His Escape from Bondage, and His Complete History: An Autobiography*. New York: Gramercy Books, 1993.

Drescher, Seymour. *Econocide: British Slavery in the Era of Abolition*. Pittsburgh: University of Pittsburgh Press, 1977.

   From Slavery to Freedom: Comparative Studies in the Rise and Fall of the Atlantic System. New York: New York University Press, 1999.

Dubois, W. E. B. *The Negro American Family*. Cambridge, MA: MIT Press, 1970. (Reprint of the 1908 edition).

Dunaway, Wilma A. *The African-American Family in Slavery and Emancipation*. New York: Cambridge University Press, 2003.

Dusinberre, William. *Them Dark Days: Slavery in the American Rice Swamps*. New York: Oxford University Press, 1996.

Egerton, Douglas R. *Gabriel's Rebellion: The Virginia Slave Conspiracies of 1800 & 1802*. Chapel Hill: University of North Carolina Press, 1993.

   He Shall Go Out Free: The Lives of Denmark Vesey. Lanham, MD: Rowman & Littlefield, 2004.

Elkins, Stanley M. *Slavery: A Problem in American Institutional and Intellectual Life*. Chicago: University of Chicago Press, 1959.

Eltis, David. *Economic Growth and the Ending of the Transatlantic Slave Trade*. New York: Oxford University Press, 1987.

   The Rise of African Slavery in the Americas. New York: Cambridge University Press, 2000.

   "The Volume and Structure of the Transatlantic Slave Trade: A Reassessment." *William & Mary Quarterly*, 3rd series, Vol. 63, No.1 (January 2001), pp. 17–46.

Eltis, David, Frank Lewis, and Kenneth Sokoloff, editors. *Slavery in the Development of the Americas*. New York and London: Cambridge University Press, 2004.

Engerman, Stanley L., Seymour Drescher, and Robert L. Paquette, editors. *Slavery*. New York: Oxford University Press, 2001.

Engerman, Stanley L., and Eugene D. Genovese, editors. *Race and Slavery in the Western Hemisphere: Quantitative Studies*. Princeton, NJ: Princeton University Press, 1975.

Escott, Paul D. *Slavery Remembered: The Twentieth-Century Slave Narratives*. Chapel Hill: University of North Carolina Press, 1979.

Estatísticas Históricas do Brasil. Séries Estatísticas Retrospectivas. Volume 3: Séries Econômicas, Demográficas e Sociais, 1550 a 1985. Rio de Janeiro: Instituto Brasileiro de Geografia e Estatística, 1987.

Fernandes, Florestan. *A Integração do Negro na Sociedade de Classe*. São Paulo: EDUSP, 1965.

Finley, Moses I. *Ancient Slavery and Modern Ideology*. London: Chatto & Windus, 1980.

Flávio Motta, José. *Corpos Escravos, Vontades Livres: Posse de Cativos e Família escrava em Bananal (1801–1829)*. São Paulo: Annablume, 1999.

Florentino, Manolo, and José Roberto Góes. *A Paz das Senzalas: Famílias Escravas e Tráfico Atlântico, Rio de Janeiro, c. 1790–c. 1850*. Rio de Janeiro: Civilização Brasileira, 1997.

Fogel, Robert William. *Without Consent or Contract: The Rise and Fall of American Slavery*. New York: Norton, 1989.

Fogel, Robert William, and Stanley L. Engerman. *Time on the Cross: The Economics of American Negro Slavery*. Boston: Little, Brown, 1974.

Fogel, Robert William, and Stanley L. Engerman, editors. *Without Consent or Contract: Markets and Production, Technical Papers (Volume 1)*. New York: Norton, 1992.

Without Consent or Contract: Conditions of Slave Life and the Transition to Freedom, Technical Papers (Volume 2). New York: Norton, 1992.

Fox-Genovese, Elizabeth. *Within the Plantation Household: Black and White Women of the Old South*. Chapel Hill: University of North Carolina Press, 1988.

Franco, José Luciano. *Afroamérica*. Havana: Publicaciones de la Junta Nacional de Arqueología y Etnología, 1961.

Franco, José Luciano. *La Conspiración de Aponte de 1812*. Havana: Publicaciones del Archivo Nacional, 1963.

Franklin, John Hope, and Loren Schweninger. *Runaway Slaves: Rebels on Plantations*. New York: Oxford University Press, 1999.

Frazier, E. Franklin. *The Negro Family in the United States*. Chicago: University of Chicago Press, 1939.

Freitas, Délcio. *Palmares: a Guerra dos Escravos*. Porto Alegre: Editora Movimento, 1973.

Freyre, Gilberto. *The Masters and the Slaves: A Study in the Development of Brazilian Civilization*. Berkeley: University of California Press, 1986.

Gaspar, David Barry, and Darlene Clark Hine, editors. *More than Chattel: Black Women and Slavery in the Americas.* Bloomington and Indianapolis: Indiana University Press, 1996.

Genovese, Eugene D. *Roll, Jordan, Roll: The World the Slaves Made.* New York: Pantheon Press, 1974.

Goslinga, Cornelis C. *The Dutch in the Caribbean and on the Wild Coast, 1580–1680.* Assen, The Netherlands: Van Gorcum, 1971.

Graham, Richard. *Britain and the Onset of Modernization in Brazil, 1850–1914.* New York: Cambridge University Press, 1972.

"Slave Families of a Rural Estate in Colonial Brazil" *Journal of Social History,* Vol. 9 (1976), pp. 382–402.

Guimarães, Carlos Magno. *Uma Negação da Ordem Escravista: Quilombos em Minas Gerais no Século XVIII.* São Paulo: Ícone, 1988.

Gutiérrez, Horacio. "Crioulos e Africanos no Paraná, 1798–1830." *Revista Brasileira de História,* Vol. 8, No. 16 (1988), pp. 161–88.

Gutiérrez, Horacio. "Demografia Escrava Numa Economia Não Exportadora: Paraná." *Estudos Econômicos,* Vol. 17, No. 2 (1987), pp. 297–314.

Gutman, Herbert G. *The Black Family in Slavery and Freedom, 1750–1925.* New York: Pantheon Press, 1976.

Haber, Stephen, editor. *How Latin America Fell Behind: Essays on the Economic Histories of Brazil and Mexico, 1800–1914.* Stanford, CA: Stanford University Press, 1997.

Haines, Michael R., and Richard H. Steckel. *A Population History of North America.* New York and London: Cambridge University Press, 2000.

Hamilton, Earl J. *American Treasure and the Price Revolution in Spain, 1501–1650.* Cambridge, MA: Harvard University Press, 1934.

Handler, Jerome S. *The Unappropriated People: Freedmen in the Slave Society of Barbados.* Baltimore: Johns Hopkins University Press, 1974.

Harris, Leslie M. *In the Shadow of Slavery: African Americans in New York City, 1626–1863.* Chicago: University of Chicago Press, 2002.

Higgins, Kathleen J. *"Licentious Liberty" in a Brazilian Gold-Mining Region: Slavery, Gender, and Social Control in Eighteenth-Century Sabará, Minas Gerais.* University Park: Pennsylvania State University Press, 1999.

Higman, Barry W. *Slave Populations of the British Caribbean, 1807–1834.* Baltimore: Johns Hopkins University Press, 1984.

Hodges, Graham Russell. *Root and Branch: African Americans in New York and East Jersey, 1613–1863.* Chapel Hill: University of North Carolina Press, 1999.

Howard, Philip A. *Changing History: Afro-Cuban Cabildos and Societies of Color in the Nineteenth Century.* Baton Rouge: Louisiana State University Press, 1998.

Iglesias García, Fe. "El Censo Cubano de 1877 y sus Diferentes Versiones." *Santiago,* Vol. 34 (June 1979), pp. 167–211.

John, A. Meredith. *The Plantation Slaves of Trinidad, 1783–1816: A Mathematical and Demographic Inquiry*. New York: Cambridge University Press, 1988.

Johnson, Michael P. "Denmark Vesey and His Co-Conspirators." *William & Mary Quarterly*, 3rd Series, Volume 63, No. 4 (October 2001), pp. 915–76.

Johnson, Walter. *Soul by Soul: Life inside the Antebellum Slave Market*. Cambridge, MA: Harvard University Press, 1999.

Jones, Jacqueline. *Labor of Love, Labor of Sorrow: Black Women, Work and the Family from Slavery to the Present*. New York: Basic Books, 1985.

Karasch, Mary. *Slave Life in Rio de Janerio, 1808–1850*. Princeton, NJ: Princeton University Press, 1987.

Kent, R. K. "Palmares: An African State in Brazil." *Journal of African History*, Vol. 1 (1965), pp. 161–75.

Kiernan, James Patrick. "The Manumission of Slaves in Paraty, Brazil, 1789–1822." Ph.D. thesis, New York University, 1976.

Kiple, Kenneth F. *African Slavery in Latin America and the Caribbean*. New York: Oxford University Press, 1986.

Another Dimension to the Black Diaspora: Diet, Disease, and Racism. New York: Cambridge University Press, 1981.

Slavery in the Americas: A Comparative Study of Cuba and Virginia. London: Oxford University Press, 1967.

The Atlantic Slave Trade. New York: Cambridge University Press, 1999.

The Caribbean Slave: A Biological History. New York: Cambridge University Press, 1984.

"The Internal Slave Trade in Nineteenth-Century Brazil: A Study of Slave Importations into Rio de Janeiro in 1852." *Hispanic American Historical Review*, Vol. 51, No. 4 (1971), pp. 567–85.

"The Nutritional Link with Slave Infant and Child Mortality in Brazil." *Hispanic American Historical Review*, Vol. 69, No. 4. (1989) pp. 677–90.

Klein, Herbert S., and Stanley L. Engerman. "Fertility Differentials between Slaves in the United States and the British West Indies: A Note on Lactation Practices." *William & Mary Quarterly*, Vol. 35, No. 2 (April 1978), pp. 357–74.

Kolchin, Peter. *American Slavery, 1619–1877*. New York: Hill and Wang, 1993.

Kulikoff, Allan. *Tobacco and Slaves: The Development of Southern Cultures in the Chesapeake, 1680–1800*. Chapel Hill: University of North Carolina Press, 1986.

Landers, Jane G., editor. *Against the Odds: Free Blacks in the Slave Societies of the Americas*. London: Frank Cass & Co., 1996.

Las siete partidas del rey Alfonso el sabio, cotejadas con varios codices antiguos, por la Real Academia de la Historia (3 vols.). Madrid: Imprenta Real, 1807.

Law, Robin, and Paul E. Lovejoy, editors. *The Biography of Mahommah Gardo Baquaqua: His Passage from Slavery to Freedom in Africa and America.* Princeton, NJ: Markus Wiener Publishers, 2001.

Lofton, John. *Denmark Vesey's Revolt: The Slave Plot That Lit a Fuse to Fort Sumter.* Kent, OH: Kent State University Press, 1983.

Lovejoy, Paul. *Transformations in Slavery: A History of Slavery in Africa.* Cambridge: Cambridge University Press, 1983.

Luna, Francisco Vidal. "Casamento de Escravos em São Paulo: 1776, 1804, 1829." In Sérgio Odilon Nadalin et al., editors, *História e População: Estudos Sobre a América Latina.* São Paulo: Fundação Sistema Estatual de Análise de Dados, 1990, pp. 226–37.

Luna, Francisco Vidal, and Herbert S. Klein. *Slavery and the Economy of São Paulo 1750–1850.* Stanford, CA: Stanford University Press, 2003.

Madden, R.R. *Poems by a Slave in the Island of Cuba, recently liberated; translated from the Spanish by R. R. Madden, M. D., with the History of the Early Life of the Negro Poet, written by Himself; to which are prefixed two pieces descriptive of Cuban Slavery and the Slave Traffic.* London: Thomas Ward and Co., 1840.

Malone, Ann Patton. *Sweet Chariot: Slave Family and Household Structure in Nineteenth-Century Louisiana.* Chapel Hill: University of North Carolina Press, 1992.

Manning, Patrick. *Slavery and African Life: Occidental, Oriental, and African Slave Trades.* New York: Cambridge University Press, 1990.

Manzano, Juan Francisco. *The Autobiography of a Slave / Autobiografía de un esclavo. A Bilingual Edition.* Introduction and modernized Spanish version by Ivan A. Shulman; translated by Evelyn Picon Garfield. Detroit: Wayne State University Press, 1996.

Marcílio, Maria Luiza. *Crescimento Demográfico e Evolução Agrária Paulista, 1700–1836.* São Paulo: Editora Hucitec, 2000.

Mattos, Hebe Maria. *Das Cores do Silêncio: Os Significados da Liberdade no Sudeste Escravista, Brasil, Eéc. XIX.* Rio de Janeiro: Editora Nova Fronteira, 1998.

Mattoso, Katia de Queirós. "Slave, Free and Freed Family Structures in Nineteenth Century Salvador, Bahia." *Luso-Brazilian Review,* Vol. 25 (1988), pp. 69–84.

Meanders, Daniel E., editor. *Advertisements for Runaway Slaves in Virginia, 1801–1820.* New York: Garland Publishing, 1997.

Mellafe, Rolando. *La Introducción de la Esclavitud Negra en Chile: Tráfico y Rutas.* Santiago: Universidad de Chile, 1959.

Metcalf, Alida. "Searching for the Slave Family in Colonial Brazil." *Journal of Family History,* Vol. 16, No. 3 (1991), pp. 283–97.

Montejo, Esteban. *The Autobiography of a Runaway Slave.* Edited by Miguel Barnet. New York: Pantheon Books, 1968.

Moreno Fraginals, Manuel. *El Ingenio: Complejo Económico Social Cubano del Azúcar* (3 vols.). Havana: Editorial de Ciencias Sociales, 1978.

Morgan, Edmund S. *American Slavery, American Freedom: The Ordeal of Colonial Virginia*. New York: Norton, 1975.

Morgan, Phillip D. *Slave Counterpoint: Black Culture in the Eighteenth-Century Chesapeake & Low Country*. Chapel Hill: University of North Carolina Press, 1998.

Mörner, Magnus. *Race Mixture in the History of Latin America*. Boston: Little, Brown, 1967.

Mortara, Giorgio. "A Família Escrava e a Penetração do Café em Bananal (1801–1829)." *Revista Brasileira de Estudos Populacionais*, Vol. 6 (1988), pp. 71–101.

"Estudos Sobre a Utilização do Censo Demográfico para a Reconstituição das Estatísticas do Movimento da População do Brasil." *Revista Brasileira de Estatística*, Vol. 3, No. 5 (January – March 1941), pp. 41–3.

Motta, José Flavio. *Corpos Escravos, Vontades Livres: Posse de Cativos e Família Escrava em Bananal (1801–1829)*. São Paulo: Annablume, 1999.

Mullin, Gerald W. *Flight and Rebellion: Slave Resistance in Eighteenth-Century Virginia*. New York: Oxford University Press, 1972.

"Newspaper Advertisements Offer Rewards for the Return of Runaways." In Robert Edgar Conrad, *Children of God's Fire: A Documentary History of Black Slavery in Brazil*. Princeton, NJ: Princeton University Press, 1983, pp. 362–6.

Nina Rodrigues, Raymundo. *Os Africanos no Brasil*. São Paulo: Editora Nacional, 1982.

Nishida, Mieko. "Manumission and Ethnicity in Urban Slavery: Salvador, Brazil 1808–1888." *Hispanic American Historical Review*, Vol. 73, No. 3 (1993), pp. 61–91.

Slavery and Identity: Ethnicity, Gender, and Race in Salvador, Brazil, 1808–1888. Bloomington: Indiana University Press, 2003.

Oliveira Vianna, Francisco José. "Resumo Histórico dos Inquéritos Censitários Realizados no Brasil." In Brazil, Diretoria Geral de Estatistica, *Recenseamento do Brasil, 1920, Vol. 1: Introdução*. Rio de Janeiro, 1922.

Ortíz, Fernando. *Hampa Afrocubana: Los Negros Brujos*. Madrid: Librería de F. Fé, 1906.

Los Negros Esclavos. Havana: Editorial de Ciencias Sociales, 1987.

Owens, Leslie Howard. *This Species of Property: Slave Life and Culture in the Old South*. New York: Oxford University Press, 1976.

Palmer, Colin A. *Slaves of the White God: Blacks in Mexico, 1570–1650*. Cambridge, MA: Harvard University Press, 1976.

Paquette, Robert L. *Sugar Is Made with Blood: The Conspiracy of La Escalera and the Conflict between Empires over Slavery in Cuba*. Middletown, CT: Wesleyan University Press, 1988.

Pearson, Edward A., editor. *Designs against Charleston: The Trial Record of the Denmark Vesey Slave Conspiracy of 1822*. Chapel Hill: University of North Carolina Press, 1999.

Pérez de la Riva, Francisco. *El Café: Historia de su Cultivo y Explotación en Cuba*. Havana: Jesús Montero, 1944.

Phillips, Ulrich Bonnell. *American Negro Slavery: A Survey of the Supply, Employment and Control of Negro Labor as Determined by the Plantation Regime*. New York: Appleton, 1918.

Postma, Johannes Menne. *The Dutch in the Atlantic Slave Trade, 1600–1815*. New York: Cambridge University Press, 1990.

Price, Richard, editor. *Maroon Societies: Rebel Slave Communities in the Americas*. Baltimore: Johns Hopkins University Press, 1979.

Raboteau, Albert J. *Slave Religion: The "Invisible Institution" in the Antebellum South*. New York: Oxford University Press, 1978.

Ramos, Donald. "Marriage and the Family in Colonial Vila Rica." *Hispanic American Historical Review*, Vol. 55, No. 2 (1975), pp. 200–25.

Rawick, George P., editor. *The American Slave: A Composite Autobiography* (19 vols.). Westport, CT: Greenwood Press, 1972–79.

Reis, João José. *Death Is a Festival: Funeral Rites and Rebellion in Nineteenth-Century Brazil*. Chapel Hill: University of North Carolina Press, 2003.

    Slave Rebellion in Brazil: The Muslim Uprising of 1835 in Bahia. Baltimore: Johns Hopkins University Press, 1993.

Reis, João José, and Flávio dos Santos Gomes, editors. *Liberdade por um fio: História dos Quilombos no Brasil*. São Paulo: Companhia das Letras, 1996.

Robertson, David. *Denmark Vesey*. New York: Knopf, 1999.

Rogers Albert, Octavia V. *The House of Bondage or Charlotte Brooks and Other Slaves Original and Life-like, as they Appeared in their Old Plantation and City Slave Life; Together with Pen-Pictures of the Peculiar Institution, with Sights and Insights into their New Relations as Freedmen, Freemen, and Citizens*. New York: Hunt & Eaton, 1890.

Russell-Wood, A. J. R. *Slavery and Freedom in Colonial Brazil*. Oxford: Oneworld Press, 2002.

    The Black Man in Slavery and Freedom in Colonial Brazil. New York: St. Martin's Press, 1982.

Saunders, A. C. de D. M. *A Social History of Black Slaves and Freedmen in Portugal, 1441–1555*. New York: Cambridge University Press, 1982.

Scarano, Julita. *Devoção e Escravidão: a Irmandade de Nossa Senhora do Rosário dos Pretos no Distrito Diamantino no Século XVIII*. São Paulo: Companhia Editora Nacional, 1976.

    Empire and Antislavery: Spain, Cuba, and Puerto Rico, 1833–1874. Pittsburgh: University of Pittsburgh Press, 1999.

Schwartz, Stuart B. *Slaves, Peasants, and Rebels: Reconsidering Brazilian Slavery*. Urbana and Chicago: University of Illinois Press, 1992.

Sugar Plantations in the Formation of Brazilian Society: Bahia, 1550–1835. New York: Cambridge University Press, 1985.

"The Manumission of Slaves in Colonial Brazil: Bahia, 1684–1745." *Hispanic American Historical Review,* Vol. 54, No. 4 (1974), pp. 603–35.

Scott, Rebecca. *Slave Emancipation in Cuba: The Transition to Free Labor, 1860–1899.* Princeton, NJ: Princeton University Press, 1985.

Scott, Rebecca, Seymour Drescher, Hebe Maria Mattos de Castro, George Reid Andrews, and Robert M. Levine, editors. *The Abolition of Slavery and the Aftermath of Emancipation in Brazil.* Durham, NC: Duke University Press, 1988.

Sheridan, Richard B. *Sugar and Slavery: An Economic History of the British West Indies, 1623–1775.* Baltimore: Johns Hopkins University Press, 1973.

Simonsen, Roberto C. *História Econômica do Brasil (1500–1820),* 6th ed. São Paulo: Editora Nacional, 1969.

Slenes, Robert W. *Na Senzala Uma Flor: Esperanças e Recordações na Formação da Família Escrava, Brasil Sudeste, Século XIX.* Rio de Janeiro: Editora Nova Fronteira, 1999.

"The Demography and Economics of Brazilian Slavery: 1850–1888." Ph.D. dissertation, Stanford University, 1976.

Solow, Barbara L., editor. *Slavery and the Rise of the Atlantic System.* New York: Cambridge University Press, 1991.

Solow, Barbara L., and Stanley L. Engerman, editors. *British Capitalism and Caribbean Slavery: The Legacy of Eric Williams.* New York: Cambridge University Press, 1987.

Stampp, Kenneth M. *The Peculiar Institution: Slavery in the Antebellum South.* New York: Knopf, 1956.

Starling, Marion Wilson. *The Slave Narrative: Its Place in American History.* Boston: G.K. Hall, 1981.

Starobin, Robert S., editor. *Denmark Vesey: The Slave Conspiracy of 1822.* Englewood Cliffs, NJ: Prentice-Hall, 1970.

Stein, Stanley. *Vassouras: A Brazilian Coffee County, 1850–1890.* Cambridge, MA: Harvard University Press, 1957.

Stevenson, Brenda E. *Life in Black & White: Family and Community in the Slave South.* New York: Oxford University Press, 1996.

Speculators and Slaves: Masters, Traders, and Slaves in the Old South. Madison: University of Wisconsin Press, 1989.

"The Demographic Cost of Sugar: Debates on Slave Societies and Natural Increase in the Americas." *American Historical Review,* Vol. 105, No. 5 (December 2000), pp. 1534–75.

Tannenbaum, Frank. *Slave and Citizen: The Negro in the Americas.* New York: Vintage Books, 1946.

Thornton, John. *Africa and Africans in the Making of the Atlantic World, 1400–1680.* Cambridge: Cambridge University Press, 1992.

Toplin, Robert Brent. *The Abolition of Slavery in Brazil.* New York: Atheneum, 1972.

Turner, Nat. *The Confessions of Nat Turner, the Leader of the Late Insurrection in Southampton, Va.* Baltimore: T. R. Gray, 1831.

Vinson, Ben, III. *Bearing Arms for His Majesty: The Free Colored Militia in Colonial Mexico.* Stanford, CA: Stanford University Press, 2001.

Wade, Richard C. *Slavery in the Cities: The South 1820–1960.* New York: Oxford University Press, 1964.

Weiner, Marli Frances. *Mistresses and Slaves: Plantation Women in South Carolina, 1830–1880.* Urbana: University of Illinois Press, 1998.

Williams, Eric. *Capitalism and Slavery.* Chapel Hill: University of North Carolina Press, 1944.

Windley, Lathan A., editor. *Runaway Slave Advertisement: A Documentary History from the 1730s to 1790.* (4 vols.), Westport, CT: Greenwood Press, 1983.

Wright, Gavin. *The Political Economy of the Cotton South: Households, Markets, and Wealth in the Nineteenth Century.* New York: Norton, 1978.

Wright, Irene. *The Early History of Cuba, 1492–1586.* New York: Macmillan, 1916.

Zanetti, Oscar, and Alejandro García. *Sugar and Railroads: A Cuban History 1837–1959.* Chapel Hill: University of North Carolina Press, 1998.

INDEX

Abakuá society, 181–2
abolition, 14–15, 251–90
  in Brazil, 11, 12, 15, 50, 251, 258–9,
    273–4, 282–90
  in British West Indian colonies, 14, 18,
    259–60
  in Cuba, 15, 21, 206–7, 258–9, 273–82,
    288–90
  Dom Pedro II and, 12, 283–5
  humanism and, 14, 252–4
  industrial revolution and, 143
  in Jamaica, 276
  in Latin America, 50
  Methodists and, 255, 273
  in northern states (U.S.), 147
  political factors in, 14, 288–90
  prior to American Revolution, 256
  in Puerto Rico, 21, 281
  Quakers and, 252, 255–7, 260, 273
  religious revivalism and, 14, 260–1
  in Spain, 21, 276, 277
  technological innovation in sugar
    production and, 143–7
  unprofitability of slave labor and, 143–51,
    252–4
  U.S. Constitution and, 27, 32, 257, 265–6
  in United States, 14, 15, 27, 32, 147,
    256–7, 260
  in United States versus Britain, 257–8
  in United States versus Cuba and Brazil,
    259
  "Williams thesis" and, 14, 143–4, 252–4
  See also British abolition and abolitionists;
    Civil War; Emancipation
    Proclamation; Moret Law; Rio Branco
    Law
African-Americans, 169, 269, 272
  in New York City, 239
  as soldiers in Civil War, 270–1
African organizations, 48
  See also cabildos de nación; irmandades
African religion, 182, 186
  Brazilian and Cuban slaves and, 41, 180–7

candomblé and, 182–4, 186–7
santeria and, 182
  in South America, 41
  U.S. slaves and, 178–80, 181
  See also Islam; religion
African slave trade, 13, 137, 162
  abolition of (Cuban), 278
  abolition of (U.S.), 30, 256–7
  African merchants in, 35
  Brazil and, 40, 50, 51, 107–12, 154
  Brazilian coffee production and, 10,
    110–12, 156
  Brazilian mining boom and, 59–60, 153–6
  Brazilian sugar production and, 39–40,
    156
  in Caribbean colonies, 33–5, 36, 41, 52,
    140
  in Caribbean versus colonial Latin
    America, 41, 52–5
  in colonial Mexico and Peru, 37, 40
  comparative impact on slave families,
    173–4
  in Cuba, 19, 24, 112–13, 208
  cultural impact in Spanish and Portuguese
    colonies, 41
  demographic collapse of indigenous
    people and, 36, 37, 50
  development of, 33
  discovery of gold and, 34
  Dutch and, 51–2
  eighteenth-century, 41, 55, 59, 154
  end of, by British, 10, 156, 251–2, 255–6,
    258
  in Haiti and Jamaica, 55
  industrial revolution and, 143
  influence on slave rebellions, 208–10
  labor demands and, 36–8
  Minas Gerais and, 109–10
  Old World destinations of (1444–1600),
    35
  origins, 134
  Portuguese colonization and, 34–5, 36–8,
    39, 51–2, 134

African slave trade (*cont.*)
  pre-European arrival, 35
  racism and, 134
  rice cultivation and, 57–8, 59
  in South Carolina, 257
  Spanish colonization and conquest and,
    35–52
  St. Kitts and, 52
  sugar production and, 19, 34, 56, 112–13,
    140
  in United States, 56–7, 59, 257
  in United States versus Brazil and Cuba,
    96–8
  volume and destinations, 61
  waning of, in colonial Spanish America,
    50
American-born slaves, 53, 57
American Colonization Society, 260
American Revolution, 18, 26–7
  antislavery sentiment prior to, 256
Amistad incident, 209
annexation movement (Cuba), 276–7
Aponte conspiracy, 206–8
Arawaks (indigenous Cubans), 12, 136–7
Articles of Confederation, 26
  replacement Constitution by, 27
Aztecs, 13, 23, 35, 36, 137

Bananal (São Paolo, Brazil), slave
    populations in, 110–11
  See also Brazil; São Paolo
bandeiras, 5, 220
baptism, 178
Baquaqua, Mahommah Bardo, 83–94
Barbados
  British occupation of, 140
  European absentee sugar producers and, 17
  indentured servants in, 23–4, 140
  slave populations in, 54
  sugar production in, 15, 23, 52, 140
  tobacco production in, 52, 140
Bill of Rights, 27
Boston, 25
Boston Massacre, 26
Boston Tea Party, 26
bounty hunters, 44, 45, 203
Brazil
  under Dom Pedro II, 10
  immigration to, 10
  indigenous slavery in, 136
  infrastructure modernization in (1850),
    10, 108
  land rights in, 23
  Paraguayan War and, 10–11
  Portuguese colonization of, 1–9
  republicanism in, 11, 12
  São Paolo, 154–6, 163

  See also Minas Gerais; population (free);
    Portuguese colonization (Brazil); Rio
    de Janeiro; São Paulo
Brazilian slavery, 14
  African religion and, 180–7
  versus Caribbean, 52–5
  coffee production and, 9, 11, 156–7,
    164
  comparative economic viability of,
    157–64
  comparative slave prices, 158
  first presence of (sixteenth century), 35
  import comparisons by country, 24
  internal slave trade of, 10, 108, 163, 176
  legal status, 40
  manumission and, 104–5
  marriage and, 173, 174
  migration of, 117–31, 152, 157, 175–6
  mining and, 59–61, 153–6, 192–3,
    216–19
  occupational diversity of, 40, 53, 152
  Palmares and, 45, 213–16, 217
  promiscuity stereotype and, 172–3
  quartados in, 198–9
  regional economic cycles and, 107–12,
    151–7
  resistance and rebellion in, 224–33, 287
  roças and, 188–91
  self-purchase and, 197–9, 285–6
  slave families and, 43, 168, 172–6
  slave labor and, 151
  as slave societies versus societies with
    slaves, 40
  in sugar cane farming and sugar
    production, 39–40, 43, 50, 59
  in sixteenth century, 36, 39–40, 43
  in seventeenth century, 38–40, 50
  in eighteenth century, 59–61
  urban, 194–6
  See also abolition; Minas Gerais (Brazil);
    mocambos; slave populations
breeding. *See under* slave populations
Britain
  challenges with French in United States,
    25–6
  in North America, 22–3
British abolition and abolitionists, 18,
    251–6, 276
  in Cuba, 21, 211, 212, 276
  Jamaica slave uprising and, 259
  versus U.S., 257–8
  in West Indian colonies, 259–60
  See also abolition
British Caribbean colonies, 54–5, 140
  eighteenth-century slave trade and, 41
  occupation of Havana, 16
  in seventeenth century, 52, 54–5

British North American colonies.
    See United States
British West Indian colonies, 15
    abolition in, 14, 18, 259–60
    import of slaves from United States, 22
    slave populations in, 98
    sugar economy and, 17, 18
    See also Barbados; Jamaica
Brooks, Charlotte, 64, 65–8, 71

cabildos de nación (Cuban African ethnic
        organizations), 180–4, 206–7
    versus secret societies, 181–2
    U.S. slaves and, 181
Cabot, John, 22
California, 28, 264
    gold in, 28
Canada, 25
candomblé, 182–4, 186–7
    See also African religion
Capitalism and Slavery (Williams), 143,
        252–4
Caribbean slavery, 41, 52
    African slave trade and, 33–5, 36, 41,
        52–5, 140
    versus colonial Latin America, 41,
        52–5
    death rates in, 54
    diets and, 99
    as slave societies versus societies with
        slaves, 40
    sugar production and, 140
Cartier, Jacques, 22
cash access, 196–7
Catholic Church, 41, 105, 180
    in Brazil, 10, 184–6
cattle ranching, in Cuba, 13, 14
Charleston, 150
    growth of (eighteenth century), 25
Chesapeake Bay region, 55–9
    conspiracies to rebel in, 238
    percentage of slaves born in (1750), 57
    prerogatives available to slaves in, 55–6
    settlement of, 22
    slave populations in (seventeenth
        century), 24, 55, 56–7
    slavery development in, versus South,
        57–9
    slavery in, 22, 24, 55–9
    tobacco production in, 22, 23, 24, 25
children, 42
    death rates of, 98
    of slaves and slave masters, 50
    See also Moret Law; Rio Branco law; slave
        families
cimarrones, 46, 205, 206
    See also runaway slaves

Civil War, 15, 28, 30–2, 251, 262, 269
    African-Americans in, 270–1
    slaves reaction to, 31, 269
coartado and *coartación*, 49, 196–7, 198–9
    female slaves and, 199
    See also freedom
Coercive Acts, 26
coffee and coffee production
    African slave trade and, 10, 156
    in Brazil, 8, 9–10, 11, 110–12, 156–7, 164
    in Cuba, 16
    destruction of during Haitian revolution,
        17
    natural reproduction and, 110–12
colonial taxation, 26
    revolutionary responses to, 26
Columbus, Christopher, 34, 40
    Cuba and, 12
communities. *See cabildos de nación*;
        irmandades; maroon communities;
        mocambos
Confederacy, 31
conspiracies. *See* rebellions and resistance
Constitution (U.S.), 27, 272
    abolition and, 27, 257, 265–6, 272
    adoption of, 27
    Bill of Rights and, 27
    states rights in, 27
    thirteenth Amendment to, 32, 272
Continental Congress, 26
Cortés, Hernán, 35
cotton and cotton production, 29, 149
    in Brazil, 8
    cotton gin and, 149
    founding of textile mills, 30
    spread of U.S. slavery in nineteenth and,
        149–50
    technological innovation in, 149
Creole slaves, 191, 199
Cuba
    annexation movement in, 20, 276–7
    cattle ranching in, 13, 14
    Columbus and, 12
    by-country comparison of colonial
        political institutions, 23, 25
    effect of sugar prosperity on, 19–20
    elites in, 19–21
    independence and, 20, 19–21
    land rights in, 23
    national identity and, 19, 20
    railroads in, 17, 18, 145, 149, 212
    Reformist Party in, 20
    secret societies in, 181–2
    Spanish conquest of, 13
    Spanish merchant class in, 20
    wealth distribution in, 19, 20
    See also Havana; Ten Years, War

Cuban slavery, 14, 137, 162, 273–4
  1842 slave code, 196
  African religion and, 180–7
  African slave trade and, 24, 208
  annexation movement and, 276–7
  Aponte conspiracy and, 206–8
  cabildos de nación and, 180–4, 206–7
  cimarrones (runaways), 46, 205, 206
  comparative economic activities and,
    143–4
  comparative economic viability of,
    157–64
  comparative slave prices, 158
  conucos and, 188–91
  economic aspects, 136–47, 273–4
  economic development in Havana and,
    138–40
  gold and, 34, 136–7
  in Havana, 34, 125, 138–40
  impact of British occupation on, 16–17
  import comparisons by country, 24
  La Escalera conspiracy and, 177, 207, 209,
    209, 210, 213, 233, 276
  manumission and, 104–5
  occupational diversity of, 15, 138–40,
    142–3, 162
  patrocinados and *patrono* period, 281–2
  rebellions and, 204–13
  slave families and, 176–7
  slave labor and, 151
  sugar production and, 15, 18–19, 125–31
  tobacco production and, 141–2
  urban, 194–6
  "whitening" and, 274, 275, 278
  See also abolition; *cimarrones*; *coartado* and
    coartación; *ingenios*; slave populations
cunucos (Cuban provision grounds), 188–91
  See also land access and rights

death rates, 97–100
  of children, 98
  climate and, 100–2
  in colonial Caribbean, 54
  disease and, 100–2
  of indigenous slaves, 34, 39, 136
  in mining regions, 104
  in sugar production areas, 43, 102–4
  of Ten Years' War, 21
  See also natural reproduction; slave
    populations
Declaration of Independence (1776), 26
demographics *See* death rates; natural
    reproduction; population (free); sex
    ratios; slave populations
diamonds, 153
  development of African slave trade and,
    59–60

exports (Brazil), 9
diets, 98–100, 189–90
disease, 34, 38, 41, 59, 100–2, 137
  immunity to, among U.S.-born slaves,
    101–2
Dolores, José, 210
Dom João, 7–8
Dom Pedro, 8–9
Dom Pedro II, 8, 10
  abolition and, 12, 283–5
domestic servants, 195
Douglass, Frederick, 261, 262
Dred Scott decision (1857), 266
Durham, Tempe Herndon, 68–71
Dutch, 4–5, 51
  African slave trade and, 51–2
  attacks on Brazilian sugar production, 51
  colonization of New York, 23, 52
  colonization of Surinam, 52
Dutch East India Company, 22, 51

economics and economies, 132–3, 164, 166
  abolition and, 14, 143–4, 252–4
  agricultural (U.S.), 30
  Brazilian slave-based regional cycles,
    107–12, 151–7
  cash access of slaves, 196–7
  of colonial Brazil, 5–6, 7, 59–61
  of colonial Cuba, 14–21, 136–47
  comparative economic activities in Cuba,
    142–3
  comparative viability of slave economics,
    157–64
  Cuban state-sponsored monopoly
    companies, 16
  export economy of Brazil (nineteenth
    century), 8, 9–10, 162
  export economy of Cuba (nineteenth
    century), 112
  of Great Britain (eighteenth century), 25
  of Havana, 138–40
  profitability of slave labor, 143–51,
    157–64
  slave prices, 158
  of United States (seventeenth century),
    59
  of United States (eighteenth century), 25
  of United States (nineteenth century),
    29–30
  See also coffee and coffee production;
    mining and mining economies; rice
    cultivation; sugar and sugar production;
    tobacco and tobacco production;
    wealth distribution
El Ingenio (Fraginals), 143
Emancipation Act (Britain), 259
  See also abolition

emancipation law (Cuban), 21, 97
  See also abolition
Emancipation Proclamation (U.S.), 31, 270,
  272
  See also abolition
Erie Canal, 29
Española (contemporary Haiti and
  Dominican Republic), 12–13
  gold deposits in, 12, 34
  indigenous slavery in, 12
  See also Dominican Republic; Haiti

factories, 30
family. See slave families
female slaves, 42, 172, 236
  coartación and, 199
  as domestic servants, 195
  health of, 98
  manumission of, 199–200
  as mistresses to slave masters, 50
  prostitution and, 195
  urban slavery and, 195
  See also children; Moret Law; Rio Branco
    Law; sex ratios; slave families
First Great Awakening, 260
Florida, 21
  slavery in colonial, 59
food. See diets
Fraginals, Manuel Moreno, 143–4
France
  attack on Havana, 137, 138
  challenges with British in U.S., 25–6
  conflict with Portuguese in Brazil, 3
  control of Canada, 25
  See also French colonies
free laborers
  in Brazil, 23, 152
  in colonial Cuba, 14, 18
free peoples of color, 24, 48, 53
  in Brazil, 61, 119–23
  by country comparison, 23–4, 53–4, 61,
    123, 195–6
  in Cuba, 18, 124–5, 206–7
  importance of, to slaves, 48
  in Old versus New South, 116
  percentage of women in colonial Latin
    America, 50
  in urban areas, 195–6
  U.S. population of, 113–14, 123, 195–6,
    236
  in Virginia, 242
  See also maroon communities; race and
    racial structure
Free Soil Party (U.S.), 262, 266
freedom, 46, 48–9, 165
  self-purchase of, by slaves, 197–9, 285–6
  for slave soldiers, 46

See also abolition; coartado and coartación;
  manumission; rebellions and resistance;
  runaway slaves
French and Indian War, 16, 25–6
French colonies, 41
  in Caribbean (seventeenth century), 52
  in Quebec, 22
  sugar economy and, 17
  See also France; Haiti
French Revolution, 7
Fugitive Slave Act (1850), 237, 264

Gabriel's Rebellion, 242–5
  betrayal in, 244–5
Ganga Zumba (Great Lord), 215–16
Garrison, William Lloyd, 261
Georgia
  rice cultivation in, 24, 148
  slave imports to, 24
German migrants, 24
gold
  in California, 28, 264
  in Caribbean, 13
  development of African slave trade and,
    34, 59–60
  development of Cuban slavery and, 34,
    136–7
  in Española, 12, 34
  exports (Brazil), 9
  gold rush to Brazilian interior, 5, 153–6
  indigenous slavery and, 12, 34
  in Minas Gerais, 5, 59–60, 153, 216
  See also mining and mining economies

Haiti
  destruction of sugar and coffee
    infrastructure and, 17
  European absentee sugar producers and,
    17
  independence of, 17
  slave imports to, 55
  sugar production in, 15, 54
Haitian Revolution, 14, 46, 205, 211, 242,
  246
  Cuban elite's fear of, 19, 274
  destruction of sugar and coffee
    infrastructure and, 17
Havana, 13, 194
  British occupation of, 16
  as colonial capital, 14–15, 34, 138–40
  economic expansion of, 17, 138–40
  French attacks on, 137, 138
  racial intermarriage in, 176
  slavery in, 34, 125, 138–40
  Spanish fleet system and, 14–15, 34
  sugar production and, 17, 160
  See also Cuba

hiring out, 194–5, 242
Hispaniola. *See* Española
Hudson, Henry, 22
humanity (slaves' assertion of), 42, 44, 55–6,
    165–8, 177–8, 200–1, 202
    cabildos de nación and, 180–4, 206–7
    cash access and, 196–7
    commerce and, 194
    land access and, 188–91
    self-purchase and, 197–9, 285–6
    See also African religion; *coartado* and
        coartación; freedom; marriage;
        mocambos; rebellions and resistance;
        religion; rituals; slave families

immigration
    to Brazil, 10
    to United States, 24, 28
Incas, 13, 23, 36, 137
Inconfidencia Mineira (colonial Brazilian
        conspiracy), 7
indentured servants, 140
    in Barbados, 23–4, 140
    in colonial United States, 55, 56, 148
independence and independence
        movements
    abolition and, 278–81
    in Brazil, 7–8, 227
    in Cuba, 19–21, 278–81
    in Spain, 278
    in United States, 26–7
    See also American Revolution; Haitian
        Revolution; Ten Years' War (Cuba)
indigenous peoples and slavery, 13, 23, 25,
        33–4, 36–7, 41, 46, 47
    in Brazil, 2, 59, 136
    Brazilian sugar production and, 3, 39, 59,
        152
    in Cuba, 136–7
    death rates, 34, 39, 136
    decline of, in Caribbean colonies, 12,
        13
    demographic collapse of, 36, 37, 38
    in Española, 12
    laws against enslavement of, 38, 135
    missionary activity to, 5
    mocambos and, 221
    population recovery of, 38, 50
    rise of, 134–6
    U.S. westward expansion and, 27
    See also Arawaks; Aztecs; Incas
industrial revolution, 143
infrastructure
    Brazilian, 10, 108
    U.S. economic growth and, 29–30
ingenios (sugar mills), 139, 141–2, 145,
    162

pre-eighteenth century, 15
    See also sugar and sugar production
Irish migrants, 24
irmandades (Brazilian religious
        brotherhoods), 184–7
Islam, 182
    See also African religion; religion

Jamaica
    abolition of slavery in, 259–60, 276
    British occupation of, 140
    European absentee sugar producers and, 17
    slave imports to, 55
    slave uprising in, 259
    sugar production in, 15, 23, 54, 140, 146
Jamestown, 22

Kansas-Nebraska Act (1854), 266, 267

La Escalera conspiracy, 177, 207, 209, 210,
    211, 213, 233, 276
labor. *See* free labor; indentured servants;
    slave labor; wage labor
land access and rights, 188–91
    by-country comparison, 23
    U.S. westward expansion and, 27–8
    See also Louisiana Purchase; Northwest
        Ordinance
Latin American independence wars, 18
Latin American slavery, 38
    versus Caribbean, 35–52, 52–5
Leeward Islands, European absentee sugar
    producers and, 17
Liberator, The (abolitionist newspaper),
    261
Liberty Party (U.S.), 262
Lincoln, Abraham, 268–70, 271
London Antislavery Committee, 259
Louisiana
    slave-based sugar economy in, 150
    slavery in colonial, 59
Louisiana Purchase (U.S.), 28, 263
Lowcountry. *See* Southern states (U.S.)

manumission, 105, 199
    Creole slaves and, 199
    female slaves and, 199–200
    rates of, by country, 104–5, 200
Manzano, Juan Francisco, 80–3
maroon communities, 44–5, 203
    of Brazilian runaway slaves (*mocambos*),
        213, 316
    palenques (Cuban maroon communities),
        203, 205, 206
    See also free peoples of color; race and
        racial structure
Marquis of Pombal, 7

marriage, 42, 167
    Brazilian slaves and, 173, 174
    racial intermarriage in Havana, 176
    right to, as social control by masters, 170
    sex ratios and, 43
    See also slave families
Maryland, 55
    settlement of, 23
Massachusetts
    founding of textile mills in, 30
    Puritan colony in, 23
mestizo (mixed Spanish/indigenous person),
    47–8, 53
    See also free peoples of color
Methodists
    abolition and, 273
    members of African descent, 179
Mexican War, 28, 262
Mexico, 36–8
    African slave trade in, 37, 40
    conflict with United States over Texas,
        28
    independence of, 28
    silver production in, 37
    Spanish conquest of, 13
mid-Atlantic states, 27
midwives, 191
migrants
    German, 24
    Irish, 24
    to United States, 24
migration. *See* slave mobility
Minas Gerais (Brazil), 60, 109–10, 184, 192,
    216–19
    gold in, 5, 59–60, 153
    importation of slaves to, 59–60, 109–10
    Inconfidência Mineira (colonial Brazilian
        conspiracy) in, 7
    mocambos in, 217, 218–19
    sex ratios in, 103
    slave populations in, 109–10, 117, 124
    See also Brazil; mining and mining
        economies
mining and mining economies, 36, 37
    bandeiras and, 5
    boom in Brazil, 5–7
    in colonial Spanish America, 37
    death rates in, 104
    sex ratios in, 103–4
    slaves in, 59–60, 153, 192–3, 216–19
    eighteenth-century Brazilian population
        and, 6
    See also gold; Minas Gerais; silver and
        silver production
missionary work, 5
Missouri Compromise (1820), 263–4, 266
mocambos (Brazilian runaway slave

communities), 203, 213–16, 217–24,
    287
    indigenous peoples and, 221
    military efforts against, 218–19
    in Minas Gerais, 217, 218–19
    See also Palmares
Montejo, Esteban, 71–80
Moret Law, 147, 279, 280, 281, 283, 285
    See also abolition; Cuban slavery
mortality rates. *See* death rates
mulattos, 24, 38
    See also free peoples of color; race and
        racial structure
Muslims. *See* Islam

Napoleon Bonaparte, 7
Napoleonic Wars, 7, 18
narratives. *See* slave narratives
Nat Turner rebellion, 247–9
natural reproduction, 28, 30, 58, 96, 100,
    106–7
    in Bananal (Brazil), 110–11
    coffee production and, 110–12
    in Cuba, 112–13
    diet and, 98–100
    disease and, 100–2
    height and, 99–100
    in Minas Gerais (Brazil), 109–10
    in mining zones, 104
    in Southern United States, 169
    in sugar plantation zones, 102–3
New Amsterdam, 23
    See also Dutch; New York City
New England
    population of (1790), 27
    shipbuilding industry in, 25
    slave populations in (1750), 24
New England Anti-Slavery Society, 261–2
New Jersey, 24
New York City
    African-Americans in, 239
    Dutch colonization of, 23, 52
    exploration and settlement of, 22–3
    as first capital of United States, 27
    growth of (eighteenth century), 25
    migrants to, 24
    slave population of (1750), 24
    slave rebellion in, 238–40
northern states (U.S.)
    abolition and, 147
    non-slave-based economy of, 30
    slavery in, 24, 56
    See also Civil War
Northwest Ordinance (U.S.), 28, 262

palenques (Cuban maroon communities),
    203, 205, 206

Palmares (Brazilian runaway slave
    community), 45, 213–16, 217
  film about, 214
  See also mocambos
Paraguay, 11
Paraguayan War, 10–11
patrocinados and patronos (Cuban slaves and
    slave masters), 281–2
Pennsylvania
  migrants to, 24
  slave populations in (1750), 24
Peru, 36–8
  African slave trade in, 37, 40
  Spanish conquest of, 13
Philadelphia, 25
plantations. See sugar and sugar production
politics
  abolition and, 288–90
  by, country comparison, 23, 25
  See also Lincoln, Abraham; Republican
    Party (U.S.)
population (free)
  of African heritage, in Portugal, 48
  Brazilian (1819), 9
  Brazilian (1872), 11
  Brazilian (eighteenth century), 6
  comparative racial structure by country,
    23–4
  Cuban (1827–62), 18
  Cuban (1650–1774), 15
  Cuban (before/after Ten Years, War), 21
  mestizo (sixteenth century), 47–8
  regional distribution of Brazilian (1872),
    11
  regional distribution of U.S. (1790), 27,
    114
  in United States (1700), 24
  in United States (1810), 97
  in United States (1860), 96, 97
  in United States (eighteenth century), 27
  in Virginia (1700), 24
  See also slave populations
Portugal and Portuguese, 7
  African slave trade and, 34–5, 36–8, 39,
    134
  population of African heritage people in,
    48
  See also Portuguese colonization (Brazil)
Portuguese colonization (Brazil), 1–9
  conflict with French, 3
  by-country comparison of political
    institutions, 23, 25
  under Dom João, 7–8
  under Dom Pedro, 8–9
  first presence of African slaves during, 35
  independence from, 8
  independence movements in, 7–8

as leading importer of slaves, 40
  rebellions under, 8
  transformation of (eighteenth century),
    5–6
  versus U.S. settlement, 23–4
  See also Brazil; Brazilian slavery
prerogatives, of slaves. See humanity (slaves,
    assertion of)
profitability. See under economics
promiscuity, 168–9, 172–3
Prosser, Gabriel, 242–5
  See also Gabriel's Rebellion
prostitution, 195
Protestantism, 178–80
  See also by denomination; religion
provision grounds, 188–91
  See also land access and rights
Puerto Rico, 18
  abolition of slavery in, 21, 277, 281
  gold in, 34
  slave population in, 277
  Spanish occupation of, 13
punishment, 202, 204
  of runaway slaves, 45
Puritans, 23

Quakers, 252, 255–7, 260, 273
quartados, 198–9
quilombos. See mocambos

race and racial structure
  colonial conceptions of, 47–8
  by-country comparison, 23–4, 47, 53–4,
    61, 273
  enslavement and, 13–14, 134
  equality and, 272–3
  in Methodist Church, 179
  rebellion and, 225
  separation of, in colonial Spanish
    America, 47
  in southern states (1700), 24
  in St. Kitts, 54
  U.S. conceptions of, 47, 272–3
  in Virginia, 24, 242
  "whitening" of Cubans and, 274, 275, 278
  See also cabildos de nación; free peoples of
    color; irmandades; maroon communities
racism, 269
  comparative conceptions of, 273
  in Cuba, 275, 277–8
  enslavement and, 134
  post-abolition, 15, 290
  slave families and, 169, 172–3
railroads, 18, 145, 212
  in Brazil, 10, 108
  in Cuba, 17, 18, 145, 149, 212
  sugar production and, 17, 18, 145, 149, 160

in United States, 29, 149
Raleigh, Sir Walter, 22
Real Compañia de Comercio de la Habana, 141
rebellions and resistance, 202–50, 233
    against abusive masters, 46
    in Bahia (Brazil), 224–33
    betrayal and, 244
    in Brazil, 7, 8, 44–6, 230, 287
    Brazilian versus Cuban, 213
    in Chesapeake region, 238
    during Civil War, 31, 271
    against colonial taxation, 26
    in Cuba, 204–13
    "day-to-day" (U.S.), 237
    fear of, by Cuban elites, 19, 20, 42, 274, 280
    impact of imported African slaves and, 208–10
    Inconfidencia Mineira (colonial Brazil), 7
    in Jamaica, 259
    in Latin America, 44–6
    in New York City, 238–40
    race and, 225
    in South Carolina, 240–1, 245–7
    in United States, 233–50
    See also Amistad incident; Aponte conspiracy; Boston Massacre; Boston Tea Party; Gabriel's Rebellion; Haitian Revolution; *La Escalera* conspiracy; *mocambos*; Nat Turner rebellion; Palmares; runaway slaves; Vesey, Denmark
religion
    abolition and (U.S.), 14, 252, 255–7, 260–1
    baptism and, 178
    Brazilian and Cuban slaves and, 180–7
    First Great Awakening (U.S.), 178, 260
    Second Great Awakening, 260
    U.S. slaves and, 178–80, 182
    See also by denomination; African religion; Islam
Republican Party (U.S.), 31, 266
    See also Civil War; Lincoln, Abraham
republicanism (Brazil), 11, 12
resistance. *See* rebellions and resistance
rice cultivation
    import of slaves for, 24, 57–8
    in southern states, 24, 29, 57–8
    U.S. slavery and, 150
Rilleux, Norberto, 146
Rio Branco Law (Brazil), 11, 283, 284, 285
    See also abolition; Brazilian slavery
Rio de Janeiro, 60, 154–6
    growth of, 60
    urban slavery in, 60

See also Brazil
rituals, 177–8
Roanoke Island, 22
roças (Brazilian provision grounds), 188–91
    See also land access and rights
Rogers, Octavia Victoria, 64, 65
Roman judicial codes, 48, 104, 196, 197
Royal Commercial Company of Havana, 16
Royal Tobacco Company, 16
Runaway Slave law. *See* Fugitive Slave Act
runaway slaves, 202–3
    Brazilian communities of (*See mocambos*)
    in colonial Brazil and Latin America, 44–6
    in Cuba, 46, 205, 206
    punishment of, 45, 203
    spontaneity of, 203
    U.S. Fugitive Slave Act (1850), 237, 264
    in United States, 202, 203, 237, 264
rural slavery, 45
    land access and, 188–91
    slave families in, 42–3

Saco, José Antonio, 275, 276, 277, 279
santeria, 182
    See also African religion
Santo Domingo. *See* Haiti
São Paolo (Brazil), 154–6, 163
    slave population of, 163
    See also Brazil
Scotch-Irish migrants, 24
Second Continental Congress, 26
Second Great Awakening, 260
secret societies
    Abakuá society, 181–2
    versus *cabildos de nación*, 181–2
Seven Years' War (1756–1763), 16, 25–6
sex ratios, 236, 237
    in colonial Brazil, 43
    in colonial Latin America, 42–3
    by-country comparison, 235
    effect on marriage, 43
    in mining economies, 103–4
    slave family formation in U.S. South and, 169
    See also female slaves
Sierra Leone, 260
Siete Partidas, 196
silver and silver production, 5, 36, 37
    in Mexico, 37
slave elders, 191
slave families, 42–4, 167–8
    in Brazil, 43, 168, 172–6
    comparative impact of African slave trade on, 173–4
    in Cuba, 176–7

slave families (*cont.*)
female-headed, 171
impact of internal Brazilian slave trade on, 175–6
impact of internal U.S. slave trade on, 170–1, 175–6
maintaining on plantations versus farms, 171
nuclear, 171–2
promiscuity stereotype and, 168–9, 172–3
racist interpretation of (Brazil), 172–3
racist interpretation of (U.S.), 169
in rural areas, 42–3
scholarly interpretations of, 168–70
social control by masters and, 167, 170
threat of destruction of, 43–4, 170, 172, 204
in urban areas, 42
in United States, 168–77
in Virginia, 171
See also marriage
slave labor
by country comparison, 151
as dominant system, 23
economics of, 132–133–164
incompatibility with technological innovation and, 143–7
occupational diversity of, 15
profitability of, 143–51
in southern U.S., 150–1
slave masters, 166–8
abusive, 40, 44, 46
children with slaves and, 50
in Cuba, 281–2
female slaves as mistresses to, 50
freeing of slaves by, 50
murder of, 46
religion and, 180, 188
resistance against abusive, 46
social control and, 42, 57, 167, 189–91
written records of, 95
slave mobility, 117–31, 152, 157, 175–6
slave narratives, 63, 64
Brazilian, 83–95
of Charlotte Brooks, 64, 65–8, 71
Cuban, 71–83
of Esteban Montejo, 71–80
of Juan Francisco Manzano, 80–3
of Mahommah Gardo Baquaqua, 83–94
of Tempe Herndon Durham, 68–71
U.S., 65–71
slave populations, 100
American-born, 53, 57
in Bananal (Brazil), 110–11
in Barbados, 54
in Brazil (1819), 9, 116–23
in Brazil (1872), 11, 116–23

in Brazil (general), 97, 116
breeding thesis and, 106–7
in British West Indies, 98
in Caribbean versus colonial Latin America, 53–4
in Chesapeake Bay region (1700), 24
in Chesapeake Bay region (seventeenth century), 24, 55, 56–7
concentration of, in southern U.S., 27, 114, 147–8
contrasts between U.S., Brazilian, and Cuban, 96–8, 113, 124–31
by-country in Americas (1790), 61
in Cuba (1650–1774), 15
in Cuba (1774 and 1792), 17
in Cuba (1827–62), 18, 19, 277
in Cuba (general), 97
in Cuba (nineteenth century), 112–13
declining (Brazil), 104–5, 119–22
declining (Cuba), 18, 104–5
in Iguaçu region (Brazil), 223
in Lima (sixteenth century), 37
in Mexico City (sixteenth century), 37
migration of, 117–31
at Minas Gerais (Brazil), 109–10, 117, 124
in New England (1750), 24
in New York City (1750), 24
in Old versus New South, 114–16
in Pennsylvania (1750), 24
in Puerto Rico, 277
in São Paulo (Brazil), 163
in southern United States (seventeenth century), 57
in southern United States (eighteenth century), 58
in Trinidad, 98
uniqueness of U.S., 96–8
in United States (1700), 24
in United States (1740), 56
in United States (1790), 27, 113–16
in United States (1810), 97
in United States (1820), 236
in United States (1860), 29, 96, 97, 113–16
in Virginia, 24, 242
See also death rates; natural reproduction; sex ratios
slave prices, 158
slave societies, versus societies with slaves, 40
slaves and slavery, 13
abuse of, 44, 202
in Africa (pre-European arrival), 35
American-born, 53
city commerce and, 194, 195
comparative height of, 99–100
control over lives and (*see* humanity [slaves' assertion of])

diets of, 98–100, 189–90
diversity of experiences of, 33, 40, 44
free peoples of color and, 48
in Havana, 34
industrial revolution and, 143
as investments, 132
legal status, of, 42
occupational diversity of, 36–8, 56
social prestige of ownership of, 132
social structure and, 191–2
as soldiers, 46
in sugar and sugar production, 23, 34, 39
See also abolition; African slave trade;
    Brazilian slavery; Caribbean slavery;
    Cuban slavery; female slaves;
    indigenous slavery; rural slavery; slave
    families; slave narratives; slave
    populations; urban slavery; U.S. slavery
South Carolina
    rice cultivation in, 24, 148
    slave imports to, 24, 257
    slave rebellion in, 240–1, 245–7
    urban slavery in, 58–9, 150
southern states (U.S.)
    absence of free labor in, 150–1
    agricultural economy of, 30
    cotton and, 30, 149
    free peoples of color in Old versus New
        South, 116
    importation of slaves to, 24, 57–8,
        149–50
    Old versus New South slave population,
        114–16
    portion of U.S. population (1860), 29
    pro-slavery lobby in, 257, 260, 265
    racial structure of (1700), 24
    rice cultivation in, 57–8
    slave-based economy of, 30
    slave populations (colonial), 57
    slave populations in (1790), 27
    slave populations in (eighteenth century),
        58
    as slave societies versus societies with
        slaves, 40
    slavery development in versus
        Chesapeake, 57–9
    technological innovation in cotton
        production in, 149
    urban slavery in, 150
    See also Civil War
Southwest Ordinance (U.S.), 262
Spain
    abolition in, 21, 276, 277
    exploration of United States, 21–2
    Spanish Caribbean colonies, 12
    Cuban state-sponsored monopoly
        companies, 16

development of African slave trade in,
    33–5
Havana as colonial capital of, 14–15
See also Cuba; Dominican Republic;
    Española; Haiti; Havana; Puerto Rico;
    Spanish fleet system
Spanish colonization, development of
    slavery in Americas and, 35–52
Spanish fleet system, 64
    attacks on, 13
    Havana and, 14–15, 34
St. Domingue. See Haiti
St. Kitts, 54
    African slave trade and, 52
    sugar production in, 52
    tobacco production in, 52
Stamp Act (1875), 26
steamboat, 29, 149
sugar and sugar production, 146, 147
    abolition and, 143–7
    African slave trade and, 56, 156
    in Barbados, 15, 23, 52
    in Brazil, 8, 9, 39–40, 50, 59, 151–2
    Brazilian versus U.S. tobacco production,
        23
    in Cuba, 14, 15, 17, 18–19, 19–20, 112,
        125–31, 141–7
    Cuban elites and, 17
    death rates in, 43, 102–4
    decline after abolition in British colonies,
        18
    destruction of, during Haitian revolution,
        17
    differences between Cuba and British/
        French colonies, 17
    Dutch attacks on Brazilian, 51
    in Dutch Surinam, 52
    in Haiti, 15, 54
    indigenous slavery and, 39, 152
    in Jamaica, 15, 18, 23, 54, 146
    in Louisiana, 150
    in Madeira and São Tomé, 2, 39
    railroad systems and, 17, 18, 145, 149
    in St. Kitts, 52
    technological innovations in, 17, 18,
        143–7
    transformation of Caribbean slavery and,
        140
    See also ingenios (sugar mills)
Surinam, 52

Tailors' Rebellion (Brazil), 227
Ten Years' War (Cuba), 21, 207, 212, 251
    abolition and, 21, 251, 273
    See also Cuba
Texas, 28, 263–4
    U.S./Mexican conflict over, 28

tobacco and tobacco production, 148
  in Chesapeake Bay region, 22, 23, 24, 25
  contraband trade of, 16
  in Cuba, 15–16, 137, 141–2
  import of slaves to United States for, 22,
    24, 56, 59, 148
  in St. Kitts and Barbados, 52, 140
  U.S. versus Brazilian sugar production, 23
  in United States, 59, 150
  wealth for British merchants from (U.S.), 25
Trinidad, slave populations in, 98
Turnbull, David, 211
Turner, Nat, 247–9

United States
  agricultural economy of, 30
  British exploration and settlement of,
    22–3, 26–7
  conflict with Mexico over Texas, 28
  by-country comparison of colonial
    political institutions, 23, 25
  first settlement in, 21
  French challenges with British in, 25–6
  immigration to, 28
  independence (1783), 27
  land rights in, 23
  population (eighteenth century), 27
  settlement of, versus Brazilian, 23–4
  Spanish exploration of, 21–2
  westward expansion and, 26, 27–8
  See also by specific state; abolition;
    Chesapeake Bay region; Civil War;
    northern United States; southern
    United States; U.S. slavery
urban slavery, 44, 193–6
  commerce conducted in, 194
  in Cuban and Brazilian cities, 194–6
  female slaves in, 195
  hiring out and, 194–5, 242
  occupational diversity of, 193–4
  in Rio de Janeiro, 60
  slave families and, 42
  in South Carolina, 58–9, 150
  in southern United States, 58, 150, 195
U.S. slavery, 14, 147–51, 257
  African religion and, 178–80, 181
  in Chesapeake Bay region, 24, 55–9
  during colonial period, 55–9
  comparative economic viability of,
    157–64
  comparative slave prices, 158
  cotton and, 149–50
  curbing of prerogatives, 57
  demand for slave labor (eighteenth
    century), 25
  development in Chesapeake versus South,
    57–9

diet and, 98–100
end of African slave trade, 30
first slaves imported, 22, 56–7
height of, 99–100
imported comparisons by country, 24
importation for tobacco, 24, 56, 148
importation to southern states (1700s), 24
internal slave trade, 170–1, 175–6
migration, 117–31
in northern states (seventeenth century),
  56
northern versus southern states, 30–1
  (see also abolition; Civil War; politics)
profitability of, 147
promiscuity stereotype and, 168–9
reaction to Civil War, 31, 271
rebellions and resistance, 233–50
religion and, 178–80, 182
rice cultivation and, 148, 150
runaways, 202, 203, 237, 264
self-purchase and, 197
slave families in, 57, 168–77
slave narratives of, 65–71
technological innovation in cotton and,
  149
territorial expansion and, 28, 30–2,
  262–70 (see also abolition; Civil War;
  politics)
tobacco production and, 150
See also by specific state and region;
  abolition; African slave trade;
  humanity; natural reproduction;
  northern United States; slave
  populations; southern United States

Varela, Father Félix, 274, 275
Verrazano, Giovanni, 22
Vesey, Denmark, 245–7
Virginia, 14, 55
  colonial settlement in, 22
  racial structure in, 24, 242
  slave families in, 171

wage labor, 151
War of 30, 259
War of the Triple Alliance.
  See Paraguayan War
warfare, 134
wealth distribution
  eastern versus western Cuba, 19, 20
  See also economics and economies
"whitening," 274, 278
Whitney, Eli, 149
Williams, Eric, 143–4, 252–4
women slaves. See female slaves

Yoruba, 181–2, 186

Zumbi, 216